Not My Mother's Sister

Not My Mother's Sister

Generational Conflict
and Third-Wave Feminism

Astrid Henry

Indiana University Press
BLOOMINGTON AND INDIANAPOLIS

This book is a publication of

Indiana University Press
601 North Morton Street
Bloomington, Indiana 47404-3797 USA

http://iupress.indiana.edu

Telephone orders   800-842-6796
Fax orders   812-855-7931
Orders by e-mail   iuporder@indiana.edu

The paper used in this publication meets the minimum
requirements of American National Standard for Information
Sciences—Permanence of Paper for Printed Library
Materials, ANSI Z39.48-1984.

Manufactured in the United States of America

Library of Congress Cataloging-in-Publication Data

Henry, Astrid, date
  Not my mother's sister : generational conflict and third-wave feminism / Astrid Henry.
      p. cm.
Includes bibliographical references and index.
  ISBN 0-253-34454-9 (cloth : alk. paper) — ISBN 0-253-21713-X (pbk. : alk. paper)
  1. Feminism—United States. 2. Feminist theory—United States. 3. Lesbian feminist
theory—United States. 4. African American women. I. Title.
  HQ1421.H43 2004
  305.42'0973—dc22
                                                                        2003027304

1 2 3 4 5 09 08 07 06 05 04

To my father
for teaching me how to live feminism

and

To Jane
for teaching me how to write it

Contents

Acknowledgments

I am very grateful to the many people who have supported me throughout the long process of writing this book. This project originated as a dissertation in the Modern Studies Program of the English Department at the University of Wisconsin–Milwaukee. I am indebted to Jane Gallop for our many conversations—intellectual, political, and personal—over the last decade. As my dissertation director, Jane never wavered in her belief in me and in this project, even as she consistently pushed me to make the work better. I am so grateful to Jane for our friendship and for teaching me both the hard work and great pleasure in writing. I would also like to thank the other members of my dissertation committee, Lynne Joyrich and Kathy Woodward. Their insightful reading of my work has been invaluable, and I have learned much from them and our conversations. Thanks also to Gwynne Kennedy and Sylvia Schafer for their many helpful ideas and suggestions.

While at UWM I was part of a community of graduate students to whom I owe an enormous debt for their support and critical readings of my work. In particular, I would like to thank Karen Boren, Eric Hayot, Jeff King, Christie Launius, and Jennifer Maher. I also want to thank the many teachers and mentors who helped me to become a feminist scholar, especially Nancy Baker, Jessica Benjamin, Susan Burgess, Greg Jay, Angel Moger, and Sara Ruddick. I owe special thanks to Shahnaz Rouse of Sarah Lawrence College. Being Shahnaz's student remains one of the most important experiences of my life, and I am forever changed by her inspiring example. I also want to thank my many wonderful students throughout the years, particularly the students in my courses on third-wave feminism and feminist generations at Saint Mary's College, Grinnell College, and the University of Wisconsin–Milwaukee. You are the reason why I love what I do.

I am indebted to my editor, Kate Babbitt, for her incisive reading of the manuscript. Her comments and questions were extremely helpful in making the final revisions. Susan Fraiman and the two anonymous readers of the manuscript also contributed many useful insights into my project. All errors and oversights are, of course, entirely my own. Thanks also to Tony Brewer, Jane Lyle, and Robert Sloan at Indiana University Press for all their help.

For their support and championing of my work, I would like to thank Jennifer Baumgardner, Rory Dicker, Paula Kamen, Andrea O'Reilly, Alison Piepmeir, and Jo Reger. I have received much support from my colleagues at Saint Mary's College over the last few years, and I would especially like to thank Ann Clark and Phyllis Kaminski for their encouragement of my work. I would also like to thank my friends for seeing me through this long process. In particular, I thank Nicole Bates, Jimmy Cox, Nina DeYoung, Dianna Diers, Joe Eisman, Malinda Foy, Cricket Keating, Amy O'Neill, Mary Porter, Mariah Schroeder, and Jennifer Zachman. Thanks also to the women of my meditation group—Theresa Priebe, Linda Reid, and Cookie Werbel—for their support and wisdom.

Some of the ideas included in chapter 1 were first worked through in "Biting the Hand that Feeds You: Feminism as the 'Bad Mother,'" in *Mothers and Daughters: Connection, Empowerment, and Transformation,* edited by Andrea O'Reilly and Sharon Abbey (Boston: Rowman & Littlefield Publishers, 2000), 213–224. Sections of the introduction, chapter 1, and chapter 5 appeared in an earlier form as "Feminism's Family Problem: Feminist Generations and the Mother-Daughter Trope," *Catching a Wave: Reclaiming Feminism for the 21st Century,* edited by Rory Dicker and Alison Piepmeir (Boston: Northeastern University Press, 2003), 209–231.

My family has been a constant source of love, support, and encouragement throughout the process of writing this book. I want to thank my cousin, Anja Laub Methling, for her compassionate heart and great insight into family dynamics. I thank my brother, Axel Henry, for helping me to appreciate that differences are inherent to families. I could not have finished this project without the support of my sister, Else Henry, whose faith in my abilities never wavers. As have many of my generation, I learned about feminism as a child, from parents whose family values were feminist. I want to thank my mother, Meser Henry, for our friendship and for helping me to understand the complexities of the mother-daughter relationship. I am indebted to my father, Harley Henry, for his enthusiastic championing of my scholarship and for his unconditional love and support. Finally, I am profoundly grateful to David Harrison for his love, understanding, and sense of humor, not to mention his dedication to this book and its ideas. His insightful criticism of all the many drafts proved invaluable to the book's completion. David, "if they asked me, I could write a book . . ."

Not My Mother's Sister

Introduction

Feminism has become a mother figure,
and what we are seeing is a daughter's revolt.[1]

—B. Ruby Rich

In the summer of 1994, I read Katie Roiphe's *The Morning After: Sex, Fear, and Feminism on Campus* for the first time. For months, the book had been receiving a lot of attention, but neither I nor any of my feminist friends had yet read it. I remember a fellow graduate student telling me that, given its politics, she would *never* read Roiphe's book, for obviously Roiphe was an idiot. After reading *The Morning After* that summer, I can't say I disagreed with her assessment. "*Whose* feminism is she talking about?" I said out loud, to no one in particular, as I sat reading. "This is ridiculous!"

I was quick to dismiss Roiphe during that initial reading in great part because, to put it bluntly, I thought she was dead wrong about the state of contemporary feminism. What she described bore little resemblance to the feminism I knew. Roiphe and I, who are approximately the same age, seemed to have read similar books and taken similar classes, both participating in a "feminism on campus," yet we emerged from these experiences with wildly different takes on feminism.

What I found most unrecognizable in Roiphe's text was the image she painted of feminism as a puritanical, regulating force. For Roiphe, feminism was like a stern mother telling women how to behave. She described feeling constrained by feminism, her individuality and freedom curbed by its long list of rules and regulations. For me, feminism had mostly been about the opposite: a way for me to be an individual and

1

break free of society's many rules about women's proper place. Feminism had given me a language and a set of tools to fight for social justice and to see the interconnectedness of all forms of oppression. Feminism had profoundly shaped both my personal and professional lives, and I felt a strong sense of loyalty and gratitude toward it.

My feelings about feminism, I came to realize, were those of a dutiful daughter. Feminism was a mother figure to me as well—but an encouraging one that had given me much support over the years. As it had been for Roiphe, feminism had been an integral part of my life since I was a little girl. In fact, one of my few clear memories of childhood is of my mother proudly telling a friend that I was "already a real feminist" at the age of nine. Feminism was a kind of mother figure to me, too, I realized, but one that I needed and loved. As a dutiful daughter of feminism, then, I can see now that part of my original intent in writing this book was to defend the feminism that I saw being attacked by so many members of my generation. Unlike them, I wouldn't abandon second-wave feminism. I would defend it as one would a mother maligned during a schoolyard battle.

A few years after reading Roiphe, I began work on a doctoral dissertation that examined contemporary representations of feminism. As I pursued my research, it became clear that what I had first noticed in Roiphe's text was, in fact, a ubiquitous phenomenon: writers of all ages, feminists and non-feminists alike, were describing feminist intergenerational relationships in familial terms.[2] My project eventually became this book, with the following focus: how the mother-daughter relationship is *the* central trope in depicting the relationship between the so-called second and third waves of U.S. feminism and how the employment of this metaphor—or matrophor—has far-reaching implications for contemporary feminism.[3]

Indeed, feminists seem to have difficulty avoiding familial metaphors in describing feminist generations. In an essay which both relies on and criticizes the use of the mother-daughter trope—aptly titled "An Open Letter to Institutional Mothers"—Rebecca Dakin Quinn coins the term "matrophor" to describe "the persistent nature of maternal metaphors in feminism."[4] The prevalence of this matrophor within myriad genres of feminist discourse suggests that there is something to be gained from turning feminism—and often feminists—into "mothers." This matrophor, I argue, appears to embolden feminism's "daughters," granting them authority and a generational location from which to speak.

The term "generation" warrants glossing. In recent years, there has been an increasing tendency to speak of feminism in terms of generations. In fact, within feminism, the 1990s may well be remembered as a decade defined by the notion of feminist generations, so commonplace was the use of this concept to mark differences among and between feminisms—and feminists. The prevalence of a generational understanding of feminism can be seen in the numerous academic texts on the subject,[5] conferences on the theme,[6] retrospectives on women's studies as a discipline,[7] and a publishing boom in feminist memoirs.[8] In its most-often-used form, the phrase "feminist generations" points to the existence of at least two—if not more—coexisting generations of U.S. feminists: second-wave feminists of the 1970s and a new generation of feminists, who emerged in the 1990s, who are being called the third wave.[9] This latter term, the "third wave," has frequently been employed as a kind of shorthand for a generational difference among feminists, one based on chronological age. Yet, as I argue, the term must also be seen as representing the desire of those who embrace it to signal a "new" feminism that is distinct from the second wave.

Though plural, the term "generations" is almost always dyadic, referring to just two generations. We seem unable to think of generations—or even of waves, for that matter—in threes or fours.[10] I am interested in how the persistent twoness of generations recalls the mother-daughter relationship. As Mary Russo has argued, the problem with the "maternal symbolic" is that it "normalizes relations between women by limiting or privileging the difference configured in the mother-daughter dyad."[11] In other words, rather than recognizing the variety of "relations between women," the matrophor reduces these potential *relationships* to a single *relationship:* that of mother and daughter. Describing second-wave feminists—and second-wave feminism—as "mothers" to the third wave may have been inevitable, given that the age difference between each wave's representatives is roughly the equivalent of one familial generation. Yet as I discuss in chapter 2, within the second wave's imagined relationship to feminism's first wave—a generational relationship that cannot so easily be represented as familial—the language of the family was already being deployed.

At first glance, the metaphor of the wave seems to offer an alternative model for describing feminist generations. What has since come to be known as the first wave encompassed such a long period of history that multiple generations of women were engaged in its struggle. Within pro-suffrage families, for example, it was not uncommon for three generations—grandmothers, mothers, and daughters—to have participated in this one "wave." The emergence of feminism's third wave seems to profoundly alter our use of the metaphor of the wave. Given the easy mapping of "mother" and "daughter" onto "second wave" and "third wave," the wave metaphor and the mother-daughter relationship increasingly have become synonymous within feminist discourse. While initially offering a generational model located outside the family, then, the wave metaphor has come to resemble the familial structure with its understanding of generations based on the human life cycle.

In his influential work on generations, Karl Mannheim argues that a new generation appears roughly every thirty years. While his understanding of generations is founded on their emergence within society, culture, and politics, he argues that "the sociological phenomenon of generations is ultimately based on the biological rhythm of birth and death."[12] Political or cultural generations, then, imitate the familial generational model with its regeneration around the 30-year point. This would suggest that the very notion of generations can only be understood in terms of the family, reproduction, and the birth cycle.[13] The movements known as feminism's second and third waves certainly fit Mannheim's paradigm. In fact, the third wave's launch is easily read as the start of a new feminist generation precisely because it adheres to the 30-year structure: the second wave was born in the 1960s, the third wave in the 1990s.

Such a view of regeneration ensures that feminists who came of age in the late 1970s to mid-1980s—and thus fall in the middle of this 30-year period—must necessarily go missing from feminism's narrative of its generational structure. They are subsumed under the category "second wave," and their inability to be read as a distinct generation is compounded by the dyadic mother-daughter relationship used to represent feminist generations. As they can be understood as neither "mothers" nor "daughters" within feminism's imagined family structure, such feminists are frequently absent from recent discourse on feminism's (seemingly two) generations.

The terms "second wave" and "third wave" appear stable and co-herent, in part, because they conform to our dominant understanding of generations within the United States. Members of the second wave can be read as Baby Boomers (people born between 1947 and 1961), while third-wave feminists are easily collapsed into the larger category Generation X (people born between 1961 and 1981).[14] As generational categories, the terms "Baby Boomers" and "Generation X" are used to mark the shared historical experience of those born within a particular time span. Central to such a notion of generations is the concept of coming of age, a phrase I use to mark the moment when one moves from childhood to adulthood, typically defined as somewhere between the ages of eighteen to twenty-five. As sociologists who study generations have argued, the historical events that surround these coming-of-age moments help to transform a random group of people of roughly the same age into a seemingly coherent generation.[15] The generation of young feminists discussed in this work, the post–baby boom Generation Xers, came of age after the leftist movements of the 1960s and 1970s and during the conservative Reagan-Bush years. Thus, it is typically defined by its (supposed) political apathy.

Mannheim outlines the two reigning models for understanding generations, generational conflict, and struggle: he calls the first the "positivist" model and the second "romantic-historical."[16] In the former, each successive generation is seen to go beyond that which came before it: a new generation is equated with progress. In the latter, the past is romanticized and idealized; in this model, the passage of time signals not progress but decline. Within recent feminist discourse, both of these models are used to describe the generational struggle between the second and third waves. As did second-wave feminists in their relationship to the first wave, third-wave feminists have often relied on a positivist notion of history to show the progress and improvement made by their feminism. In contrast, many second-wave feminists have criticized third-wave (or "younger") feminists through a romantic-historical model that expresses nostalgia for their own historical moment and experience.[17] Some younger feminists have also looked back on the early second wave with a kind of romantic longing for a time they never knew.

Of course, the term "generation" has additional connotations outside the familial or sociopolitical contexts described so far. Since the 1960s, generations have increasingly been defined as market groups to whom products and lifestyles can be sold. While "Generation X" and "Baby Boomers" may describe some form of shared political and personal identity, as these generational labels are more commonly conceived they function as consumer groups to be targeted by advertisers.[18] In the last few years, "third-wave feminists" have themselves become just such a consumer group, targeted by numerous websites and magazines. Such merchandising ultimately suggests an anxiety at the heart of generational discourse: as one generation goes out of fashion, it is inevitably replaced by the younger generation that follows.[19] Within contemporary feminist writing, certain feminisms are depicted as old or outdated in order to posit the new generation's progress and improvement. The term "old" signifies the inverse of both "new" and "young," two terms that are frequently collapsed within feminist generational discourse.

So far I have been speaking of generations as though they should be—or even can be—understood as coherent. My goal, however, is to interrogate precisely this imagined unity of generations, exploring how and why feminists represent generations, or waves, in monolithic terms. As Joan W. Scott argues, "The emphasis on generational differences, in fact, seems to me to displace or paper over these other [ideological] differences, creating an illusory unity for feminism, taking as representative of feminism whatever discourse seems dominant at a particular moment."[20] Central to this book is the notion that a cohesive generational unit is itself always a fiction. A generation is an imaginary collective that both reveals truths about people of a particular age and tries to mold those people into a unified group. Even as we use the often-productive concept of generations, we must be wary of the ways in which it provides a reductive image of relationships between women, between feminisms, and between historical periods. As Lisa Marie Hogeland cautions: "Generational thinking is always unspeakably generalizing."[21]

Although one is invariably placed within a generation by accident of birth, in fact generations also constitute what Mannheim has called a kind of "identity of location."[22] Generational units must bring themselves into being through an active identification with their particular historical moment.[23] For political generations, in particular, this active identification is crucial. Within recent feminist writing, however, such a vision of political generations is rarely articulated. Rather, it is all too frequently assumed that feminists of a certain age will, *naturally,* share a generational identity. Political generations, unlike familial ones, require intentional identification. To paraphrase Simone de Beauvoir, one is not born a feminist but rather becomes one. What gets lost in the use of the matrophor is precisely the will behind this identification, for once feminism becomes a mother, the generation that follows her will consist (merely) of her daughters.[24] When young women's identification with feminism becomes naturalized in this way, we lose sight of what is, in fact, a deliberate political act: choosing to identify with feminism.

Throughout this study, I describe the importance of identification—both with and against other feminists—to the formation of feminist generations. As discussed in chapter 2, the second wave's identification with the first wave granted feminists in the 1960s a group identity: women involved in the historic struggle for women's rights. For third-wave, or "younger," feminists, their simultaneous identification with and rejection of second-wave feminism is what grants them an identity to call their own. *Not My Mother's Sister* examines how such cross-generational identifications—and disidentifications—have been politically emboldening to feminists of both waves.

In using the term *disidentification,* I mean to suggest an identification *against* something. My understanding of this term is based, in great part, on the work of Diana Fuss in *Identification Papers.* Building on the work of Judith Butler, Fuss develops the following account of disidentification. "What at first may appear to be a refused identification," she writes,

> might in some cases more accurately be termed a disavowed one—an identification that has already been made and denied in the unconscious. A disidentification, in other words, may actually represent "an identification that one fears to make only because one has already made it."[25]

For third-wave feminists, this refused identification, or disidentification, is frequently with or against second-wave feminism. In fact, it appears that for many younger feminists, it is only by refusing to identify themselves with earlier versions of feminism—and frequently with older feminists—that they are able to create a feminism of their own.

In its suggestion of a disavowed or feared identification, the concept of disidentification resonates with the mother-daughter relationship, or matrophor, used to describe feminist generational relationships. Many second-wave feminists—white, middle-class women in particular—have described how joining the women's movement enabled them to escape their mothers' fate. Ann Snitow, for example, remarks: "Some of us early [feminists] were too afraid of the lives of our mothers to recognize ourselves in them. But I remember that this emotional throwing off of the mother's life felt like the only way to begin."[26] In her description of her fear of "recognizing herself" in her mother's life, Snitow offers an illustrative example of disidentification: she suggests that the desire to escape her mother's life was particularly strong because she could—all too clearly—recognize herself in this life and in the female role it mandated. Thus, for many white, middle-class feminists of the second wave, according to Marianne Hirsch, mothers "become the targets of this process of disidentification and the primary negative models for the daughter."[27]

The noted second-wave writer Phyllis Chesler provides another example of this disidentificatory process in her book *Letters to a Young Feminist*. Published at the end of the 1990s, the volume is a collection of twenty-two letters addressed to an imaginary reader—"a young woman, possibly a young man, somewhere between the ages of eighteen and thirty-five." In her first missive to this "young feminist," Chesler writes, "When I was your age, I did not know what I needed to know in order to understand my life—anybody's life. Perhaps in writing to you, I wish to correct that, to make amends."[28] Chesler envisions her epistolary collection as passing down some of the wisdom she has gained from her 30-plus years in the feminist movement. Yet as the above passage suggests, she also sees her letters as "correcting" something that was missing from her own life; she imagines that she can give "young feminists" something she never had and that they will want to hear what she has to say.[29]

Chesler's presumptuousness is illustrative, if not typical, of a particular kind of generational relationship, one in which young feminists are expected to learn from the wisdom of their elders. As one such young feminist, Devoney Looser, so aptly writes, "Second-wave feminists—like it or not—are destined to fail in their mission to 'pass on' feminist knowledge."[30] Chesler seems unaware of the patriarchal nature of this model of authority in which it is the duty of the sage old ones to pass on knowledge. Nor does she seem aware that her book's very format of a series of letters written to an unnamed, unspecified, and (most important) unresponsive young feminist posits the exchange of knowledge as instruction rather than dialogue. As Jennifer Baumgardner and Amy Richards write in their critique of Chesler's collection, "You have to stop treating us like daughters. You don't have the authority to treat us like babies or acolytes who need to be molded."[31]

Putting aside these reservations about *Letters to a Young Feminist* for a moment, one of Chesler's letters may be instructive here for what it reveals about the process of disidentification. She argues that the women who initiated the second wave of U.S. feminism experienced their movement as a motherless one, driven by the power of sisterhood.

> Like the goddess Athena, newly hatched from her father Zeus's brow, we, too, wanted to experience ourselves as motherless "daughters." We were a sibling horde of "sisters" . . . we lived in a universe of same-age peers. We knew of no other way to break with the past. . . . When we stepped out onto the stage of history we did so primarily as motherless daughters/sisters/sibling rivals. Psychologically, we had committed matricide.[32]

Here Chesler implies that in order to bring their new movement to life—to make history, to effect change—second-wave feminists had to imagine themselves as motherless. They had to disconnect themselves from the generation of women who came before them; in effect, they had to reject their mothers. Chesler suggests that there is something politically empowering about psychological matricide that allowed the now-unfettered daughters to "step out onto the stage of history" as political agents and makers of change.

For many among the new generation of feminists who have both claimed and been given the title "third wave," feminism also appears like "a universe of same-age peers." Naomi Wolf, a key spokesperson for this new generation, said in 1991 of the then-burgeoning third wave: "[I]t would need to be, as all feminist waves are, peer-driven: no matter how wise a mother's advice is, we listen to our peers."[33] Like Chesler, Wolf suggests that there is power to be found in a peer-driven movement. More than that, in arguing that "all feminist waves are peer-driven," she, like Chesler, defines feminism as a daughter's movement. Unlike the mothers rejected by Chesler's generation, the older generation described here *is* feminist. In fact, the mother whose advice Wolf cautions us against taking appears to be feminism itself; Wolf turns second-wave feminism into the mother of the third wave. Paradoxically, then, the very advice

Chesler wishes to impart to young feminists will not be heard—"no matter how wise"—precisely because of this psychological matricide, which ensures that we listen to our peers, not our mothers.

As feminism itself has become a mother to the third wave, the various imagined familial relationships with feminism have transformed. When second-wave feminists committed psychological matricide they became motherless daughters who could then join forces in an orphan tribe of sisters, "a sibling horde." As Chesler describes her generation, a new political family replaced her former biological one: sisterhood replaced daughterhood. Yet for the next generation of feminists, feminism's family appears quite different.[34] As one third-wave writer claims, "notions of sisterhood seldom appeal to women of my generation."[35] Because they have rejected the "sibling horde," many young feminists seem to remain within the imagined mother-daughter relationship precisely in order to give them a position from which to speak—as daughters rather than sisters. In rejecting a notion of collective sisterhood—but without another model, familial or otherwise, to supplant it—they remain within the mother-daughter relationship, albeit as only children to a controlling mother feminism. "Sisterhood is powerful" has been replaced by a new slogan: "Daughterhood is powerful."[36]

In Chesler's description of psychological matricide, she suggests that this act is essential to freeing oneself and gaining one's individuality, particularly when the mother "remain[s] in the position of dreaded other, of object to the daughters' emerging subjectivity."[37] As Snitow's earlier comments suggest, however, this "matricide" might also be understood as expressing a fear—a fear of recognition, a fear of identification. As outlined by Adrienne Rich in *Of Woman Born: Motherhood as Experience and Institution*, the concept of matrophobia provides a useful frame for understanding this fear. Rich writes: "Matrophobia can be seen as a womanly splitting of the self, in the desire to become purged once and for all of our mother's bondage, to become individuated and free." She continues:

> Matrophobia . . . is the fear not of one's mother or of motherhood but of *becoming one's mother.* . . . But where a mother is hated to the point of matrophobia there may also be a deep underlying pull toward her, a dread that if one relaxes one's guard one will identify with her completely.[38]

Matrophobia shares with Fuss's notion of disidentification the fear of an identification that one doesn't want to make, that one "fears to make only because one has already made it." What Chesler terms psychological matricide, then, can perhaps be viewed as one form that matrophobia takes, but its disidentification masks a fear of identification. This "matricide," then, keeps at a distance the disavowed identity.

For third-wave feminists, the disavowed identity that must be kept at bay is often second-wave feminism itself. However second-wave feminism is described—puritanical, dated, dowdy, asexual, to name but a few common traits attributed to this mother—she has become an easy figure to reject. She stands in the way of the daughters' freedom.

In critically analyzing these maternal metaphors, or matrophors, I have invariably relied upon them myself. Like the mother-daughter relationship itself, the matrophor seems difficult to escape even as one attempts to critique it. This is, admittedly, one of the contradictions of my project—that the very structure I hope to question, if not disrupt, is one that I repeatedly reinforce. If so difficult to disrupt, why, then, examine the mother-daughter metaphor at all? The answer, for me, comes in part from what this metaphor allows us to see and what it reveals about feminist conflict. As Susan Fraiman notes, "Family metaphors do not exacerbate tensions so much as they help to get a handle on them."[39] Elaborating on the matrophor's value, Rosi Braidotti writes:

> [T]he mother-daughter nexus has reached the status of a political paradigm. As such, it fulfills two crucial functions: firstly, it points to a specific type of woman-to-woman bonding. Secondly, it spells the conditions of negativity and violence that are specific to that type of bonding. It is precisely on these two accounts that I wish to defend it as a very adequate political metaphor.[40]

The mother-daughter relationship—with both its implied connection and aggression—is a particularly female political metaphor, and thus has particular resonance within feminism. Like sisterhood, it has its limits as a political metaphor, to be sure, but I agree with both Fraiman and Braidotti that we must try to think through its signification rather than abandoning it at the outset.

Some feminists have cautioned against continuing to discuss feminist conflict in generational terms, arguing that to do so only serves to solidify the troubling familial metaphors used to describe generations. To be sure, the insistence of speaking of feminisms in terms of distinct—and discrete—generations obscures the ways in which continuity exists across feminisms and prevents us from recognizing other forms of difference among feminists of different ages.[41] As Diana Elam reminds us, "Generation stands alongside race, sexuality, and class as a form of difference among women."[42] While historical generation and chronological age are but *one form* of difference, in the last decade, feminist conflict has almost exclusively been understood in generational terms.

I believe it is vitally important that feminists critically examine the metaphors and tropes we use to describe our ideological and political debates. While the recent focus on generations should not lead us to believe that all forms of feminist conflict are, in truth, generational, neither should we treat as irrelevant the apparent persistent need to describe this conflict in generational terms. "If there is now a growing body of writing on second-wave and third-wave feminist experiences, beliefs, and platforms, little has been written on the traffic between each so-called camp," writes Devoney Looser. "Very little indeed has been published on the caricatures of each generation and on the basis of these, if any, in fact." Encouraging feminist scholars to analyze these caricatures, Looser writes, "[W]e should continue to examine what are already quite entrenched and *perceived* feminist generational differences and alliances. These deserve to be further theorized now, even if they are ultimately cast out of our critical vocabulary."[43] It is my hope that *Not My Mother's Sister* will add to the project called for by Looser in trying to theorize how—and particularly why—feminist differences and alliances are conceived in generational terms.[44]

Throughout working on this project, I have frequently reflected on Katie King's oft-quoted statement that "[o]rigin stories about the women's movement are interested stories, all of them."[45] King reminds us that all narratives about feminism and its history reflect more than the truth or an accurate accounting of facts. The stories we tell about feminism also reveal the desires of those who tell them. In analyzing the rhetoric and tropes by which third-wave feminists describe second-wave feminism, my intent is to explore the motivations behind these representations, the ways in which creating a particular feminist past proves emboldening. *Not My Mother's Sister* does not set out to give its readers a complete and accurate history of the second wave; rather, my goal is to examine the second wave as it has been envisioned by a wide range of next-generation feminists. Neither do I intend this work to offer a full accounting of the third wave; I am not sure that a complete history is even possible at this time, although I am sure that this work doesn't live up to the task. While I originally envisioned *Not My Mother's Sister* as a way by which to counter what I saw as my generation's inaccurate representations of the second wave, I now recognize all too clearly that such a rescue mission is inevitably futile. As Elam astutely points out, "There is no one feminist who can do justice to all other feminists of all generations."[46] My own allegiances and my own subjective perspective invariably inform the feminisms I chose to criticize here and those I try to salvage.

Not My Mother's Sister begins by describing the political and cultural events that led to the emergence of feminism's third wave. As I discuss, in order for this birth to effectively appear as the start of a new wave in feminism, the 1980s had to be represented as a post-feminist decade, defined by its lack of feminist activity. Central to this chapter are three writers, Rene Denfeld, Katie Roiphe, and Naomi Wolf, who were some of the first next-generation feminists to articulate a critique of the second wave in generational terms. While they were given much media attention, to be sure, they also had a profound effect on the ways in which subsequent third-wave feminists positioned themselves *against* the second wave. Through a close analysis of the works of these three writers, among others, I explore how feminism has been described as a "birthright" passed down from mother to daughter. In its association with childhood rules, however, this representation has led many younger feminists to want to rebel against second-wave feminism.

Chapter 2 returns to the beginning of the second wave of U.S. feminism to explore how feminists from this period constructed a relationship to the first wave. When the women involved in the second wave revitalized U.S. feminism in the late 1960s, they not only continued a political movement from the past; in effect, they invented our contemporary notions of feminist generations and waves. The second wave's development of the metaphor of the wave, along with a penchant for speaking about feminism in generational terms, has had a powerful influence on the recent articulation of a third wave of feminism. Through an analysis of radical feminist journals and books from 1967 to 1975, I examine how second-wave feminists developed their feminism through both identifying and disidentifying with their feminist "foremothers."

After this brief historical turn, I return to third-wave writing from the last decade in order to address the ways in which sexuality has become the central means by which third-wave feminists have asserted generational differences. Chapter 3 explores how younger feminists have represented feminism's debates around sexuality, its sex wars, as it were. The third wave's depiction of these debates often makes second-wave feminism appear both prudish and puritanical. Rejecting the so-called victim feminism of Catherine MacKinnon and Andrea Dworkin, with its focus on the danger of rape and women's lack of agency, third-wave feminists have instead celebrated a woman's right to pleasure. At times ignoring or misrepresenting pro-sex feminisms of the second wave, the third wave has stressed its innovation by celebrating a "new" feminist (hetero)sexuality, one that is being posited in generational terms.

Chapter 4 continues this theme through reading recent queer and lesbian writing on generational divides. I discuss how 1970s lesbian feminism is represented in ways that are remarkably similar to the puritanical portrait of feminism discussed in chapter 3. In particular, I examine how transforming lesbian feminism—and feminism generally—into a mother requires that she be stripped of her sexuality; in fact, she must be asexual, if not explicitly anti-sex, to represent the maternal. And, as I argue, it appears that feminism must be maternalized for the "daughter" generation to have a movement of its own.

Not My Mother's Sister concludes with a chapter that addresses the ways in which race has functioned within third-wave writing. I examine the central role played by feminists of color, black feminists in particular, in the development of third-wave feminism. The mainstream media has virtually ignored third-wave feminists of color in its coverage of feminism and its newly emerged next generation, instead preferring to focus on more conservative white feminists, such as Roiphe. A central figure in chapter 5 is Rebecca Walker, daughter of second-wave feminist Alice Walker, who has been credited with coining the term "third wave" and is one of this wave's main spokespersons. Through an analysis of writing by Walker, Joan Morgan, and Danzy Senna, among others, I explore how feminist generational relationships are depicted by young feminists of color and the differences in the feminism both rejected and claimed by this new breed of writers. As I discuss, the ruling mother figure that has been made out of second-wave feminism is distinctly raced as white, creating a more complicated generational picture for third-wave feminists of color than is seen in the work of many white writers.

In the ten years that have passed since my initial reading of *The Morning After*, I have read it a dozen more times. In all honesty, I have come to appreciate this book. Though extremely subjective and deeply flawed, Roiphe's text offers one young woman's honest attempt to think through her (our?) generation's relationship to feminism. This isn't to say that I agree with Roiphe any more than I did during that summer day a decade ago, but I appreciate what I now see as her attempt to figure out something important about her relationship to the feminisms which surrounded her: at home, on campus, in books, in her bedroom.

While I still have reservations about claiming the title "third-wave feminist" for myself, through the process of writing *Not My Mother's Sister* I have developed more of an identification with this new breed of feminists than I originally imagined I would. I have had to confront what it means to write as a "daughter" in the face of "mother feminism." We younger feminists may not be able to write the story of the second wave in such a way as to highlight our easy alliance with it, nor will we be able to effortlessly posit the superior nature of our feminism. It is to a more expansive vision of generational dialogue and exchange that I hope *Not My Mother's Sister* can contribute.

1.

Daughterhood
Is Powerful

THE EMERGENCE OF FEMINISM'S THIRD WAVE

Around 1991, feminism resurfaced in the public imagination.[1] After a decade in which feminism seemed to have disappeared into the academy, feminism was once again a hot topic—one that people were reading about, organizing around, and discussing. The fall 1991 Senate confirmation hearings for Clarence Thomas's and Anita Hill's testimony regarding Thomas's sexual harassment of her have often been cited as the wake-up call which roused a great number of U.S. women back into feminist activism.[2] In the political arena this undoubtedly was the case; the Thomas hearings galvanized millions of women to action, from running for office to organizing campaigns to voting. The elections of 1992 saw women elected into office in record numbers, and the conservative anti-feminist politics of George H. Bush, preceded by eight years of the same from Ronald Reagan, were replaced with the first baby-boomer president: Bill Clinton, a man whose personal and political lives were shaped, in part, by the ideals of the second wave of the women's movement.[3]

While the television spectacle of the Thomas-Hill hearings certainly played a major role in the reemergence of women's issues in the public imagination, the hearings were not the only event in 1991 that suggested the beginning of a new moment in feminism. The year 1991 also saw the publication of two best-selling feminist books: Susan Faludi's *Backlash: The Undeclared War Against American Women* and Naomi Wolf's

The Beauty Myth.[4] Receiving a great deal of critical and media attention, these two books signaled a new generation of popular feminist writing. *Backlash* and *The Beauty Myth* were widely read and discussed by women and men across the U.S., as *Sisterhood Is Powerful* and other second-wave books had been two decades earlier.

Backlash was particularly influential in the resurgence of feminism during this period, both in drawing a new generation of young women into feminism and in restarting a much-needed dialogue about sexism, misogyny, and women's inequality. The thesis of Faludi's book—that the gains made by the women's movement in the 1970s were followed by a "backlash" against feminism and women in the 1980s—challenged the complacent attitude espoused by many men and women alike: that the women's movement was over, all the necessary gains having been made, and that we were now in a "post-feminist" period in which feminism was no longer necessary. In its challenge to the conservative claim that women had achieved full equality in the U.S., *Backlash* was a clarion call for feminist action. Feminism was not irrelevant; in fact, it appeared more relevant and necessary than ever.

The shift in consciousness around women's issues during this period—what Naomi Wolf has called a "genderquake"—was the product of several other important feminist cultural events.[5] The film *Thelma and Louise,* released in May of 1991, was both heralded and criticized for its image of women fighting back against male misogyny and violence. While the politics behind the film's feminism have since been much analyzed by cultural critics, *Thelma and Louise* played an important role in the discussion about the meaning and importance of feminism in the early 1990s. On the small screen, feminist characters were also gaining attention. In the late 1980s and early 1990s, the success of television shows such as *Roseanne* and *Murphy Brown,* both of which premiered in 1988, showed that strong women characters espousing feminist ideals could get high ratings and public support. These events in the early 1990s suggested that something was stirring in feminism. The claim that we were "post" feminism no longer made sense; feminism was not something women had left behind but in fact was something women were reclaiming and reconceptualizing in an enthusiastic way.

One event that was characteristic of this moment was the revamping of the feminist magazine *Ms.* In July of 1990, *Ms. Magazine* returned in a new format after an eight-month hiatus.[6] First hitting newsstands in the spring of 1972, *Ms.* had become an increasingly mainstream women's magazine during the 1980s, its feminism watered down to meet advertisers' demands. The new *Ms.*—free of advertising, committed to its feminist roots, and under the helm of the well-known second-wave writer Robin Morgan—would be, in Morgan's words, "unashamedly *feminist.*" In her editorial in the inaugural issue, "Ms. Lives!" Morgan writes:

> They said it couldn't happen. They said no periodical should even try to get along without advertising. They said readers wouldn't want a major feminist magazine of substance, audacity, quality. They said this is a "postfeminist" era, that younger women weren't interested and older women were burned out. They said *Ms.* was dead.[7]

In arguing against the premature "death" of *Ms.*, like the premature death of feminism itself, Morgan's title "*Ms.* Lives!" recalls the early second-wave slogan, "Feminism Lives"—a rallying cry used by early second-wave feminists to proclaim the "rebirth" of feminism after the "death" of the first wave with the success of women's suffrage in 1920. What is striking about Morgan's use of this death and birth imagery, however, is that it works to signal the "rebirth" of feminism at a moment when second-wave feminism and second-wave feminists were, literally, still very much alive. While many in the popular press have tended to depict feminism as disappearing in the 1980s—whether because it became academicized, achieved its goals, or lost its appeal for women—feminism did not, in fact, die out.[8] Feminism's resurrection in the 1990s, then, is significantly different than its previous "rebirth." In the late 1960s, the claim that feminism had been "reborn" relied on the notion that feminism had been dormant—even dead—for the forty-some years after the passage of the Nineteenth Amendment. It was only because feminism's history was narrated in this fashion that the second wave's imagined resuscitation of feminism was possible. The revitalization of feminism in the 1990s relies on a similar—albeit much shorter—period of feminist dormancy: the post-feminist 1980s, an era in which "younger women weren't interested and older women were burned out."

If the late 1960s through the 1970s were years of feminist activity, the 1980s have routinely been characterized as a time when feminism was no longer necessary. The first text to apply the term "post-feminist" to both the 1980s and the generation of women who came of age during the late 1970s and early 1980s is Susan Bolotin's "Views from the Postfeminist Generation," published in the *New York Times Magazine* in 1982. Bolotin laments the fact that the women she interviewed—who were all born between 1957 and 1964, and thus on the cusp between the Baby Boomers and Generation X—viewed feminism as something passé.[9]

The term "post-feminism" warrants glossing. On the one hand, the term has been used to mark historical periods when feminism and women's movements are in decline or abeyance; it has often been used to indicate a rejection of feminism.[10] This rejection, then, serves as proof of the *failure* of feminism. On the other hand, the prefix "post" points to a time *after* feminism—in other words, a time when feminism is no longer needed precisely because its goals have been achieved. Thus, "post-feminism" would also seem to signify the *success* of feminism. Paradoxically, then, the term signals both failure and success, both an anti-feminist critique of the misguidedness of feminism and a pro-feminist nod to feminism's victories.

In what might well be the first documented use of the term, a women's literary group described themselves as "post-feminist" in 1919. In the group's journal, they elaborate on the term's ideology: "[W]e're interested in people now—not in men and women."[11] As historian Nancy F. Cott demonstrates in *The Grounding of Modern Feminism,* the success of feminism during the early part of the twentieth century, particularly in achieving women's suffrage, was what allowed feminism to seem obsolete to the generation of young women who came of age in the 1920s. For these women—"interested in people" rather than women—feminism appeared outdated in its devotion to the limits imposed by gender. Paradoxically, it was precisely because those limits appeared to have been lifted by feminism that feminism seemed passé. Women could now reject the group identity reinforced by feminism in favor of the more enlightened identity of modern individualism. As Cott writes, however, "The resort to individualism took the feminist standpoint that women's freedom and opportunities should be no less than men's, but individualism offered no way to achieve the goal except by acting as though it had already been obtained."[12]

Moving ahead sixty years, the past was repeating itself. For the "post-feminist generation" of the 1980s, women had gained their freedom and equal opportunity. If many women felt grateful to the women's movement for achieving these goals, they also assumed that feminism's success indicated its obsolescence.[13] Others felt "anger toward Second Wave feminism" for eliminating the comforting, if nonetheless oppressive, old rules of the game surrounding heterosexuality and the family.[14] For such women, feminism had indeed had a radical effect on society, but it had failed in substantially replacing the old pre-feminist ways of living with workable alternatives. Still others felt that feminism had passed them by. As one 24-year-old in Bolotin's article laments: "The revolution wasn't ours. So we put together our own kind of feminism, which has very little activism in it. I wish that I had had a revolution to go to, a cause to believe in. My life has been lacking in the kind of *upheaval that allowed* women to become feminists."[15]

On the surface, what seems to distinguish young women in the 1990s from their immediate predecessors—women who appeared to reject feminism in favor of a Reaganite notion of individualism—is that they *do* want to identify themselves as feminists, even as they criticize much about contemporary feminism.[16] Clearly, some kind of upheaval occurred in the late 1980s and early 1990s which allowed women to become feminists again. Unlike their "post-feminist" predecessors, many in this new generation do not view feminism as passé or irrelevant to their own lives. They are not apathetic toward feminism; quite the opposite, they are actively engaged with it. In fact, it is their desire for feminism that makes them struggle with it.[17]

In narrating this most recent portion of feminism's history, it is tempting to divide the 1980s and 1990s into wholly discrete decades: the former characterized as post-feminist, the latter as feminist. Such a partition is difficult to resist, in part, because for many of us who lived through the transition from the 1980s to the 1990s, a real and noticeable shift *did* occur within feminism. Although this "new feminist generation" has certainly been propped up by much media hype, there was and is something very real about the changes that have occurred over the last fifteen years. Yet all of us who attempt to chronicle contemporary feminism, myself included, must be wary of this division of decades and how it inevitably ends up reproducing an all-too-pat vision of generations and their political consciousness.

Feminism did not die out in the 1980s. In addition to the ongoing feminism of women active in the women's movement of the 1960s and 1970s, many women who came of age in the late 1970s and 1980s embraced feminism as eagerly as women had before them and women would after them.[18] Similarly, celebrating the 1990s as a time of un-adulterated acceptance of feminism is simply wrong. As every opinion poll on feminism over the last decade has shown, the majority of women—young and old—do not identify with the term "feminist," even as they support most of the changes made by the feminist movement over the last thirty-five years. In fact, two recent nationwide polls suggest that the percentage of women who identify as feminist has actually dropped over the last decade.[19] Whatever post-feminism means then, it is not a concept that disappeared in the early 1990s. Many young women today define themselves as post-feminist even as some of their contemporaries deliberately reject the term in order to signal their own, "new" feminism.

While expressing some truth, the notion that the 1980s can be dismissed as a post-feminist decade is, in great part, a fiction that has helped to propagate conservatives' view of feminism and that now serves to grant a new generation of feminists a way by which to distinguish themselves from their immediate predecessors. The mainstream media has played an important role in the construction and maintenance of this chronology of feminism's history. In the 1980s, popular-press coverage of the women's movement was characterized by articles proclaiming the failure of feminism—to transform women's lives, to make women happy, to effect social and political change.[20] In essence, feminism was blamed both for not doing enough and for doing too much to change the lives of women. In the early 1990s, however, a noticeable shift began to take place in the media's coverage of feminism, the women's movement, and women's relationship to feminism. To begin with, feminism was once again in vogue as a topic of discussion. More important, it was no longer possible to simply proclaim that feminism had failed, for however contradictory, women appeared to be rejecting and reclaiming feminism simultaneously. The early 1990s saw a series of such articles, most of which addressed the double-edged response U.S. women have to feminism: on the one hand, the overwhelming majority strongly believe in women's equality; on the other hand, many women are reluctant to identify themselves as feminists, often due to the belief that one must subscribe to a particular set of feminist ideals, or conform to a particular "feminist type," in order to be a "real"—or "good"—feminist.[21]

If in the early part of the 1990s feminism was being reclaimed and reconceptualized—both in the press and in women's lives—this phenomenon cannot be understood without looking at the larger social and political shifts that were occurring during, and just prior to, this period. Undoubtedly twelve years of conservative policies instituted by Reagan and Bush did a great deal to spark women's activism around issues such as abortion and reproductive rights, gay and lesbian rights, equal wages and treatment in the workplace, AIDS, and sexual harassment. In addition, gains made by the second wave of the women's movement in the areas of rape law and victims' rights had slowly filtered into the culture. By the late 1980s and early 1990s, feminist issues such as date rape were receiving a great deal of national attention. Similarly, the great number of high-profile sexual-abuse cases during this period—particularly those involving children in day-care centers and adults with recovered memories of abuse—increased mainstream awareness of feminist tenets such as believing the victim. While much of this feminist legal and social reform was undoubtedly long overdue, the high visibility of cases of sexual violence and abuse, combined with the increasing attention paid to sexual harassment following the Thomas-Hill hearings, led some to argue that "sexual correctness" had gone too far.[22] An offshoot of political correctness, sexual correctness has often been described as a product of the feminist movement and its attention to women's victimization. The notion of sexual correctness has been used by many anti-feminists to argue that feminism itself has gone too far.

At the same time that some feminists were being indicted for their promotion of sexual correctness, other feminists were advocating a noticeably different kind of feminist approach to sexuality, one that emphasized women's pleasure and power over their victimization. As many feminist historians and theorists have discussed, a tension between these two opposing views of sexuality and women's victimization has been a part of feminism since its inception. It is beyond the scope of this project to trace the history of this debate within feminism, and others have already done so quite well.[23] Rather, what I am interested in here is how at this particular moment in feminism's history—around 1991—this internal debate within feminism increasingly moved into the public arena. Like other trends within the popular representation of feminism during this period, the high visibility of conflicts within feminism seemed to signal a renewed interest in feminism and its goals. It has been suggested that the enactment of these conflicts in the public arena can only have negative consequences, such as accusations of "cat fights" and "sibling rivalry" among women, the triumph of the most conservative form of feminism, and ultimately the repudiation of feminism itself.[24] This is undoubtedly true in many instances, yet I would also argue that something positive is to be gained by this supposed airing of dirty laundry; namely, the public exposure of the differences and diversity within feminism. In presenting feminism as contested ground, it appears both alive and lively, open and eager for a new generation to engage with it. And so, it seems, a new generation has.

THE DAWNING OF THE THIRD WAVE

Simultaneous to this activity of the early 1990s, a new movement in feminism was being heralded: the third wave. The term "third wave" has been attributed to Rebecca Walker, who first used it in a 1992 *Ms.* essay; later that same year, Walker co-founded a national organization called Third Wave Foundation devoted to young women's activism.[25] In fact, however, the term "third wave" originally surfaced, to my knowledge, five years earlier in an essay titled "Second Thoughts on the Second Wave," by Deborah Rosenfelt and Judith Stacey. In describing the ebbs and flows of feminism throughout the late 1970s and 1980s, Rosenfelt and Stacey write that "what some are calling a third wave of feminism [is] already taking shape."[26] Naomi Wolf, in her 1991 *Beauty Myth*, first imbued the term with a specifically generational meaning, referring to the "feminist third wave" as women who were in their twenties in the early 1990s.[27]

During the late 1980s and early 1990s, the term "third wave" was also being used by some feminists "to identify a new feminism that is led by and has grown out of the challenge to white feminism posited by women of color." The text which is often cited as making this claim is an anthology which never materialized in book form, due to financial problems at Kitchen Table: Women of Color Press.[28] Though never actually published, *The Third Wave: Feminist Perspectives on Racism* continues to inform the way some feminists employ the term "third wave," using it to signal a new wave of feminism led by women of color that is specifically anti-racist in its approach. As Lisa Albrecht, one of this text's editors, reports, however, within the context of this anthology, the term "third wave" was not meant to be understood as a generational term.

> Third wave feminism as we used it was NOT about young feminists or generational feminism. It was/is about a movement beyond the first two waves of feminism, which we saw as [focused on] white women. . . . We defined third wave feminism as emerging with *This Bridge Called My Back* and the rise of vocal women of color challenging white women.[29]

Albrecht's use of "third wave" to indicate a challenge by women of color to white feminists and the racism within the second wave continues to shape contemporary uses of the term.[30] However, by the mid- to late 1990s, the term "third wave" had become synonymous with younger feminists and with stressing generational differences from the second-wave feminists of the 1970s.[31]

The use of the term "wave" long predates its use in the 1990s. Women involved in the women's liberation movement of the late 1960s and early 1970s adopted the term "second wave" in order to signify their connection to the feminism of the nineteenth and early twentieth centuries, which from that moment on became known as the first wave of feminism.[32] The term "wave" served to indicate a resurgence of a previously existing movement. However, the second wave's use of the term "first wave" to mark the earlier period in feminist activity frequently carried with it an assumption about the superiority of their own movement, using the numerical delineation of a "second wave" to signify feminism's progress.

The wave metaphor signals both continuity and discontinuity; in fact, both are essential to its rhetorical effectiveness. Continuity is suggested in the very notion of a wave, which is inevitably followed by successive waves cresting on the shore. The term "wave" is rarely used to stress the singularity of something but rather emphasizes the inevitability of—and connection to—other such waves. Discontinuity—and often progress and improvement—is highlighted by the numerical delineation of a new, in this case second, wave. While waves may inexorably be connected to other waves, and thus never stand alone in isolation, the announcement of a new wave is typically meant to stress the *evolution* of ideas and political movements. The wave metaphor, then, manifests the same contradictory take on the earlier women's movement that I have been emphasizing: it allows one both to identify and disidentify with the past.[33]

In her 1992 article "Becoming the Third Wave," written in response to the Clarence Thomas hearings, Rebecca Walker uses the term to emphasize both that feminism is not dead and that a new generation of feminists is beginning to mobilize. As she states, "I am not a postfeminism feminist. I am the Third Wave."[34] In defining herself as not post-feminist, Walker insists that she has not moved beyond the space created by the second wave; she is not beyond feminism. Her denunciation of the category post-feminist can be read as an indictment of the media's labeling of all women who chronologically follow the second wave as such. Moreover, Walker's claim can also be read as a way to distance herself from the group of women—whether organized generationally or not—who have embraced the term "post-feminism." Her claiming of the title "feminist" maintains a link with second-wave feminists while simultaneously enabling her to distance herself from the generation that immediately precedes her.

Yet the fact that Walker's "I am not a postfeminism feminist" is immediately followed by "I am the Third Wave" suggests that, for her, merely adopting the label "feminist" is not sufficient. As she later notes, third-wavers "modify the label [feminism] in an attempt to begin to articulate our differences."[35] Walker's use of the term "third wave," like the second wave's self-baptism two and a half decades earlier, represents a desire to be a part of something new, a movement distinct from the previous wave. In fact, the term "third wave" can only be understood within the context of its two preceding waves, the first and, more important, the second wave of U.S. feminism. In the move from second to third, the naming of a new wave relies upon the connotation of progress implied by the metaphor of the wave. The bravado behind Walker's claim—"*I am* the Third Wave"—would further seem to suggest a breaking away from second-wave feminism even as it disavows this break.[36]

Like Walker, Naomi Wolf's 1991 description of the then-burgeoning third wave is concerned with remaining within an ongoing feminist tradition—that is, she does not describe herself as beyond or "post" feminism—while simultaneously breaking away from second-wave feminism.

I have become convinced that there are thousands of young women ready and eager to join forces with a peer-driven feminist third wave that would take on, along with the classic feminist agenda, the new problems that have arisen with the shift in Zeitgeist and the beauty backlash. . . . While transmitting the previous heritage of feminism intact, it would need to be, as all feminist waves are, peer-driven: no matter how wise a mother's advice is, we listen to our peers. It would have to make joy, rowdiness, and wanton celebration as much a part of its project as hard work and bitter struggle, and it can begin all this by rejecting the pernicious fib that is crippling young women—the fib called postfeminism, the pious hope that the battles have all been won.[37]

Within this relatively short passage from *The Beauty Myth*, a number of the distinguishing characteristics of the "new" feminism called the third wave are evident, ideas that would be explored in greater detail by a wide range of young feminists as the 1990s rolled on. This generation enters into feminism through both rejecting the imagined post-feminism of their immediate predecessors (and some of their peers) and reclaiming the feminism of the early second wave.

The identificatory relationship established between second- and third-wave feminists, however, has as much to do with disidentifying as it does with identifying. Like the relationship constructed by second-wave feminists to their first-wave predecessors, in this relationship it is the ambivalence or tension between acceptance and rejection—moving closer and breaking away—that is most interesting. In Wolf's text, while it is not particularly zealous in trying to break free from second-wave feminism, one can see tendencies that point toward this disidentifying trend within third-wave writing.[38] Wolf writes that "along with the classic feminist agenda," third-wave feminism would also need to address "the new problems that have arisen with the shift in Zeitgeist." Thus, while this feminism would need to transmit "the previous heritage of feminism intact," it would also need to go beyond that heritage and offer something new. But what exactly would be new about this feminism, and what would it look like?

Wolf does not explore this question in much detail in *The Beauty Myth*, but she does offer us some clues. In defining this new wave as peer-driven, she unequivocally divides coexisting generations of feminists into age-based camps. Furthermore, the way she describes this generational division—"No matter how wise a mother's advice is, we listen to our peers"—stresses that it is predicated on the difference between the familial and the non-familial, mothers and peers. Within this structure, second-wave feminists become the mothers of the new wave. Their feminism is reduced to advice which, "no matter how wise," can, and perhaps should, be rejected in favor of what non-familial co-horts have to offer.

In describing second-wave feminism as a figurative mother figure to the third wave, Wolf provides an early example of what was to become a ubiquitous trope within subsequent writing on feminist generational relationships. The reliance on the mother-daughter trope to describe the relationship between the second and third waves may have been inevi-table given that the age difference between each wave's representatives is roughly the equivalent of one familial generation. The effectiveness of this metaphoric familial relationship is compounded by the fact that for some third-wave writers and activists, their real mothers are, in fact, second-wave feminists: this is the case for both Rebecca Walker and Naomi Wolf, for example.[39] Second-wave feminists, then, are literally mother figures to the third wave, even as they are given this figurative role in their writing.

Central to this imagined mother-daughter relationship, however, is the absence of the generation of women who came of age in the late 1970s and 1980s: the so-called post-feminist generation. This generation has slipped through the cracks of the current generational structure being used to talk about feminism, feminist generations, and feminist waves. Its disappearance is no accident. This generation cannot be a branch on feminism's family tree if the wave structure and the family structure are to be mapped onto one another. Had Wolf included this missing generation into her description of feminism, her easy characterization of second-wave feminists as mothers would never have been possible.[40] The overwhelming preference for talking about feminist generations in terms of second and third waves—a generational structure modeled on the familial structure of the mother-daughter relationship—has meant that women who were in their twenties and early thirties in the 1980s must be metaphorically exiled from feminism's imagined family.

In her attempt to visualize the possible feminism of a third wave, Wolf provides the following image of pleasure, which would become central in defining generational differences between the two waves: "It would have to make joy, rowdiness, and wanton celebration as much a part of its project as hard work and bitter struggle." Wolf did not set these contrasting images of how feminism *feels* to those who engage with it in opposition in this passage; in fact, she argues that both must be central to the third-wave project. As the 1990s continued, however, "joy, rowdiness, and wanton celebration" would increasingly come to define third-wave feminism, while "bitter struggle" would be almost exclusively attributed to the second wave, with the emphasis on bitterness.

In the years immediately following *The Beauty Myth,* several other books were published which were significant in attempting to define this new feminism and its relationship to feminisms of the (recent) past. Wolf's own *Fire with Fire: The New Female Power and How It Will Change the 21st Century,* published in 1993, signaled a sharp change of course in the feminism of this writer, who was thirty-three at the time of its publication.[41] While *The Beauty Myth* was criticized for contributing to women's sense of themselves as powerless victims of the patriarchal beauty industry, *Fire with Fire* is an argument for what Wolf terms "power feminism," a feminism in staunch opposition to "victim feminism."[42] Like Wolf's first book, *Fire with Fire* received a lot of critical attention in the popular press, although it did not have the same impact as *The Beauty Myth.*[43] Even as it purports to argue for "power feminism" and against "victim feminism," it defines these two "opposing" sides so broadly that the thrust of Wolf's argument tends to get lost. One critic wrote that Wolf advocates "a feminism so inclusive it has no specific content."[44]

A book that garnered a much more polarized response from its critics was Katie Roiphe's *The Morning After: Sex, Fear, and Feminism on Campus,* also published in 1993.[45] Whereas *Fire with Fire* is surprisingly non-confrontational, Roiphe sharply attacks contemporary feminism by examining what she terms "the date rape movement" and its negative effect on young women's perception and experience of sexuality. At the time of the book's publication Roiphe was a 25-year-old graduate student at Princeton University. She first gained public attention in 1991 with her *New York Times* op-ed piece entitled "Date Rape Hysteria"; in the summer of 1993, "Date Rape's Other Victim," an adapted version of a chapter from *The Morning After,* was published in the *New York Times Magazine.*[46] Roiphe's book and the articles that preceded it received an enormous amount of critical attention from both supporters and detractors.[47] *The Morning After* was reviewed on the front page of the *New York Times Book Review,* a rather remarkable accomplishment for a first book by a relatively young and unknown author.[48] Roiphe was applauded for what one critic called her "brave" stand in opposition to the feminist "doctrine" surrounding date rape and women's victimization.[49] It was "the first intelligent cry of protest from Roiphe's generation against what feminism hath wrought in the name of woman," said another.[50] Yet others lambasted her for her inaccurate and unsympathetic discussion of date rape on college campuses and for her overly simplistic portrayal of contemporary feminism.[51] This representation of feminism enabled Roiphe to depict herself as on the cutting edge of feminist critique—distinctive and alone "aside from the lone dissenting voice of Camille Paglia," as she herself put it.[52]

Two years later another book challenging second-wave feminism appeared on the scene: Rene Denfeld's *The New Victorians: A Young Woman's Challenge to the Old Feminist Order,* published in 1995. Denfeld, a 28-year-old journalist at the time of the book's publication, repeats the rhetorical strategy used by Roiphe and Wolf: she constructs a nightmarish vision of contemporary feminism, one built on its excesses, so that she can knock it down and offer another feminism in its place. Like Roiphe and Wolf, Denfeld relies on a particularly skewed understanding of academic feminism and feminist theory to make her case that feminism has gone off course. *The New Victorians* did not receive as much critical attention as had either *The Morning After* or *Fire with Fire.* This occurred, I think, in part because many familiar with the history of feminism and the women's movement found Denfeld's thesis—that contemporary feminism is repeating the mistakes of nineteenth-century feminism—to be a topic that, as one critic wrote, "has been thoroughly explored by historians and journalists."[53] Denfeld did not enter feminism in the same controversial manner as did Roiphe, although they share many of the same gripes.

All three of these books are popular (and popularized) mainstream feminist texts of the 1990s, texts that have been identified—by either their authors or their commentators—as representative of the next generation of feminists' critique of the second wave. Although the theoretical bent of each of these authors is different, each attempts to define feminism at the end of the twentieth century by positing a generational divide between third- and second-wave feminisms and feminists. Denfeld, Roiphe, and Wolf were early influences on the generationally focused direction that feminism took in the 1990s. In creating a monolithic, irrelevant, and misguided second wave against which to posit their own brand of feminism, they defined a rhetorical structure that many other third-wave writers would duplicate as the 1990s progressed, even as these later writers would do so for different means and ends.[54]

Some commentators, including Leslie Heywood and Jennifer Drake in *Third Wave Agenda,* refer to Roiphe, Denfeld, and Wolf as post-feminists in order to distinguish their own version of third-wave feminism from that of this more conservative trio.[55] While I sympathize with their desire to distance themselves from this other group of young feminists, I disagree with their method. As Jennifer Baumgardner and Amy Richards note in *Manifesta: Young Women, Feminism, and the Future,* "Failing to distinguish between Roiphe and the right wing, regardless of legitimate critiques of her work, is where feminists did themselves damage."[56] Separating young feminists into two camps—third-wave feminists and post-feminists—can be useful in order to outline the ideological differences between them; yet I believe we must be wary of how the term "post-feminist" is ultimately used to dismiss those with whom we might disagree. While it is disturbing and worthy of criticism that it is generally more conservative feminists—usually white, usually straight—who tend to get the headlines, this in and of itself does not warrant rejecting them from the feminist camp. In fact, in their critique of the very notion of a feminist camp, I agree with these more conservative writers: feminism must have room for dissent.[57]

By the mid-1990s, other next-generation writers began to participate in the dialogue that had been initiated, in part, by this group of dissenting feminist voices. While the feminism of Denfeld, Roiphe, and Wolf primarily focused on the perceived orthodoxies of the monolithic feminism they wished to challenge, the texts that emerged in the mid- to late 1990s offered a more complex representation of second-wave feminism to a popular audience.[58] This later group of writers stressed their connection to the feminisms of the past even as they sought to posit themselves as new—both generationally and ideologically. In 1995, two now-classic third-wave anthologies were published: *Listen Up: Voices from the Next Feminist Generation,* edited by Barbara Findlen, and *To Be Real: Telling the Truth and Changing the Face of Feminism,* edited by Rebecca Walker. As Findlen says of *Listen Up,* "The spirited voices in this collection are not 'daughters' rebelling against the old-style politics of their 'mothers.'"[59] Both anthologies address a wide range of feminist perspectives, and the authors included represent a spectrum of racial, ethnic, gender, and sexual identities. Subsequent third-wave anthologies—such as *Third Wave Agenda: Being Feminist, Doing Feminism* (Heywood and Drake, 1997); *Adiós Barbie: Young Women Write about Body Image and Identity* (Edut, 1998); *Letters of Intent: Women Cross the Generations to Talk about Family, Work, Sex, Love and the Future of Feminism* (Bondoc and Daly, 1999); *Colonize This! Young Women of Color on Today's Feminism* (Hernández and Rehman, 2002); and *Catching a Wave: Reclaiming Feminism for the 21st Century* (Dicker and Piepmeier, 2003)—repeat the framework of the 1995 collections in their vision of a third-wave feminism in which both race and sexuality are centrally located alongside gender.[60] Cross-generational dialogue has also become more common within this new wave's texts.[61] In addition to these anthologies, several new feminist magazines—aimed at feminists in their twenties and thirties—began publishing during the 1990s, including *Bust* and *Bitch: Feminist Response to Popular Culture*.[62] The 1990s also witnessed an explosion of independent feminist publications, such as fanzines and webzines, and musical and cultural movements, such as Riot Grrrls and the Radical Cheerleaders.[63] And outside the United States, a "new feminism" spearheaded by young women was also being proclaimed in Australia, Canada, and the United Kingdom.[64]

In both *Catching a Wave* and *Colonize This!* September 11, 2001, and its aftermath are discussed, and when compared to the earlier collections of the mid-1990s, these more recent anthologies suggest that third-wave discourse is beginning to move beyond the autobiographical essay that has so defined its rhetorical style toward a more overtly political agenda. As Rory Dicker and Alison Piepmeier describe their volume, *Catching a Wave*

> contends that this generation needs a politicized, activist feminism that is grounded in the material realities and the cultural productions of life in the twenty-first century. We need a feminism that is dedicated to a radical, transformative political vision, a feminism that does not shy away from hard work but recognizes that changing the world is a difficult and necessary task.[65]

A more overtly political third wave is also called for in *Manifesta: Young Women, Feminism, and the Future* (2000) by Jennifer Baumgardner and

Amy Richards, which provides readers with a thirteen-point political agenda for feminism's next wave, an appendix with resources for activist work, and a guide for voter registration activism.[66]

The third-wave feminism represented in these more recent texts paints a very different portrait of contemporary feminism than the one offered by third-wave writers such as Katie Roiphe and Naomi Wolf, most specifically because these latter writers rarely engage with feminism that isn't produced by and about white women.[67] The intense media focus given to Roiphe and other white "dissenter" feminists has tended to obscure one of the most exciting aspects of this burgeoning movement: namely, that the third wave is truly a multiracial, multiethnic coalition of young activists and writers. At least, that is how many third-wave writers have tried to describe this new wave. As Catherine Orr notes:

> [T]he contradictory character of the third wave emerged not from the generational divides between second wavers and their daughters, but from critiques by Cherríe Moraga, Gloria Anzaldúa, bell hooks, Chela Sandoval, Audre Lorde, Maxine Hong Kingston and many other feminists of color who called for a "new subjectivity" in what was, up to that point, white, middle-class, first world feminism. These are the discourses that shaped, and must continue to shape, third wave agendas in the years to come.[68]

An early example of this conceptualization of the third wave is found in Sandoval's 1991 essay, "U.S. Third World Feminism: The Theory and Method of Oppositional Consciousness in the Postmodern World." In it she writes, "the recognition of differential consciousness" coming out of U.S. Third World feminism "is vital to the generation of a next 'third wave' women's movement and provides grounds for alliance with other decolonizing movements for emancipation."[69] As seen in much third-wave writing by writers of all races, the central insight of U.S. Third World feminist thought regarding the interlocking nature of identity—that gender, race, ethnicity, sexuality, and class never function in isolation but always work as interconnected categories of oppression and privilege—has been described as the second wave's most influential and vital lesson. For many third-wavers, critiques of feminism's racism, its homophobia, and its inattention to other forms of oppression among women have been at the center of what they have learned as feminist theory and the history of the women's movement.[70] As Ednie Kaeh

Garrison noted in 2000, "It is clear now that feminist critiques of feminism are part of the very origins of Third Wave feminism rather than trailing behind an already unitary model of the movement."[71]

While Garrison is correct to note that these critiques are "part of the origins" of the third wave—at least for many of the writers included in the more recent anthologies noted above—a "unitary model of the movement" still circulates within third-wave writing: namely, a unitary second wave in which women of color are relegated to the sidelines. Even when second-wave feminists of color are recognized as foundational to the third wave, such feminists seem unable to represent feminism itself.[72] On one hand, depicting the second wave as primarily white can be read as an acknowledgment of the secondary status given to feminists of color during the last forty years of feminist theory and movement. On the other hand, this gesture enables third-wave feminists to position themselves as superior to the feminists of the past in their seeming ability to make *their* feminism anti-racist from its inception. An emblematic example of this gesture can be found in *Colonize This!*, where one contributor writes:

> The predominantly white and racist feminist movement of the 1970s ignored the relationship between racism, classism and homophobia. This pervasive feminist thinking has denied the complexities of the oppression I fight everyday [*sic*]. In the growing emergence of "third wave" feminism, feminism isn't reduced to one English-speaking white face from North America.[73]

While I don't mean to suggest that the feminist movement of the 1970s was not "predominantly white and racist," I am interested in how repeating this representation enables younger feminists to present their new wave as more progressive and inclusive than that of their second-wave predecessors. As Lisa Marie Hogeland rightly points out, "It's become a truism that the second wave was racist, for instance, no matter that such a blanket argument writes out of our history the enormous and important contributions of women of color in the 1970s."[74] For feminism to truly be transformed from within, as the most optimistic third-wave writers argue it has been, it must incorporate a history of the struggles that got us next-generation feminists to where we are today.[75] Feminism's history cannot be reduced to a simple narrative in which the "bad" white racist second wave was replaced by the "good" racially diverse and anti-racist third wave.[76]

As it has developed over the last decade, the third wave has been given a variety of meanings, particularly with regard to what makes it new or different from second-wave feminism. As of this writing, third-wave feminism refers to at least three distinct, albeit interconnected, concepts: generational age, ideological position, and historical moment. In its primary use, "third wave" signifies the age of its adherents; that is, "third wave" refers to the feminism practiced and produced by women and men who were born after the baby-boom generation.[77] In its earliest formulation, "third wave" was frequently conflated with Generation X (those born 1961–1981) because Gen X feminists were in their twenties and early thirties when the third wave first emerged in the early 1990s.[78] By the turn of the twenty-first century, however, segments of Generation X had moved into their late thirties and (gasp!) early forties, raising interesting questions about the ways in which "third wave" denotes age and generational location. In *Manifesta*, Baumgardner and Richards claim that "third wave" refers to feminists "under thirty-five," while Third Wave Foundation, the organization co-founded by Richards and Rebecca Walker, describes its mission as "support[ing] the leadership of young women 15 to 30."[79] While Generation X ages, the third wave remains young, unhinging the relationship between the two terms. It would appear, then, that "third wave" remains a signifier of youth rather than of a particular generation. Like the 1960s slogan "don't trust anyone over 30," this meaning of third wave suggests that a particular politics is the province of the young. This understanding of the term radically alters our use of the wave metaphor in describing feminist generations. Just as Baby Boomers remain within their demographic category even as they age, second-wave feminists remain "second wave" even as they grow older. (One could even say that this aging has been central to the third wave's representation of the second wave.) However, if Generation X feminists are no longer third wave once they reach thirty-five, what wave are they a part of? Does aging make one second wave? No matter what their year of birth or demographic generation is, will feminists under thirty-five own the third wave?[80]

A second understanding of "third wave" stresses its value as an ideology independent from a demographic generation. In this understanding of the term, the third wave represents a shift within feminist thought, moving it in a new direction by blending aspects of second-wave feminism with other forms of contemporary critical theory, such as queer, post-colonial, and critical race theories. As Heywood and Drake describe this ideological shift, third-wave feminism "contains elements of second wave critique of beauty culture, sexual abuse, and power structures while it also acknowledges and makes use of the pleasure, danger, and defining power of those structures."[81] This ideological understanding of third-wave feminism leads to a third meaning which sees it as developing out of the realities of the current historical moment, "a world of global capitalism and information technology, postmodernism and postcolonialism, and environmental degradation," as Dicker and Piepmeier write in *Catching a Wave*. "We no longer live in the world that feminists of the second wave faced." Third-wave feminists, they continue, "are therefore concerned not simply with 'women's issues' but with a broad range of interlocking topics."[82]

The ways in which historical moment, ideology, and age are frequently conflated within third-wave discourse complicates any easy separation of the term's meanings. In fact, if the third wave's ideology is seen as an *inevitable* by-product of either this current historical moment or the age of its practitioners, there seems to be little difference between the terms.[83] Yet, if the term "third-wave feminism" is meant to describe a particular ideological stance in relation to contemporary social and political realities, it could, of course, be adopted—or rejected—by feminists of all ages. Writing as a, generationally speaking, second-wave feminist, Carol Siegel notes: "Lately, among some of the self-described third-wave feminists, I have finally started to feel, once again, at home in feminism. Could feminism's third wave be my wave?"[84] Siegel's comments point to the possibilities of cross-generational identification, cautioning us against permanently affixing ideologies to people simply because of their chronological age.

In none of these various understandings, however, is the term "third wave" used to describe a political movement in the 1960s sense; rather, the third wave functions more like "an ideology without a movement."[85] As Ednie Kaeh Garrison argues, "In the Third Wave, feminist collective consciousness may not necessarily manifest itself in a nationalized and highly mobilized social movement unified around a single goal or identity. At the moment, this hardly seems imaginable."[86] In fact, in its current manifestation, third-wave feminism is more about textual and cultural production, local forms of activism, and a particular form of feminist consciousness than it is a large-scale social justice movement.

ENTERING FEMINISM

"Women's rights are my generation's heritage and we've taken their promise to heart. And now we need to take back feminism."[87] This passage, which concludes Rene Denfeld's introduction to *The New Victorians,* is emblematic of how many young feminist writers enter into feminism. On the one hand, they describe themselves as the beneficiaries of feminism, raised with an unshakable belief in their own equality. Yet that equality—or women's rights—is frequently juxtaposed with feminism, as if to suggest that feminism is no longer concerned with women's rights but rather with women's powerlessness. Central to this argument is the notion that while contemporary feminism may not be doing its job right, these women can rehabilitate it; they can save it, as it were. The call to "take back feminism" seems purposely designed to recall the second-wave feminist slogan and movement "take back the night." The premise behind that earlier movement—that women should take back the night and the streets from men—suggests that it is men who stand in the way of women's liberation. In reworking this slogan, Denfeld gives it an interesting spin. It is now feminists, not men, who stand in the way of women's liberation; it is feminists who have what must be taken back.

Denfeld's edict to "take back feminism" is puzzling, though, given that it seems to imply that feminism was once rightfully ours—that is, belonging to the generation of women who came of age in the late 1980s and early 1990s. Feminism *is* ours in that we have lived our entire lives with the political and social gains made by the second wave of the women's movement, we have been educated by women's studies programs and feminist theory, and we have grown up taking for granted the success and victories of our mothers' generation of feminism.[88] But is feminism ours in such a way that we can "take it back"? And what would it mean to "take it back" from the women who gave it to us in the first place?

Denfeld's call to take back feminism points to a significant difference in the ways in which the women of the two waves enter into feminism and identify as feminists. When she writes that "[w]e are living lives radically different from the ones the current feminist leadership did at our age," I believe Denfeld means more than just the fact that young women today are raised with a belief in their own abilities and equality.[89] While second-wave feminists could believe, as Vivian Gornick has written, that "we were making the revolution," third-wave feminists do not enter feminism with the same sense of their own power to change history.[90] In great part, this can be attributed to the very different political climate of the contemporary U.S. as compared to that of the 1960s and early 1970s, as well as the new global realities that face all citizens of the world at this current historical moment. Women entering feminism today are much less idealistic—and hopeful—about the possibility of revolutionary social change than were early second-wave feminists. Paradoxically, then, younger women may have a strong sense of their own personal power while feeling ambivalent about their power to effect real change.

Indeed, there is no indication that the third wave believes it is "making the revolution" in the same sense as did Gornick's generation. Rather, the opposite is true; third-wave texts are replete with images of having been born too late to effect real change. "I used to think I had missed my time. I thought the flame lighting the hearts of activists had been snuffed."[91] "I have always been upset that I missed the protests of the sixties and seventies. Lots of women in my generation have felt that there was no way to actively fight for our rights."[92] Throughout this project, I discuss how third-wavers have frequently created a feminism of their own by pitting their wave against the second wave. For other young feminists, however, this new wave lacks any unifying objective, eliciting feelings of loss and disappointment over what our generation has missed out on.[93] As Meg Daly so accurately writes, "We use our anger at our 'mothers' as an excuse for inertia and lack of focus. We're jealous that they got an exciting revolution and we got . . . Bill Clinton?"[94] In this reoccurring motif, the third wave expresses a longing for a political movement to call its own.[95]

Another important distinction marks the ways in which the two waves enter into feminism. In inaugurating their movement, second-wave feminists did not have to confront an established feminist generation in their immediate present. The first wave of feminism was long since "dead" by the time they emerged on the political scene. They could thus identify with feminists of the previous century without really having to contend with them. First-wave feminists could be embraced as foremothers precisely because they were no longer around to contest the "new" feminism—not to mention the second wave's depiction of their movement. In contrast, when third-wave feminists come to feminism, they confront a social and political movement and theory that already exists. Moreover, second-wave feminists are still very much a part of the feminist landscape. In fact, for many young feminists, second-wavers appear to "control" feminism, prompting one contributor to *Listen Up* to note that "[y]oung feminists have long felt we needed to be invited to our mothers' party."[96]

In their desire to have a movement of their own, third-wave feminists share sentiments expressed by the second wave in its early period. Yet the third wave's use of the wave metaphor to mark what may more accurately be described as a *generational shift* within feminism is troubling for what it suggests about how new movements within feminism must articulate their emergence. Third-wave feminists do not bring feminism into being; they do not create feminism from within. This is not to imply, of course, that second-wave feminists invented feminism. However, their experience of becoming feminists and developing a women's movement had a sense of newness, discovery, and rebellion about it that cannot be said to characterize the third wave. The newness, discovery, and particularly the rebellion offered by third-wave writers lies somewhere else than in the act of making feminism. It lies in the confrontation with feminism.

When second-wave feminists began to organize in the late 1960s, they were reacting, in great part, to the sexism of both the New Left and the civil rights movement. Thus, the development of an autonomous women's movement was a kind of rejection of and rebellion against both the other leftist and freedom movements of the period and the misogyny of society at large. Second-wave feminism did not initially develop in opposition to other forms of feminism. As the second wave developed, conflicts between various kinds of feminism emerged; divisions among feminists increasingly became feminism's focus. However, it is important to remember that when the second wave emerged, it seemed (and was) revolutionary precisely because it had a formidable *external* foe: sexism, misogyny, the patriarchy.[97]

From an analysis of some third-wave writing, it would appear that, in the thirty-five years since the second wave's inception, our notions of what feminism is fighting against have dramatically changed: we've moved from taking back the night to taking back feminism. The next generation of feminists do not appear to experience their enemy as external. Rather, the battles are internal. In its most extreme formulation, it is feminism itself that has become the enemy.

> From Catherine MacKinnon to the protesters against the *Sports Illustrated* swimsuit issue to more mainstream theorists of sexual harassment, feminists are on the front lines of sexual regulation. . . . [F]eminism has come more and more to represent sexual thoughts and images censored, behavior checked, fantasies regulated. In my late adolescent idiom, feminism was not about rebellion, but rules; it was not about setting loose, as it once was, it was about reining in.[98]

In Roiphe's description of contemporary feminism, it is no longer misogynist men, patriarchal attitudes, or a sexist culture which "regulate" women's behavior. The task of regulating women's lives has been taken over by feminists, the very group who were concerned with freeing women from oppressive control. Feminism, then, seems to stand in the place that once was occupied by the external forces against feminism. Feminism is what stands in the way of women's liberation.[99]

A feminism that seeks to regulate rather than liberate will obviously be, as Roiphe describes it, "not about rebellion, but rules." And rules are what we rebel against, just as the early second wave rebelled against the "rules" of society constraining women's behavior, rights, and opportunities. In her topsy-turvy world of feminism, Roiphe offers a paradoxical position: if feminism is about rebellion, to be true feminists we should rebel against the thing that most oppresses us as women—feminism.

FEMINISM AS BIRTHRIGHT
AND THE IDEOLOGY OF INDIVIDUALISM

"For anyone born after the early 1960s," write Jennifer Baumgardner and Amy Richards, "the presence of feminism in our lives is taken for granted. For our generation, feminism is like fluoride. We scarcely notice that we have it—it's simply in the water."[100] Put another way, "feminism is our birthright," as Denfeld writes in *The New Victorians*.[101] This ubiquitous phrase within third-wave discourse highlights the third wave's unique and historically unprecedented relationship to feminism, one that grants women my age a noticeably different experience of feminism than that of our mothers' generation. Particularly for those of us who were raised by feminist parents to be feminists, feminism is a given, handed to us at birth. It is often not something we need to seek out or fight for. "I didn't spend much time thinking about feminism," writes Roiphe, "It was something assumed, something deep in my foundations."[102] Roiphe's description of feminism as that which is "deep in her foundations"—like Rebecca Walker's statement that feminism "has always been so close to home"—suggests that feminism is indeed "our birthright," a kind of genetic inheritance, passed down at birth.[103] (One critic went as far as describing Roiphe as a woman "who could be said to have imbibed feminism with her mother's milk."[104])

Handed to us at birth, feminism no longer requires the active identification that it once did.[105] We often don't need to get to feminism through some means—whether consciousness-raising, activism, or reevaluating our personal relationships—because feminism is already there for us.[106] As Barbara Findlen writes in *Listen Up*, "My feminism wasn't shaped by antiwar or civil rights activism; I was not a victim of the problem that had no name."[107] We don't need to create feminism, it already exists. We don't need to become feminists, we already are. Because women of my generation often do not experience feminism as a process—that is, as something we actively choose or help to create—we have a much more ambivalent identification with it. Even for those of us who see ourselves as aligned with second-wave feminism, our sense of owning feminism can still feel tenuous. We own feminism in the sense that it is our birthright, yet in other ways it is not ours. It belongs to another generation, another group of women: second-wave feminists. They were the ones who went through the heady experience of *creating* feminism; we just get to reap the benefits.

In order to get a sense of how different feminism felt for second-wave feminists, one need only look at Gloria Steinem's introduction to Walker's anthology, *To Be Real*. In it, she writes, "Because I entered when feminism had to be chosen and even reinvented, I experienced almost everything about it as an unmitigated and joyful freedom—and I still do."[108] When one compares Steinem's "unmitigated and joyful freedom" with the depressing sense of confinement and curbed independence found in some third-wave texts, it is clear that there has been a definite generational shift in the way that women experience feminism. Perhaps the third-wave complaint that feminism feels constricting—as opposed to feeling like "unmitigated freedom"—should be read as a lament for what we missed out on: entering feminism when it had to be chosen and reinvented.[109]

The tendency within much third-wave writing toward making a clean break with the past, rather than maintaining a sense of connection, may be inevitable given the language used to describe the third wave's relationship to feminism. Conceiving of feminism as a birthright passed from mother to daughter undoubtedly influences the third wave's understanding of and relationship to feminism. It may be that something inherited from one's mother is likely to be rejected, no matter what it is. It may be that a birthright, bound up as it is with one's mother, is unable to produce individuality. Defining what she terms "matrophobia," Adrienne Rich writes of "the womanly splitting of the self, in the desire to become purged once and for all of our mother's bondage, to become individuated and free."[110] Given this matrophobia, identifying with one's mother and with her feminism may ultimately incite rebellion, a desire "to move away," as Denfeld calls for.[111]

In fact, I would argue that the excessive focus on individualism by many third-wavers reveals more than just a preference for liberal feminism. In their descriptions of what this individuality is set in opposition to, one gets the sense that individuality provides a means of resisting the group identity implied by the terms "feminists" and "women." Beyond simply disidentifying with these two identity categories, this resistance might also suggest a desire to break away from their mothers, both real and figurative. In *Fire with Fire,* for example, Wolf describes power feminism, the feminism she advocates, as that which "[e]ncourages a woman to claim her individual voice rather than merging her voice in a collective identity."[112] Wolf gives us a clue about what individuality represents for many third-wave feminists: it is the antithesis of "merging her voice in a collective identity." What is to be resisted is staying (sub)merged in collectivity. Wolf's description suggests that in order to retain—or even to gain—one's identity and autonomy, one must unmerge, move away, break free.

In psychoanalytic terms, the notion that one achieves autonomy and individuality through making a clean break from the mother has traditionally been ascribed to the male experience. As part of the individuation process, girls must also separate from their mothers, but because of the gender identification between a girl and her mother, this process is often more difficult, more confusing, and more incomplete. It has been argued that the inability to make such a clean break from the mother—which is, of course, itself an impossible fantasy—leads women to experience their identity as relational. That is, self-identity is always interconnected with the identity of the other, causing girls and women to have less investment in the defensive clean-break model of autonomy exhibited by many boys and men.[113] While this theory has been adopted by many feminists in order to stress the positive psychological traits produced by such identity formation, in general, it has not been able to account for the more negative—or perhaps less idealized—aspects of the female individuation process. In particular, feelings such as ambivalence and even outright hostility toward the mother have gone relatively unexplored.[114]

In the third wave's relationship to the second wave, I believe we see signs of the difficulty that individuation poses for women, particularly in the face of a powerful mother figure: in this case, feminism. As one third-wave writer notes, "A daughter fears that she will somehow be co-opted by her mother's desires, drives, and idiosyncrasies and will become the mother at the expense of the self."[115] In both their retaining of the identity "feminist" and in the rare moments when they champion second-wave feminism, third-wavers maintain a connection to their mothers' generation—and often to their real mothers. Like the shared gender identity between mother and daughter, they are not easily able to extricate themselves from the shared identity of feminist. In their frequent attempts to radically break free from the feminism of the past, however, their desire for autonomy and their own individual identity is revealed. They want a shared connection through feminism, but they want their freedom and individuality too.[116]

In her introduction to *To Be Real,* Walker describes a new generation of feminists that seeks to challenge many of the second wave's perceived orthodoxies; she argues for a feminism that includes contradictions and an ability to go beyond political correctness. As she describes the feminism of the previous generation: "For many of us it seems that to be a feminist in the way that we have seen or understood feminism is to conform to an identity and way of living that doesn't allow for individuality, complexity, or less than perfect personal histories."[117] Challenging the perceived dogmatism of second-wave feminism, third-wavers have steered clear of prescribing a particular feminist agenda and instead have chosen to stress individuality and individual definitions of feminism.[118] As Heywood and Drake note, "[T]he ideology of individualism is still a major motivating force in many third wave lives."[119] Individualism as a shared ideology makes for a political paradox, of course, since historically women's liberation movements, like other civil rights movements, have required some sense of collectivity to pursue political goals. Yet this collectivity—or what a previous generation may have termed "sisterhood"—no longer seems available or even desirable. "The same rights and freedoms feminists won for us have allowed us to develop into a very diverse generation of women, and we value our individuality," writes Denfeld. "While linked through common concerns, notions of sisterhood seldom appeal to women of my generation."[120]

Third-wave feminists' preference for defining feminism in their own terms—that is, for each individual feminist to define feminism *for herself individually*—can be seen in the original declaration of the third wave, Rebecca Walker's 1992 statement "*I am* the Third Wave." In calling for a new wave, Walker does not speak in a collective voice. There is no "we" in this statement, just an "I."[121] An early expression of what was to become a common theme within third-wave discourse, Walker's essay does not attempt to speak in the name of other women. Rather, she writes about her own, individual desire to devote her life to feminism.[122]

The third wave's "ideology of individualism" has found its perfect form in the autobiographical essay, the preferred writing genre of third-wavers and one that shares little with the group manifestos of a previous generation. The majority of third-wave anthologies published since the mid-1990s have been structured around such personal essays and, correspondingly, personal definitions of feminism. Such essays can be seen as the first step in the consciousness-raising process developed from the earlier women's liberation movement. That is, they provide a means by which to express individual experiences and to analyze those experiences in larger social and political terms. Where the third wave has often appeared stuck, however, is in moving from this beginning consciousness-raising stage of self-expression to developing a larger analysis of the relationship between individual and collective experience, culminating in theory and political action.[123]

The third wave's individualistic form of feminism also has an interesting relationship to another second-wave concept: identity politics. As it was conceived by second-wave feminists, as well as other groups from the period, identity politics posits a relationship between one's gender, racial, and class experience and one's political interests. While these identity categories are also routinely stressed in third-wave texts, there is little sense that they can provide a coalescing structure to bring people together, nor are claims in the name of any one group, such as "women," likely to be found in these texts. A good example of how identity categories are stressed in order to further individual expression, as opposed to a collective political agenda, can be found in Barbara Findlen's introduction to *Listen Up*, where she describes the authors in her collection:

> Women in this book call themselves, among other things, articulate, white, middle-class, college kid; wild and unruly; single mother; Asian bisexual; punk; politically astute, active woman; middle-class black woman; young mother; slacker; member of the Muscogee (Creek) Nation; well-adjusted; student; teacher; writer; an individual; a young lady; a person with a visible disability; androgynous; lapsed Jew; child of professional feminists; lesbian daughter; activist; zine writer; a Libra; an educated, married, monogamous, feminist, Christian African American mother.[124]

In its attention to speaking from an embodied and particular position, one that is always inflected by race, class, sexuality, religion, and educational status, this litany of identity categories reveals the influence of second-wave feminism. Yet unlike the second wave, the third wave does not move beyond these individual assertions of identity to a larger, collective political identity. The Asian bisexual can only speak for herself, not for other Asians nor other bisexuals. For the third wave, identity politics is limited to the expression of individual identity.

Within this "ideology of individualism," feminism has frequently been reduced to one issue: choice. In its most watered-down version, this form of third-wave feminism is appealing to many since it rarely represents political and social issues in ways that suggest the need for collective action or change other than on the individual level. As Elspeth Probyn has noted, it is a "choice freed of the necessity of thinking about the political and social ramifications of the act of choosing."[125] Feminism thus becomes an ideology of individual empowerment to make choices, no matter what those choices are.[126]

For the more conservative of this new breed of feminists, this focus on choice and individualism is conceptualized as a return to "the original ideal of feminism," in which "women have ultimate responsibility for their problems, happiness, and lives." As Karen Lehrman argues in advocating what she terms "real feminism," "The personal, in other words, is no longer political."[127] In its worst form, this feminism marks its progress by the status of white middle-class women; as long as this group is doing well, there's clearly no longer a need for a mass movement. This position is the main thesis of Lehrman's 1997 *The Lipstick Proviso: Women, Sex and Power in the Real World*, where she argues that "discrimination is not as bad as it's made out to be," adding, "Women are not 'oppressed' in the United States, and they're no longer (politically at least) even subjugated."[128] In this narrow view, feminism is exclusively concerned with gender equality and fails to recognize the interconnectedness of race, class, and sexuality, let alone connect feminism to other social and economic justice movements.[129] In an essay entitled "Betty Friedan's Granddaughters: *Cosmo,* Ginger Spice & the Inheritance of Whiteness," Jennifer Harris argues that economic and racial privilege enable white, middle-class feminists to solipsistically explore their own identities. These "granddaughters," she argues, "must move beyond reading the 'problems' of contemporary women, as well as the concerns of feminism and the freedom of women, in particularly narrow ways."[130] If the third wave has been schooled in the lessons of the second wave, as some third-wavers argue it has been, then it must conceive of feminism as more than just a movement to empower white economically privileged women. Yet clearly the various articulations of feminism's next generation suggest that there are as many competing narratives of the third wave as there are of the second.

FEMINISM AS MOTHER

In her introduction to *Daughters of Feminists* (1993), Rose Glickman writes:

> In a profound sense all women roughly between the ages of eighteen and thirty-five, whether they embrace or reject feminism, are *the daughters of feminism*, heir to its struggles, failures, and successes; inheritors, willy-nilly, of the heroic phase of the modern women's movement.[131]

Here feminism is described as a mother figure, giving birth, as it were, to a generation of women whose lives will be radically different than those of the women who came before them. Glickman's reliance on the mother-daughter trope to describe the relationship between the second and third waves of U.S. feminism is emblematic of writing by and about young feminists over the last decade. Yet when the mother-daughter trope is relied upon to describe generational conflicts between feminists, feminism often appears as "an embittered, puritanical mother," to quote one commentator.[132] Thinking of feminism as a mother—let alone a "puritanical" one—profoundly shapes the kinds of relationships that will be possible between successive generations of feminists.

Given feminism's tendency to ebb and flow as a political movement, it may be that feminist generational conflict will inevitably be mapped onto the mother-daughter relationship, which has its own set of dynamics surrounding change, progress, and regression. One generation—whether feminist or familial—may reject the past, the next may carry on its tradition. One generation may be conservative, the next radical. A woman's relationship to feminism, then, may invariably be bound up with her relationship to her mother and her mother's generation of women. A first-wave feminist writing in 1871, according to historian Carroll Smith-Rosenberg, "experienced her feminism as a revolt against her mother's ways."[133] A young anti-feminist woman interviewed for Bolotin's 1982 article said, "My feelings about feminism are at least partially a reaction to my [feminist] mother."[134] Feminism may be embraced as either a "revolt" against one's mother or as a way of identifying with her, while the same may be true of the rejection of feminism.

Many of the authors examined here were raised by feminist mothers, including Rene Denfeld, Katie Roiphe, Rebecca Walker, and Naomi Wolf.[135] These "real" mothers are unequivocally described in positive terms in their texts.[136] What they bequeath these women is desired and praised.[137] These are the "good mothers" of third-wave feminism. However, relationships to these "real" mothers coexist alongside relationships to mother feminism: a mother who more often than not is described as confining, regulating, and puritanical. What this mother feminism bestows is unwanted, and these third-wave writers seem to reject what she has to offer. She is the "bad mother" of these texts.

In Roiphe's *The Morning After*, for example, these two relationships are represented by two central figures in the text. The first is Roiphe's biological mother, Anne Roiphe, herself a well-known feminist author. She represents Roiphe's notion of "good feminism": equality feminism that advocates sexual liberation and is against censorship. She is the "good mother" of Roiphe's text.[138] The other figure is Catherine MacKinnon, who plays an equally pivotal role in *The Morning After* as the dour feminist who "looks like someone's aunt" and acts as the strict, prohibitive voice of contemporary feminism and all that is wrong with it.[139] The contrasting relationships that Roiphe has to these two women is indicative of the relationship between the third and second waves as described in much third-wave discourse. While these writers frequently represent their relationships to their own mothers as being positive, especially when those mothers are feminists, there is nevertheless the sense in which feminism itself—whether embodied in a figure such as MacKinnon or not—has come to stand for the "bad mother" of second-wave feminism: the mother who lays down the rules and insists on a curfew.[140]

A central problem with relying on the mother-daughter trope to describe intergenerational conflict is that it forces us to remain within a familial model which lends itself too easily to a psychoanalytic interpretation. It is unfortunate that, unlike with the father-son relationship, classic psychoanalysis has very little to offer us in terms of an understanding of the mother-daughter relationship, especially when it comes to conflict. Even within feminist psychoanalytic work, like that of Nancy Chodorow or Jessica Benjamin, for example, very little has been said about the role of antagonism within this relationship.[141] Part of the problem is that within the psychoanalytic framework there is no equivalent of the Oedipal model for women, leaving us without a means by which to discuss the daughter's desire to "kill the mother." This has caused many feminists, I think, to downplay what is a fairly strong expression of hostility in some of these third-wave texts. Susan Faludi, for example, has argued that "[t]he old Oedipal thing of killing one's father is not what this is about."[142] And Gloria Steinem offers:

> [I]t would help to remember that a feminist revolution rarely resembles a masculine-style one—just as a young woman's most radical act toward her mother (that is, connecting as women in order to help each other get some power) doesn't look much like a young man's most radical act toward his father (that is, breaking the father-son connection in order to separate identities or take over existing power).[143]

In this, I would disagree with Steinem. In fact, many of the young women I have discussed here see their most radical act toward mother feminism as breaking the mother-daughter connection precisely in order to create separate identities or take over existing power.

In her essay "Mothers and Daughters," Erica Duncan argues that the story of Electra is often offered as a competing narrative to the Oedipal model; however, "the Electra story, frequently presented as the paler parallel of the Oedipal myth, deals with revenge for the death of the father and not with any autonomous desire to possess what the mother possesses."[144] Duncan's essay stresses the fact that we have no tradition of "the usurper daughter" from which to begin thinking about such conflicts between mothers and daughters; there is a "total absence of competitive daughters in our literature."[145]

Relying on a non-confrontational model of the mother-daughter relationship not only hampers our ability to discuss the daughter's feelings of hostility and competition toward her mother; it also offers little understanding of the mother's hostility or competition toward her daughter. Beth Schneider has argued that "generational succession is different for women, since through their children, women experience succession as an extension and perhaps natural replacement for themselves rather unlike men who think in terms of displacement."[146] Yet if the second-wave reaction to third-wave feminists is any indication, this can hardly be said to be true. As Rebecca Walker comments on the responses *To Be Real* has generated from second-wave feminists: "I think some of the older women have been a little threatened. It's a fear about being somehow displaced."[147]

CHILDREN OF FEMINISM

Describing feminism as a birthright suggests that feminism is passed down within the home, a familial space of mothers and daughters. Such a spatial image can be seen in Walker's introduction to *To Be Real*, where she writes:

> Linked with my desire to be a good feminist was, of course, not just a desire to change my behavior to change the world, but a deep desire to be accepted, claimed, and loved by a feminist community that included my mother, god-mother, aunts, and close friends. . . . Because feminism has always been so close to home, I worried that I might also be banished from there.[148]

For Walker—the daughter of a famous feminist and the goddaughter of another, Gloria Steinem—feminism is indeed "close to home." Feminism is both family and community; it shapes who she is. Yet her trepidation that she might "be banished from there" would seem to insist that feminism is more than a way of being in the world or acting politically. The possibility of being cast out of feminism suggests that feminism is not just about ideology or political conviction. Rather it functions as a home, a place where feminism is passed down in childhood. Contrast this with Gloria Steinem's foreword to *To Be Real:* "In my generation we came to feminism as adults."[149] The work of third-wave writers suggests that coming to feminism as children has deeply influenced the ways in which they experience feminism. A feminism acquired in childhood *feels* substantially different than one chosen later in life.

In some third-wave texts there is an interesting correlation between understanding feminism as something given to children as a birthright and the frequency with which feminism is described as *childish*. Like something played with as a child, it would seem that feminism forever carries the taint of immaturity. Feminism's association with childhood is central to Katie Roiphe's critique of "victim feminism" in *The Morning After*. In arguing that feminists have gotten to the point where they view any form of unsolicited sexual attention as sexual harassment, for example, she compares feminism's "rules" on sexual harassment to her 3-year-old sister's point of view, implying that while her sister's perspective eventually matured, that of most feminists has not.[150] The connection between feminism and childishness is further stressed in Roiphe's critique of Take Back the Night marches. She mocks such events as furthering an archaic—and child-like—view of female purity and innocence: "Take Back the Night marches are propelled by this myth of innocence lost. All the talk about empowering the voiceless dissolves into the image of the naive girl child who trusts the rakish man." She continues:

> As long as we're taking back the night, we might as well take back our own purity. Sure, we were all kind of innocent, playing in the sandbox with bright red shovels, boys too. We can all look back through the tumultuous tunnel of adolescence on a honey-glazed childhood, with simple rules and early bedtimes.[151]

In pairing "taking back the night" with "taking back our purity," she suggests that both involve a return to childhood: a simpler time. For Roiphe, this return is clearly about regression, moving backward rather than forward to maturity. Becoming a feminist, then, is like returning to childhood, to an "innocent" and "honey-glazed" time "with simple rules and early bedtimes." Roiphe uses childhood as a synecdoche for everything she deplores about contemporary feminism: simplicity, rules, innocence, purity, and a lack of agency. If feminism wants to return us to the simple clarity of a "honey-glazed childhood," with clear rights and wrongs, inevitably it must make children out of adults. It must desexualize us. Her message to feminists appears to be this: grow up.

In *Fire with Fire*, Wolf makes a similar point when she critiques the feminist focus on similarities rather than differences among women. She writes, "[M]any women are still thinking in terms of schoolyard intimacy rather than political power; that we cannot get beyond the idea that a group of women is held together by shared personal closeness rather than specific shared goals."[152] Like Roiphe's image of "playing in the sandbox with bright red shovels," Wolf's "schoolyard intimacy" suggests that feminists are stuck in preadolescent childhood. For Wolf, however, this childhood doesn't represent a pre-sexual period so much as it does a time when women, or should I say girls, are "held together by shared personal closeness." If feminism is based on feeling, Wolf appears to say, feelings are bound to get hurt. In another section of *Fire with Fire*, in fact, she argues that victim feminists "fear ostracism from the group, a childhood sting that never healed. If alliance is seen as intimate friendship, conflict is seen as 'betrayal.'"[153] The problem with so-called victim feminists, then, is that they behave like schoolgirls guided by sentiment rather than grown women with political agency.

The claim that feminism is childish is often coupled with the claim that it is old or old-fashioned. On the surface this seems to be a contradiction; after all, how can something be old and young simultaneously? In these texts, however, the figure of "the grandmother" is used to link these two ideas, specifically around the issue of sexuality. Roiphe writes, "The assumption embedded in the movement against date rape is our grandmothers' assumption: men want sex, women don't. . . . [T]he rape-crisis movement recycles and promotes an old model of sexuality."[154] She later compares guidelines for preventing date rape with her grandmother's warnings to her mother about drinking on dates.[155] The "grandmother"—standing in for women from the generation preceding our mothers'—is both old (and old-fashioned) and naive (or childish) when it comes to sex.[156] Relying on the cultural associations of asexuality which surround the young and the old, the two can thus be used interchangeably to represent the non-sexual.

From a generational perspective, the grandmother plays a critical role in the construction of feminism offered by these third-wave writers. If the mother in these texts (both literal and figurative) represents second-wave feminism, the grandmother embodies the generation of women *before* the second wave: the pre-feminist woman of the 1950s.[157] The grandmother, then, symbolizes the type of woman second-wavers didn't want to be: *their* mothers. As with the allusions to childhood in these texts, the argument here is that feminism involves going backward. Feminism returns us to the past—a time which we have already moved beyond, a time our mothers already "ran away from" and "escaped."[158] Feminism, paradoxically, returns us to a time *before* feminism.

2.

Finding Ourselves in the Past

FEMINIST GENERATIONS AND THE
DEVELOPMENT OF SECOND-WAVE FEMINISM

In the late 1960s in the United States, women around the country were beginning to meet, talk, and organize around the issue of women's liberation. Fed up with the secondary status given to women's issues on the left and emboldened by the black power rhetoric that had emerged from the civil rights movement, these women decided that the time had come for their own issues and goals to be placed at the forefront of their political work. For many of the women involved in this burgeoning movement, the idea that women could work together in the name of women seemed new, exciting, and without much historical precedent. From their perspective, the earlier women's movement of the nineteenth and early twentieth centuries seemed removed and without much relevance to the lives and politics of the new breed of feminists. While many women were certainly aware that a women's movement had existed in the previous century, they looked instead toward the New Left and civil rights movements of the 1960s as the forerunners to their feminism.

As the women's movement of the late 1960s and early 1970s evolved, however, the earlier women's movement and its leaders increasingly came to be seen as *the* historical and political precedent to the new feminism. Originally an offshoot of the New Left, the women's liberation movement soon came to identify its origins in a political and historical moment far removed from its own present. Returning to the nineteenth and early twentieth centuries to establish their historical roots, the feminists of the late 1960s created a generational structure between the two eras of feminism, classifying them as two moments in the same movement: the first and second waves of U.S. feminism.

This deliberate affiliation with the nineteenth-century women's movement had a profound effect on the rhetoric, both written and oral, of second-wave feminists. The most notable was a legitimization of feminism itself. The majority of the feminist activists and writers of this period had come out of the New Left, a movement that had clearly relegated women's issues to a secondary position. For these women, the knowledge that there was a historical precedent for their blossoming movement helped to validate feminism at a time when it was often ridiculed as silly and not politically serious. This return to the past, however, provided contradictions as well as confirmation. By linking themselves to the first wave, second-wavers raised the possibility of generational conflict with the past. In identifying themselves as "the second wave"—and often "the second generation"—of feminist activism, the feminists of the 1960s and early 1970s acquired a group of foremothers with whom to both identify and struggle.[1]

During this fervent period in feminism's history, in the year 1969 to be precise, an event occurred which helped to construct the relationship between these late-twentieth-century women and their nineteenth-century counterparts. On the occasion of Richard Nixon's inauguration in January 1969, various women's groups, most of which had been meeting for less than a year, took part in an anti-inaugural protest held in Washington, D.C. This protest rally had been organized the previous fall at a national women's conference. During Thanksgiving weekend of 1968, approximately 200 women from thirty cities in the U.S. and Canada met to commemorate the 120th anniversary of the first women's rights convention in Seneca Falls, New York. At this national conference, organized primarily by feminist activists from New York City and Washington, D.C., one of the topics addressed was the upcoming anti-inaugural demonstration to protest Nixon's presidency, an action that was being organized by the National Mobilization Committee to End the War in Vietnam.[2] It was decided that women's groups should organize their own protest at this event, one they would take part in separately from the men of the leftist groups with which most of these women were affiliated. During the planning of this demonstration, members of New York Radical Women, the first women's liberation group in New York City and a group which produced many of the movement's future leaders, suggested that they organize a protest in which they would "give back the vote" for which the suffragettes had struggled.[3]

As Ellen Willis, a member of the New York group, notes in "Women and the Left," her 1969 essay on this demonstration:

> The theme of the women's liberation [group at the anti-inaugural] was "Give back the vote." Since women's 80-year struggle for the vote had achieved a meaningless victory and vitiated the feminist movement, we planned to destroy our voter registration cards publicly as a symbol that suffragism was dead and a new fight for real emancipation was beginning. Some women wanted to invite men to burn their voters' cards with us during or after our action. This idea was rejected on grounds that it would change the action from a repudiation of suffrage as a sop for women to a general protest against the electoral process.[4]

Willis's choice of rhetoric offers an illustrative example of the early second wave's relationship to the achievements of the women's movement of the nineteenth and early twentieth centuries: dismissal as something worthless. The vote meant nothing. In arguing that the struggle for the vote had vitiated the earlier movement, Willis suggests that suffrage itself had been the downfall of the previous feminist movement. That movement had failed because first-wave feminists had not fought for "real emancipation" but rather had allowed themselves to be placated by "sop." For feminists looking for a history they could reclaim and celebrate, the suffragettes appear not to have provided them with the kind of foremothers they desired.[5] As one sign carried at the protest proclaimed, "the vote wasn't worth the struggle."[6]

In arguing that suffrage had corrupted the early movement, feminist protesters at the anti-inaugural developed two distinct yet related accounts of feminism's history, both of which would profoundly shape the early writings of second-wave feminists and their relationship to the past. The first argued that suffrage had led to a meaningless victory, yet it simultaneously retained the notion of a nineteenth-century women's movement separate from suffrage. In effect, this allowed feminists of the late 1960s to salvage a segment of the early women's movement which preceded its perceived myopic drive for the vote—a version of the first wave that would later prove quite useful for early second-wave politics. By arguing that "suffragism was dead and a new fight for real emancipation was beginning," the second historical trajectory divided feminism into two parts: the "dead" suffrage movement was defined as conservative, misguided, and over so that the "new," "real" feminism of the present could assert itself as truly radical and thus, ultimately, a better kind of feminism.

If the feminists of the 1960s and early 1970s hadn't had this group of historical foremothers with whom to compare themselves, it is unclear whether their own radicalism could have been so easily asserted. Given that other leftist movements of the time were critical of the women's liberation movement for not being radical enough because of its focus on sex rather than class, the second wave's oppositional relationship to more conservative aspects of the first wave may have been an attempt to legitimate the new movement as radical in the eyes of its leftist contemporaries. According to accounts from the period, the feminist protest at the anti-inaugural primarily revolved around the confrontation between white leftist men and white leftist women, not the ideological split between second- and first-wave feminists. Perhaps second-wave feminists trashed their historical predecessors to advance their own radicalism in front of the men of the New Left. Yet it is itself an interesting contradiction that this demonstration to "give back the vote" was organized during a conference celebrating the 1848 Seneca Falls convention—the foundational moment of U.S. feminism. While honoring their feminist predecessors, these feminists simultaneously chose to distance themselves from them and their political objectives.

Shortly after the anti-inaugural, Anne Koedt and Shulamith Firestone, both of whom had been active with other feminist groups in New York during this period (such as New York Radical Women, The Feminists, and Redstockings), broke off to form their own group, New York Radical Feminists (NYRF).[7] As did most feminist groups of this period, NYRF outlined their beliefs and goals in a manifesto and a set of principles: both "Politics of the Ego: A Manifesto for N.Y. Radical Feminists" (adopted December 5, 1969, at NYRF's founding meeting) and "Organizing Principles of the New York Radical Feminists" were first published in the feminist journal *Notes from the Second Year*.[8] As these texts document, Koedt and Firestone envisioned that NYRF would both be aware of feminism's history and ground itself in it. In that spirit, NYRF would consist of several subgroups—15-person "brigades"—each one named after a famous historical pair of women. As the group notes in its "Organizing Principles":

> We are dedicated to a revival of knowledge about our forgotten feminist history, and to a furthering of the militant tradition of the old radical feminist movement. We define this roughly, as: The whole American Women's Rights Movement until 1869, the Stanton-Anthony group thereafter (National Woman's Suffrage Association) and much later the revived militant tradition associated with Harriet Stanton Blatch in the U.S. (the Congressional Union, later the Woman's Party) and with the Pankhursts in Great Britain (The Woman's Social and Political Union). We also include various feminist independents such as Simone de Beauvoir. To this end each cell group of New York Radical Feminists will be named after a different radical feminist (or, where possible, a team of radical feminists, who worked closely together, such as the Grimké sisters, or the Pankhursts) and will put out as their first group project a booklet biography on their chosen name.[9]

The first such subgroup, headed by Koedt and Firestone, was dubbed the Stanton-Anthony Brigade, named after two of the most celebrated feminists of U.S. history, Elizabeth Cady Stanton and Susan B. Anthony.

Naming the founding cell of New York Radical Feminists the Stanton-Anthony Brigade had historical relevance beyond the names of these two feminists. The very word "brigade" also alluded to two past events within feminism's history. The first occurred in January 1968 when a coalition of women's peace groups calling themselves the Jeanette Rankin Brigade demonstrated against the Vietnam War at the opening of Congress.[10] Rankin was the first woman in the United States to serve in Congress (1917–1919 and 1941–1943), voting against both world wars while in office. This is the first instance of which I am aware in which women's groups from the 1960s named themselves after a figure from women's history, an act honoring the past. The second precedent for the brigade structure is articulated by NYRF in their "Organizing Principles":

> Nuclear leaderless/structureless groups of no more than 15, together with some minimal coordination between them, have already, in the short history of feminism, proven to be the organizational method best suited to our needs and goals. . . . Further, we have found that women within this cadre function best in units of two, occasionally three, of their own personal choice. Such a *Sister System* was common to the old feminist movement, and was a valuable aid in overcoming, by means of close mutual reinforcement and intersupplementation, the weakness and lack of confidence we have each acquired in different areas due to the constant battering from without.[11]

New York Radical Feminists' decision to name their founding brigade after not one but two earlier feminists—as opposed to the singular figure evoked by the Jeanette Rankin Brigade—would appear to be based on their notion of this "Sister System." This system, which was inaccurately accredited to "the old feminist movement," no doubt was appealing to NYRF because of the twin aspects of feminist ideology, particular to the late 1960s and early 1970s, which it picks up on: sisterhood and leaderlessness. It is ironic that it was a battle over these very issues which led to the disintegration of New York Radical Feminists' brigade structure only a year later.[12]

Taken together, these two events in 1969—the anti-inaugural protest, which used as its grounding principle the *misguidedness* of first-wave feminism, and the formation of a feminist group, which in its name *honored* two of the very women who had been an integral part of that earlier movement—suggest the contradictory nature of the second wave's relationship to the first wave of feminism. On the one hand, the past was repudiated and viewed with disdain. On the other hand, it was honored as a rich source of knowledge and guidance. This contradiction, I contend, was not only irreconcilable but was, in fact, vital to the development of second-wave feminism. It was precisely the productive tension between these two contrasting relationships to the first wave that emboldened the second wave to see itself as a powerful political movement.

DISCOVERING HISTORY AND MAKING WAVES

Initially, women in the feminist movement of the mid- to late 1960s did not conceive of the women's movement of the previous century as the historical predecessor to their own activism. Rather, as is clear from the accounts and histories of this period, other leftist movements of the 1960s were seen as the origins of what would become second-wave feminism. As my concern is with the ways in which a generational relationship between first- and second-wave feminisms begins to take shape during this period, in what follows I focus on texts written during the initial period of second-wave writing, from 1966 to 1975; most of my sources were published between 1969 and 1971. During this early period of second-wave feminism, the idea of tracing feminism's origins back to the nineteenth century was one which slowly began to take hold as women began to identify the previous century's movement as their history and their political foundation.

A crucial component in the development of this chronology of feminism's history was the use of the metaphor of the wave to articulate the relationship between the two imagined eras of feminist movement. During the late 1960s and early 1970s, feminists first began to identify themselves as "the second wave" of the women's movement while simultaneously designating the period between 1848 (the Seneca Falls Convention) and 1920 (the gaining of the vote) as "the first wave." From the vantage point of late-twentieth-century feminism, it is almost impossible even to think about feminism's history without describing its ebbs and flows in terms of waves, so entrenched has this metaphor become within feminist discourse.

The term "second wave" is attributed to Marsha Weinman Lear, who uses the term in a *New York Times Magazine* article from March 1968 to describe the then-burgeoning movement: "In short, feminism, which one might have supposed as dead as the Polish Question, is again an issue. Proponents call it the Second Feminist Wave, the first having ebbed after the glorious victory of suffrage and disappeared, finally, into the great sandbar of Togetherness."[13] In identifying themselves as the second wave, women active in the women's liberation movement were able to position themselves within the longer trajectory of feminism's history while simultaneously putting themselves at the forefront of something new, as the third wave also would do when it announced itself in the early 1990s. This is an important two-pronged effect of the metaphor of the wave as it was deployed by feminists in the late 1960s: namely, it legitimized feminism as a serious and ongoing political struggle with a history while simultaneously granting the second wave a means by which to posit themselves as the vanguard.

The contradictions inherent in the metaphor of the wave become clear when examining its use by feminist writers in the late 1960s and early 1970s. Shulamith Firestone, for example, uses "the second wave" to designate the ways in which this later movement follows in the path of the earlier movement and continues its fight for women's equality:

> In the radical feminist view, the new feminism is not just the revival of a serious political movement for social equality. It is the second wave of the most important revolution in history. . . . In this perspective, the pioneer

Western feminist movement was only the first onslaught, the fifty-year ridicule that followed it only a first counteroffensive—the dawn of a long struggle to break free from the oppressive power structures set up by nature and reinforced by man.[14]

Here Firestone suggests that the fight for women's rights is an ongoing battle, one where successive troops will be needed to continue the onslaught. She implies that if the period between the passage of the vote and the beginning of the second wave was "only a first counteroffensive," the second wave will itself be followed by another period of ridicule. Firestone utilizes the wave metaphor to stress the continuity of feminist movement, the many phases within a long struggle.

In contrast, Germaine Greer, in her 1971 *The Female Eunuch*, uses the term "second wave" to suggest that her movement has gone beyond the first wave. Her book begins with this passage:

> This book is a part of the second feminist wave. The old suffragettes, who served their prison term and lived on through the years of gradual admission of women into professions which they declined to follow, into parliamentary freedoms which they declined to exercise, into academies which they used more and more as shops where they could take out degrees while waiting to get married, have seen their spirit revive in younger women with a new and vital cast. . . . The new emphasis is different. Then genteel middle-class ladies clamored for reform, now ungenteel middle-class women are calling for revolution.[15]

For Greer, "second" is tantamount to "new" (and "improved"), making the first wave analogous with "old"; "new" and "old" are clearly synonyms for good and bad, radical and conservative, respectively. Even her use of "ladies" to denote first-wave feminists, in contrast to the word "women" she uses to describe those active in the second wave, indicates a binary between the old and the new, the old and the young, the conservative and the radical. While Firestone's use of the term "second wave" signifies a sense of continuity with the past, Greer's use of the term suggests a break with that past.

In these two examples one can see the contradictions implied in using the term "second wave" to speak of the women's movement that began in the late 1960s. On the one hand, the metaphor of the wave allowed feminists to make connections across time, enabling women to see themselves as part of an ongoing movement for women's rights and equality. On the other hand, this metaphor has often relied on a positivist understanding of generations founded on the idea of progress, in which each generation is understood to go beyond the generation which came before it.[16] In this construction, the use of the wave metaphor expresses a desire for separation over identification, a use of the past to mark the superiority of the present.

The always-dual meaning intrinsic to the metaphor of the wave is emblematic of the second wave's relationship to feminists of the nineteenth and early twentieth centuries. The ways in which second-wave feminists described their knowledge—or lack thereof—of the previous era of feminism is similarly contradictory. In her preface to the 1970 edited volume *Voices from Women's Liberation,* Leslie Tanner offers one example of a ubiquitous narrative of ignorance followed by discovery:

> As I gathered papers and became more involved in the physical aspect of putting the book together, I became aware of the historical aspect of Women's Liberation. I found out how little I (and most women I talked to) actually knew about our own heritage. A minimal amount of research soon showed me how deliberately women had been left out of our history books. Strong, courageous women! I became angry. I felt cheated.[17]

As Tanner suggests, many feminists did not even know that a women's movement had existed in the previous century. In passages such as these, second-wave feminists describe the first wave as their "heritage," a history that had been intentionally hidden but that once discovered could embolden them. In this regard, the second wave's relationship to the first is noticeably different from the third wave's relationship to the second. In constructing a relationship to the past, second-wave feminists had to first unearth first-wave feminism; their recovery of the past and, ultimately, their identification with it did not involve a direct confrontation with feminists of the nineteenth and early twentieth centuries. The encounter with feminism looks decidedly different to third-wave feminists who grew up with feminism "in the water" and with second-wave feminists as teachers, mentors, family, and friends.[18]

For second-wave feminists, a second mode of articulating feminism's relationship to the past recognized that a previous women's movement had existed but tended to dismiss the value of this movement for the present. Second-wave discourse which stressed the need to reject the past was most frequently produced by women who, while self-described feminists, were more aligned with the New Left than with the radical feminist groups of the period. As Marilyn Webb writes in a 1968 essay in *New Left Notes*, "The women's movements of the past are irrelevant."[19] From the point of view of Webb and others, the "bourgeois and reformist" suffrage movement, which represented the entire previous women's movement, was a haunting presence that caused many feminists to want to distance themselves from the first wave.[20]

The person credited with initiating a new mode of relating to the past, one that would ultimately lead to locating 1960s feminism's origins in the nineteenth century, is Shulamith Firestone. More than any other feminist activist and theorist of this period, Firestone stressed the need, first, to make visible the history of the past and, second, to identify with this past and learn from it.[21] In her writing on the early women's rights movement, Firestone addresses both of the prevailing models of relating to the past: ignorance and dismissal. In 1968, for example, Firestone described the paucity of affirmative history given to women: "Little girls are taught to believe that all their rights were won for them a long time ago by a silly bunch of ladies who carried on and made a ridiculous display, all to get a piece of paper into a ballot box."[22] "For all practical purposes," women of her generation, Firestone claimed, did not even know "there had been a feminist movement."[23]

More important than simply acknowledging the previous movement, Firestone devoted much of her writing to combating the tendency of viewing women's history as irrelevant for contemporary feminist concerns by reclaiming the earlier women's movement as the foundation of late-twentieth-century *radical* feminism. She says of her 1968 essay, for example, "In this article I shall attempt to show that the WRM [women's rights movement] was a radical movement from its very beginning, in the early nineteenth century, and that a strong radical wing of the movement existed up to and through the bitter end in 1920."[24] In positing that the earlier movement was not just feminist but in fact radical feminist in its approach, Firestone was able to configure a relationship between the two eras in which the later movement could be seen as following in the earlier one's footsteps:

> The contemporary radical feminist position is *the direct descendant* of the radical feminist line in the old movement, notably that championed by Stanton and Anthony, and later by the militant Congressional Union subsequently known as the Woman's Party. It sees feminist issues not only as women's first priority, but as central to any larger revolutionary analysis.[25]

For many, Firestone's formulation of the past as radical had the effect of making the earlier movement a desirable predecessor, one that could be claimed without anxiety. For those women on the left who viewed the nineteenth-century movement as reformist, Firestone's rehabilitation of the first wave provided a clear challenge: feminism's foremothers were indeed revolutionary in their approach, long before the civil rights movement or the New Left had articulated a radical politics of their own. In this regard, Firestone's contribution to feminism and to its narration of its history was particularly important in refuting many radicals on the left, who used the deficiencies of the suffrage movement to argue that "an autonomous women's movement would inevitably be counterrevolutionary."[26]

This shift in identification with the past, however, made a clear distinction between what parts of that past were to be reclaimed and what parts were to be left aside. In salvaging the women's movement of the nineteenth century, those figures and theories seen as radical were stressed over those—like much of the later suffrage movement—that were deemed conservative. The following passages from Firestone's influential 1970 text *The Dialectic of Sex: The Case for Feminist Revolution* indicate the ways in which "the radical" was claimed as a basis for identification while simultaneously distancing second-wave feminism from "the conservative" aspects of the earlier women's rights movement:

> The early American Woman's Rights Movement was radical. In the nineteenth century, for women to attack the Family, the Church . . . and the State (law) was for them to attack the very cornerstones of the Victorian society in which they lived—equivalent to attacking sex distinctions themselves in our own times.
> [By 1890] Conservative feminism, with its concentration on broad, unitive, single-issues like suffrage, with its attempt to work within and placate the white male power structure—trying to convince men who knew better, with their own fancy rhetoric yet—had won. Feminism had sold out, languished.[27]

Firestone's tactic was to focus on the early period of the nineteenth-century movement, a period in which a woman's general right to equality in society and the law was at the forefront of the movement's agenda, not the more specific focus on the vote. Since many of Firestone's contemporaries on the left considered the vote to have had little effect in eradicating sexism or dismantling the patriarchal structure of U.S. society—as witnessed by the protest at the anti-inaugural demonstration—they no doubt appreciated her rehabilitation of the first wave against its later, "suffrage-driven" period. In other words, Firestone's narrative of the past was able to reclaim a radical, thus positive, early period precisely because it simultaneously acknowledged what many women on the left believed to be true: namely, that the suffrage movement (and thus the nineteenth-century women's movement in general) had been conservative and thus an unappealing site in which to locate present-day feminism's roots.

Firestone's division of the nineteenth-century movement into a "good/radical" early period and a "bad/conservative" later period can also be seen in the ways in which leading feminists of this earlier movement were either embraced or rejected. In particular, Susan B. Anthony and Elizabeth Cady Stanton—the two women most identified with the post–Seneca Falls early period of the women's movement—were celebrated for embodying the radical dimensions of first-wave feminism. In *The Dialectic of Sex,* Firestone refers to Anthony and Stanton as "the healthily selfish giants of the radical feminist rebellion," language that clearly illustrates the ways in which late 1960s leftist politics infused her reading of the past.[28] While "radical" and "rebellion" were ubiquitous terms in feminist discourse of this period, it is "the healthily selfish giants"—an image with Amazonian overtones—that is perhaps most revealing of Firestone's imagined relationship to Anthony and Stanton and her desire to locate feminism's origins in the past. Not just giants, not just selfish, but *healthily* selfish giants: women who fought for their own rights but were not unhappy or bitter because of it. Rather, these women eagerly reached for what was theirs with gusto.

It's important to note that the version of first-wave feminism that was being put forward by Firestone and her contemporaries during the late 1960s and early 1970s was one which preceded the discipline of women's history, a field which was in its infancy during this same period. Later feminist historians would offer a more complex and troubling understanding of the politics of first-wave feminism, including critiques of Stanton and Anthony's at-times xenophobic and racist arguments for why white, middle-class women needed the vote. Firestone's enthusiastic embrace of Stanton and Anthony as feminist foremothers was made possible in great part because of the paucity of women's history available to her in the late 1960s, particularly history written by feminist scholars.

She could thus construct a narrative of nineteenth-century feminism that emboldened feminists in the present, without having to explore the first wave's more troubling legacy.

In order fully to appreciate the shift in identification with these historical figures that Firestone was advocating, one need only look at the very different representation of Susan B. Anthony presented by Betty Friedan in her 1963 *The Feminine Mystique:*

> Painfully insecure and self-conscious about her looks—not because of treatment by men (she had suitors) but because of a beautiful older sister and mother who treated a crossed eye as a tragedy—Susan Anthony, of all the nineteenth-century feminist leaders, was the only one resembling the myth [of the "embittered shrew"]. She felt betrayed when the others started to marry and have babies. But despite the chip on her shoulder, she was no bitter spinster with a cat.[29]

Friedan's image of Anthony relies upon a definition of female happiness in which beauty and heterosexual romance are equated with fulfillment. Although Friedan no doubt intended her caveat—"despite the chip on her shoulder, Anthony was no bitter spinster with a cat"—as a positive spin on poor Anthony's predicament, this passage nevertheless betrays an allegiance to a view of single womanhood (and, one might add, some aspects of feminism) as ultimately unsatisfying, irrespective of the role political activity may play in one's life.

Although *The Dialectic of Sex* was published only seven years later, Firestone's "healthily selfish giants" can be read as both an implicit critique of this image of Anthony (and other feminists) and as an indication of the changes that had occurred within feminism since the 1963 publication of *The Feminine Mystique*. No longer were looks and marriage status something which needed to be justified lest feminism be equated with the ugly image of the "embittered shrew."[30] Rather, by the time Firestone's book was published, feminism had amply critiqued both beauty and marriage. A healthily selfish feminist giant would, ideally, not need to trouble herself with either: she was free to pursue her own happiness without constraint.

As feminists from the late 1960s and early 1970s began reclaiming these freedom-pursuing women of the nineteenth century as their political predecessors, writings from this period became increasingly focused on highlighting the similarities between the two movements. As Judith Hole and Ellen Levine note in their 1971 essay, "The First Feminists":

The contemporary women's movement is not the first such movement in American history to offer a wide-ranging feminist critique of society. In fact, much of what seems "radical" in contemporary feminist analysis parallels the critique made by the feminists of the nineteenth century.[31]

Hole and Levine's rhetorical strategy here was a common one: namely, to suggest that the contemporary movement was repeating efforts made by earlier feminists.[32] Another frequently used tactic was to highlight the common struggle for women's rights shared by both movements while simultaneously pointing out the differences in the two historical periods. An example of this approach can be seen in the blurb on the back cover of Tanner's *Voices from Women's Liberation*, a passage in which the differences stressed seem particularly dramatic:

> The Unfinished Revolution. They used to gather in great conventions for eloquent speeches. Now they meet in private apartments and rap among themselves. They used to fight for legal rights and the vote. Now they focus on human rights, and the scope of their struggle includes such matters as the plight of the black woman, sexist brainwashing in high school, male chauvinism, and the myth of the vaginal orgasm. But one thing has not changed. Women want their freedom. And they want it now. Listen to them.[33]

Both ways of identifying with the past served their purpose: the women's movement of the nineteenth century came to be seen as a source of history, knowledge, and connection. Groups such as New York Radical Feminists integrated this new relationship to the feminist past into their activist goals. In their mission statement they require that group members have "a minimum of three months of 'consciousness-raising,'" "a minimum of three months of reading and discussion," and "six weeks of intensive reading and discussion of feminist history and theory (preferably direct sources)" in order "to acquaint each member of the group with her own history and *to give her a sense of continuity* with the feminist political tradition."[34]

Throughout the 1970s, this new way of conceptualizing present-day feminism's relationship to its past became integrated into feminist discourse and analysis. What had originally been seen as a bold move in Firestone's assessment of nineteenth-century feminists—"pointing out that they were predecessors we could be proud of"—soon became a matter of course within the ruling narrative of U.S. feminism's history.[35] From the vantage point of late-twentieth-century feminism, there have been important and lasting consequences of this relationship to the past: not just the creation of a generational structure between these two "waves" of feminism but the construction of a particular narrative of feminism's history.

As they turned backward in time to locate their feminist origins, many feminists of the late 1960s and early 1970s began to construct a chronology of feminism's history, a timetable that has had a powerful and lasting effect on the way successive feminists have interpreted this past. Feminists of this period saw themselves as reviving a movement that had, for all intents and purposes, died with the passage of the Nineteenth Amendment in 1920. Consequently, it became quite popular to conceptualize feminism as something that had been reborn at the end of the 1960s. From the ubiquitous slogan "Feminism Lives" to the title of Hole and Levine's history of this movement, *The Rebirth of Feminism*, feminism's resurrection was proclaimed. To get a sense of the frequency of this metaphor, one need only look at the litany of death and rebirth images that can be found in the feminist writing of this period: "when the ballot was won, the feminist movement collapsed in what can only be described as exhaustion";[36] "to women born after 1920, feminism was dead history";[37] feminism "has been revitalized only as recently as the last five years, and after some forty years of dormancy";[38] after dying with the passage of the Nineteenth Amendment, "[feminism] arose again in the late 60's to proclaim self-determination the ultimate good."[39]

Marking feminism's death and subsequent rebirth in this manner created a chronology in which no feminism or women's movement was seen to exist in the period between 1920 and the late 1960s. Additionally, since second-wave histories of earlier feminism focused almost exclusively on the women's movement between 1848 (the Seneca Falls Convention) and 1920 (the gaining of the vote), any feminism prior to 1848, such as that of British feminist Mary Wollstonecraft, was also ignored.[40] Feminist historians have demonstrated that feminist ideology continued to exist after the Nineteenth Amendment was passed.[41] Thus, the issue is not whether one version of feminism's history is more accurate than the other; but rather, why the early second-wave feminists found it valuable—perhaps even necessary—to stress the death and subsequent rebirth of feminism, demarcating two discrete eras of women's movement.

Designating the parameters of feminism's history in this way enabled second-wave feminists to see themselves as the "next" (or "new") generation of the women's movement, a task which would not have been as easily accomplished had they taken into account these missing periods of feminist activity. By demarcating the period which subsequently came to be known as the first wave, these later feminists created a structure to describe feminism's history in which only two distinct periods of feminist movement could be said to exist: the years between 1848 and 1920 and the period which began in the late 1960s. This formulation proclaimed the second wave as only the second such movement in U.S. history and so granted second-wave feminists a kind of political power and clarity that would not have been available to them otherwise.

Describing the past as containing only one preceding wave of feminism allowed women of the late 1960s to create a narrative of feminism in which they were its inevitable second chapter, its second wave. It was not just past history that had to be wrestled with, however, for this trajectory of feminism to be fully persuasive. The young, self-described radical women I've been discussing in this chapter also distanced themselves from their more liberal, and often older, feminist contemporaries in order to herald themselves as the harbingers of something new. The most glaring example of this can be seen in accounts of the official starting date of the second wave. Radical feminists consider 1968 to be the first year of the U.S. women's movement of the late twentieth century. According to Robin Morgan, the protest at the Miss America Contest in Atlantic City on September 7, 1968, organized by the New York group Radical Women, was "the first major action of the current Women's movement."[42] The status of 1968 as second-wave feminism's "first year" was further stressed by the title of the influential radical feminist journal *Notes from the First Year*, published in 1968, and followed by *Notes from the Second Year* in 1969 and *Notes from the Third Year* in 1970.[43] While 1968 was a singularly important year for feminist and other leftist, student, and anti-war movements around the world, 1968 could only be credited as the revived U.S. women's movement's "first year" by ignoring significant feminist events from earlier in the 1960s.[44] Most notable of these is the 1966 founding of the National Organization for Women, a group started by Betty Friedan.[45] As Cellestine Ware notes in *Woman Power*, "NOW is reformist, works from within the system, and is referred to . . . as the *forerunner of new feminism.*"⁴⁶ Radical feminists were eager to distance themselves from Friedan's brand of liberal feminism and the older (read: over thirty) women with which it was associated. Classifying their feminism's starting date as 1968 over 1966 allowed radical feminists to disassociate from their older, more liberal feminist contemporaries while simultaneously stressing a connection to their younger, radical peers in other leftist movements of the late 1960s.

For Firestone and her radical feminist peers, liberal feminists were "more a leftover of the old feminism," a type of "old feminism"—specifically, the conservative turn in the suffrage movement of the late 1800s and early 1900s—"rather than a model of the new."⁴⁷ In defining her liberal contemporaries as old while positing her radical cohorts as new, Firestone attempted to partition both the past and present feminist eras along the binary of old/conservative versus new/radical. Thus, her peers could be aligned with Stanton and Anthony in the radical camp, while her liberal contemporaries were united with what Firestone perceived as the suffrage-driven, obsolete feminists of the late first wave—an interesting parallel, considering that the "radical" Stanton and Anthony were chronologically "older" than the conservative suffragettes. Like using 1968 to mark the beginning year of radical feminism, Firestone's intention was to distance radical feminists from their liberal counterparts. It is curious that at the same moment that she critiqued liberal feminists for their similarity to "the old feminism," she argued that radical feminists needed to construct a similar affiliation to the feminism of the past, or what was perceived as its earlier radical segment.

An example of how this desire for radical roots worked itself out within second-wave discourse can be seen in radical feminists' treatment of Betty Friedan. While the 1963 publication of *The Feminine Mystique* is often considered to mark "the beginning of the second feminist wave," to quote Germaine Greer, most of the feminists I have been discussing here rejected Friedan as a role model and foremother because of her association with liberal feminism.⁴⁸ Instead, these women embraced another earlier feminist, Simone de Beauvoir, as a source of inspiration and knowledge. Shulamith Firestone dedicated *The Dialectic of Sex* to her, writing "For Simone de Beauvoir: who kept her integrity."⁴⁹ And the radical feminist group Redstockings' 1975 journal, *Feminist Revolution*, has the following inscription: "This journal is dedicated to Simone de

Beauvoir, the French woman who exposed male supremacy for this era, and gave us our feminism."[50]

The declaration that Beauvoir "gave us our feminism" must, I think, be read in relationship to Friedan and her important role within U.S. feminism during this period. By all accounts, Friedan's *The Feminine Mystique* had an enormous impact on the national discussion about women in U.S. society; her 1963 analysis of the limits of women's traditional roles as housewives and mothers lit a fuse that would eventually lead to the explosion of women's rights groups in the late 1960s. The fact, then, that many feminists of this period argued, as Redstockings member Kathie Sarachild does, that "we derived from Beauvoir, not Friedan" seems a noteworthy site of disidentification given the historical importance of Friedan and her influential bestseller.[51] On the surface, the rejection of Friedan in favor of an identification with Beauvoir clearly comes out of a preference for radicalism over liberalism. As one radical feminist writes, "We, in this segment of the movement, do not believe that oppression of women will be ended by giving them a bigger piece of the pie, as Betty Friedan would have it. We believe that the pie itself is rotten."[52] At the time of these early second-wave writings, Friedan's home within liberal feminism was well known to feminists: she was actively involved with NOW and frequently spoke out against what she saw as the radical extremes of the new movement. Beauvoir, on the other hand, represented a more radical brand of feminism: "Beauvoir's book was the best, most radical, and comprehensive analysis up to its time and remains so. It was crucial to the development of the WLM [women's liberation movement]."[53]

More important, Beauvoir's alignment with French intellectualism made her a more attractive foremother than the American Friedan, forever associated with the unexciting world of the housewife. Friedan may indeed have begun second-wave U.S. feminism, but for many of the young white women involved in this burgeoning movement, she was too close to home. As historian Paula Giddings has remarked, the second wave of the women's movement was begun by "the daughters of the women Friedan had written about."[54] For these feminists, Friedan and the women she spoke for represented that which they were trying to escape, not imitate: the lives of their mothers. Ann Snitow, for example, remarks: "The usually white and middle-class women who were typical members of early women's consciousness raising groups often saw their mothers as desperate or depressed in the midst of their relative privilege."[55]

Friedan was—in both a literal as well as figurative sense—too much of a real mother figure to these young feminists for her to successfully play the role of mentor to their burgeoning movement. Beauvoir, on the other hand, represented the kind of emancipated woman many radical feminists wanted to emulate. An intellectual and writer, someone who was virtually against the reproductive role of women and had chosen not to participate in the institution of marriage, Beauvoir had made many of the life choices that radical feminists were just beginning to consider for themselves. To radical feminists such as Firestone, Beauvoir symbolized the antithesis of Friedan and the domestic female world she represented.[56]

In constructing a chronology of feminism in which they could be said to "derive from Beauvoir, not Friedan," radical feminists employed one of the strategies I have already discussed, namely locating their roots in the past in order to grant them political clout with their radical contemporaries. In part, this was accomplished by the mere fact of claiming *The Second Sex* over *The Feminine Mystique;* published in France in 1949 and followed by a 1952 U.S. edition, Beauvoir's text was over a decade older than Friedan's. In addition to its themes and analysis, then, *The Second Sex*'s "age" also made it worthy of radical feminists' veneration. Like their affiliation with the early, radical wing of the first wave, second-wave feminists avoided the complications of dealing with their immediate feminist contemporaries by locating their origins in the past. In the case of Beauvoir, this distancing was made even stronger by the fact that she was French, not American. Rejecting the feminism that was nearest to them nationally and generationally, radical feminists developed a particular origin story of their feminism.

Their desire to distance themselves from Friedan, however, led some radical feminists to describe the relationship between the two celebrated feminists in curious terms. "In fact," Kathie Sarachild argues, "Simone de Beauvoir is the *mother* of Betty Friedan, which is only dimly acknowledged in Friedan's book."[57] Given what appears to be a strong wish to disassociate from the overly domestic (in both senses of the word) Friedan, radical feminists' use of familial language to facilitate this separation seems particularly startling. Why make Beauvoir—admired precisely for being a non-maternal figure—a "mother" to anyone? In making Beauvoir the mother to Friedan, who was commonly considered the mother of 1960s feminism, Sarachild makes Beauvoir a kind of "grandmother" to modern feminism, a figure that radical feminists seem to have less trouble identifying with than their more immediate mothers, both literal and figurative. Granting Beauvoir the status of wise elder to Friedan—even when the French feminist was only thirteen years older than her American counterpart—reveals a wish on the part of radical feminists to locate the birth of their movement elsewhere: in another place, in another woman far removed from the all-too-near Friedan.[58]

Arguing that feminism died in 1920 only to be reborn in 1968 created a neat and tidy narrative to account for what is actually a much more complicated feminist history. Why, for example, did many women (especially young women) abandon feminism after the vote was won?[59] In what ways did the feminists energized by Friedan's *The Feminine Mystique* coexist in the same political generation as radical feminists such as Morgan and Firestone? By not recognizing the ways in which feminism continued to exist—or accounting for why and how it may have been transformed—during the period after 1920 but before the second wave's "first year" in 1968, feminists of the late 1960s and early 1970s virtually ignored any kind of identification with the generation of women who had immediately preceded them: namely, their mothers and their mothers' generation.[60] The death-and-rebirth imagery that proliferated during this period may have been a way for second-wave feminists to imagine that they were giving birth to themselves. This metaphoric parthenogenesis allowed them to evade the more complicated relationship to their mothers' generation of women, women's rights, and feminism, which they could avoid grappling with by imagining themselves as springing to life in the late 1960s. Perhaps it was only by going back in history 100 years that second-wave feminists were able to find feminist mentors, the "healthily selfish giants" they were looking for.

It is ironic that while feminists of the late 1960s stressed the importance of affiliating with feminists of the past, it was only by disconnecting themselves from women in their immediate present—their older feminist contemporaries, such as Friedan, as well as their mothers and their mothers' generation of women—that they were able to construct their identification with feminism. The regularity with which writers from this period describe feminist generational relationships in familial terms suggests that differentiating themselves from their mothers was an intentional effect of stepping onto the stage of history. Firestone, for example, refers to second-wave feminists as "the rebellious daughters of [the] wasted generation" of women who came of age immediately after suffrage was won, while in Jo Freeman's terms, second-wavers are "the granddaughters of those suffragettes."[61] These imagined familial relationships position second-wave feminists as feminism's heroic daughters gaining wisdom through their connection to the past—their figurative "grandmothers," the suffragettes. Again, second-wave feminists emboldened themselves as political agents through identifying with one group of women at the same time that they disidentified with another.

Yet their reliance on the language of the family to make this break is revealing for what it suggests about the symbolic value of "the daughter" as an agent of rebellion. Recalling Rich's concept of "matrophobia," the daughters' desire to, as one commentator put it, "extricate themselves from the role that their mothers had occupied" led some second-wave feminists to describe generational relationships among women generally in familial terms.[62] Within this framework, "mothers" are inevitably lacking so that "daughters" may succeed where they have failed.

HISTORY IS POWERFUL

In an essay on political generations, Beth Schneider argues that "a generation must be self-conscious about its own role in history." She asks, "Can a generation affect political change if it is not aware of its historical place?"[63] Schneider's question can be applied to the writing of the early second wave; it is clear that second-wave feminists were unusually self-conscious of their role in history, which had a powerful effect on feminist discourse. The second wave's understanding of its historical importance was, in great part, shaped by its relationship to the movement it conceived of as its historical predecessor. In recuperating that past and constructing a relationship to it, women of the second wave began to understand themselves as part of history, as making history even as they were living through their own historical moment. For women of the early second wave, history was no longer seen as something beyond the control of its players; rather, through their affiliation with the first wave, they became empowered to see themselves as *agents* in history, as opposed to mere pawns. Their identification with the first wave granted feminists a group identity: women involved in the historic struggle for women's rights. In discovering written documents from feminism's earlier era, second-wave feminists began to recognize the necessity of writing the history of their own movement. In understanding that feminists of the first wave "also faced very similar criticism" and "encountered resistance" in their attempts to define their movement, second-wave feminists were more able to counter the charge that, as Kathie Sarachild put it, "It was arrogant for us to compare ourselves to the glorious sisters of the past, to put ourselves into history."[64]

The cumulative effect of this identification with the past was that women of the early second wave began to document their own movement in a meticulous fashion. From chronicling protest demonstrations to publishing the manifestos of groups that were only in existence for six months, every aspect of this movement was recorded. In looking back on this period in feminism's history, I have often found myself feeling envious of the enthusiasm and confidence with which feminists of the early second wave were able to write about their own historical moment. One can't help but notice a great sense of exuberance in these early second-wave texts, a feeling of being a part of something larger than oneself, of being an agent in history. While the fastidiousness with which they recorded every facet of their struggle may seem a bit presumptuous at times, it indicates a kind of assuredness of the mark they were, in fact, making on society. Women, like myself, who have come to feminism after this initial period of second-wave activism and writing have, by and large, been unable to take ourselves as seriously—or at least we have been unable to feel so sure about our own place in history. Located after the second wave but with no real foreseeable next wave to pull us in, we may feel adrift, lacking the presumption of a political and historical purpose that so anchored the women of the late 1960s and early 1970s.[65]

The value of documenting history can also be seen in the ways in which feminist journals and anthologies of this period included texts from both the previous and present centuries. During the early second wave, it was not uncommon for the past and the present to play co-starring roles in feminist texts; writings from the two waves were placed side by side, linking them as part of one common movement for women's rights. For example, the proceedings of Susan B. Anthony's trial for illegally voting in the presidential election of 1872 were published in *Notes from the Third Year: Women's Liberation* alongside essays by second-wave radical feminists.[66] One-third of Leslie Tanner's edited anthology *Voices from Women's Liberation* consists of nineteenth- and early-twentieth-century pieces, while the remaining two-thirds is made up of writings from the late 1960s and early 1970s.[67] And the journal published by the New York radical feminist group Redstockings, *Feminist Revolution*, has excerpts from nineteenth-century feminists leaders interspersed throughout.

In pairing their writings with important historical documents—such as the "Declaration of Sentiments and Resolutions" from the Seneca Falls Convention of 1848—second-wave feminists were, in effect, positing that their tracts carried, or eventually would carry, the same kind of historical and political weight.[68] Perhaps the most notable indication of this is the number of texts published between 1968 and 1975 which record the incipient movement's early history. Judith Hole and Ellen Levine's 488-page history of the women's liberation movement, *The Rebirth of Feminism* (1971), exhaustively chronicles the movement's origins, its organizations and leaders, its protests and activism, and feminist positions on everything from fashion to child care to religion.[69] Cellestine Ware's *Woman Power* (1970) also details the history of the movement, which at the publication of Ware's book was only in its third "official" year of existence. And, the best-selling 1970 *Sisterhood Is Powerful*, edited by Robin Morgan, contains a section entitled "Historical Documents," which, contrary to what is suggested by the name, contains organizational principles and manifestos from feminist groups of the late 1960s, such as Valerie Solanas's SCUM Manifesto, documents from radical feminist groups WITCH and Redstockings, and NOW's "Bill of Rights" from 1967. These examples indicate the degree to which second-wave feminists perceived that what they were doing was of historical importance and thus in need of documentation and recording for posterity—a perception that seems extraordinary given the fact that the movement was in its infancy. The second wave's sense of itself as history in the making is particularly striking in comparison to the third wave's sense of itself. By and large, third-wave essays and anthologies published at the end of the twentieth century suggest that younger feminists feel quite tentative about their place within history and their ability to make history and effect change.

Nowhere is the second wave's sense of its historical importance more evident than in the journal edited by Shulamith Firestone and Anne Koedt. In calling their 1968 journal *Notes from the First Year* and the subsequent issues *Notes from the Second Year* and *Notes from the Third Year,* Firestone and Koedt seem to have had an awareness of the significance of their historical moment for the future of U.S. feminism. In using the very title of the journal to mark the progression of their movement, Firestone and Koedt attest to both the need for historical reflection and the fact that they were taking part in a new wave of feminism, one which was still in its infancy. In their editorial statement in *Notes from the Second Year,* they write, "We needed a movement periodical which would expand with the movement, reflect its growth accurately, and in time become a historical record, functioning politically as did Stanton and Anthony's *Revolution* exactly a century ago."[70] Their sense that they were creating a historical record although they were in the first years of a new movement offers another example of how early second-wave feminists saw themselves as being part of history even as they demarcated themselves as new and vanguard. As was the case with many feminist journals of this period, *Notes* quickly went out of existence, leaving only three issues to serve as its historical record.

In her 1975 essay "The Power of History," Kathie Sarachild describes reactions to Firestone's insistence on documenting the incipient movement: Firestone, she writes, "dare[d] to embarrass herself by taking the history of the movement, taking herself and the others who began it, absolutely seriously."[71] In retrospect, the seriousness with which Firestone and others documented the early days of the women's movement of the late 1960s and early 1970s has proved invaluable for subsequent feminists' understanding of the development of late-twentieth-century feminism. Because feminists of this period "took themselves seriously," even when to do so might have seemed presumptuous, there is a wealth of texts that chronicle the movement's early history. As someone who first encountered these texts a decade and a half after they were first published, I can remember feeling in awe of the political urgency expressed in these writings. These are texts written to change things and the authors believe that, in fact, they will bring change. Perhaps the early years of any political movement is bound to produce writing which excites and motivates its readers in this manner; after all, new movements want to draw people in. The texts from the early second wave seem to be doing something more than just recruiting new members, however. They enthusiastically offer their readers the possibility of changing the course of history. This is not a common feature of third-wave feminist texts, which are more accurately characterized by their lack of a shared collectivity and by a reluctance to claim their generation's ability to effect dramatic social change.

RACE AND THE FORMULATION OF FEMINISM'S WAVES

In constructing a relationship between themselves and feminists of the nineteenth and early twentieth centuries, second-wave feminists often made a point of stressing the similarities between the two movements. Race was one of the key issues used to develop this connection as feminists stressed the ways in which race-centered political movements were the catalysts for both the first and second waves: the abolitionist movement for the suffrage movement of the nineteenth century, and the civil rights movement for the women's movement of the 1960s. Characteristically put by Firestone, "So just as the issue of slavery spurred on the radical feminism of the nineteenth century, the issue of racism now stimulated the new feminism."[72] This formulation of the genesis of both movements granted second-wave feminists another means by which to stress the continuities between themselves and the first wave; the two movements could be said to mirror each other in their origins.

It is unfortunate that formulating feminism's history in this manner—as a trajectory in which the struggle for racial equality inevitably leads to the struggle for gender equality—tended to obliterate the intersections between race and gender. One movement was seen as focusing solely on race, the other solely on gender. The consequence is that black women from both eras effectively disappeared. In Jo Freeman's *The Politics of Women's Liberation*, her reliance on this structure leads her to write of first-wave feminists, "American women discovered they could not work to free the slaves without working to free themselves."[73] In this passage, "slaves" and "American women" are used to denote two distinct groups. Narrating first-wave history in this manner greatly influenced, often with dire consequences, the ways in which an attention to race was incorporated (or not) into early second-wave feminism. It is a paradox that even as they attempted to assert the more progressive racial politics of their own movement, white second-wave feminists ended up reproducing the troubling first-wave structure of pitting rights for black men against rights for white women, a structure which emerged when both groups struggled to gain the vote following the Civil War. Black women, of course, would not get the vote until both African Americans and women were legally enfranchised.

As has been widely critiqued by black feminist scholars, this model of understanding the interrelationship between struggles for racial equality and struggles for gender equality—in both the first and second waves—produced the image that "all the women are white and all the blacks are men."[74] In "Double Jeopardy: To Be Black and Female," published in both *Sisterhood Is Powerful* and *The Black Woman: An Anthology* in 1970, Frances Beale coins the term "double jeopardy" to account for the particular position of black women, one which neither the black civil rights movement nor the white feminist movement could successfully address in isolation.[75] During the late 1960s and early 1970s, many black women writers were calling attention to both the male bias of the civil rights movement and the white bias of the feminist movement, yet this critique was not incorporated into white feminism in any substantial way until a number of years later, if it was addressed at all.

It may be that their desire to identify with historical foremothers caused white feminists to adopt, often uncritically, the analogy used by first-wave feminists in which oppression on the basis of race and oppression on the basis of sex were seen as separate but equivalent. Historians of the first wave have documented how white women involved in the abolitionist movement of the nineteenth century used this analogy to articulate their own right to enfranchisement.[76] In 1860, for example, Elizabeth Cady Stanton argued that "[p]rejudice against color, of which we hear so much about, is not stronger than that against sex."[77] A common second-wave strategy in making this analogy was to point out the similarities between the status of African Americans and the status of women, as seen in Beverly Jones and Judith Brown's 1968 essay, "Toward a Female Liberation Movement," in which they state, "There is an almost exact parallel between the role of women and the role of black people in this society."[78] The problem with this parallel, of course, is that it cannot account for those located at the intersection of these two groups: black women. As Deborah King has noted,

> We learn very little about black women from [the race-sex] analogy. The experience of black women is apparently assumed, though never explicitly stated, to be synonymous with that of either black males or white females; and since the experiences of both are equivalent, a discussion of black women in particular is superfluous.[79]

Since white second-wave feminists tended to define the women's movement in terms of its relationship to the first wave of feminism and to the contemporary civil rights movement—both of which failed to think through the intersections between race and gender—many of their early texts reproduce the damaging theoretical blind spot of these two movements.

This blind spot can also be seen in the ways in which white feminists of the early second wave virtually ignored black feminists of the nineteenth and early twentieth centuries. Not only were the most celebrated first-wave feminists white, such as Anthony and Stanton, but the early second wave's version of the prior women's movement often entirely overlooked the participation of black women in the political movements of the nineteenth century. For example, Leslie Tanner's 1970 anthology *Voices from Women's Liberation,* in which one-third of the material is from the nineteenth and early twentieth centuries, contains only one essay by an African-American woman from the first wave, "The Women Want Their Rights," by Sojourner Truth.[80] White feminists' neglect of black women involved in the first wave is brought into relief by the many texts written by black feminists during the late 1960s and early 1970s about the role of African-American women in the abolitionist and suffrage movements—women such as Truth, Harriet Tubman, Ida B. Wells-Barnett, Mary McLeod Bethune, and Mary Church Terrell.[81] The fact that their black feminist contemporaries were writing about black first-wave feminists at the same moment that white feminists neglected them suggests that the representation of first-wave feminism as virtually all white cannot be attributed solely to ignorance.

It could be argued that white feminists' desire to identify with the past manifested itself as a longing to find women who mirrored their own race and class perspectives; given the overwhelmingly white and middle-class composition of early second-wave feminism, this led to a whitewashed account of the first wave.[82] Even if they had been aware of the many black women involved in the earlier movement, it may be that few white women would have looked to black women as foremothers to their own feminism.[83] Their use of the present to analyze the past caused white feminists to recognize only those women in the nineteenth century who articulated the need for an independent women's movement, as many white feminists had done coming out of the civil rights movement. Unfortunately, their desire to find historical parallels between the two movements caused white feminists to ignore the more complicated intersections between race and gender in the discourses of both the abolitionist and suffrage movements—not to mention within the black feminism of their own day. In this regard, it is worth noting that few of the historical accounts of the first wave from this early second-wave period (1968–1972) fully address the ways in which white women employed a racist ideology of white womanhood to argue for their right to suffrage over the right of black men.[84]

The second wave's desired identification with the first wave played an important role in shaping their discourse around race. The fact that white feminists tended to focus their attention primarily on white feminists of the past while simultaneously overlooking the role of black women in the earlier women's movement reinforced many black women's already skeptical view of feminism. If the new feminist movement intended to ground itself in a past whose leaders were white and whose story was that of white women, it was, in effect, defining feminism as a white movement.

What began as an attempt to stress the common oppression shared by blacks and women—where their situations were seen as analogous—quickly evolved into an attempt by many white feminists to stress the more fundamental, and thus more damaging, nature of sexism over racism. Ellen Willis's "Women and the Left" provides an example of this frequent argument:

> Femaleness, like blackness, is a biological fact, a fundamental condition. Like racism, male supremacy permeates all strata of this society. *And it is even more deeply entrenched*. Whites are at least defensive about racism;

men—including most radicals, black and white—are proud of their chauvinism. Male supremacy is the oldest form of domination and the most resistant to change.[85]

Once male supremacy was defined as the root of all other forms of domination—that "racism is sexism extended," as Firestone argued—it could then be asserted that "[t]here cannot be real restructuring of this society until the relationships between the sexes are restructured."[86] Aiming to eliminate the root cause of all other forms of oppression, then, the feminist movement—not the civil rights movement or the New Left—could claim the title of the truly radical movement of the 1960s.

From the standpoint of black feminists of the period, the common claim that "[m]ale supremacy is the oldest, most basic form of oppression" was an attempt by white women to view their subjugation as equivalent to that experienced by black women.[87] This argument was hardly persuasive to African-American women, who tended to find the analogy insulting and dismissive, not to mention ignorant of the real privileges enjoyed by many white feminists. As Toni Morrison argued in a 1971 essay in the *New York Times Magazine*, "[S]ome black women [think] that Women's Lib is nothing more than an attempt on the part of whites to become black without the responsibilities of being black."[88] A similar point was made by Linda La Rue in her 1970 "The Black Movement and Women's Liberation":

> The surge of "common oppression" rhetoric and propaganda may lure the unsuspecting into an intellectual alliance with the goals of women's liberation, but it is not a wise alliance. It is not that women ought not to be liberated from the shackles of their present unfulfillment, but the depth, the extent, the intensity, the importance—indeed, the suffering and depravity of the *real* oppression blacks have experienced—can only be minimized in an alliance with women who heretofore have suffered little more than boredom, genteel repression, and dishpan hands.[89]

La Rue counters the argument that all women are "sisters" in their common oppression with a representation of white womanhood which seems straight out of Friedan's *The Feminine Mystique:* "boredom, genteel repression, and dishpan hands." It is ironic that the radical feminists who were most likely to use the argument of a common oppression were also those who would have been most offended by the comparison to Friedan's liberal feminism. White feminists who had deliberately rejected Friedan as a political ally precisely in order to stress their own radicalism were now being charged with sharing the bourgeois lifestyle she represented.

Since second-wave feminists tended to depict the first wave as made up solely of white women, the fact that their own movement was racially integrated—at least in name if not always in numbers—helped to further the notion that they had moved beyond the segregation of the earlier movement.[90] Like the metaphor of the wave itself, second-wave discussions of race were a way to stress the parallels between the two movements while simultaneously marking their superiority over the first wave. The belief in a revolutionary multiracial feminism is perhaps most evident in the ubiquitous slogan of the period, "Sisterhood is Powerful," which stresses a common sisterhood based on the shared oppression of all women. Much early feminist theory was founded on this vision, such as the "Redstockings Manifesto," where the radical feminist group relies on a shared sisterhood to call women to action: "We identify with all women"; "We repudiate all economic, racial, education, or status privileges that divide us from other women"; "We call on all our sisters to unite with us in struggle."[91] In its best intentions, the feminist argument that all women are sisters in a common struggle was an attempt to look beyond race and class divisions toward a definition of sisterhood that included all women. This position does mark a substantial change in the construction of the political group "women," particularly when compared with much first-wave feminism, particularly the post–Civil War white suffrage movement. Second-wave feminists attempted to posit a more progressive feminist politics than their foremothers, and they perceived themselves as doing just that. As has been widely discussed by feminist scholars over the last thirty years, however, the rhetoric of universal sisterhood was often not accompanied by a careful analysis of differences between women, whether of race, class, or sexuality. As the second wave of feminism moved into the 1970s, these differences would ultimately unravel the optimism and idealism expressed in the frequent claim of sisterhood. Feminism would be forced to address the very real differences that divided women and complicated any monolithic definition of "woman"—or of feminism itself.

SEXUALITY AND THE NEW FEMINISM

Although second-wave feminists connected to many facets of first-wave feminism in order to stress the similarities between the two movements, one issue was rarely discussed in generational terms but rather was used to stress the newness of the second wave: sexuality. The relative absence of direct comparisons between the first and second waves on the question of sexuality is striking in the feminist texts from the late 1960s and early 1970s, particularly in light of the frequency with which such contrasts were made with regard to the other topics examined in this chapter. Certainly the sheer abundance of texts which explore issues unexamined by the first wave serve as a strong indicator of the second wave's difference from the first: these include second-wave discussions of clitoral orgasms, lesbianism and bisexuality, and monogamy, not to mention the second wave's reevaluation of issues covered by the first wave, such as marriage, housework, and women's "nature."[92]

There is one notable exception to this lack of direct comparison between the waves on the topic of sexuality. It comes from Betty Friedan, who assesses the progress of the burgeoning second wave in her 1973 epilogue to the tenth-year edition of *The Feminine Mystique*. In describing her contemporaries as compared to feminists of the past, Friedan points to the progress made by the modern movement: "Women also had to confront their sexual nature, not deny or ignore it as earlier feminists had done."[93]

Friedan's point regarding the role of sexuality in second-wave feminism can be seen in much of the writing by the radical feminists discussed here, who stressed the central importance of sexual liberation to feminism. In this regard, Kate Millett is emblematic in her call for "the end of sexual repression—freedom of expression and of sexual mores."[94] In *The Female Eunuch,* Germaine Greer makes a similar point, arguing that women must claim their sexuality, take responsibility for their own pleasure, and demystify the power granted to men, heterosexual intercourse, and the penis. As she puts it, "The cunt must come into its own."

> [W]omen will have to accept part of the responsibility for their own and their partners' enjoyment, and this involves a measure of control and conscious cooperation. Part of the battle will be won if they can change their attitude toward sex, and embrace and stimulate the penis instead of *taking* it.[95]

While there was a wide debate within early second-wave discourse about what the place of sexuality within feminism should be—a debate which would eventually culminate in the sex wars of the late 1970s and early 1980s—feminists of this period clearly understood sexuality to be a major issue for feminism. As Alice Echols puts it, "while nineteenth-century women's rights activists equated sex with danger, radical feminists believed that sexuality is simultaneously a realm of danger and of pleasure for women."[96]

The text that came to epitomize the early second wave's stance on sexuality is Anne Koedt's influential "The Myth of the Vaginal Orgasm" of 1968. Based in part on the findings of Masters and Johnson's 1966 *Human Sexual Response,* the essay describes how women have been socialized and psychologized into believing "the myth" that orgasms occur in the vagina rather than in the clitoris. Koedt argues that the importance of the clitoris to female orgasm had been hidden from women in order to ensure their dependence on men and the institution of heterosexuality. She writes:

> The recognition of clitoral orgasm as fact would threaten the heterosexual institution. For it would indicate that sexual pleasure was obtainable from either men or women, thus making heterosexuality not an absolute, but an option. It would thus open the whole question of human sexual relationships beyond the confines of the present male-female role system.[97]

For Koedt, the recognition of clitoral orgasm would achieve far more than the pleasure experienced by individual women: confronting the myth of vaginal orgasm would also help to dismantle the institution of heterosexuality and the male-female role system.

Koedt was criticized for what some perceived to be proselytizing for lesbianism and her overly negative (mis)representation of the sexual experiences of women. Germaine Greer pondered, "One wonders just whom Miss Koedt has gone to bed with," while Betty Friedan noted, "I thought it was a joke at first—those strangely humorless papers about clitoral orgasms that would liberate women from sexual dependence on a man's penis."[98] Nevertheless, "The Myth of the Vaginal Orgasm" had a profound effect on feminist discourse on sexuality, particularly its claim that "[w]hat we must do is redefine our sexuality. We must discard the 'normal' concepts of sex and create new guidelines which take into account mutual sexual enjoyment."[99] Koedt's call for "new guidelines" became the central principle for much early second-wave analysis of sexuality.[100]

Although it does not do so directly, Koedt's landmark essay does seem to offer a kind of comparison between generations of feminists. I remember the first time I read this essay, seventeen years after its publication, and the image it gave me of the women's movement during the late 1960s. I remember wondering if prior to Koedt's analysis women had even known they had clitorises. As she writes, "Considering that women know little about their anatomy, it is easy to be confused."[101] It seemed shocking to me: how could women not know? Yet the essay also thrilled me; or rather, I found the idea of living through such a monumental discovery thrilling, if somewhat inconceivable. If second-wavers had discovered the clitoris, what could my generation accomplish that could come anywhere near this feat?[102]

In hindsight, I can see that my original reading of this essay was colored by my newly discovered identification (and obsession) with the early second wave, particularly its radical wing. The texts I was reading from this period excited me; their energy, exuberance, and sense of purpose left me breathless. I wanted to devour everything I could from this period—the heyday of contemporary feminism. Yet my identification with—or perhaps more accurately, my desire for—early second-wave feminism also revolved around feelings of envy. I had found feminism too late. Everything new and exciting had already happened. I tried to find a way to incorporate my passion for these texts and what they offered into my everyday life, but it was a doomed project. The discovery of the clitoris was old news. Most of the women I knew had grown up reading *Our Bodies, Ourselves* or *Cosmopolitan* magazine; we grew up with information about female orgasms, like feminism itself, "in the water."[103] The notion that "the recognition of clitoral orgasm" could be a radical and transforming act seemed strange and far removed, yet I found myself envying second-wave feminists and the clarity of their purpose. The feminism I had inherited seemed far more complicated and therefore less exciting.

I believe that my response says something about how early second-wave feminists saw themselves as following—or moving beyond—the first wave. The vision of the past offered by "The Myth of the Vaginal Orgasm" seems to suggest that prior to the late 1960s, few women had orgasms. It is as if second-wave feminists were the first generation of U.S. women actually to enjoy sex. Perhaps the exuberance around sexuality that I so clearly felt in these writings is one of the most significant differences of second-wave feminists from their first-wave foremothers.

This difference seems particularly noticeable in the plethora of second-wave texts that address lesbianism, a topic that, not surprisingly, given the sexual mores of the nineteenth and early twentieth centuries, was not addressed by first-wave feminists. Like the discourse on clitoral orgasms, early second-wave discussions of lesbianism began as a way by which to critique the institution of heterosexuality and the inevitable centering of female sexuality around the male body. Although this argument was clearly pro-lesbian, its force came more from its critique of heterosexuality and patriarchy than from an outright celebration of female sexuality and the joys of lesbian sex. A classic example can be found in Radicalesbians' "The Woman Identified Woman" from 1970:

> Our energies must flow toward our sisters, not backward toward our oppressors. As long as woman's liberation tries to free women without facing the basic heterosexual structure that binds us in a one-to-one relationship with our oppressors, tremendous energies will continue to flow into trying to straighten up each particular relationship with a man, into finding how to get better sex, how to turn his head around. . . . This obviously splits our energies and commitments, leaving us unable to be committed to the construction of the new patterns which will liberate us.[104]

Rather than arguing for lesbianism as a pleasurable sexual (or even emotional) choice on its own merits, Radicalesbians posit lesbianism as a way by which to "free women" by breaking them out of the confines of heterosexuality. In essence, this is a polemic *against heterosexuality* and "male-identified women" rather than an argument *for lesbianism.* Throughout "The Woman Identified Woman," lesbian sex is never mentioned; rather, female "energy" and "connection" are heralded. Lesbianism would appear, in fact, to stand for a kind of asexuality, a sexuality that is characterized more by what it is not—heterosexuality—than what it is. While certainly not representative of all the writing on lesbianism during this period, this line of reasoning did have enormous resonance throughout early second-wave theorizing on sexuality, culminating in the notion that "feminism is the theory, lesbianism is the practice."[105] By 1972, the Washington, D.C., lesbian feminist collective The Furies were arguing that "[l]esbianism is not a matter of sexual preference, but rather one of political choice which every woman must make if she is to become women-identified and thereby end male supremacy."[106]

Articulating the political value of lesbianism had the effect of desexualizing it and, ultimately, silencing the incipient discussion of female sexuality which began in the late 1960s. Ironically, what was originally conceived of as a radical critique of heterosexuality—one that distinguished second-wave feminists from their first-wave predecessors—ended up mirroring the first wave's stance on sexuality. First-wave feminists had gone from advocating a multi-level women's rights agenda, one which embraced female emancipation on all levels, to a more specific agenda focused around women's virtues and moral superiority, one which saw sexuality as a danger to women.[107] Similarly, while early radical feminism stressed the importance of sexual liberation for feminism, much of the lesbian feminism and cultural feminism that came out of this movement increasingly focused on the dangers of male sexuality and the need to protect women from its harm. Sexuality, heterosexuality in particular, became aligned with men and was thus deemed dangerous for feminism and women.

A text that is emblematic of this position is Robin Morgan's 1973 "Lesbianism and Feminism," in which she states:

> Every woman here knows in her gut the vast differences between her sexuality and that of any patriarchally trained male's—gay or straight. That has, in fact, always been a source of *pride* to the lesbian community, even in its greatest suffering. That the emphasis on genital sexuality, objectification, promiscuity, emotional noninvolvement, and of course invulnerability was the *male style,* and that we, as women, placed greater trust in love, sensuality, humor, tenderness, commitment.[108]

Most of the traits Morgan characterizes as "the male style"—genital sexuality, promiscuity, emotional non-involvement, and invulnerability—could just as easily have been advocated by Germaine Greer two years earlier in *The Female Eunuch*. As the seventies rolled on, however, the feminist call for sexual liberation and "freedom of expression and of sexual mores," as Kate Millett had argued, was increasingly replaced by a single definition of what it meant to be a good feminist: someone who "placed greater trust in love, sensuality, humor, tenderness, commitment" than in getting it on. As the 1970s progressed, Greer's proclamation that "[t]he cunt must come into its own" was drowned out by statements such as "the real issue is simply that women *don't* like [sex] either with the same frequency or in the same way as men."[109] Paradoxically, the very issue that had made second-wave feminism seem most new, daring, and radical evolved into that which made it seem most old-fashioned, moralistic, and conservative to many in the next generation of women to encounter feminism. As some began to view second-wave feminism itself as a historical artifact—to be reclaimed or rejected—a particular representation of the second wave came to dominate the narrative of feminism as told by this new generation: the puritanical second wave. Constructing their own version of an emboldening feminist past, a new generation would go on to proclaim the next wave of feminism.

3.

Taking Feminism to Bed

THE THIRD WAVE DOES THE SEX WARS

As a review of third-wave writing makes clear, "Sexuality, in all its guises, has become a kind of lightning rod for this generation's hopes and discontents (and democratic vision) in the same way that civil rights and Vietnam galvanized [a previous] generation in the 1960s."[1] When they emerged in the early 1990s, third-wave feminists entered into an ongoing debate within feminism about sexual freedom and agency. While many second-wave feminists argued that sexual freedom and pleasure were central to women's political liberation, others insisted that sex was primarily a site of oppression and danger to women. When they have studied this history at all, third-wave feminists have gravitated toward the former position, stressing the liberating potential of sexuality. Rejecting the so-called victim feminism of Catherine MacKinnon and Andrea Dworkin, with its focus on the danger of rape and women's lack of agency and power, third-wave feminists have instead celebrated those aspects of second-wave feminism that assert a woman's right to pleasure.

An example is the 2000 anthology *Sex and Single Girls: Straight and Queer Women on Sexuality*. As with Seal Press's other third-wave anthologies over the last decade, this collection includes a wide range of young authors writing on a particular theme, in this case sexuality at the turn of the twentieth century.[2] Describing the sexual world that young women faced as they grew up, editor Lee Damsky writes:

Women in my generation were born in the '60s and '70s with the sexual revolution and the feminist movement, but we grew up with a mix of socio-sexual contradictions: the conservative backlash and the AIDS epidemic, the queer movement and genderfuck. We got divorced parents and "family values," homophobia and lesbian chic, "Just Say No" and "Ten Ways to Drive Him Wild."[3]

Damsky attributes these "socio-sexual contradictions" to coming of age at a particular moment in history, one that included both the feminist movement and conservative backlash. Like other third-wave anthologies, *Sex and Single Girls* is generational in its focus, especially in its discussion of sexuality *after* the women's movement of the 1960s and 1970s. Yet Damsky does not conceive of her collection as an attack on the second wave. Rather, she sees *Sex and Single Girls* as building on earlier feminist anthologies from the 1980s, such as *Powers of Desire: The Politics of Sexuality* (1983) and *Pleasure and Danger: Exploring Female Sexuality* (1985), which she describes as influencing her to publish a collection on women's sexual experiences at the beginning of the twenty-first century.[4] Coming out of feminism's sex wars, these earlier texts politicized sexuality, which, Damsky argues, "was essential to the progress of second-wave feminism." As she continues,

In retrospect, the sex wars can be seen as a struggle over what the relationship between the personal and the political should be. . . . What I took from those anthologies compiled in the early '80s was a feminist examination of sexuality that included personal experiences of sex by women of diverse backgrounds and sexual interests and that also seriously addressed the questions of women's sexual oppression.[5]

In Damsky's view, second-wave feminism was concerned with both sexual pleasure and sexual oppression; it was not committed solely to one side of this putative divide. She offers a nuanced representation of feminism's sex wars and their effect on her generation, seeing these wars as an essential part of the second wave's legacy to the third wave.

The term "sex wars" has been used to describe the intense debates that took place within feminism during the late 1970s through the mid-1980s. For feminists who participated in these debates, they "did indeed feel like 'war,'" to quote Lisa Duggan.[6] In broad terms, these debates focused on the role of sexuality for women's liberation and freedom. More specifically, feminists argued over pornography, sex work, censorship, sadomasochism and other sexual practices, and what constituted "good" feminist sex—or whether there should even be such a concept in the first place. As Duggan notes, "The porn wars more or less subsided in the mid-eighties as the antiporn position lost favor among most feminists, and lost in the courts and legislatures of the United States. But they have had consequences which are with us still."[7] These "wars" continue to play out in the ways in which sexuality is debated within feminism at large, to be sure. For third-wave feminists, however, these second-wave conflicts have dramatically influenced how younger women enter into feminism and position themselves in relation to it. As Damsky writes, "When we first discovered feminism, porn became anathema, and by the time we got to college-level women's studies it was part of the curriculum."[8] Thus, while an earlier generation of feminists may have been caught in the middle of an ideological battle over the meaning of sexuality, many third-wavers take for granted a particular sexual sensibility.

Third-wave feminists see their sexual freedom as a fundamental right, much like the right to vote. As Paula Kamen chronicles in her study of this generation's sexual attitudes, young women today "feel more comfortable than did earlier generations in aggressively and unapologetically pursuing their own interests in sexual relationships."[9] This perspective informs *Sex and Single Girls* as well as other third-wave texts, such as Rebecca Walker's "Lusting for Freedom," in which she says of her generation, "We need to learn that bodily pleasure belongs to us; it is our birthright."[10] Walker's use of "birthright" echoes the ubiquitous slogan "feminism is our birthright," suggesting that the inheritance passed to us by the second wave is one that is sexual as well as political.[11] Other third-wavers argue that feminism gave them the tools and analytical skills to develop new kinds of romantic and sexual relationships. In *Young Wives' Tales: New Adventures in Love and Partnership*, editors Jill Corral and Lisa Miya-Jervis argue that "[f]eminism's messages of self-reliance and critique of heterosexuality" have "transformed the way we see relationships."[12] And still others describe how feminism has given them a language for expressing their sexuality and a license to explore their desires. *Sex and Single Girls* contributor Meg Daly describes feminism's effects in a particularly vivid way when she writes, "Learning how to orgasm was, in a sense, a physicalization of all the feminist theory and sisterhood-is-powerful feeling I'd been immersed in for four years."[13] Daly credits feminism with liberating her sexuality (and making her come).

Daly's description provides a powerful counterexample to the arguments made by Katie Roiphe and Rene Denfeld in their works from the mid-1990s, where feminism was under attack for its anti-sex—particularly its perceived anti-heterosexual sex—moralizing. As Denfeld and Roiphe represented feminism, it was a movement and theory obsessed with controlling women's sexuality: "[F]eminists are on the front lines of sexual regulation."[14] Roiphe's attack on feminism and what she termed "date rape hysteria" was quickly challenged by feminists, both young and old.[15] As Jennifer Baumgardner and Amy Richards write, "Roiphe's instinct not to restrict sex is shared by many other young women, but she doesn't appear to understand that one can be both pro-sex *and* anti-rape. . . . Celebrations of women's sexuality coexist with stories of abuse in plenty of Third Wave zines."[16] Roiphe and Denfeld's representation of feminism as a moralizing force, however, continues to hover over third-wave discourse, shaping the ways in which some younger feminists position themselves against the second wave.

As Duggan notes, the sex wars "more or less subsided in the mid-eighties," although one wouldn't know it from reading Roiphe and Denfeld. For them, as well as for some of the other third-wavers who would follow in their footsteps, feminism has remained at war. Conceiving of feminism as a battle, such young feminists have entered the combat zone ready to fight on the side of pleasure, even though, as Linda Garber notes, "[t]he Sex Wars had happened, and sex clearly had won."[17] As one contributor to *Sex and Single Girls* suggests, the end of these "wars" has meant that "[n]o one thinks twice before calling herself 'sex-positive'—after all, who wants to be anti-sex?"[18] As with "power" feminism and "victim" feminism, "pro-sex" and "anti-sex" are terms that are used almost exclusively by those advocating one position in order to denounce the other.[19] While many feminists, both second- and third-wave, describe themselves as pro-sex, I can think of no feminist who describes herself as anti-sex. When Generation X "does the Sex Wars," however, it seems to want to have a war of its own, recreating a battle to fight.[20] In order to have such a battle, some third-wavers ascribe the anti-sex position to the second wave in order to grant themselves an unrivaled claim to pro-sex feminism, thereby obscuring the ways in which the original "war" was *intra*generational, not intergenerational. This reductive categorizing risks making what are, in fact, political and ideological differences among feminists—of all ages—into generational attributes.[21]

This is not the case for Damsky's collection, however; while decidedly generational in its focus on the sexual experiences of women "born in the '60s and '70s," neither her organization of the book, nor its essays, posit the third wave as a pro-sex challenge to the second wave. Included in *Sex and Single Girls* is an essay entitled "Blow Job Queen," in which author Merri Lisa Johnson explores her sexual fantasies, in particular her favorite masturbation fantasy of "a girl giving me head (that's right—sucking my dick)."[22] In its discussion of one woman's particular sexual fantasies and desires, "Blow Job Queen" is not unlike the other essays in Damsky's collection in its vision of sexual possibilities and female pleasure, of sexual limits and transgressions. Within her essay, neither Johnson's self-described "off-limits" desire to have a penis of her own, nor her sexuality generally, is described in generational terms.[23] Rather, her focus is on the pleasures and dangers of transgression, particularly how this blow job fantasy allows her to transgress the feminine role prescribed by her class and region. "Growing up in an upper-middle-class family in the South," Johnson writes, "eager to escape the constraints of traditional femininity, giving blowjobs meant being dirty and bad—sexual, and therefore dangerous and powerful."[24] For Johnson, the transgressive pleasures of both giving and, in her fantasies, getting blow jobs have to do with escaping the constraints that bind her, constraints which she describes as gender and class based. She desires to be bad because being bad means being sexual—someone powerful and dangerous, unlike the good girl she is raised to be.

After taking the reader through a detailed account of her masturbation fantasies, Johnson still remains tentative about them and what they suggest. She expresses ambivalence about even articulating these fantasies, expressing her feelings as a mix of emotions—"pleasure and guilt, shame and bravado." Describing these "transsexual fantasies" as a betrayal of the men she has sex with, she seems unable to reconcile her desire to receive a blow job with her heterosexuality.[25] She remains conflicted. Intent on proving how "terrible and dangerous I was," she ultimately confesses to the reader, "So I admit it. I didn't give many blowjobs as a girlfriend, wife, or one-night stand. This feels like a failure to measure up to my own bad girl image. . . . I hate to admit it; sexual bravado is more my style."[26] Describing as a failure her inability to truly be a bad girl, she comes clean. While proclaiming her sexual bravado, she ultimately reveals her timidity.

In "Blow Job Queen," Johnson's apprehensions about her fantasies have little to do with feminism and more to do with the constraints of traditional femininity and her own ambivalence about being a good girl. In one notable passage, however, she describes her "conflicting emotions on this subject" in terms that are infused with what might be called a feminist critique. As she writes at the very end of her essay, "I had crossed a line. In imaging that other female body servicing me as if I were a man, I feared that I'd bought into the cultural subordination of women."[27] Johnson again expresses reservation about the fantasy, but in this instance her fear has as much to do with her feminism as it does her traditional femininity. While the essay is initially about the pleasures of being off limits, she ultimately ends "Blow Job Queen" by pondering whether she should cross those limits at all.

Two years after the publication of *Sex and Single Girls,* Johnson published her own anthology, *Jane Sexes It Up: True Confessions of Feminist Desire.* Like Damsky's volume, it explores sexuality at the turn of the twentieth century, offering a range of perspectives on the topic. Like Damsky's collection, *Jane Sexes It Up* is characteristically third wave in its embrace of sex work and pornography, topics that an earlier feminism debated with much acrimony. In contrast to Damsky, however, Johnson positions her volume against second-wave feminism in terms that are both generational and, at times, antagonistic. Billed as a "much-needed discussion of feminism and sex," *Jane Sexes It Up* often relies on a narrow representation of the second wave's sexuality in order to stress its own supposed radicalness.[28]

In her introduction to the collection Johnson writes, "Rather than forcing ourselves on feminism, then, the *Jane* generation means to reconnect with our movement."[29] Johnson proposes that feminism already is "our movement"—belonging to the "*Jane* generation," Generation X, the third wave. Her use of "reconnect" also suggests that a connection to feminism existed in the past and can now be reclaimed, a gesture which is not unlike Denfeld's call for young women to "take back feminism."[30]

Young women of the *"Jane* generation," then, won't force themselves on feminism but rather will attempt a rapprochement, become reacquainted, as it were.

Included in the anthology are three essays by Johnson, one of which, "Pearl Necklace: The Politics of Masturbation Fantasies," repeats the subject matter of "Blow Job Queen." Both essays are about Johnson's fantasy to have a penis and receive oral sex from a woman. By the publication of the second essay, however, her earlier reservations about these fantasies have disappeared. In "Pearl Necklace," Johnson no longer depicts much anxiety around this fantasy; she no longer appears concerned that it might signal a breach of her proper Southern femininity. Rather, what was a brief point at the end of "Blow Job Queen"—the potential conflict between this fantasy and her feminism—has become her later essay's driving force. Both pieces take up the relationship between her feminism and her fantasy, but by the later essay Johnson's qualms about buying into the cultural subordination of women are gone. Instead, she uses her fantasy to express her reservations about feminism.

In "Pearl Necklace," Johnson again presents a masturbation scene in which she is fantasizing about having a penis. Only now, she's found a particularly resistant sexual partner. She writes, "With my hand between my legs, I become feminism's enemy number one. Crude, forceful, selfish. I put my dick in her mouth, and she does not like it."[31] Transforming feminism into her imaginary partner, Johnson becomes feminism's bad date—a boorish lover who is going to have her way with feminism whether feminism likes it or not. (And she doesn't.) Given the intense media hype over date rape in the early 1990s, precipitated in part by Katie Roiphe's attacks on feminism, Johnson's use of date-rape imagery adds another layer of meaning to her attempt to "become feminism's enemy number one." She appears to get off on the idea of being feminism's enemy; one might say she becomes the crude, selfish, and potentially violent man that feminism warns us about. Continuing to think through the pleasures of making it with an apparently resistant partner, she writes, "Who is this girl I picture with my dick in her mouth? Why do I take pleasure in tricking her into crossing her erotic boundaries? Why do I want her to go further than she wants to?"[32] As in "Blow Job Queen," Johnson again explores the possibilities of crossing boundaries and transgressing limits. But whereas she previously remained tentative about such border crossing, she now takes pleasure in it and wants to push feminism to the limit as well.

In their frequent references to crossing the line and being off limits, Johnson's essays recall Gayle Rubin's 1985 "Thinking Sex: Notes for a Radical Theory of the Politics of Sexuality," in which she analyzes the hierarchies of sexual values institutionalized by religious, medical, psychiatric, and popular discourses of sexuality. Within such hierarchies, she argues, there appears to be a "need to draw and maintain an imaginary line between good and bad sex."[33] For Rubin, "the line appears to stand between sexual order and chaos," a sort of "erotic DMZ" where "[o]nly sex acts on the good side of the line"—heterosexual, married, monogamous, intragenerational—"are accorded moral complexity."[34] While it is true that feminists have been among the most vocal critics of these sexual hierarchies, other feminists have been active in drawing more such lines, creating a feminist sexual value system of "good" and "bad" sex. Recall Robin Morgan's definition of "male" (that is, "bad") sexuality with its "emphasis on genital sexuality, objectification, promiscuity, emotional non-involvement, and of course invulnerability."[35] Feminism, then, has sometimes functioned like other forms of authority—religious, medical, psychiatric—in regulating sexual behavior, in this instance, the sexual behavior of feminists themselves.

Describing her pleasure in masturbating to her blow job fantasy, Johnson writes, "This was off-limits (where I love to be right before I come)."[36] Johnson suggests that her own notion of the line between "good" and "bad" sex has developed, in part, from feminism: "Taboo images often spring to mind when I masturbate, so it makes sense that the commitment I developed to feminism in graduate school would designate a new field of possibility for transgression."[37] Here she suggests that feminism creates the moral line and thus makes possible the taboo transgression entailed in crossing it. Feminism, then, builds the very boundary that Johnson wants to cross. But in order to have such a boundary, Johnson must represent feminism as an authority who designates certain areas as sexually off limits.

Indeed, Johnson appears to want more than to just cross the line herself. She is interested in tricking feminism into crossing its own erotic boundaries. Although she later claims to want to reconnect with feminism rather than force herself on it, Johnson's desire to have her way with feminism and take it with her across the "good-bad" sex divide is also evident in her introductory essay to *Jane Sexes It Up*. "When I first imagined this project," she writes, "I thought that in writing it I would force feminism's legs apart like a rude lover, liberating her from the beige suit of political correctness. I wanted feminism to be *bad like me*. A young feminism, a sexy feminism."[38] Like the passages from "Pearl Necklace," these rely on decidedly aggressive imagery in order to convey the idea of what Johnson wants from feminism. Gone are any mentions of Johnson's "failure to measure up to [her] own bad girl image." She's "bad"—"sexual, and therefore dangerous and powerful," as she writes in "Blow Job Queen"—and she's going to make feminism "bad" too, even if what she's doing constitutes assault.

Johnson imagines not only sexually freeing feminism but also updating its wardrobe. This narcissistic makeover requires that feminism adopt Johnson's look—"young," "sexy," and, as she stresses, "bad like me." She attributes a certain sexual attitude to her age, imagining that, with her youth, she can revitalize feminism, bring it up to date, make it hip again. Describing what she terms a "particularly third wave" form of feminist desire, one that is "immodest and cocky," she writes of the "sheer fun my generation pursues in the performance of our erotic personas."[39] Johnson thus makes desire age-based, attributing erotic sensibility to generation rather than to any particular sexual proclivities or ideological stance. The implication, of course, is that the sexual desires and experiences of second-wave feminists, with what Johnson calls their "nicey-nice persona[s]," were decidedly different than the third wave's.[40]

While admittedly singular in its overt expression of sexual aggression toward feminism, Johnson's work shares with some other third-wave discourses an interest in being "bad." Her "sexual bravado"—with its revelations of "perversion[s]" and "shameful secret[s]"—seems like it is trying to measure up to Johnson's own bad-girl image.[41] She appears intent on proving how "bad" she really is, to shock her audience, perhaps, although her fantasies hardly seem shocking to this jaded reader.[42] (I'm reminded of *The Sexual Life of Catherine M.*, in which Catherine Millet writes, "In my naïveté I initially thought that a blow job was a deviant sexual practice."[43]) When this "bad-girl" feminism is pitted against what Johnson perceives as the "nicey-nice" feminism of the past, it appears that the good-girl/bad-girl divide is generational. A central theme in the second-wave project of liberating women's sexuality was the critique of the sexual double standard and of "the view that sexuality was bad for women and that only 'bad' women were sexual."[44] It is unfortunate that in their investment in retaining a good-girl/bad-girl divide, so that they can be feminism's "bad girls," some third-wavers uphold this double standard, a sexist paradigm that feminists might be better off dismantling rather than perpetuating.[45]

It is worth noting that this debate between so-called anti-sex, or victim, feminists and pro-sex, or power, feminists is one that has had little interest for women of color. In fact, I would go so far as to say that feminism's wars over sexuality have primarily been fought between white women—both intragenerationally within the second wave of the late 1970s and early 1980s and cross-generationally in the last decade as white third-wavers criticize their white feminist "foremothers."[46] In what they term "a womanist critique of the current feminist conflict," Barbara McCaskill and Layli Phillips argue that "African American women have been virtual, conspicuous absentees at worst and passive observers at best, in the assessments and debates that entangle victim and power feminists."[47] Historically, it has typically been white, economically privileged women who have had the luxury to define their liberation exclusively in terms of their individual sexual freedom. As Jane Gerhard notes in her study of second-wave feminism, in focusing on sexuality as its central feminist issue, white cultural feminists "minimized the intersection of sexuality with other axes of identity, namely, race and class."[48] In much of the new "sexy" feminism of the third wave, a similar lack of attention to class and race is taking place. It is a paradox, then, even as some third-wavers use the "newness" of their sexuality to assert a new wave, they end up repeating a white second-wave inattention to the intersectionality of identity.

DOMINATING FEMINISM

In *Jane Sexes It Up*, Johnson has feminism on its knees. Since her original essay in *Sex and Single Girls*, she has become more cocky (pun intended), and consequently, it would seem, her relationship to feminism has changed. "Forc[ing] feminism's legs apart like a rude lover" and "put[ting] my dick in her mouth," Johnson's description of what she wants to do to feminism is unmistakably aggressive. She describes imposing herself on feminism, violating it. It might be feminism's "first time," but Johnson is going to get what's she after. In the process, Johnson intends to sexualize feminism, to make feminism "bad like her."

In her image of dominating feminism, Johnson turns the tables: while once feminism had authority over her, it is now she who is in control, forcing feminism to go farther than it wants to go. This image only works because of the power Johnson has already attributed to feminism, as when she writes that feminism is like "a strict teacher who *just needs to get laid.*"[49] Her depiction of violating feminism is premised on two distinct although interconnected traits: feminism as authority figure (the "strict teacher") and feminism as uptight prude ("who just needs to get laid"). Indeed, feminism's authority is inextricably linked to its prudishness. In essays so explicitly concerned with dominating feminism, it appears that feminism can never be the dominatrix herself. Her authority is always non-sexual and boring, "beige" and "politically correct."

Theorist Cathryn Bailey offers a useful perspective for analyzing Johnson's rhetoric. Using Michel Foucault's work on power to discuss the ways in which feminism functions as an authority, Bailey argues that although feminist power is not located in any one centralized figure, it nevertheless is experienced as quite real. As Bailey argues,

> [T]he fact that we cannot speak of a singularly identifiable feminist power does not mean that it does not exist with the capacity to affect subjects. In the wake of the current backlash against feminism, many of us are accustomed to thinking of it as an increasingly disempowered movement, but we need to see how it continues to be enmeshed in power relations. If not, we can never comprehend why someone who has some appreciation for feminism might, nevertheless, feel a need to resist aspects of it, as many younger women clearly do.[50]

Resistance is built into all forms of power, according to Bailey's Foucauldian analysis. Impossible as it might seem to some second-wave feminists, feminism itself is now perceived as just such a power, ensuring that it too will be resisted. Bailey continues:

> Many younger women see themselves as struggling against becoming the kind of feminist subjects they thought they were supposed to become. As such, they may be offering a kind of resistance that is not immediately

directed at actual feminists, but rather to an internalized version of a feminist governor—a "panoptical feminist connoisseur."[51]

In their struggle against becoming the kind of feminist they imagine feminism wants them to be, some third-wave feminists resist feminism—at least, the "feminist governor" they have internalized—even as they create new forms of feminist identities for themselves. Bailey's discussion of resistance resonates with what I have earlier described as disidentification, namely the third wave's refused identification with second-wave feminism precisely in order to create a feminism of their own. Bailey's analysis also helps explain why this "feminist governor"—as in Johnson's "strict teacher who just needs to get laid"—is rarely given a name. In other words, attacks are not directed at actual feminists but at feminism itself, or rather the version of feminism that many third-wave feminists have internalized.

It is worth noting that the authority granted to feminism—"the Feminism that gets to wear a capital 'F'"—is a sign of the important role of the movement in third-wave lives.[52] As Bailey points out, "to some extent it is a testament to the success of feminism that such teaching produces younger feminist subjects who resist, on feminist terms, the very feminism that has helped to shape them."[53] Johnson's "strict teacher," then, may be more than a metaphor. For her, as for many of us in the next generation, feminism has indeed been a teacher, one that has helped to shape who we are. Yet the teacher-student relationship, like the mother-daughter one, can be fraught with tensions. As with other clichés of generational succession, the trope of the student who surpasses the teacher is rife with generational rivalry and anxieties about replacement.

Writing as a student in the face of a powerful "strict teacher," Johnson on one hand grants all the authority to feminism, making it the instructor who tells her what to do. Yet she also imagines herself as having the power to dominate feminism, to top it, as it were. Unlike many of her generational cohort who express feelings of powerlessness in the face of feminist authority, Johnson imagines that she can transform feminism. In order to do so, she relies on imagery derived from S/M culture. As Pat Califia has noted, S/M sexual roles are not fixed but rather can be taken on and transformed in the pursuit of pleasure. Some of these roles, Califia notes, include teacher and student, adding that roles can be reversed within S/M encounters such that "the child may be chastising the parent," and the student may be dominating the teacher.[54] In making feminism a strict teacher, Johnson frees herself to play with the power structure inherent in the roles of teacher and student. Her use of S/M imagery enables her to escape merely being a "bottom" to feminism's "top." Thus, while Johnson imbues feminism with authority, because she writes not as a daughter but as a fellow participant in an erotic (if dominating) S/M scene, she too can walk away with a sense of power.

WHO IS FEMINISM?

As Bailey's analysis suggests, younger feminists often resist second-wave feminism through rebelling against an "internalized feminist governor," one that may have very little relation to any particular feminist (or any particular feminism). This "governor" often goes unnamed and is just called "feminism," an amorphous category that includes both everything and nothing. Johnson's representation of second-wave feminism shares similarities with that of the feminists who began developing "next-generation" feminism in the early and mid-1990s—writers such as Katie Roiphe and Rene Denfeld. In this early work, the argument was made that feminism is both childish and old-fashioned; as such, feminism offers a regressive return to the past rather than a progressive step forward. Sexuality has been central to this claim, for it is in its discourse on sexuality that feminism appears both most immature (too young) and most archaic (too old-fashioned). More than any other aspect of contemporary feminism, the so-called dominant feminist perspective on sexuality is what seems to signal regression. "It is the passive sexual role that threatens us still," as Roiphe writes in *The Morning After*, "and it is the denial of female sexual agency that threatens to propel us backward."[55]

In their "histories" of feminist theorizing on sexuality, Denfeld and Roiphe argue that contemporary feminism is anti-sex and, in particular, anti-heterosexuality. In their version of second-wave feminism, whereas once feminists celebrated the pleasure and power of sexuality, today's feminists only see its dangers: rape, pornography, and domestic violence. As Denfeld writes in a characteristic bit of hyperbole, "to be a feminist today one must support the censorship of sexual material."[56]

In their attacks on feminism, Roiphe and Denfeld contributed to the granting of omnipotent power to feminism's "governor" and thus had a major influence on how some subsequent young feminists positioned themselves in relation to feminism.

Denfeld and Roiphe did more than just attack feminism, however. They singled out certain feminists for condemnation, thereby adding to the perception that these women function as the movement's supreme leaders, standing in for feminism as a whole. The hit list of feminist leaders put forward by *The Morning After* and *The New Victorians* is predictable: Catherine MacKinnon is Roiphe's main target, while in Denfeld's text she is joined by Robin Morgan and Andrea Dworkin to form the feminist troika responsible for the rise of "victim feminism." In their representations of these feminists and their influence, they suggest that MacKinnon, Dworkin, and Morgan are the main feminist theorists of our time, thereby ignoring a wide range of other feminist thinkers and leaders and myriad forms of feminist theory.

Even as they make this claim, however, they are forced to concede that it is precisely because of the feminism that came before them—the one that championed female sexual agency—that they are able to construct their own pro-sex platform. They are thus left with a complicated set of relationships to feminism: on the one hand, they must acknowledge and celebrate what was (and is) powerful about feminism's effect on women's sexuality, for how else to account for their own position? On the other hand, in arguing against second-wave feminism and positing themselves as new vanguards, they must represent the bulk of feminism as being anti-sex. Whereas in moments Roiphe and Denfeld appear quite able to present feminism as a straw woman all too ready to be knocked down, in their discussions of sexuality they are thus left in a quandary: they must somehow hang on to the "good feminism" of the second wave, the pro-sex feminism that empowered them to be sexual, even as they trash what they see as contemporary feminism's anti-sex bias.

Rather than finding support in the many other pro-sex feminisms of the 1990s and even 1980s, however, they return to the 1970s to find their allies. Paradoxically, then, even as they suggest that feminism signals a return to the past, they themselves make such a return in order to reclaim what was empowering about early second-wave feminism.

Denfeld, for example, praises the original *Our Bodies, Ourselves* as an example of a pro-sex feminism that dealt with sexuality in an explicit way and taught her "that other women masturbated and had sexual fantasies." As she writes, growing up with the book on her mother's bookshelf, she "looked forward to having sex" and embraced the positive image of female sexuality of *Our Bodies*.[57] In both *The Morning After* and *The New Victorians*, Germaine Greer (her work from the 1970s anyway) plays a prominent role as the "good feminist" of the second wave, the one who got it right. Greer offers a model of the kind of writing on sexuality that these writers think is needed, but find absent, in contemporary feminism. Roiphe praises *The Female Eunuch* for having offered a "brand-new, explosive, a tough and sexy terrorism for the early stirrings of the feminist movement."[58] Denfeld adds, "A woman who has shaped her perception of feminism on older feminist works such as Nancy Friday's *My Secret Garden* or Greer's *The Female Eunuch* will find herself in for a shock when she encounters the movement itself. Rarely do today's feminists even acknowledge these books exist."[59]

When they try to describe their fellow feminists who might share their anti-censorship and pro-sexuality views, they appear to be at a loss for words. Roiphe concedes that there are "a few feminists" who object to the expanding definition of date rape, and Denfeld acknowledges that there are "several feminist writers" who have spoken out against censorship and "a handful" who challenge what she terms "antiheterosexuality theory."[60] Neither writer, however, explores these anomalous "minority" feminist positions in any detail, leaving their readers to assume—quite inaccurately—that they basically speak alone.

In their desire to reclaim the "early stirrings" of the second wave, while dismissing what followed as puritanical and anti-sex, Denfeld and Roiphe have a relationship to history which is uncannily reminiscent of the relationship constructed by second-wave feminists to the first wave. Namely, the early period of the former movement is praised as offering the kind of feminism that can empower us in the present, while the later period is dismissed as restrictive and ultimately irrelevant. This time around, however, there is a twist. In the case of the second wave, late first-wave feminism was rejected because it was not radical enough, while these third-wave writers reject late second-wave feminism because it is *too* radical, albeit in a sexually conservative way.

Denfeld's relationship to feminisms past and present gets tricky when she laments the dearth of pro-sex writing for today's young feminists. As she writes, "With the exception of a few fringe works written primarily by lesbians (such as Susie Bright) and reprints of *Our Bodies, Ourselves,* there hasn't been a celebratory book on female sexuality written by a feminist since the mid-seventies."[61] Leaving aside the fact that Denfeld's claims are absurd, as any trip to a feminist bookstore could tell you, her rhetoric deserves further scrutiny. Paradoxically, it would seem that while lesbians are anti-sex, they are simultaneously the only ones currently writing "celebratory books on female sexuality." Although lesbianism for Denfeld symbolizes all that is repressive and puritanical about feminism today, lesbians are apparently the only ones, outside of reprints of *Our Bodies, Ourselves,* who offer an alternative to anti-sex feminism.

Denfeld's use of the word "fringe" here is worth examining. If lesbians and bisexual women—"such as Susie Bright"—are writing "fringe works," this would apparently contradict the authority accorded to lesbians in the rest of Denfeld's text. To give but one example of a ubiquitous argument in *The New Victorians,* Denfeld writes, "[A] powerful school of feminist thought teaches that only lesbian relationships are acceptable for enlightened feminists. This topic is often shrouded in silence because feminist leaders consistently condemn as homophobic those who would discuss it."[62] The idea that feminism is synonymous with lesbianism—or that one must be a lesbian to be a "good" feminist—has a long history within both the women's movement and its representation in the larger culture.[63] As historian Nancy F. Cott has described, when young women rejected feminism in the 1920s they did so, in part, because of the newly created association between feminism and lesbianism, an association advanced by the new fields of psychoanalysis and sexology in which "[w]omen's desire to team with other women was labeled lesbianism."[64] In her article on "postfeminism" from 1982, Susan Bolotin quotes a 24-year-old who says, "I don't label myself a feminist. Not for me, but for the guy next door that would mean that I'm a lesbian and that I hate men."[65] As this account suggests, "I'm a lesbian" and "I hate men" are often seen as synonymous by the general, nonfeminist public. Lesbianism is defined not in terms of desire for women but in terms of hatred of men: that is, lesbians are *against* men rather than *for* women.

In this construct, "the lesbian" serves only as a signifier of women's oppositional relationships to men. Unfortunately, some third-wavers end up validating this view of lesbianism, as when Denfeld describes feminism's critique of "compulsory heterosexuality" as "antiheterosexuality theory."[66] To analyze heterosexuality is to be antiheterosexual, just as to be a lesbian is to be anti-male.

In her argument about how feminism has gone wrong, Denfeld stresses that feminists have forgotten about the pleasure that heterosexuality and men can provide. She writes,

> In discounting the role that men play in women's lives, the women's movement today has made a serious mistake. As long as feminism stands for male bashing, mandated lesbian sexuality, separatism, and repressive sexual mores, countless women will turn their faces away from a movement that stands for hostility and discrimination.[67]

In Denfeld's account, male-bashing, mandated lesbian sexuality, separatism, and repressive sexual mores are all linked, forming an image of *the* feminist "position" on sexuality. Not only is lesbian sexuality mandated—that is, forced, not desired—it is equated with male-bashing and repressive sexual mores. The image of lesbianism offered here is anti-male, anti-sex, and prudish. This lesbianism is not about pleasure, but about the *absence* of pleasure.

Let's return to Denfeld's claim that "[w]ith the exception of a few fringe works written primarily by lesbians," "there hasn't been a celebratory book on female sexuality written by a feminist since the mid-seventies." If lesbians control a "powerful school of feminist thought" which mandates lesbianism, how is it, then, that lesbians are simultaneously on the fringe of feminism? If lesbians play such a dominating role in feminism today, wouldn't it follow that their "celebratory books on female sexuality" would be seen as mainstream rather than fringe?

Because anti-heterosexuality—and thus anti-sexuality generally—is defined as lesbianism, it is often incorrectly assumed that the anti-sex position is solely, or even primarily, advocated by lesbians. This argument is put forward by Roiphe, in an article entitled "Men: What's to Be Afraid of?" where she argues that women's negative personal experiences with men shape feminist arguments about (male) sexuality. That is, women who don't like men construct anti-heterosexuality theory.[68] A crucial point which often gets overlooked in the critique of feminism's perceived anti-sex agenda is that the writers who are most often cited by Denfeld and other third-wavers as arguing against heterosexuality—Catherine MacKinnon, Andrea Dworkin, and Robin Morgan, to be specific—are, in fact, *not* lesbians.[69] As Ellen Willis reminds us, "lesbians have been among" this form of feminism's "loudest critics; this is not a gay-straight split."[70]

Denfeld's argument begins to unravel when her imaginary anti-sex lesbian comes face to face with *real* pro-sex lesbians, such as Bright, Gayle Rubin, and Joan Nestle, all of whom she cites as positive influences on contemporary feminism.[71] To support the view that feminism is repeating its first-wave history, Denfeld relies on Rubin's 1981 text "The Leather Menace," in which Rubin argues that anti-S/M feminists of the late 1970s reproduced Victorian sexual mores. Ironically, an essay on sadomasochism within the lesbian community, published by a self-described butch dyke in the early 1980s, appears to be the text which most influenced Denfeld's thinking, not to mention the general thesis of her book. Denfeld, however, simply refers to Rubin as a "feminist writer."[72] Rubin seems unable to stand for feminism itself because that spot is permanently reserved for MacKinnon and company. As a pro-sex, radical feminist, then, Rubin seems permanently left out on the fringe rather than occupying feminism's center as its "governor."

In "Pearl Necklace," Merri Lisa Johnson also references an early 1980s text by a pro-sex radical dyke, in this case Pat Califia. In a parallel to Rubin's role in Denfeld's book, Califia is cited but Johnson seems unable to allow her to stand for feminism itself. Her essay begins with an epigraph from Califia's essay "Feminism and Sadomasochism," which reads: "My sexual semiotics differ from the mainstream. So what? I didn't join the feminist movement to live inside a Hallmark card."[73] Taken from a text that defends sadomasochism against, in Califia's words, "feminist theorists who believe it is the epitome of misogyny, sexism, and violence," this quote is cited approvingly, as are all subsequent references to Califia throughout *Jane Sexes It Up*.[74] A self-described sex radical, Califia has spent much of her writing career criticizing feminism's sexual moralism, but she has always done so as a feminist and in the name of feminism. In "Feminism and Sadomasochism," Califia notes, "I've been a feminist since I was 13," later explaining to her reader "why I call myself a feminist."[75] Her work has had both an explicit and implicit effect on third-wave writing about sexuality and the third wave's own critiques of feminism's sexual ethics. In *Jane Sexes It Up* and other work, it appears that Califia is a feminist foremother whom Johnson's branch of the "bad girl" third wave can embrace without hesitation.[76]

In Johnson's epigraph, the title of Califia's essay is given without any mention of the year of its publication. When readers turn to the bibliography, they find that Califia's essay comes from a 1996 anthology, *Feminism and Sexuality: A Reader.* To some readers—and perhaps to Johnson herself—this might suggest that "Feminism and Sadomasochism" is relatively recent, published after the third wave's launch in 1991, well after the sex wars of the late 1970s and early 1980s. In fact, Califia's essay was originally published in the controversial *Heresies 12: The Sex Issue* from 1981, a journal that appeared at the very height of the sex wars. Written over twenty years ago, Califia's essay is not some recent intervention into an otherwise prudish feminism. It is not a product of the "*Jane* generation" but rather is second wave, generationally speaking at least. Johnson doesn't mention this fact, however, leaving her readers to assume, unless they know otherwise, that Califia's work is, like her own, a late-twentieth-century challenge to feminism's perceived orthodoxies.

Perhaps I am making too much of what is, after all, just a citational oversight. Yet I would argue that the way in which Califia's essay is used in Johnson's work is emblematic of a certain kind of third-wave relationship to second-wave feminism. Second-wave feminism, in all its many varieties, has clearly had a profound influence on third-wave thought, yet some young feminists have a difficult time crediting this earlier work or acknowledging that it even existed at all. As Bailey notes, "There is a level of ignorance about second-wave feminism in some third-wave critiques that is disappointing. Even worse, it is an ignorance that is rarely acknowledged."[77] This ignorance is particularly glaring in the third wave's depiction of pro-sex second-wave feminism. Indeed, reading some self-described third-wave texts—whether in the "dissenter" ranks with Denfeld or members of the "*Jane* generation"—one wouldn't know that feminists in the 1970s and '80s even considered some of the issues that the third wave now champions as its own: masturbation, nonmonogamy, bisexuality, pornography, sex work, and, of course, orgasms. Some third-wavers seem to have followed the lead of the larger, nonfeminist culture in ignoring this segment of feminism. As Ellen Willis reminds us, "While pro-sex feminism has considerable influence among feminist and gay activists, intellectuals, and artists, it has little public visibility; the mass media have more or less ignored its existence."[78]

In *Jane Sexes It Up*, Johnson herself describes coming to this realization, writing that Carole Vance's 1985 collection *Pleasure and Danger: Exploring Female Sexuality*

> would have been our template—if we'd ever heard of it. But revolutionary ideas about sexual politics are consistently misrepresented or simply "disappeared" in most narratives of U.S. history. This face of feminism—the *smart-ass take-no-shit anarch-orgasmic feminist persona* Gen X-ers thought we invented—is suppressed in the mainstream media.[79]

Johnson is right to point out that this face of feminism is consistently misrepresented or otherwise absent in mainstream representations of the movement, yet what I find puzzling is why it is also absent in much of her own writing within *Jane Sexes It Up*. It appears that in order to get the patent for inventing an "orgasmic feminist persona," third-wavers must habitually repress the knowledge of an earlier movement that could contest their claim. It is regrettable that "third wave feminists are sometimes surprised by this history," but I have to wonder why this history is not available to younger feminists.[80] Why, as Johnson argues, do many young feminists think they invented this feminist persona? Is it because the knowledge of this face of feminism is truly being suppressed, or is it because remaining ignorant allows the third wave to assert itself as feminism's innovators?

Unlike Denfeld, the "*Jane* generation" has not completely ignored the pro-sex second wave. In addition to both Vance and Califia, Johnson cites Germaine Greer, Amber Hollibaugh, and Anne Koedt, noting that "these women laid the groundwork for a feminism that gives women permission to explore, discover, reveal, and celebrate what gets us off. No matter what."[81] Yet even as she references these earlier feminists, she appears to need to have some other feminism to write against.

It appears that when this earlier pro-sex feminism is acknowledged at all, its status as second-wave feminism is untenable. Feminism, capital F, must remain anti-sex so that third-wavers can announce their generation's arrival with its "much needed" intervention into feminist thought. The question raised by these examples is, Why is it impossible to hold together two different versions of feminism simultaneously—the pro-sex and the anti-sex, assuming we want to keep using such reductive formulations in the first place? Why is it impossible for us to hold a complex and multi-dimensional view of feminism?

In *New Millennial Sexstyles*, Carol Siegel gives the third wave's ahistorical tendencies a more positive spin than, admittedly, I have been doing. It is worth noting that Siegel writes as a second-wave feminist who is disgruntled with what she sees as the limits of *her* generation, so perhaps we share something in this regard. As she argues:

> One of the favorite poses of the second-wave feminist here at the end of the twentieth century seems to be exhausted scanning of the horizon for reinforcements, for younger women who have a complete enough commitment to feminism to carry on the struggle. The subtext of this self-representation is that we not only have a prior claim to feminist radicalism, but also continue to set the standards by which the usefulness of feminisms should be judged.

Siegel criticizes second-wave feminists for their desire for reinforcements to carry on the struggle in the same manner that it has always been carried out. She faults her generation for its insistence that younger feminists follow, lockstep, in the second wave's footsteps. (Phyllis Chesler's *Letters to a Young Feminist* comes to mind, for example.)

Siegel continues: "But I also see women of another kind in the new generation, women who dare to be different from what we so often were . . . women who *in their apparent ahistorical ignorance* of the fairy tales that have defined us may break into something new."[82] Rather than criticizing third-wave feminists for "their apparent ahistorical ignorance," Siegel suggests that this ignorance makes possible "something new." She implies that ignorance may even be necessary for the development of new forms of feminism—feminisms unlike anything second-wavers have ever seen. Siegel's use of "apparent" here corresponds with my own sense that this ahistorical ignorance may not always be based in a real lack of knowledge but rather in something else, perhaps a desire to be unfettered from the demands of the past, to be free to carve out a new feminism. Historical memory, she seems to suggest, weighs us down, prevents us from creating something new. History can't just be passed down like fairy tales. A bit of forgetting, Siegel suggests, is just as empowering as knowledge.

In thinking about why I've been so puzzled by some third-wave feminisms, I have had to analyze my own fantasies—namely my fantasy that a complete (and complex) feminist history is available, ready to be passed down to the next generation. I want to resist the idea that each generation must reinvent the wheel—or that, apparently, reinventing the wheel is so pleasurable for some. There is no such complete feminist history, of course, and even if there were, every generation will have to find and make its own history, perhaps forgetting along the way.

HETEROSEXUALITY: THE LOVE THAT FINALLY DARE SPEAK ITS NAME?

"[F]eminism isn't dead," writes Patricia Payette in *Jane Sexes It Up*, "it's merely undergoing a transformation at the hands of young women like myself who are refusing to submit to outmoded paradigms that tell us what we should and shouldn't desire for ourselves."[83] Payette's comments point to the central role played by desire in the third-wave's "transformation" of feminism. For many in this new generation, the assertion of desires is at the heart of this "new" and "sexy" feminism, one that is being used to stress generational differences between the waves.

It is an understatement to say that the last thirty-five years have led to a remarkable expansion in the sexual freedom taken for granted by most women, young and old. "Most women I know personally take for granted a range of options for their sexual behavior, whether or not they are interested in or comfortable with all of the alternatives," writes Lee Damsky in *Sex and Single Girls*. Such options include: "serial monogamy (plus or minus cohabitation), recreational sex with dates or fuckbuddies, abstinence, using sex toys or porn, trying S/M, having children, getting married, experimenting with open relationships."[84] For third-wave feminists, growing up with these options "in the water," to use Baumgardner and Richards's phrase, has meant that they often feel entitled to pursue their pleasure in ways which an earlier generation of women might not have felt so comfortable in doing or may have been prohibited from doing altogether. From HBO's *Sex and the City* to *Bust* magazine to the women in hip-hop and rock, a new breed of sexual woman is being celebrated in our culture.[85] As *Bust* editor Debbie Stoller writes, "In the '90s, the women of the New Girl Order are ready to go out and get what's cumming to us. Our mission is to seek out pleasure wherever we can find it. In other words, if it feels good, screw it. Vibrators in hand, we're ready to fight the good fight."[86] (Perhaps it's no coincidence that vibrator sales went from $15,000 in 1977 to $6.5 million in 1998.[87])

Rather than seeing themselves as part of an ongoing debate within feminism—one that can be traced back to the first wave—about the meaning of sexuality for women's liberation, some third-wavers describe as a generational perspective what is more accurately a particular feminist philosophy of sex. These "women of the New Girl Order" celebrate sexuality as the third wave's particular contribution to feminism, that which makes third-wavers unlike the feminists who came before them. Describing the sexual credo of feminism's "next generation," *Bust* editor Stoller writes:

> In our quest for total sexual satisfaction, we shall leave no sex toy unturned and no sexual avenue unexplored. Women are trying their hands (and other body parts) at everything from phone sex to cybersex, solo sex to group sex, heterosex to homosex. Lusty feminists of the third wave, we're more than ready to drag-race down sexual roads less traveled.[88]

Ads for feminist sex-toy shops such as Toys in Babeland and Good Vibrations, along with articles extolling the joys of sex toys, are monthly staples of *Bust* and other third-wave magazines. "In contrast to the typical notion of their activist 1970's foremothers," one journalist commented, "the women who publish these magazines will discuss lipstick and liberation in the same breath."[89]

This "new" feminism is, in part, a reaction to the negative and stereotypical image of "the feminist" that both the popular press and occasionally third-wave writers help to perpetuate. The same anti-male and anti-sex image of feminism that early second-wave writers had to contend with continues to live on, shaping the various defensive ways that people enter feminism. In claiming the identity of feminist, many writers seem to bend over backward not to fit its perceived negative stereotypes, particularly that of the "unattractive," "man-hating dyke."[90] In its coverage of feminism, the media has often focused more on how feminists look than on what they have to say. In the popular press's representation of feminism, this focus on style and appearance has contributed to the often-negative image of feminism presented to the general public. As Australian feminist Kathy Bail points out, many women have embraced the "new" feminism because they "don't want to identify with something that sounds dowdy, asexual or shows them to be at a disadvantage. They don't want to be seen as victims."[91] One way, then, that the supposed anti-sex bias of feminism can be countered is by presenting an image of feminism as sexy, attractive, and fun: a "do-me feminist" who desires men rather than a castrating man-hater.

In his 1994 *Esquire* article, Tad Friend coined the phrase "do-me feminism" to describe a rather all-encompassing group of feminist writers that included Susie Bright, Pat Califia, Rene Denfeld, Mary Gaitskill, bell hooks, Lisa Palac, Katie Roiphe, Rebecca Walker, and Naomi Wolf. Not only was this group fairly disparate in their feminist beliefs, but they also represented a range of ages, not just the "young and sexy" crowd later championed by the "*Jane* generation." Describing what was, in 1994, perceived as a "new" breed of feminists, Friend writes:

> The do-me-feminists are choosing locker-room talk to shift discussion from the failures of men to the failures of feminism, from the paradigm of sexual abuse to the paradigm of sexual pleasure. They want to return sex from the political realm to the personal. In short, they want to have fun.[92]

Friend explicitly attributed this "do-me feminism" to a new generation of women thinkers.[93] Yet the list of women he sees as coming under the "do-me" banner represented both Generation Xers and Baby Boomers, suggesting that the ideology of "do-me-ism" wasn't necessarily the sole possession of one generation, even as he quotes NOW president Patricia Ireland as saying, "This is not your mother's feminism."[94] Friend's term "do-me feminism" was quickly followed by other descriptive adjectives to christen the feminism of this new generation—"babe feminism,"[95] "bimbo feminism,"[96] and "vibrator feminism"[97]—adjectives that work to differentiate this new breed from their feminist foremothers.

Central to this new generation's claim of transforming feminism has been its celebration of heterosexuality. In her description of feminism's "mandated lesbian sexuality," Denfeld, among others, helped to promote the idea that second-wave feminism had completely silenced hetero-sexual women, giving them no means by which to express their desires. In *Fire with Fire,* Naomi Wolf echoes this point, writing:

> Victim-feminist anxiety over robust female heterosexuality has led to situa-tions in which there is an elaborate vocabulary with which to describe sexual harm done by men, but almost no vocabulary in which a woman can celebrate

sex with men. Indeed, there is almost no feminist culture in which I can recognize my own sexual life.[98]

Without a vocabulary for her heterosexual desires, feminism seems to have little to offer Wolf. It can give her nothing in which she can recognize her own sexual life; rather, it only gives her a distorted image of that life in its "victim-feminist anxiety." Wolf suggests that feminists have dropped the ball when it comes to addressing her needs. This point is echoed by Merri Lisa Johnson in her reflections on the power of Andrea Dworkin's rhetoric. "Sex-positive writers," she argues, "have established no corresponding framework for understanding what we—as women, as feminists—*like* about sex."[99] Johnson, like Wolf, wants something from feminism, but feminism doesn't appear able to give it.[100]

When they turn to feminism to find a vision of what Wolf terms "radical heterosexuality," third-wave feminists find nothing but silence, a silence that is deafening in what it says about feminism's inability to theorize heterosexuality.[101] In their critique, third-wavers suggest that heterosexuality has come to be the new love that dare not speak its name. Ellen Willis provided an early alarm about this silence in her 1982 essay, "Toward a Feminist Sexual Revolution," in which she writes: "Many feminists who are aware that their sexual feelings contradict the neo-Victorian ideal have lapsed into confused and apologetic silence. No doubt there are also thousands of women who have quietly concluded that if this ideal is feminism, then feminism has nothing to do with them."[102] Many of the young feminists who have followed Willis's generation, let alone members of Willis's own generation, feel angry and betrayed by a feminism that has kept so quiet on the pleasures (although not the dangers) of heterosexuality. Third-wavers have demanded that feminism change. As British next-wave feminist Natasha Walter writes: "Unless feminists acknowledge the confidence and pride women have often felt within heterosexual culture they run the risk of placing women as victims even when they are not, and so reducing women's potential power."[103] Or as Sarah Smith, a contributor to *Jane Sexes It Up* puts it in her essay extolling the joys of dildos: "Women who are not sexually disenfranchised by fucking put a different face on the women's liberation movement, with an outrageousness, pleasure, and effrontery I find far more appealing, one I feel better about advocating to would-be feminists."[104] Smith argues for a feminism rooted in sexual pleasure, even when that pleasure includes sexual practices, such as intercourse, which some feminists have argued are inherently oppressive to women. In calling for a feminism led by women who are not "disenfranchised by fucking," Smith, like many of her generational cohorts, deliberately positions her feminism against the anti-intercourse MacKinnon-Dworkin second wave. The third wave wants to expand the sexual possibilities available to women and sees sexual pleasure as central to women's power outside of the bedroom. In their championing of a positive and empowered vision of female heterosexuality, many third-wavers seek to end the perceived silence on the subject, opening up the discussion of sexuality begun by the second wave in the late 1960s.

Unfortunately, the claims of a "new" feminism rooted in (hetero)sexual pleasure has led some third-wavers to depict straight women as outcasts within feminism. Rene Denfeld often makes this claim, as does the Milwaukee-based group Feminists for Fornication. In the group's 1996 "Mission Statement" they write:

> Feminists for Fornication is a community-based not-for-profit group of women who like sex, especially with men. We are tired of being called sluts and anti-feminists. Our concern is that the anti-pornography feminist movement is prescribing sexual norms that will label women who enjoy sexually explicit material as deviant.[105]

Feminists for Fornication provides an interesting twist on the usual correlation between homosexuality and deviancy. The new deviant, they suggest, is the straight woman.[106] It is her sexuality that is outlawed within feminism. Straight women, then, become feminism's ultimate outlaws, its bad girls, a role that some third-wavers, such as Johnson, are all too eager to embrace as they launch their critiques of the second wave.

Feminists for Fornication is but one example of how younger feminists have tried to assert their own form of sexual feminism in the face of a "feminist governor" who restricts their right to pleasure. Reacting against what they find missing in second-wave feminism, many younger feminists are trying to create a feminism which can give them what they want: a sexual culture that includes joy, pleasure, and freedom, no matter what the sexual orientation of one's partner. Such a feminism must include an attention to the real sexual dangers still confronted by women without assuming that those dangers encompass the sum of what sexuality can mean in each of our lives.[107] Rather than flattening out the debates within feminism into caricatures of bad and good, pro and anti, third wave and second wave, third-wave feminists should form alliances across the generations with like-minded feminists, no matter what their age. As a third-wave contributor to *Colonize This!* writes: "I reveled in a feminism that included the rage of Catherine MacKinnon as well as the joy of Susie Bright."[108] Or, to give this sentiment a second-wave spin, in the words of Joan Nestle, "It's not women's shelters or writing about fucking. We need to have both."[109] At its best, this is a vision of feminism that women of all generations can embrace.

4.

Neither My Mother nor My Lover

GENERATIONAL RELATIONS IN QUEER FEMINISM

One of the defining issues of the generational struggle between feminism's second and third waves is sex. According to some third-wave feminists, the second wave represents a movement and a theory stripped of sexuality whose only power comes from stridently saying no. Second-wave feminists are accused of puritanism and of imposing their sexual morality on other feminists and society at large. Arguing that there is "almost no feminist culture in which [heterosexual women] can recognize" their sexual lives, some straight third-wavers complain that feminism has never given them a way to express the pleasures of sexuality.[1] The second-wave feminism that they ubiquitously critique—and thus ironically confirm as all-powerful—is anti-sex.

One might assume that lesbians of the next generation would avoid pitting themselves against the past because of the volume of second-wave writing celebrating lesbianism—that sexual bonds, as opposed to familial or political ones, might offer an alternative model for understanding generational relationships.[2] It comes as some surprise, then, to discover that young lesbians have also employed a generational model to separate themselves from the second wave. Like "third wave," the term "queer" has been used to mark a new formulation of politics and identity, one that emerged in the late 1980s and early 1990s. While "queer" is not always deployed to mark a generational changing of the guard in the manner intended by the third wave, many self-described queer writers have used the term precisely in order to mark a generational shift that identifies them as distinct from the lesbians and gay men who came of age in the 1970s and 1980s.

In many of the mainstream texts written by straight third-wavers, third-wave "daughters" battle against their second-wave "mothers" over the meaning and value of feminism. The fact that these daughters are—often quite literally—the daughters of feminists is important; the mothers they write about and rebel against are both their real biological mothers and symbols of a figurative mother feminism. Since feminism for them is already so located *within* the family, their rejection of feminism often becomes a family problem as well.

I initially assumed that this family drama might take a different form in lesbian and queer discourse. I was quickly proven wrong when I came across a description of lesbian generational conflict that again relies upon the matrophor, although in this case from the rejected mother's point of view.[3] The self-described "mother" is noted second-wave lesbian-feminist historian Lillian Faderman, and the essay is her afterword to the anthology *Cross Purposes: Lesbians, Feminists, and the Limits of Alliance,* an anthology which, as the title suggests, examines the tensions between lesbians and feminists since the second wave of the women's liberation movement.

Faderman's afterword sums up the arguments that came before it and literally has the last word, in the anthology at least, on how we might think about the relationship between lesbianism and feminism at the end of the twentieth century. It is interesting, though, that Faderman centers her final words not on the alliances between lesbian and straight feminists, as others in the collection do, but on the relationship between lesbian feminists and queer feminists. She begins her essay with the following set of questions:

> Is the lesbian-feminist of the older generation feeling like the mother—who had been "very advanced" in her youth—whose daughter, having just come of age, rudely rejects all mama's ideas as dated and dowdy though she only half understands them? Does the mother feel a sting of injustice in her daughter's lack of desire to listen to what mama had already been about in her shining youth? Does mama, with menopause looming on the horizon, feel betrayed and abandoned and worried sick by the favorite daughter who should now be paying her the tribute of wanting to follow closely in her footsteps instead of running off with strange young men?[4]

At first glance, Faderman's use of "mother" and "daughter" to describe lesbian feminists and queer lesbians respectively doesn't seem that unusual, given the tendency to make all feminist generational conflict familial. Yet the fact that it is not just "older" feminists but "older" *lesbian* feminists who are the "mothers" in this passage warrants a second look. Does the *lesbian* mother-daughter pair described in Faderman's essay offer a different image of the daughter's rebellion than that seen in so much of the current writing by young feminists? Faderman levies the exact same accusations at young lesbians that many other second-wave feminists have charged of the third wave. For this new generation, the feminism of the past is "dated and dowdy," making the feminism of the present cutting edge and exciting: a generational relationship in which old is bad, new is good, and daughters must reject their mothers in order to move forward.

Relying upon the mother-daughter trope to explain all intergenerational relationships between women creates an impasse in understanding the *lesbian* "mother-daughter" pair. Building on feminist psychoanalytic writing on the mother-daughter relationship, the feminist project to develop positive models of this relationship has tended to downplay or ignore the hostility that may be involved in relationships between women.[5] While feminist theorists have argued for the necessity of representing the mother-daughter relationship within our culture and within theory, their emphasis on the pre-Oedipal stage of childhood development, in which the mother has tended to play the primary if not the exclusive role, has lent itself to a vision of mother-daughter relationships in which individual identities are unproblematically (and often quite idealistically) merged.

This pre-Oedipal conceptualization of the mother-daughter pair has informed a variety of feminist theories on lesbianism.[6] Perhaps the most influential second-wave theorist in this regard has been Adrienne Rich, in whose work the parallels between mothers and daughters and lesbian lovers are repeatedly stressed. In her now-classic 1980 essay "Compulsory Heterosexuality and Lesbian Existence," she argues for the key place of the mother-daughter relationship on her "lesbian continuum." "All women," Rich argues, "exist on a lesbian continuum"—"from the infant suckling at her mother's breast, to the grown woman experiencing orgasmic sensations while suckling her own child, perhaps recalling her mother's milk smell in her own."[7] Because these two mother-daughter pairs make up half of Rich's list of continuum possibilities, the suggestion is that the mother-daughter relationship has more than just an incidental connection to lesbianism. This point is also stressed by Rich in *Of Woman Born,* where, in a chapter on mothers and daughters, she approvingly cites the words of lesbian poet Sue Silvermarie:

> In loving another woman I discovered the deep urge to both be a mother to and find a mother in my lover. At first I feared the discovery. . . . Now I treasure and trust the drama between two loving women, in which each can become mother and each become child.[8]

When put together, these texts suggest that we can reinterpret the mother–suckling child pair as lesbian as well as imagine the lesbian couple as mother and child. In other words, both couples appear to be able to slide back and forth between a maternal and a lesbian relationship.

To characterize these two "couples" as both maternal and lesbian, however, is to flatten out the differences between the familial and the sexual—to make them one and the same. Or perhaps it is not so much that the two types of relationships become identical but that sexuality must drop out in the face of the familial. The fact that Rich chose to stress the maternal over the erotic in her discussion of lesbian relationships had its rhetorical purpose at the time when her texts were first published, when the lesbian was still very much the outsider of feminism. Only by understanding this historical context does Rich's choice to rehabilitate the lesbian by associating her with the maternal make sense. Using the mother-daughter relationship to define her lesbian continuum was a powerful strategic move on Rich's part, given the universal experience of childhood and the centrality of motherhood to the feminist project. She defined a "lesbian existence" that was unthreatening and so broadly defined as to be welcoming to all women. Yet the legacy of this intervention into the discourse on lesbianism is troubling. Conceptualizing the lesbian couple as a mother-child redux tends to obliterate some of the very real problems in *adult* relationships between women, and it leaves us with little by which to understand sexual dynamics between women.

All this brings us back to the "daughter" described by Faderman. While the lesbian feminist in Faderman may simply "*feel* like the mother," by the end of this passage Faderman seems to have erased all traces of the metaphoric aspects of this reproduction, naturalizing the lesbian feminist of the 1970s as mother and the 1990s queer dyke as daughter. Her use of the mother-daughter trope to describe the relationship between lesbian feminists and queer feminists, then, not only picks up on the prevalent structure used to describe the second and third waves, it also seems to rely upon Rich's notion that relationships between lesbian women constitute a kind of mother-daughter dyad. Might it be, then, that there are two distinct, albeit connected, mother-daughter pairs operating in Faderman's essay: one based on generational location/age and one based on a shared lesbian identity? It appears that the mother-daughter relationship is mapped onto both the intergenerational pair and the lesbian couple. Neither of these are literally mother-daughter pairs, of course; in both, the maternal relationship is intended to be read as figurative. I am not convinced, however, that reading either relationship as such—whether generational or sexual—will allow us fully to understand debates within contemporary feminism. Sexuality, or more precisely desire between women, must complicate our understanding of generational relationships within feminism.

RUNNING OFF WITH STRANGE YOUNG MEN

"Does mama, with menopause looming on the horizon, feel betrayed and abandoned and worried sick by the favorite daughter who should now be paying her the tribute of wanting to follow closely in her footsteps instead of running off with strange young men?" Faderman's description of the mother-daughter relationship centers around rejection, which she describes as the daughter's rejection of her mother, a mother who now appears to sit anxiously at home waiting for her daughter's return. As the now-familiar story goes, the daughter no longer finds worthwhile what her mother has to offer. The mother has been replaced.

Given the slippage in some lesbian-feminist theory between the maternal and the sexual, not to mention Faderman's choice of words, this description of the mother's rejection takes on a double meaning. Her emphasis on feeling "a sting of injustice in her daughter's lack of desire" and finding herself "betrayed and abandoned," suggests more than just maternal rejection. Here we see sexual rejection, a lover's rejection. Though couched in the language of the family, I would argue that this rejection actually seems to spring from a relationship between women which exists outside the family, a relationship of desire. Is the "daughter's lack of desire" to listen to and respect "mama" the problem? Or is it the "daughter's lack of desire" *for* "mama"?

Faderman's words would suggest that these "strange young men" have taken over the lesbian feminist's rightful place: as respected parent and as potential lover. Although the passage from Faderman is rich with anxieties about aging and the inevitability of being replaced, what is perhaps most striking about the generational struggle she describes is the key role that men seem to play in it. The fact that her "favorite daughter"—the lesbian daughter, the one who is like her—has chosen to run off with men rather than stay by her side suggests that the queer third wave's rejection of its mothers is, in fact, strikingly similar to the rejection made by the straight third wave.

In the writing by both queer "daughters" and straight "daughters," relationships to men are used to distinguish the feminists of the next generation from those of the previous one. In the writing by many straight third-wave authors, this gets channeled into being sexy for men, as in the "bimbo feminism" or "do-me feminism" discussed in chapter 3. In making men as central to feminism as women are, these straight third-wave writers attempt to counteract what they perceive as the "male-bashing" of the past. In contemporary queer feminism, this newfound affinity with men usually revolves around working with gay men in activist groups and adopting what many term a gay model of sexuality.[9] In both these versions of late-twentieth-century feminism, relationships to men are used to separate younger feminists from the (s)mothering feminists of the past and all they represent—their asexuality, their separatism—whether those attributions are caricatures or real.

A review of the writing by young lesbians and queer dykes since the late 1980s would suggest that the desire to "run off with strange young men" is a predominant and recurrent theme in much of this work. This period has seen a proliferation of writing by women about their relationships to gay men: from AIDS activism to the burgeoning field of queer theory to adopting a gay model of sexuality, lesbians are working with and sometimes sleeping with men.[10] For a variety of historical and sociocultural reasons, in the last decade and a half lesbians and gay men have joined forces in a way not seen since the gay liberation movement of the early

1970s. While the homophile organizations of the post–World War II, pre-Stonewall period allowed for some interaction between gay men and lesbians, both the organizations and the bars of this earlier period were fairly segregated by sex.[11] Gay liberation brought lesbian women and gay men together, working politically alongside each other for the first time. As the 1970s went on, however, this earlier segregation reemerged as the political solidarity of gay liberation slowly dissolved and gay men and lesbians again began to do their political work and their socializing separately. This segregation along gender lines was further solidified by the rise of lesbian feminism as the predominant theory for understanding lesbian experience. With its critique of male power and privilege, whether gay or straight, lesbian feminism argued that lesbians' natural allies were straight women, not gay men. The lesbian separatist movement which developed from this theory, along with the concomitant expansion of gay male subcultures centered in urban cities, kept lesbians and gay men even further isolated from one another. It wasn't until the AIDS crisis that this began to change.

In an essay which addresses the effect of the AIDS crisis on relationships between gay men and lesbians, aptly titled "New Alliances, Strange Bedfellows: Lesbians, Gay Men, and AIDS," Ruth Schwartz argues that the experience of joining forces with gay men has had a profound effect on her generation of lesbians. She writes:

> [W]e found that those men had something we wanted for ourselves—a feeling of entitlement, the ability not to hesitate, not to wonder whether you could get what you wanted or whether you deserved it, but just to go for it, whatever it was. There was something in that arrogant energy—which made gay male sexual culture so different from our own—that we craved.[12]

Here we see Faderman's "daughter" from her own point of view. She craves these strange young men and what they have to offer; they have something that she wants, something "mama" and her lesbian feminism cannot give her.

Schwartz states that what is appealing about these young men is the "arrogant energy" of their sexual culture; she writes that "their enthusiastic embrace of the sexual made me experience my own gayness as a proud, *lustful* identity."[13] In emphasizing the word lustful, Schwartz suggests that what she and other lesbians crave is, in fact, *sexual*, yet the desired object is not gay men but a lustful identity of one's own, a sexual lesbian culture. In running off with strange young men, queer women aren't abandoning mama's lesbianism so much as her desexualized lesbian-feminist culture.

Through their relationships to men, queer women have been able to distance themselves from their lesbian-feminist predecessors as well as from feminism itself. From allegiances with gay men to an affinity for male theorists to dalliances with male sex partners, these men seem to offer young queer women something "mama" can't. This has produced a distinct generation gap between the two current generations of lesbian and queer women. For one generation, men were often the opposition, even when those men were themselves gay. For the other, their queer identities, their sense of the gay community, and frequently their sexual practices have been strongly shaped by gay men.[14] Men are more often seen as allies rather than part of the problem to be overcome.[15] This heterosociality suggests a desire to bond within one's age group as well as along political lines, but it can also be seen as a reaction against lesbian-feminist identity politics in which women's natural allies are other women.

Central to this generation gap is the distinction between coming to lesbianism through feminism versus coming to it through something else, such as one's sexual desire.[16] While the Radicalesbians' "The Woman Identified Woman" and Adrienne Rich's "Compulsory Heterosexuality and Lesbian Existence" may have argued that through feminism women could become the natural allies and lovers of women, for the queer generation, this allegiance has lost both its political imperative and its radical sexual possibilities.[17] Today's young lesbian is often a male-identified woman; it just so happens that the men she identifies with are most often also queer. And it is no longer compulsory heterosexuality which feels constricting to her but feminism's compulsory lesbianism which does.

In fact, feminism may play little to no role in the young queer woman's lesbianism. As one writer notes when describing the "new lesbian" of the 1990s: "In 1970, the Radicalesbians declared, 'A lesbian is the rage of all women condensed to the point of explosion.' Today we've lightened up."[18] The suggestion is that the lesbian no longer stands for feminism personified; she can "lighten up" and release that burden from her shoulders. The difference in these two affective tones from the 1970s and 1990s—"rage" and "arrogant energy"—is that one is sexually draining, the other sexually empowering. This might be what is particularly attractive about gay men: theirs is a sexuality about desire, not politics. Because there is no gay male equivalent of lesbian feminism—a theory which describes the sexual as springing from the political—gay male sexual culture appears unfettered by the demands of a political agenda. It doesn't have a feminism to keep it in check.

Turning to gay men, then, appears to offer young queer women a sexual culture, although one that often seems founded on a rejection of feminism. In this Faderman is absolutely correct: these daughters are rejecting mama, but it is her feminism that necessitates this abandonment. As one commentator notes, "Viewing feminism as the repressive mother, many younger lesbians have come to frame their identities on the basis of a shared 'queerness' with gay men."[19] Another adds, "For some lesbians and gay men, feminism seems to have become the wicked stepmother, originator of the hated political correctness against which it's become so important to rebel."[20] In both these statements it is the maternalization of feminism—feminism *as* mother/stepmother—which demands that feminism must ultimately be rejected.

As in much straight third-wave writing, contemporary queer writing is filled with descriptions of the ways in which feminism has become a repressive and intrusive force, dictating how lesbians should dress, act, and have sex. One woman writes: "It is apparent from the rigorous specifications a woman must meet before she dare call herself a lesbian that the freedoms proclaimed in the early days of women's liberation have now become tyrannies of their own."[21] She adds that lesbian feminists "should not deter women from loving women by harassing them for not loving a woman in the official, approved lesbian-feminist community manner. But they do."[22] In a statement to lesbian feminist Janice Raymond, a member of the activist group Transsexual Menace writes: "[Y]ou [have] become an agent of the very oppressions we as queers seek to confound and overturn"[23] Finally, one self-described queer woman notes: "Feminism as it has evolved can no longer accept difference and can only accept an orthodoxy."[24] Taking out the references to queer sexuality, these statements could just as easily have been written by "a dissenter feminist" from the third wave. Viewing feminism as orthodoxy, oppressor, and stern patroller of behavior would appear to be a generational thing, not just a straight thing.

If being queer represents a turning toward men—gay or straight—in developing a new form of female sexuality, we might wonder what is being rejected in the process and what it has to do with mothers. In a 1992 essay about female participation in the queer activist group ACT UP, one lesbian member writes:

> The boys promised us equality in the queer nation. We knew they didn't really mean it, but despite protests, we were basically willing to settle for a smaller piece of the pie. It tasted so good. In those heady days, it was all too easy for us girls to dismiss the older lesbian feminists as flabby ferocious frumps and trot off to join the boys at ACT UP, where the cash was flowing and T.V. cameras were rolling.[25]

Here the older lesbian feminist is rejected as a flabby frump, an image which echoes Faderman's "dated and dowdy." While this may seem in line with a daughter's description of her aging mother, it can also be read as dismissive in another sense. The "flabby frump" is unattractive and undesirable sexually.

In other words, as in straight third-wave writing, young dykes tend to portray the previous generation of feminists as frumpy and unsexy. The word "frumpy," like "dowdy," suggests a look that is not only unsexy but out of fashion. Fashion plays a central role in staging this generational divide, both in terms of literal fashion—that is, style of dress—and in terms of the desire to be "in fashion" in a larger sense. In order to present their generation as new and different, many queer writers depict lesbians of the previous generation as a monolithic group with not only a prescribed sexual practice but a dress code: the "Birkenstock and flannel wearing, radical separatist feminist lesbian culture."[26] For many young women, the past represents both bad fashion, or rejection of fashion altogether, and being outdated in terms of sexual practices and theories. As Arlene Stein notes in her article on the "style wars and the new lesbianism," the "new" lesbian is into fashion while she considers the lesbian feminist to be "anti-style."[27] This point is echoed by a member of the early 1990s activist group Queer Nation: "The problem I have with older lesbians is that they really hate me for the way I express myself through how I dress and behave. . . . They tell me I'm objectifying myself. They need to get over it. Fuck em."[28]

By representing older lesbian feminists as regulating, as well as unstylish and prudish, young dykes can appear free, sexy, and fun.

In a 1990 letter to the now-defunct gay and lesbian journal *Outlook,* one reader wrote:

> The dominance of lesbian-feminism as the paradigmatic experience of lesbian sexuality for the past, say, 25 years, should fool no one into believing that things were always this way, or that they will or should be this way in the future. Lesbians are doing and talking about things we have never done or talked about before. We are moving beyond the realm of Sisterhood into the world of the nasty, the tasty, and the sexy. We are pushing the boundaries of what is acceptable lesbianism. We use the word "fuck" like the boys used to, we wear lipstick, and we lust openly and pridefully. We dance and sweat and tease, and we Have Sex.[29]

The fact that these last two words—"Have Sex"—are capitalized stresses the point that it is *having sex* which most distinguishes 1990s lesbianism from that of the 1970s. As if to say: we have sex; you didn't. We have a lustful sexual culture; you just had a dour political one.

Caricaturing lesbian feminists as asexual and anti-sex, as well as charging them with desexualizing lesbianism altogether, gives these "daughters" of the queer 1990s a mother figure to rebel against, which may be the whole point.[30] Within contemporary third-wave feminism, this is a common depiction of the second wave. Yet within lesbian and queer writing, it is precisely this representation of 1970s lesbianism which makes what might otherwise have been a potential erotic relationship familial. If the previous generation of lesbians can be understood as mothers, the incest taboo will ensure that intergenerational relationships between women remain non-sexual. In this regard, it is worth noting that the gay male model of sexuality adopted by many queer lesbians does not include a celebration of intergenerational sexual relationships, particularly given the important status of these relationships within gay male culture from antiquity to the present. Defining intergenerational relationships as familial bars the possibility of sex; it also ensures that the rejection of the mother is inevitable.

Underneath all these staged family dramas, however, lie deep-rooted associations between feminism, lesbianism, and the maternal, all of which make it difficult to unravel the various intergenerational relationships that are taking place within contemporary feminism. Even more troubling is the persistent use of the maternal to signal puritanism, repression, and asexuality. In order to argue that feminism embodies all these characteristics, we need only describe it as maternal; the rest will follow.

The mother-daughter relationship is too near, too easy, too ripe with associations, too tempting as an effective shorthand for generational relations, so we, as feminists, find ourselves using it again and again. The application of the mother-daughter trope to lesbian generations only reifies this imaginary relationship. This rhetorical sleight of hand should alarm feminists: the maternal once again signifies puritanism and control, and female sexuality is once again eradicated by motherhood.

Within writing by young queer women, the repressive "mother" rebelled against is not just the lesbian of the past; it is crucial that she is the lesbian *feminist*. I would argue that feminism carries the rhetorical weight of distancing these two generations of women from each other, both ideologically and sexually. Because feminism is so bound up with morality and maternalism, a daughter's only choice is to rebel.[31] Given that the mother is already stripped of her sexuality—in fact, she must be asexual, if not explicitly anti-sex, to represent the maternal—the daughter's rebellion will necessarily center on sexuality, as it is here where she can most effectively distance and differentiate herself from her mother. Of course, this is a circular process since it is only by first defining feminism as maternalistic and, more important, asexual that the daughter's rebellion becomes possible.

In the history of the second wave as written by queer lesbians, feminism all too often plays the role of desexualizer. As one author in the 1993 collection *Sisters, Sexperts, Queers* notes: "By the seventies, feminism had sanitized lesbianism. Lesbophobia forced lesbians to cling to feminism in an attempt to retain respectability."[32] Adds Susie Bright: "Status-quo feminism did everything it possibly could to make lesbianism seem like the most sexless intellectual exercise imaginable."[33] Both these points seem to echo one made by Pat Califia in a collection of stories from 1988:

> Feminist erotica that presents a simplistic view of lesbian sex as two women in love in a bed who embody all the good things the patriarchy is trying to destroy isn't very sexy. This stuff reads as if it were written by dutiful daughters who are trying to persuade Mom that lesbian sex isn't dirty, and we really are good girls after all.[34]

This narrative suggests that it is not lesbianism itself that is asexual; it is feminism that has the power to desexualize.

This understanding of the relationship between lesbianism and feminism has its origins in the late 1970s and early 1980s when, as B. Ruby Rich notes, "[t]he lesbian moved from a position of outlaw to one of respectable citizen" within feminism.[35] In the early stages of the women's movement, lesbians were often ostracized and excluded from feminist groups, a point perhaps best represented by the Lavender Menace protest held in 1970.[36] As lesbians increasingly began to coalesce around the banner of feminism rather than gay liberation, their place within the feminist movement became secured. The alignment of feminism with lesbianism eventually rehabilitated the lesbian from sexual outlaw to model feminist.[37] Through its ability to turn lesbianism into a political rather than erotic choice, feminism, as the above comments suggest, made lesbianism "respectable."

Joan Nestle also makes this point; she argues that the lesbian-feminist notion that "every woman is a potential Lesbian" downplayed the erotic and sexual dimensions of lesbianism and thus ultimately served the "rhetorical purpose of carrying the discussion of Lesbian-feminism into more respectable places."[38] She describes asking a group of women:

> how many would feel comfortable using the word *Lesbian* alone without the adjunct *feminism*. I was curious about the power of the hyphenated word when so few women have an understanding of the Lesbian 1950s. Several of the women could not accept the word *Lesbian* alone, and yet it stood for women who did stand alone. I suggest that the term *Lesbian-feminist* is a butch-femme relationship, as it has been judged, not as it was, with *Lesbian* bearing the emotional weight the butch does in modern judgment and *feminist* becoming the emotional equivalent of the stereotyped femme, the image that can stand the light of day.[39]

Nestle's formulation of feminist as the equivalent of the stereotyped femme resonates with Adrienne Rich's attempt to mainstream lesbianism by linking it to the maternal. Femmes and mothers are two female roles that can, as Nestle puts it, "stand the light of day." Both femmes and mothers can remain within the dominant society's concept of what a woman should be; both are potentially non-threatening.

Yet there is something more here than just the non-threatening spin put onto lesbianism via feminism. The recurrence of the term "respectability" to describe what feminism has granted lesbianism is striking.

When Califia argues that feminist erotica is made by "dutiful daughters who are trying to persuade Mom that lesbian sex isn't dirty, and we really are good girls after all," she suggests that the desire to be seen as respectable is part of a family drama: a daughter wanting her mother's approval, a daughter wanting to remain "good" in her mother's eyes. The mother that is imagined here is like the dominant stereotype of feminism: against "dirty" sex, preferring "good girls" to bad. Sharing the same values and, it would seem, the same level of authority, feminism and Mom become one and the same. Both offer respectability, as long as you follow their rules.

If in the past, feminist as adjective to lesbian served to rehabilitate, mainstream, and desexualize the dangerous and sexual aspects of lesbianism, I would argue that today's young lesbian frequently rejects "feminist" in favor of "queer" precisely because of this fact. In its allegiance with gay men, queer identity appears to offer younger lesbians a new form of outlaw status. It is no longer the separatist lesbian feminist who is the renegade but the dyke who protests, parties, and occasionally sleeps with gay men. As the "stable lesbian family unit" has increasingly gained "bourgeois respectability," to quote Jan Clausen, this respectability can only be shrugged off by rejecting a certain kind of lesbianism.[40] "Queer has given lesbianism a new lease on life," to quote one writer.[41] "[Q]ueer allows lesbians to explore their sexuality in a way that lesbian feminism never could."[42]

Eve Sedgwick's point that queer is "a word that can't be sanitized" might shed light on why this term has so often been used to signal the new lesbian relationship to both gay men and "unsanitized" sexual practices.[43] Replacing feminist (the sanitizer) with queer (the unsanitizable) as an adjective for "lesbian" has kept things sexy and links lesbians with those "strange young men" Faderman warns us about. Queer identity, according to Michael Warner, "offers a way of basing politics in the personal *without* acceding to [the] pressure to clean up personal identity."[44] Queer can't be cleaned up; it can't be rehabilitated. Queer makes lesbian sex dirty again.

The distinction between the terms "feminist" and "queer" can also be seen in the ways in which feminism is described as "simple" in contrast to the complicated unruliness of queer.[45] In its simplicity, feminism is represented as outdated, boring, and ultimately too easy. As one twentysomething lesbian notes: "I went through a period where I identified with 'sisterhood is powerful' and all. . . . But as I get older, I think that the whole era was simplistic in a lot of ways. There are a lot of rules. . . . And that's a little too simplistic for me."[46] Other writers note how queer signals chaos, something "ambiguous, frightening," the desire to accept all of life's contradictions without flattening them out, as lesbian feminism has tried to do.[47]

Queer is messy; it can't be sanitized. Its messiness is its power—its inability to be defined.[48] Unlike the specificity implied by "feminist," it would seem that "queer" can thus fulfill the needs of all who want to use it; this is its imagined strength. Because it is undefined, queer identity can become all that feminism isn't: it becomes the panacea for all the so-called ills of feminism because it is about both everything and nothing specific.

This becomes apparent when one looks at the disparate claims made about the term "queer" throughout the 1990s: "[Q]ueer posits a commonality between people which does not disallow their fundamental difference."[49] Queer is mainly about white men.[50] Queer signifies a racial diversity and anti-racist politics not seen in the previous gay, lesbian, and feminist movements.[51] Queer is about transgressive sexual practices and sexual openness.[52] Queer is just another name for gay and lesbian. Queer includes bisexuals, transgendered and transsexual people, SM practitioners, and leather folk, whether straight or gay; queer even has room for the average heterosexual, as long as s/he is willing to challenge society's dominant conceptions of gender and sexuality.[53] Queer excludes bisexuals.[54] Queer is explicitly hostile to gays and lesbians such that "It is our duty as queers to expose the lie of 'gay and lesbian' identity, to humiliate them with otherness. We must puke on their shoes, shit in their faces, and *kick their asses*."[55] Queer signals "a celebration of difference across sexualities, across genders, across sexual preference and across object choice."[56] Queer heralds "a new wave of lesbian and gay studies."[57] Queer is academic.[58] Queer is activist.[59] Queer is just another commodity, a lifestyle being sold to us.[60] And finally, queer is "not about the mainstream, profit-margins, patriotism, patriarchy or being assimilated. It's not about executive director, privilege, and elitism. It's about being on the margins."[61]

Given the many claims made in its name, I think we need to be wary of the ways in which queer is being posited as the solution to problems within feminist, as well as within gay and lesbian, politics and identities. In particular, my concern is with what happens to feminism as queer becomes the hot new theory and identity. This concern involves not only what literally happens to feminism (Are people abandoning feminist politics?), but also how feminism and its history is being represented (Which particular feminism will be made to stand for feminism as a whole?) and for what ends (Does queer identity necessitate the rejection of feminism?). As Katie King reminds us, "Origin stories about the women's movement are interested stories, all of them."[62] The same, of course, is true when it comes to queer's origin stories. A recurring theme in this story is that queer is a return to the gay liberationist ethos of the early 1970s, a move that effectively returns queer to a time before lesbian feminism.[63] This allows queer to be both new—and therefore exciting, trendy, sexy—while giving it roots in such a way that it is also old—and therefore legitimate, continuing in a fine tradition, the inheritor of the past.[64] Queer, then, is able to be both post-feminist and pre-feminist simultaneously. The more troubling question, however, is why it is that feminism must be abandoned in the process. Why must Faderman's "mama" be left sitting home alone?

I am also skeptical of the flattening out of difference that occurs in many narrations of both feminist and lesbian history.[65] For example, one account of shifting lesbian identities divides the generations as follows: "the shadowy figures lurking in the twilight world of the 1950s and 1960s, to the out, proud, politicized lesbians of the 1970s and early 1980s, to the 1990s lesbians who have abandoned radical politics but have found radical chic."[66] Such clear lines between time and people inevitably make it impossible for us to recognize the different types of lesbians and feminists who have existed within each generation. No one "type" can ever represent an entire generation or historical era. Where are we to put Pat Califia or Dorothy Allison, two lesbian writers who challenged lesbian feminism during its heyday and whose work has influenced a generation of queer dykes but, by virtue of their dates of birth, would be considered members of the second wave? Where are we to put lesbians in their twenties who practice lesbian separatism in the late 1990s?[67]

By describing the feminism of the past as monolithic, younger women have been able to situate themselves as oppositional. Therefore, second-wave feminism must ubiquitously be characterized by Catherine MacKinnon and Andrea Dworkin, while lesbian feminism must be seen as the only kind of lesbian culture to be found in the 1970s and early 1980s. Contemporaries of MacKinnon and Dworkin such as Allison, Califia, Joan Nestle, Gayle Rubin, and other feminists writing during this same period become excluded from the category "feminist," not to mention the category "lesbian." Differences among one feminist generation, then, are squashed in order to facilitate an attack against it. As more and more writers reproduce this caricatured version of second-wave feminism, it begins to take on the appearance of truth.[68]

DILDOS AND DESIRE:
LESBIAN SEXUALITY AT THE MILLENNIUM

As I've noted, queer women's interest in "strange young men" extends beyond merely working with them on activist projects; in recent years, young lesbian and bisexual women have publicly embraced what a previous generation may have termed a "male style" of sexuality. Recall, for example, the 1973 statement by Robin Morgan discussed earlier:

> Every woman here knows in her gut the vast differences between her sexuality and that of any patriarchally trained male's—gay or straight. That has, in fact, always been a source of *pride* to the lesbian community, even in its greatest suffering. That the emphasis on genital sexuality, objectification, promiscuity, emotional non-involvement, and of course invulnerability was the *male style*, and that we, as women, placed greater trust in love, sensuality, humor, tenderness, commitment.[69]

This vision of non-patriarchal sexuality is further defined by a 1971 essay entitled "Smash Phallic Imperialism," in which author Sue Katz describes lesbianism as

> an end of sex. . . . Physical contact and feelings have taken a new liberatory form. And we call that sensuality. . . . Physicality is now a creative non-institutionalized experience. It is touching and rubbing and cuddling and fondness. Its only goal is closeness and pleasure. It does not exist for the Big Orgasm.[70]

While the idealized "female style" of sexuality was always just that—an ideal which never represented the range and complexity of actual lesbian sexual practices or desires—this vision of sexuality has helped to construct the stereotypical lesbian feminist that many queer women at the end of the twenty-first century have rebelled against. Against the view that lesbian sexuality is defined by "touching and rubbing and cuddling," many young lesbians have publicly celebrated a number of sexual practices that earlier lesbian feminists would have decried as male-identified and heterosexist. In particular, penetrative sex has been touted as a new lesbian sexual practice, one which serves to distinguish the next generation from its 1970s foremothers.

Within the last 30-plus years of lesbian theorizing, sexual practices have assumed an important role in discussions of lesbian identity and the political dimension, when claimed, of lesbian sexuality. Sexual practices have often been sources of intense debate within lesbian and feminist theory, as witnessed by the sex wars of the late 1970s and early 1980s.[71] Such debates helped to solidify the perception that all forms of lesbian sexuality, by definition, should have an ethical and political component and that penetration, in particular, is politically suspect for its ties to hetero and male sexuality.[72] As Esther Newton and Shirley Walton describe this anti-penetrative tenet in their 1984 essay:

> Sexual interaction should not be genitally focused. More specifically, lesbians should not engage in any form of "hetero" sex. This includes both penetrations, either by fingers or dildoes, and tribadism (rubbing the cunt against the partner's body) which can resemble the heterosexual missionary position.[73]

During the 1970s and 1980s, Newton and Walton—among many, many others—criticized this regulatory ideal and addressed the real-life effects of an officially sanctioned feminist sexuality. Like their straight third-wave counterparts, however, many young queer writers appear to disregard—whether out of ignorance or willful neglect—pro-sex, anti-moralistic versions of second-wave feminism. Rather, they prefer to engage solely with a one-dimensional—and often caricatured—representation of second-wave sexual practice and theory. Doing so has allowed younger writers to assert their sexual practices as new and daring while simultaneously bolstering their claim about the dogma imposed by lesbian feminism. Sarah Smith, for example, a contributor to the 2002 anthology *Jane Sexes It Up*, writes:

> I wanted so badly to be a "real" lesbian that I resigned myself to throwing my pearly vibrator and favorite pink jelly dildo in the trash, my eye cast toward the emerald city of lesbian utopia. Step one in feminist-approved lesbian sex is ridding one's self of the sexual repertoire of the dick (in flesh or form).[74]

Although Smith spends time rehearsing the 1980s debates about penetration in order to gloss the sex wars, like many of her contemporaries, the war she describes appears to have had only one army: the anti-intercourse battalion of Andrea Dworkin, Sheila Jeffreys, and the like. It thus appears that the purpose of giving the reader this history is not to show the range of perspectives within feminist, or lesbian-feminist, theory over the last thirty years; rather, the argument being forwarded is that when sex is "feminist approved" it is inevitably regulating and oppressive, not to mention anti-pleasure.

In this new queer writing, a generational debate about penetrative sex is staged in which one generation is described as absolutely against it, the other completely for it. Sexual practices, like much else about contemporary lesbian and bisexual life, are described in generational terms: that is, one's generational location and age seem to dictate the kind of sex one desires and has.[75] Exemplifying this trend is the treatment of the dildo, which is routinely cited as *the* marker of a shift in lesbian sexual practice. Emma Healey, author of *Lesbian Sex Wars*, describes what she terms the "new 1990s dildocracy":[76]

> If in the 1980s the typical dyke about town owned a cat and a bicycle, her 1990s sister seems much more likely to possess a dog and a dildo. The dildo, reviled by lesbian feminism as a tool of the patriarchy, has now become a potent symbol of lesbian sexuality. It has also become a totem for the new queer sexuality, a sexuality which, at its best, both challenges and subverts.[77]

The fact that a phallic object has become a symbol for lesbian sexuality says much about the shifting definitions and mores of lesbian sexuality that have occurred since the beginning of the second wave. If the dildo was repudiated as a tool of the patriarchy, it was typically because penetration itself was seen as patriarchal. As the non-sexual bicycle is replaced by the hedonistic dildo, the anti-patriarchal politics of lesbian feminism are replaced by a sexuality that values pleasure over politics. Celebrating the dildo as "a potent symbol of lesbian sexuality" suggests a new relationship to the patriarchy as well as to penetration.[78]

Not only has the dildo been heralded as the must-have lesbian accessory, but the 1990s also saw an increasing focus on the G-spot. *On Our Backs* founder Debi Sundahl, writing under the name Fanny Fatale, championed the G-spot and even produced a popular video on the subject, *How to Female Ejaculate*.[79] While feminists and lesbians of the early 1970s celebrated the clitoris and decried "the myth of the vaginal orgasm," by the early 1990s, vaginal penetration was decidedly in vogue.[80] In the lesbian press, sex manuals, and sex-toy catalogs, the G-spot was quickly replacing the clitoris as the locus of lesbian pleasure.[81] A new lesbian sexual practice was officially proclaimed.[82]

These shifting attitudes toward penetrative sex and the public acknowledgment of dildos as an essential part of lesbian sexual practice also signal a new attitude toward penises. As one 20-something queer woman, Alison, notes when discussing her "post-lesbian" take on the male organ:

> I think the problem with a lot of lesbians is that because they haven't ever really slept with men they take the penis far too seriously, they confuse it with the phallus. In my experience penises are not the big, permanently rock-hard thrusting manifestations of male potency that your boyfriend would have you believe, but instead are rather unreliable little creatures that usually don't last long enough! . . . I think lesbians have overemphasized masculine power and take men on the level of myth, not reality. . . . The good thing about defining yourself as a *post-lesbian* is that you can go out and explode the myth. You can fuck a few guys and realize that there's a lot of fuss about nothing. Dicks can be nice and everything, but they're definitely not the phallus. Once lesbians realize that, they can go out and really get hold of the phallus. Get some real power.[83]

Perhaps Alison's post-lesbianism is similar to what other young feminists describe as "post-feminism," for it is not lesbianism as a whole that is being rejected, just a particular version of lesbianism: anti-phallic lesbian feminism.[84] If Judith Butler is correct that the "phallus is that which is excommunicated from the feminist orthodoxy on lesbian sexuality," it would seem that the phallus can be recuperated by lesbians as long as they distance themselves from this orthodoxy.[85] That is, it is feminism which is against the phallus, not lesbianism per se. Lesbians can embrace the phallus, the penis, and men once "lesbian" and "feminist" are disjoined.

Alison's comments speak to the mythology surrounding both the penis and the phallus in a certain kind of feminist—particularly lesbian-feminist—theorizing on sexuality. This mythology is also discussed by Pat Califia in her book *Public Sex*. Writing about her experiences with dildos, penises, and having sex with gay men, she notes:

> As for penis envy, I often think it would be nice to have a cock. . . . But I'm better with a strap-on dildo than most straight boys are at using their

own cocks, and besides, I can change sizes. . . . I'd like to see more women become more phallic (i.e., more powerful). Cocks seem more fragile than thermonuclear to me. There's a vulnerability about getting an erection that I'm really grateful I don't have to experience before I can give someone a night to remember.[86]

Alison's "Dicks can be nice and everything, but they're definitely not the phallus" and Califia's "Cocks seem more fragile than thermonuclear to me" both indicate that the male organ leaves something to be desired. Moreover, their comments would suggest that the lesbian feminist fear of and/or disdain for the penis is misguided. Today's lesbian can be more phallic than any man. She can use a dildo that never loses its erection, she can change her size at will, and her sexual potency isn't tied to a biological organ that runs the risk of being vulnerable.[87] It would seem that once separated from feminist hang-ups about the male body, lesbians are actually in the unique position of being able to get "some real power" by really getting hold of the phallus, the dildo being far superior to the mere penis that men possess.[88]

As the taboo on penetration dissolved in the 1990s, lesbians also started writing about having sex with men. As one lesbian recounts, "maybe penises weren't so bad after all."[89] The last decade has seen a number of high-profile lesbians publicly proclaim their desire for men.[90] For example, Susie Bright, a former editor at *On Our Backs* and a well-known sex guru and author, has been very public about her relationships with men. Lesbian sex therapist and author JoAnn Loulan has appeared on *Oprah* and *20/20* discussing her new identity as a "lesbian who is in a relationship with a man." And *On Our Backs* founder Debi Sundahl describes becoming a "traitor to the lesbian nation" through her sexual and romantic involvements with men.[91] Sundahl describes herself as a "traitor" both because she enjoys penetration and because she desires to be with a man.[92] The word "traitor" denotes the regulatory aspects of the lesbian-feminist community, implying that anyone who steps outside its bounds becomes an enemy. In a 1994 article, Sundahl, who came out in the 1970s and once defined herself as a lesbian feminist, recounts her work as a stripper and as the editor of a lesbian sex magazine, asserting that these professions taught her to be "a man's sexual equal" so that she could imagine having a relationship with a man again. In a decidedly queer description of her sexuality, she writes, "Though I had learned to eroticize the masculine with Nan" (Sundahl's longtime butch girlfriend), with John (her boyfriend), "I now learned what it was like to kiss a lesbian, among other things."[93] In other words, her relationship with a woman led her to desire masculinity which led her to a relationship with a man which led her back to what she terms lesbianism, with a queer twist.

While I do not mean to imply that these recent highly publicized transformations are merely due to trends within lesbian subcultures, I am interested in what is making such sexualities possible at this particular moment in lesbian history, both on the individual level and in terms of their public expression. One answer can be found in Jan Clausen's notable essay from 1990, "My Interesting Condition." Clausen, a poet and novelist, had lived as a lesbian feminist for twenty years before beginning a relationship with a man. In her essay, she discusses how her relationship with her male lover has affected both her sense of self and her place within her lesbian-feminist community.

> My new relationship affords an exhilarating sensation of risk-taking only partially attributable to the fact that it involves physical acts which lesbian-feminism has placed beyond the bounds of its revisionist norm of healthy womanhood. At this moment in the dialectic, heterosex ironically represents for me the anarchic power of the erotic, in contrast to the bourgeois respectability of a stable lesbian family unit.[94]

Clausen's comments would suggest that by the late 1980s and early 1990s, the sexual excitement and risk that had formerly been associated with lesbianism had shifted its location to heterosexuality. The "lesbian family unit" had so normalized and domesticated lesbianism that, in another queer twist, heterosexuality became a new form of the love that dare not speak its name.[95] This point is also echoed by a lesbian contributor to *Sex and Single Girls*, who describes her experience sleeping with a man: "I was very curious and was aroused by the idea of sex with him, because it felt so 'naughty'—which was refreshing for a jaded ole dyke like me. Going all the way back to straight boys almost seemed like the final frontier."[96] Heterosex becomes transgressive sex when lesbian sex becomes routine.[97]

While penetration need not involve one of Faderman's strange young men, it is interesting that penetrative sex—whether with dildos, with men, or by other means—has been used to mark a generational shift between lesbians. Within radical feminist and lesbian-feminist theory there is a long tradition of viewing penetration as a male sexual practice. Given the role this theory has had in shaping lesbian identity, I think it is important to read the celebration of penetration as yet another way in which young lesbians are challenging their predecessors' feminism and calling attention to the ways in which they are not like "mama."

In her book *Public Sex,* self-proclaimed radical sex activist Pat Califia explores the ways in which shifting sexual mores and practices within gay, lesbian, and queer communities have continually redefined what is seen as radical sex and what is seen as normal sex, adding that she "love[s] it when a new perversion appears."[98] Califia, like Clausen, points to the fact that one's sexual identity and sexual practices are not fixed but rather continue to change during the course of one's lifetime, often because of the sexual and political communities one inhabits. This is exemplified by her comment that "[v]anilla lesbian sex can seem pretty risqué to us hardened perverts."[99] A slang term for "non-kinky" sex, "vanilla" is often used pejoratively to mean bland, boring, even respectable sex. Within a lesbian-feminist context, vanilla has also meant politically correct sex: without penetration, without power games. Here Califia suggests that what is most outside one's normal sexual practice—in her case, vanilla sex—can, by virtue of its exclusion, become that which appears most tantalizing, most transgressive.

In thinking about the relationship between politics and sexuality, I find it extremely helpful to use Califia's description of perversion to think through the ways in which feminism continues to influence individual sexual practices. On the one hand, feminism has provided a set of sexual guidelines (however changing) that many feminists have put into discourse and practice. This might be called the feminist thesis: that is, that penetrative sex is harmful to women or that lesbian sex is the most feminist form of sex, and so forth. Inevitably, however, this thesis will be followed by its antithesis, a reaction to the first, a response inherently built into it. This may be one model of how perversions are created, how transgressive or taboo sex gains its status. In an example of precisely this process, Califia writes, "I love being fucked on my back," then wonders in a parenthetical remark, "will a penchant for the missionary position become a secret feminist perversion?"[100] Here, what might usually be considered the least radical form of sex—the missionary position—becomes a "perversion" precisely because it is otherwise unpracticed in the feminist and S/M worlds Califia inhabits.

The new queer lesbianism, with its embrace of male sexual culture, celebrates what had previously been demarcated as out of bounds, as forbidden, as politically incorrect. It may be that from Faderman's lesbian-feminist perspective, this sexuality is, in fact, truly queer. That is, queer as unexpected, odd, and deviating from the norm. Following Califia, I would suggest that within the history of lesbian identity, perhaps it is inevitable that lesbian feminism would be followed by queerness followed by something altogether different yet again.

QUEERING LESBIANISM, ABANDONING FEMINISM

While the influential 1994 anthology *The Lesbian Postmodern* is not titled *The Lesbian Queer,* throughout much of the queer and lesbian-feminist writing of the 1990s, "queer" and "postmodern" are in fact used synonymously to mark an ideological and often generational shift.[101] Both queerness and postmodernism have a particular relationship to lesbian feminism, which accounts for the predominance of what one critic called the narrative in which "lesbian-feminism becomes lesbian postmodernism simply by deep-sixing feminism."[102] Queerness and postmodernism serve to mark a break with past understandings of gay and lesbian studies, identities, and, frequently, sexual practices. They are also used to signal a new relationship between lesbianism and feminism.

In a 1997 book which uses postmodernism in just this way, *Po-MoSexuals: Challenging Assumptions about Gender and Sexuality,* editors Carol Queen and Lawrence Schimel argue that postmodernity and queerness go hand in hand in making possible a new way of theorizing and living sexuality and gender. Central to their book's thesis is the notion that we have seen the demise of an essential gay male or lesbian subject whose gender identity and sexuality can easily be traced back to either biological sex or politics. "Pomosexuals," according to the editors, are often bisexual, transgendered, or otherwise situated outside the bounds of the gay and lesbian community because of their sexual practices and/or gender identities. This new queer subject neither desires her proper object choice nor does she only have sex in a politically correct feminist fashion. Queen and Schimel write:

> If queer women have shown increasing regard for gay men, it's hardly surprising that some have wanted to adopt the very sexual possibilities queer men represent to them. So it has been that in one of the strange twists of postmodern sexual culture, just as scores of gay men have "gone lesbian" and retreated to the emotional and hopefully physical safety of monogamous partnerings, scores of queer women have "gone fag," constructing male personas, daddy/boy (or daddy/girl) relationships, and women's sex clubs on the ashes of the bathhouse era. For women raised to be good girls it's a walk on the wild side; for girls who grew up under feminism, it's a way of taking postmodern queer theory to the streets.[103]

This passage reveals the shifts in gay and lesbian life since the 1970s, the changing meaning of what "gay" and "lesbian" signify, and the relationship of feminism to this current moment. Yet it is unclear how Queen and Schimel are using the term "postmodern." In their latter use of the term—"postmodern queer theory"—"postmodern" and "queer" would seem to be synonymous: both are types of theory that challenge the unified subject presumed to know her desire. However, in their first use of the term, "postmodern sexual culture" would seem to mean queer life since AIDS; that is, postmodern would mean post-AIDS. While AIDS is not mentioned directly here, it haunts this passage in the desire to see gay men "physically safe" and in its allusion to the "ashes of the bathhouse era." The AIDS epidemic has not only forced gay men and lesbians to work together politically; if this passage is any indication, it has also caused a seeming reversal in sexual practices: gay men "going lesbian" and queer women "going fag."

Behind this construction, however, lies an account of gay, lesbian, and feminist history that warrants a second look. Though not stated explicitly, this passage relies on a particular narrative of the last thirty years that goes something like this: the post-Stonewall, pre-AIDS gay liberation period of the 1970s and early 1980s gave men an opportunity to explore their sexualities publicly and unabashedly. During this same period, however, lesbians were more concerned with fleshing out their politics and ethics than in exploring all the dimensions of lesbian sexuality. In this common narrative of the 1980s, the emergence of AIDS signals the end of gay male promiscuity and the beginning of a new sexy lesbian subculture. This is why the unmentioned but central AIDS epidemic signals a shift to a postmodern sexual culture, in which "scores of gay men have 'gone lesbian' and retreated to the emotional and hopefully physical safety of monogamous partnerings," and "scores of queer women have 'gone fag', constructing male personas, daddy/boy (or daddy/girl) relationships, and women's sex clubs."

What is troubling about Queen and Schimel's account is that their postmodern queer theory seems to leave unchallenged the assumptions behind the phrases "going lesbian" and "going fag." It appears that "running off with strange young men" won't exactly deconstruct traditional gender roles; queer women can "adopt the very sexual possibilities queer men represent to them," but these possibilities remain on loan. That is, queer women may "go fag," but what fag represents continues to be the province of gay men: sexuality that involves power and difference, role-playing, sex clubs, and non-monogamy. To "go fag" is to be public, to be dangerous, and, most important, to be sexual. "Lesbian" would seem to signal the exact opposite: retreat, safety, coupledom, monogamy. To "go lesbian" is to be private, to be safe, and most important, to be emotional. With its public/private split and its traditionally gendered understanding of sex and emotions, this hardly seems like a brave new world.

It would seem that even within this new pomosexuality, men continue to represent the possibility of sexual agency—a way for women to escape the emotional safety and boredom of lesbianism. What, then, does feminism represent? To repeat Queen and Schimel, "For women raised to be good girls," this new sexual culture is "a walk on the wild side; for girls who grew up under feminism, it's a way of taking postmodern queer theory to the streets." Originally, my understanding of this sentence was that the two groups of women mentioned were one and the same. That is, girls who grew up under feminism are, in fact, those who were raised to be good girls. This is a reading which seems fitting given the way feminism is posited in much queer writing as an arbiter of rules, a stifler of sexuality and freedom. Describing women as growing up "under feminism" certainly adds to this impression, with its allusion to living under some sort of tyrannical state. Queer, then, would mean a rebellion against or escape from feminism.

However, there is another way of reading this sentence, namely, that "women raised to be good girls" are lesbians from the second wave, while "girls who grew up under feminism" are Generation X lesbians, the generation often referred to as the third wave of feminism. Reading Queen and Schimel this way would suggest that queerness has something to offer *both* generations of women, that neither group need remain stuck in the past. Such a reading provides a helpful departure from the usual divisions cut solely along generational lines, and it could suggest that queer identity, like other political/sexual movements, needn't be the province of a particular age group. Read this way, Queen and Schimel provide a useful intervention in thinking about queer identity's relationship to lesbian feminism, as well as other branches of feminist theory.

Within academic scholarship, lesbianism and postmodernism are also joining forces. As in the sexual culture described in *Pomosexuals,* academic young dykes are running off with strange young men, participating in what Robyn Wiegman calls the "ironic wedding of seemingly subversive sexuality [lesbianism] to the body of postmodern theory." In *The Lesbian Postmodern,* a book explicitly concerned with this new union, Wiegman argues that "through this incipient terminological marriage, some of the founding assumptions of contemporary feminist theory can be challenged and, at least potentially, displaced."[104] Continuing with Wiegman's matrimonial metaphor, it appears that the "breakup" between feminism and lesbianism is also occurring in academia. Now married to postmodernism, even if ironically, lesbianism has ended its relationship to feminism. Like an abandoned wife after a divorce, feminism becomes "displaced."[105] Fittingly, this "heterosexual" marriage of feminism and postmodernism appears new precisely because it offers an alternative to the now-old-fashioned—but never lawful—same-sex union of lesbianism and feminism, an image that resonates with Califia's comment that the missionary position has become feminism's most risqué sexual practice.

Given the breakup described above, it may be useful to explore the relationship between feminism and queer theory. Overviews of the history and development of queer theory usually point to the role that feminism and feminist theory have played in its evolution. This role is usually limited, however, to the ways in which feminists pointed to what Gayle Rubin terms "the limits of feminism"; namely, that a theory of gender is not sufficient to theorize sexuality.[106] In the introduction to *Fear of a Queer Planet,* one of the first texts of queer theory, editor

Michael Warner puts it this way: "[F]eminism has made gender a primary category of the social in a way that makes queer social theory newly imaginable."[107] In this common construction of the relationship between queer theory and feminism, feminism did something—usually in the past—that allows for queer theory's emergence in the present. This construction is often supplemented by the role of the 1970s gay liberationist movement. Queer theory is posited as a return to gay liberationism with the addition of what feminism made possible in the interim. As Linda Garber notes, "With few exceptions, queer theorists have obscured [the] genealogy" of lesbian feminism's role in queer theory.[108] Feminism, then, serves as a kind of midwife to queer, helping to bring forth the nascent queer theory that gay liberationism only began.[109] To push the familial lineage to its extreme, gay lib may be the father of queer theory, while feminism is its mother.

In the last few years, several books have attempted to describe the relationship between feminism and queer theory in generational terms: what gave birth to what, what is new and what is old, and what was in fashion but has since become outdated (along with its practitioners). However, the kinship relationship between feminism and queer theory is often staged in very antagonistic terms. Take for example the 1997 *Feminism Meets Queer Theory*. In her introduction, Elizabeth Weed writes:

> When feminism meets queer theory, no introductions seem necessary. . . . Queer theory, like lesbian and gay studies, has acknowledged its intellectual debts to feminist theory and women's studies, just as feminist theory has recognized the influence of queer theory. For many in the academy, feminism and queer theory are most easily understood as two branches of the same family tree of knowledge and politics.[110]

Weed's phrase "two branches of the same family tree" makes queer theory and feminism kin, yet she also reveals that these branches do not carry equal weight. To say that queer theory owes its intellectual debts to feminism is, in effect, to assert that queer theory follows feminism; it comes after feminism in time. Thus, it has to pay its dues to its elder. And Weed's "just as feminist theory has recognized" would treat the branches as parallel, when in fact they aren't. The intellectual debts owed to feminism are described as equivalent to the influence of queer theory, yet queer theory depends upon feminism in a way that feminism does not depend on it in turn. Something about this description seems resonant with the mother-child relationship.

In the 1997 anthology *Cross Purposes: Lesbians, Feminists, and the Limits of Alliance*, the "natural" relationship between queer theory and feminism—and correspondingly, the "natural" relationship between lesbianism and feminism, lesbians and feminists—is under dispute. In her introduction to this volume, editor Dana Heller argues, "I also suspect that feminism was queer studies before queer studies was queer studies, although feminism still remains to be productively expanded by lesbian, gay, and queer studies."[111] In Heller's description, we see the relationship between feminism and queer theory pushed to its farthest conclusions. Not only is queer theory a by-product of feminism, as in Warner's description, not only does it owe its intellectual debts to feminism, as in Weed's account, but in fact "feminism was queer studies before queer studies was queer studies." Feminism, then, becomes not just the originator of what Heller terms "queer studies," it becomes queer studies itself.

Clearly queer theory is doing more than just following in feminism's footsteps or copying it outright. As with Weed's understanding that feminism must recognize the influence of queer theory, Heller argues that feminism can be "productively expanded" by queer studies. Feminism may have been queer studies in the past, but it could nonetheless stand to learn a few things from it in the present. The feminism described here seems dated. It may once have been on the cutting edge, but it has fallen behind.

The representation of feminism within queer theory is discussed by Biddy Martin in her essay "Extraordinary Homosexuals and the Fear of Being Ordinary," where she suggests that "we stop defining queerness as mobile and fluid in relation to what then gets construed as stagnant and ensnaring, and associated with a maternal, anachronistic, and putatively puritanical feminism." She adds that this formulation reproduces

> stereotypes of femininity and emotional bonds between women as quasi-natural, undifferentiated enmeshments that can only be shorn by way of identifications with (homosexual) men or with sexuality. Given the culture in which we live, it is no surprise that queer theorists, too, would repeat the age-old gesture of figuring lesbian desire in phallic terms in order to distinguish it from what then appears to be the fixed ground or maternal swamp of women-identification.[112]

Martin's "maternal swamp of women-identification" is obviously linked to feminism, particularly the feminism described in much of the writing by young lesbians that I have discussed here. In positing queer as the fluid antithesis of the static maternal swamp of feminism, these queer writers seem to be grounding their position in a repudiation of both feminism and the maternal, which in this case become equated as one.

The maternal swamp seems linked to an image of motherhood as oppressive, entrapping, a mother's womb without an escape. Feminism may be the mother which gives birth to queer theory, but this reproduction must be denied lest queer theory get bogged down in the sticky mess of the feminine, not to mention the sticky mess of feminism. Like their straight third-wave contemporaries, many queer writers would prefer to be orphans. In order to be truly new, they must have no roots, no origins. "Implicit in these constructions of queerness," Martin writes, "I fear, is the lure of an existence without limit, without bodies or psyches, and certainly without mothers."[113]

Feminism's inescapable link to women makes it maternal, yet it is also this association with mothers which creates a desire to escape it, echoing Adrienne Rich's concept of "matrophobia." The femaleness of feminism ensures that feminism must be rejected in order for a new theory to be born. It is this inability of queer theory to recognize feminism's generative possibilities that makes lesbian feminists writing in the 1990s feel abandoned and bitter. As Lillian Faderman writes in her afterword to *Cross Purposes:*

> At the least, lesbian-feminists would like some acknowledgment of the ways in which they have contributed to queer thought, perhaps even some admission that so many of the ideas of the mothers were as seminal to contemporary queer thought as the work of the poststructuralist fathers, who are invariably cited in queer scholarship, to the all-but-total neglect of the mothers.[114]

One reads here a mother's desire to be recognized, to be valued for her contribution. This recognition, however, would seem to demand identification with the mother, something that seems dangerous, a return to the maternal swamp. The queer child doesn't want to identify with her mother but prefers the excitement, the autonomy of her father. These "poststructuralist fathers" offer something new and thrilling; meanwhile, feminism remains linked to women and the maternal, and thus the risk of identification is too great.

It is unfortunate that in response to their perceived abandonment, some lesbian feminists have tried to argue that queer is too theoretical and thus is politically suspect. In a review of two books of queer theory, for example, a writer in the journal *Signs* says that such theory is "a politics formulated from a point beyond the body by people who are not hungry or cold, people who can theorize in comfort, peering at the world through computer screens, reconfiguring its surfaces endlessly, like a floppy disk."[115] Such arguments only serve to prop up the paradigm in which theory is the domain of the privileged, and thus is, by definition, anti-feminist, while feminism is always about "the real world," the body, the nitty-gritty. Thus, while many queer lesbians seem to be celebrating queer identity for precisely its sophisticated theoretical possibilities, for those against queer theory, these possibilities are ridiculed as politically naive for failing to take into account people's material needs.[116]

Along with the feelings of abandonment expressed by Faderman, one can't help but notice the real sense of danger that preoccupies much lesbian-feminist writing in the 1990s.[117] Queer identification is clearly seen as a threat, something which has the potential to destroy lesbians as well as lesbian feminism. This viewpoint is frequently expressed by Australian feminist Sheila Jeffreys, who argues that "[t]he appearance of queer theory and queer studies threatens to mean the disappearance of lesbians."[118] Writers such as Jeffreys suggest that it is not just lesbian feminism which is at risk, or any other form of lesbian specific theorizing; it is lesbians themselves who are threatened with annihilation.[119]

Jeffreys concludes her essay "The Queer Disappearance of Lesbians," by arguing that queer affiliations enable women to assimilate into and gain prestige in the academy. In other words, it is now queer identity which grants respectability. If queer identity now represents the mainstream within contemporary academia, lesbian feminists, according to Jeffreys, "are the bad girls who fail to love the male frame of mind that currently dominates lesbian and gay studies."[120] We appear to have come full circle. If queerness has become respectable, lesbian feminists can once again become "bad girls"—the outlaws of contemporary theory because they are the most excluded. Jeffreys suggests that theoretical positions, like the sexual practices and identities discussed earlier, go through cycles. Moving in and out of fashion, theories gain their allure because of their outsiderness, only to lose that appeal when they move too firmly toward the center. What was most "good girl" about lesbian feminism now makes it a theory for "bad girls." What was kinky becomes routine, making vanilla the new perversion.

The young women Faderman describes as running off with strange young men may feel compelled to do so because the feminism they would otherwise identify with seems stifling and entrapping. When Biddy Martin notes that this construction of feminism relies on "stereotypes of femininity and emotional bonds between women as quasi-natural, undifferentiated enmeshments that can only be shorn by way of identifications with (homosexual) men or with sexuality," she points to perhaps the most troubling dimension of the current generational struggle within feminism: namely, the role that men play in providing a sense of autonomy. What initially appear to be two sources of escape from the feminine/feminist swamp—"identifications with men or with sexuality"—turn out to be one and the same. Throughout most of the writing I've discussed here, it is men who represent sexuality, excitement, autonomy, and freedom, suggesting that choosing to identify with men is also a way of claiming a sexuality of one's own.

The association between men and sexuality is, of course, partly a product of the way in which feminism has increasingly been caricaturized as asexual and anti-sex. Given this representation of feminism, it is no surprise that men and male theorists come to be seen as providing a sexual alternative. This is compounded by the overmaternalization of feminism which ensures that, following the Oedipal drama, maleness is required in order to gain distance and differentiation from the mother.

I would argue, however, that at least part of the blame for the continued power of the association between men and sexuality, men and autonomy, must lie within feminism itself, particularly in terms of the paucity of feminist theorizing about the mother's sexual agency. Even within a discourse that has attempted to redefine motherhood in a non-misogynist way, we still have difficulty theorizing a mother who is actively sexual. There seems to be something about motherhood that erases sexuality. This, of course, produces a catch-22 for theories such as lesbian feminism which have, at times, relied on the valorization of the maternal to argue for a utopian vision of female sexuality. If mothers can't be sexual, and feminism is like a mother, then feminism can't be sexual. In particular, when one looks at lesbian feminism, it is clear that many of the generational impasses that currently confront lesbian and queer women have to do with the ways in which lesbian feminism has theorized—or failed to theorize—sexuality. From Adrienne Rich's maternal lesbian to politically correct dogma about sexual practices, lesbian-feminist theorizing has run away from sexuality, thereby leaving it to the men to tempt today's strange young women to run off with them.

5.

To Be, or Not to Be, Real

BLACK FEMINISTS AND THE EMERGING THIRD WAVE

In Cheryl Lynn's popular 1978 disco hit "Got to Be Real," the singer exhorts the listener to take "what you find, what you feel, what you know, to be real. . . . It's got to be real, it's got to be real." In the context of her song, Lynn's "to be real" suggests a refusal to play games in a romantic relationship; she urges her listeners, female ones in particular, to take themselves and their feelings seriously. In the twenty years since Lynn's song first got people grooving on the dance floor, the cultural significance of the phrase "to be real" has expanded beyond the mere trusting of one's intuition, to take what you feel to be real. Disco has been replaced by new musical forms, and within the vernacular of the rap and hip-hop music of the late 1990s and early twenty-first century, "to be real" has come to signify authenticity, something that can't be faked.

Within the recent explosion of new writing by young black feminists, "realness" or "being real" has emerged as a central and recurring theme. The most obvious example, of course, is the title of the now-canonical third-wave text, *To Be Real: Telling the Truth and Changing the Face of Feminism*, the 1995 anthology edited by Rebecca Walker. In her opening essay to the volume, entitled "Being Real: An Introduction," Walker expresses her hope that the essays in her collection will "create feminist space in which you can be real."[1] Her desire for an alternative space stems from her formulation of second-wave feminism as confining, a space of regulation or entrapment, as it was for Roiphe and Denfeld. She begins her introduction:

> A year before I started this book, my life was like a feminist ghetto. Every decision I made, person I spent time with, word I uttered, had to measure up to an image I had in my mind of what was morally and politically right according to my vision of female empowerment. Everything had a gendered explanation, and what didn't fit into my concept of feminist was "bad, patriarchal, and problematic."[2]

In the feminist ghetto described by Walker, political correctness governs its inhabitants, establishing a clear-cut moral universe in which feminism provides all the easy answers. Walker uses the word "ghetto" to depict feminism as a prison-like space, appearing to rely on the word's meaning as a restricted area, as in the walled Jewish ghettos of Nazi Europe. Within a U.S. context, however, the word "ghetto" is most often associated with the impoverished, black inner city, making the phrase "feminist ghetto" particularly paradoxical given the common critique that feminism is dominated by white middle- and upper-class women. The pairing of "feminist" with "ghetto" juxtaposes two terms which are each distinctly raced, the phrase suggesting a kind of contradiction in meaning.

While several of the essays in *To Be Real* do make a point of critiquing the racial biases of feminism, in fact the anthology's clearest argument against feminism's "whiteness" can be seen in its diverse list of authors. The white writers included in *To Be Real* account for just over one-third of its contributors; the other writers are predominantly African American, with several Asian American, Latina, and Southeast Asian writers included in the mix.[3] More important, however, the majority of these authors unmistakably claim feminism as their generation's inheritance—theirs to own, theirs to challenge, theirs to shape for the future.[4] Within the context of a text so centrally concerned with reconceptualizing feminism for a new generation, this matter-of-fact representation of feminism as something that belongs, indisputably, to a racially diverse group of people might be its most revolutionary statement.

This unambiguous claiming of feminism as "mine" is perhaps most evident in Walker's introduction, a piece in which she describes feminism as a kind of "home" that she comes from.[5] Walker is the daughter of one of the most influential writers of the second wave, Alice Walker, and it is precisely Rebecca Walker's sense of feminism as so deeply hers, so deeply a part of her daily life, that causes her to worry about the repercussions of challenging the established order: the rules that govern the feminist ghetto. That it is Walker who is the editor of this collection—combined with the fact that *To Be Real* is, in great part, a black feminist text—suggests another way of interpreting the phrase "feminist ghetto." Rather than necessarily reading contradiction into the pairing of the two terms, the phrase may instead point to the ways in which, for Walker, feminism and blackness are not in opposition to one another. They are not independent concepts; they are not inherently in conflict. In beginning her introduction to *To Be Real* by declaring that "my life was like a feminist ghetto," Walker picks up on the dual meaning of the word "ghetto"—as both a space of confinement and as a black space. Feminism, she suggests, is both.

My reading of the phrase "feminist ghetto," while admittedly tentative, also points to the fundamental theme of contradiction within Walker's introduction specifically and *To Be Real* generally. As the editor, she describes "looking for essays that explored contradiction and ambiguity" in living feminist lives in the 1990s and says that she is interested in "using the contradictions in our lives" as the basis for feminist theory.[6] Embracing these contradictions is central to the new vision of feminism put forward in her introduction—a feminism founded on the notion of being real. Walker describes her decision not to abandon feminism but rather to try to change it from within:

> Neither myself nor the young women and men in this book have bowed out. Instead, the writers here have done the difficult work of *being real* (refusing to be bound by a feminist ideal not of their own making) and *telling the truth* (honoring the complexity and contradiction in their lives by adding their experiences to the feminist dialogue).[7]

Within the pages of *To Be Real,* as in most other self-described third-wave texts, the complexities and contradictions within the lives and politics of this new generation are heralded as the third wave's greatest innovation and intervention into feminism. The argument that attention to complexity is what makes the third wave of feminism new and different has often been bolstered by the claim that second-wave feminism is overly simplistic and dogmatic. In the case of *To Be Real,* however, its argument isn't so much *against* one-dimensional feminism as it is *for* valuing and building on the contradictions that are inherent in living in a post–second-wave era.

For Walker, using contradictions as the basis for a new feminism involves "telling the truth" about our lives, even when those truths contradict the feminist party line. By linking "being real" with "telling the truth," both in the title of the anthology and in the passage quoted above, Walker relies on the association of being real with honesty. Doing so, however, would seem to imply that what will distinguish this new generation is their refusal to live a lie—"a feminist ideal not of their own making." Being real, she implies, is about rejecting the previous generation's definition of feminism when it doesn't fit with our experience. Like other modes of third-wave disidentification, the claim of realness is posed as the third wave's challenge to the second wave: *our* generation will tell the truth about our lives.

Although the title of Walker's introduction, "Being Real," picks up on "the real" in the volume's title, in fact the title of the anthology comes from the title of another of its essays, "To Be Real" by Danzy Senna. In an essay that problematizes the call for authenticity espoused by Walker, Senna uses the concepts of "realness" and "the real" to discuss a variety of her identities: racial, sexual, and political.

> Growing up mixed in the racial battlefield of Boston, I yearned for something just out of my reach—an "authentic" identity to make me real. Everyone but me, it seemed at the time, fit into a neat cultural box, had a label to call their own. Being the daughter of both feminist and integrationist movements, a white socialist mother and a black intellectual father, it seemed that everyone and everything had come together for my conception, only to break apart in time for my birth. I was left only with questions. To Be or Not to Be: black, Negro, African American, feminist, femme, mulatto, quadroon, lesbian, straight, bisexual, lipstick, butch bottom, femme top, vegetarian, carnivore.[8]

Like Walker, Senna is black and biracial and the daughter of a feminist mother. Like Walker, she describes feeling like a generational outsider to the movements that came before her. Yet the quest for realness which Senna portrays throughout "To Be Real"—for "an 'authentic' identity to make me real"—ultimately reveals such realness to be an impossibility. For her, realness offers only the illusion of a transparent identity.

The yearning for realness, Senna implies, is part of a nostalgia that haunts this generation, a desire for an authentic political identity and a political movement of their own. Describing her participation in a political protest during college, she comments on the political differences between the 1980s and the 1960s:

> I realized that in fact the whole protest had seemed simply a cheap imitation of the 1960s protests I had seen and heard so much about, not only in war stories from my parents, but also on television and the movies. It was a crude imitation of my parents' life experience. While our protest was about actual issues, we had recycled the language and tactics of another era, leaving the whole event with a NutraSweet aftertaste—close, but not quite the real thing.[9]

Members of the younger generation—Generation X, the third wave—have only a synthetic version of the political movements of the 1960s: NutraSweet instead of sugar. For Senna, the desire for realness reveals a yearning for a political movement with real substance; more important, however, finding realness would mean building a genuinely new movement rather than merely imitating those of the past.[10]

Throughout Senna's essay, the word "imitation"—"cheap imitation," "crude imitation"—is used to illustrate the contrast between her identities and politics and that of "the real thing": the civil rights and feminist movements of the 1960s and 1970s. When paired with another important theme within her essay, that of being biracial and too light to be "really black," the word "imitation" recalls Fannie Hurst's novel (and its two film adaptations) *Imitation of Life*. In *Imitation of Life*, a story about two mother-daughter pairs—one white, one black—the light-skinned daughter of the black mother rejects her mother in order to pass as white. In Senna's essay, this "imitation" is reversed. The light-skinned daughter of a white mother, Senna describes trying to pass as black—the "authentic identity" that will make her real. This allusion to *Imitation of Life* is made even more powerful when she employs the concept of passing to describe what it would mean to be "really" any one of her identities:

> It is perhaps because of, not in spite of, the intense confusions of my childhood and adolescence that I have come to embrace feminism in my twenties. Today I no longer yearn for a "real" mother; I can see now that I had one all along. I also no longer believe in a single "authentic Negro experience." I have also come to understand that multiplicity is inherent in my blackness, not opposed to it, and that none of my "identities" are distinct from one another. To be a feminist is to be engaged actively in dismantling all oppressive relationships. To be black is to contain all colors. I can no longer allow these parts of myself to be compartmentalized, for when I do, I pass, and when I pass [according to the *American Heritage Dictionary*], I "cease to exist."[11]

Here Senna describes passing as the opposite of complexity and multiplicity; to effectively pass as a particular identity, one must compartmentalize all other facets of oneself. She links the notion of passing to the desire for an authentic, "real" identity, suggesting that any such call for realness will necessarily entail artifice. Further, by playing with the dictionary's various definitions of passing, she suggests that to pass involves a kind of death of the self, as in the phrase "she passed on." It is interesting that Senna suggests that her embrace of feminism is grounded in the very rejection of one authentic definition of identity, whether black, feminist, or even maternal. Senna's vision of feminism as encompassing multiple perspectives, confusions and all, parallels what Walker terms "being real," or the incorporation of contradictions and complexity into feminism.

What is striking is the distinct ways in which each writer uses the notion of "the real" to articulate this new multifaceted feminism. Realness for Walker is clearly good: it represents the goal and the gift of third-wave feminism, that which can change feminism's face and move us in a new direction. For Senna, however, the goal of realness—whether as a feminist or a racial identity—is ultimately undesirable, something she associates with an earlier, and thus less mature, stage in her political development. For example, in describing her former college self, she writes:

> Once again, I found myself falling within the borderlines of identities, forever consigned to the Never-Never Land of the Mulatto Nation. How could I be black but look so white? How could I be a feminist but continue to wear lipstick and shave my legs? How could I feel attracted to men as well as to women? To escape from these dreaded multiplicity blues, I had once again constructed a "real" image of myself.[12]

Senna's use of spatial metaphors to illustrate the arenas of identity is familiar to readers of the third wave, given the frequency with which second-wave feminism is described as a confining space within this writing; that is, Walker's "feminist ghetto." Yet what is unusual in this passage is how Senna describes the construction of a "real" identity as that which will save her from "falling within the borderlines," "the Never-Never Land of the Mulatto Nation." It is realness, she suggests, that offers an *escape* from contradiction. In contrast to Walker, Senna views the aspiration to realness as a rejection of complexity rather than an embrace of it.

The juxtaposition of Senna's essay with Walker's introduction creates a kind of internal rift within the book's logic and central framing device. Both Walker and Senna, along with the rest of *To Be Real*'s contributors, critique what they see as the simplistic form of identity politics espoused by earlier generations of black, women's, and gay and lesbian liberationists. While Walker seems to hold out hope for a new, "real" form of feminism, one that will authentically express her generation's experience, Senna would seem to suggest that any such search for realness will ultimately lead this generation into the same constricting definition of feminism that they are trying to escape. She writes:

> I have become suspicious of kente cloth and womyn symbols, the sale and mass consumption of cultural artifacts. My yearning to be real has led me in circles, to red herrings called identity, those visible signifiers of liberation that can be bought and sold as easily as any other object.[13]

Senna argues that the desire for realness inexorably leads to identity, which then becomes hardened, commodified, and stripped of its internal contradictions. Within the context of the rest of *To Be Real*, her essay should be read as a warning: even a third-wave feminism premised on complexity and contradiction can lead to another prison-house of identity, creating its own definition of realness and its own revamped version of the feminist ghetto.

In a 1995 *New York Times Magazine* article on the upcoming generation of black feminists, Kristal Brent Zook argues that "[t]he choice between 'keeping it real' (whatever that means) and not being 'black enough' has become an increasingly pressing one for my generation."[14] Here Zook defines "keeping it real" as the opposite of "not being 'black enough,'" picking up on the former phrase's meaning within the hip-hop lexicon as a term that denotes staying on the level of the people and not assimilating into white culture. To "keep it real," then, *is* to be "black enough."

Zook's article and the picture she paints of the dilemma young black feminists face—whether or not to "keep it real"—appears to have inspired at least one young writer to argue for a new breed of feminism. In her 1999 *When Chickenheads Come Home to Roost: My Life as a Hip-Hop Feminist*, a book in which Zook's essay figures prominently in the footnotes, Joan Morgan argues that "more than any other generation before us, we need a feminism committed to 'keeping it real.'"[15] In fact, the claim that feminism needs to "keep it real" appears to be the over-riding thesis of Morgan's book. The phrases "keeping it real" or "let's keep it real" are used throughout *When Chickenheads Come Home to Roost* to argue for a feminism that retains the concerns of the average black woman at its core. As Morgan writes, "If feminism intends to have any relevance in the lives of the majority of black women, if it intends to move past theory and become functional it has to rescue itself from the ivory towers of academia."[16] In her argument that feminism has become overly elitist and academic, Morgan echoes the criticism made by other third-wave critics of second-wave feminism, such as Rene Denfeld and Naomi Wolf. Yet what is distinct about her argument is that her vision of a feminism that can "keep it real" allows her to critique both the whiteness of feminism and its academic elitism in one fell swoop. She writes, "When I thought about feminism—women who were living and breathing it daily—I thought of white women or black female intellectu-als. Academics. Historians. Authors. Women who had little to do with my everyday life."[17] Here the category "white women" is conjoined with "black female intellectuals" to form a group which Morgan might dub "feminists who aren't keeping it real." For Morgan, then, it is not just white feminists who are unable to "keep it real"; she also criticizes black academic feminists for closing themselves off in the ivory tower where the everyday concerns of the majority of black women go unnoticed. In pairing "black female intellectuals" with the overly general "white women," Morgan seems to suggest that academia is like a bleaching agent, inevitably whitening those who choose it as a career path. White-ness and intellectualism both have the same effect: a feminism that is out of touch with young black women.

Like many of the third-wave writers discussed earlier, Morgan's call for a new feminism is founded on the notion that her generation—the generation which follows the second wave—brings a different agenda to feminism precisely because of the second wave's successes. She writes:

> Ironically, reaping the benefits of our foremothers' struggle is precisely what makes their brand of feminism so hard to embrace. The "victim" (read women) "oppressor" (read men) model that seems to dominate so much of contemporary discourse (both black and white), denies the very essence of who we are. We are the daughters of feminist privilege. The gains of the Feminist Movement (the efforts of black, white, Latin, Asian, and Native American women) had a tremendous impact on our lives—so much we often

take it for granted. We walk through the world with a sense of entitlement that women of our mothers' generation could not begin to fathom.[18]

Like other third-wave critics, Morgan faults the second wave for its promotion of what Naomi Wolf terms "victim feminism."[19] In describing her generation's rejection of such feminism in familial terms—"we are the daughters of feminist privilege"—she seems to suggest that this rejection is expected, even inevitable.

While crediting a diverse group of women for the gains of the feminist movement, Morgan simultaneously faults white and black feminists alike for their promotion of victim feminism. Her inclusive vision of the second wave is unusual for third-wave writing, and it is noteworthy that she both praises and blames black feminists for their involvement in the development of feminism. In her critique of victim feminism, she does not single out white feminists for attack, nor does she absolve black feminists. Both groups of feminists, she suggests, have contributed to the victim-oppressor model of feminism which "denies the very essence of who we are."[20]

Morgan's notion that contemporary feminism denies the very essence of the women it seeks to address is reminiscent of Walker's statement, quoted earlier, that "being real" entails "refusing to be bound by a feminist ideal not of [one's] own making." In both statements, second-wave feminism is described as not understanding or recognizing the women of the next generation—the very women it produced.[21] Feminism appears staid, unable to adapt to the changing circumstances it helped to bring about. And so, according to Morgan, a young woman today is "going to have to push her foremothers' voices far enough away to discover her own."[22]

Like Walker, Morgan uses the concept of realness to argue that her generation needs a new feminism that speaks to its experience, picking up on the term's association with contradiction: "I wanted a feminism that would allow me to explore who we are as women—not victims. One that claimed the powerful richness and delicious complexities inherent in being black girls now—sistas of the post-Civil Rights, post-feminist, post soul, hip-hop generation."[23] Morgan's desire for a feminism that would "*allow* [her] to explore who we are as women—not victims" suggests that previous feminisms have curtailed what could be explored and what could be thought under the name of feminism. Like Walker's description of second-wave feminism as enforcing a politically correct code of behavior, Morgan implies that there are certain things that feminism simply won't allow: namely, the exploration of complexities. She rejects the ready-made feminism she inherits in favor of a feminism that addresses her experience, what it means to be "black girls now," in the late 1990s.

In describing her generational cohorts as "sistas of the post-Civil Rights, post-feminist, post soul, hip-hop generation," Morgan uses the prefix "post" to situate her generation after the liberation movements of the 1960s and 1970s; that is, after the civil rights movement and the second wave of the feminist movement. Yet her inclusion of "post soul" is an interesting use of musical and cultural styles to mark generational shifts. Since the 1990s, the phrase "hip-hop generation" has increasingly been used by young African-American writers to describe the distinct new realities faced by the generation who came of age after the civil rights and black power movements of an earlier period.[24] The phrase "hip-hop generation" functions as does "Generation X" in signifying the generation born during or after the 1960s. While on the face of it, both terms denote a demographic population, both "Generation X" and "hip-hop generation" more accurately point to a shift in aesthetic and cultural values within the culture at large. As Shani Jamila writes in *Colonize This! Young Women of Color on Today's Feminism:*

> Hip hop is the dominant influence on our generation. . . . Those of us who embrace feminism can't act like hip hop hasn't been an influence on our lives, or vice versa, simply because claiming them both might seem to pose a contradiction. They are two of the basic things that mold us.[25]

While ostensibly referring to the same chronological generation, "hip-hop generation" and "Generation X" also mark cultural distinctions *within* the post-1960s generation which must be read in terms of race. The term "Generation X" has been used, like "Baby Boomers," to mark an entire group of people born within a certain period (in this case, between 1961 and 1981), yet it has also been used to signify a particular ideology and aesthetic, a playful and ironic appropriation of previous cultural forms in a kind of postmodern pastiche.[26] Within this understanding of the term, "Generation X" has primarily been used by white writers, performers, and artists and has had little meaning within distinctly African-American cultural productions. The term "hip-hop generation" has functioned as a kind of parallel to "Generation X," marking a particular population demographic while simultaneously pointing to a particular aesthetic and set of values rooted in black culture.[27] For Morgan, then, the adjective "hip-hop" can be read as a way of designating her generational location. "Hip-hop" might also serve as a replacement for "third wave," another mode of marking generational differences between second- and third-wave feminisms, civil rights movement and post–civil rights movement generations. As Kimberly Springer argues, "There are still young Black women continuing feminist analyses of Black life, but they are not necessarily claiming the label of *third wave*."[28] Indeed, as an adjective to describe their feminism, many young African-American feminists are employing "hip hop" as an alternative to "third wave."[29]

Elaborating on what she means by a feminism able to claim the "delicious complexities" of her experience, Morgan writes, "I discovered that mine was not a feminism that existed comfortably in the black and white of things. . . . In short, I needed a feminism brave enough to fuck with the grays. And this was not my foremothers' feminism."[30] Morgan's longing for a feminism at "the juncture where 'truth' is no longer black and white but subtle, intriguing shades of gray" offers an interesting image of color within a book so centrally concerned with black feminism and black women.[31] Although Morgan uses "gray" to describe what one might call a middle ground between extremes, when read alongside other third-wave writing, her allusion to "the juncture" of black and white recalls another kind of merger: biracial children of black and white parents.

Many of the most visible members of this new generation of feminist writers, particularly within the group of young black women discussed here, are biracial or interracial—writers such as Danzy Senna, Rebecca Walker, Kristal Brent Zook, and Lisa Jones.[32] It is not only that the authors of many of these texts are themselves biracial, but within this work biraciality is frequently used as an example of the kind of complexity that this generation brings to feminism. Frequently linked to biraciality is bisexuality which, like its racial counterpart, is typically described as an identity *beyond* the simplistic categories of the past with their limiting binaries: black or white, straight or gay. "We are pushing, expanding and exploding ideologies of multiplicity and intersectionality," writes a contributor to *Colonize This!* of her generation. "We come as transracial adoptees, women of mixed race, bisexuals, refugees and hundreds of other combinations."[33] Thus, it is not just truth which is no longer black and white in the same way it was for second-wave feminists but feminists themselves that can no longer be put into such clear-cut categories. An example of such an argument can be seen in the following passage from Walker's introduction to *To Be Real:*

> For many of us it seems that to be a feminist in the way that we have seen or understood feminism is to conform to an identity and way of living that doesn't allow for individuality, complexity, or less than perfect personal histories. . . . This way of ordering is especially difficult for a generation that has grown up transgender, bisexual, interracial, and knowing and loving people who are racist, sexist, and otherwise afflicted. We have trouble formulating and perpetuating theories that compartmentalize and divide according to race and gender and all of the other signifiers. For us the lines between Us and Them are often blurred.[34]

Here Walker suggests that this new feminism involves more than just a shift in philosophy or ideology; rather, it represents a demographic shift in those who make up the next generation of feminists—"a generation that has grown up transgender, bisexual, interracial" and thus has trouble thinking in such binary terms. In other words, racial, sexual, and gender identities have become more complex and so, correspondingly, must feminism.[35]

A reading of Walker's "being real" alongside Morgan's "keeping it real" suggests that there are at least two meanings of realness being employed by this new generation of black feminist writers: in the first, realness denotes complexity, authenticity, and truth; in the second, realness signifies an unassimilated black perspective. Although these two definitions of realness undoubtedly share the same linguistic origin, when read in dialogue with each other the third-wave goal of realness seems more elusive than ever. Within the variety of "reals" being used in this writing, a representation of the feminism(s) of the past emerges, one that is clearly not real enough. When real is used to signify complexity and the truth of people's lives, second-wave feminism is critiqued for being simplistic and moralistic. When real is used to connote biraciality and bisexuality, second-wave feminism is critiqued for its limited notion of identity categories. When real is used to imply some form of authentic blackness, second-wave feminism is critiqued for its whiteness and for being too academic, which is perhaps another way of saying too white.[36] All these meanings converge in the sense that the call to "keep it real" is used to argue for a new breed of feminism that has at its core the authentic experiences of its participants. Yet as Senna's essay seems to caution us, how would this authenticity be defined and by whom? What is to prevent a new feminism premised on "keeping it real" from becoming another regulator of identity and behavior?

RACE AND THE EMERGENCE OF THE THIRD WAVE

In the fall of 1991, the Senate Judiciary Committee held its confirmation hearings on Clarence Thomas's nomination to the Supreme Court; Thomas had been selected by President George H. Bush to replace the retiring Justice Thurgood Marshall, who was known as a civil rights advocate. From the moment Bush's choice was announced, Thomas was criticized for his conservative judicial record, particularly on civil rights legislation such as affirmative action. The president was ridiculed for his cynical attempt to appeal to black voters by filling the seat vacated by Marshall with another African-American judge, no matter how stark the ideological differences were between the two men. The politics involved in Thomas's appointment ensured that the hearings would be lively, but no one was prepared for the spectacle that eventually emerged. Toward the end of the hearing process, Anita Hill, an African-American law professor from Oklahoma, came forward to announce that a decade earlier she had been sexually harassed by Thomas while he was her boss at the Equal Employment Opportunity Commission. A second set of confirmation hearings was then scheduled to begin on Friday, October 11. During the three days of testimony that weekend, it seemed as if the entire nation was transfixed in front of its televisions as Thomas, Hill, and countless witnesses testified to the veracity of Hill's claims and to the fitness of Thomas for the high court.

An event that almost didn't happen—Hill was reluctant to come forward until the last minute—has since gone down in history as a pivotal moment in U.S. gender and race relations. Anita Hill's testimony and the condescending response given to it by the Senate Judiciary Committee inspired a feminist political reawakening in women across the U.S., providing the catalyst for what we now call the third wave of feminism.[37] It was the Thomas hearings that Rebecca Walker was responding to in her 1992 *Ms.* essay, "Becoming the Third Wave," where she says of herself: "I am not a postfeminism feminist. I am the Third Wave."[38] The Thomas hearings mobilized women of all ages into action; they worked to elect record numbers of women into political office in 1992. The Thomas hearings helped put feminist issues back into the media spotlight after the bleak anti-feminist 1980s.

For African-American women, the hearings were particularly important in highlighting the need for a revitalized black feminist movement. As Beverly Guy-Sheftall notes, the Thomas hearings "sparked perhaps the most profound intraracial tensions around sexual politics that the modern African American community had ever experienced."[39] A month after the hearings had concluded with Thomas's appointment to the Supreme Court, a six-paragraph statement entitled "African American Women in Defense of Ourselves" was published in the *New York Times.*[40] A reader of this particular Sunday *Times* could not have failed to notice the advertisement. Bordered by an African-inspired pattern and filling three-quarters of the page, the written statement sits in the middle of the ad surrounded by the names of its 1,603 signatories. The alphabetical list in tiny print—made up of the names of celebrity feminists and average citizens alike—runs back and forth across the page, the sheer number of names creating a powerful image of feminist collectivity.

Detailing their opposition to the "nomination, confirmation and seating of Clarence Thomas as an Associate Justice of the U.S. Supreme Court," the group's statement goes on to say: "Many have erroneously portrayed the allegations against Clarence Thomas as an issue of either gender or race. As women of African descent, we understand sexual harassment as both." It concludes, "We pledge ourselves to continue to speak out in defense of one another, in defense of the African American community and against those who are hostile to social justice no matter what color they are. No one will speak for us but ourselves." At the bottom of the ad, included with a request for funds to help reprint it in African-American newspapers, is the following declaration: "We would also like to hear from those interested in establishing a progressive network among women of African descent so that we may more effectively make our voices heard in the future." In the months that followed its publication, a new black feminist organization was formed named after the statement's title: African American Women in Defense of Ourselves.[41]

The statement, and particularly its concluding sentence—"no one will speak for us but ourselves"—is reminiscent of the manifesto of an earlier black feminist group, the Combahee River Collective. Written in 1977, the Collective's "A Black Feminist Statement" argues that identity politics offer "the most profound and potentially the most radical" form of politics for black women. They write: "We realize that the only people who care enough about us to work consistently for our liberation is us."[42] In its claim that only black women "care enough" about black women to work for their liberation, a kind of resigned pessimism hovers over the statement, suggesting that the identity politics espoused by the Combahee River Collective are motivated by necessity born of neglect. The closing words of the "African American Women in Defense of Ourselves" statement builds on the Collective's notion of identity politics, pushing the message one step further. "No one will speak for us but ourselves" can be read in two ways. In the first, "no one will speak for us" can be read as parallel to no one "cares enough about us." In this reading, the 1991 statement builds on the argument of its 1977 predecessor: multiply oppressed by racism and sexism, as well as classism and homophobia, black women are the most disenfranchised group within U.S. politics, their needs unlikely to be met by white feminists, black nationalists, gay liberationists, or any other group with a single political focus. Yet the 1991 statement can be read in another way as well: "No one will speak for us but ourselves" poses a direct challenge to those who dismissed, appropriated, or spun Anita Hill's testimony for their own purpose. This reading suggests that others have, in fact, tried to speak for black women but have done so only to further their own agendas: from Clarence Thomas and his supporters to both the black and white media to black male and white female supporters of Hill.

The "African American Women in Defense of Ourselves" statement marked the beginning of a resurgence in black feminist activism and a renewed focus on black feminism within the popular press. In her 1991 essay "The Invisible Ones," published shortly after the hearings, Lisa Jones calls on black women to (re)claim feminism in the wake of the Thomas hearings. She writes:

To Be, or Not to Be, Real

The battle of Hill/Thomas also taught us how invisible we (black) women are as black people. . . . Black women need feminism more than ever. Who else, after all, has a stake in our visibility—in an affirming community, in our power and representation—but ourselves and all those children we're raising?[43]

In this and other essays she has written for the *Village Voice*, Jones has been at the forefront in calling for a revitalized black feminist movement among young women, a call which has also been taken up within the pages of the *New York Times* as well as black and feminist publications such as *Essence* and *Ms.*[44]

As key spokespersons and writers of this new generation, African-American feminists are leading the third wave. Some of the more visible members of this new publishing boom in feminist writing include Veronica Chambers, staff writer for *Newsweek*, contributor to *Listen Up: Voices from the Next Feminist Generation* (1995), and author of *Mama's Girl*, her 1996 memoir; Lisa Jones, staff writer for the *Village Voice*, contributor to *To Be Real: Telling the Truth and Changing the Face of Feminism* (1995), and author of *Bulletproof Diva: Tales of Race, Sex, and Hair* (1994); Joan Morgan, staff writer for *Essence* and author of *When Chickenheads Come Home to Roost: My Life as a Hip-Hop Feminist* (1999); Danzy Senna, frequently published essayist, contributor to *To Be Real*, and author of the 1998 novel *Caucasia;* and finally, Rebecca Walker, co-founder of the activist group Third Wave Foundation, editor of *To Be Real*, contributor to *Listen Up*, and author of the memoir *Black, White, and Jewish: Autobiography of a Shifting Self* (2001).[45] In the anthologies cited above and others, third-wave feminism is frequently presented as a racially and ethnically diverse movement, with black women moved from the margin to the center of this new wave.[46]

The notoriety given to a small subset of primarily white feminist writers combined with the popular media's seeming inability to acknowledge feminism as anything other than a white middle-class movement has created a fairly whitewashed representation of the third wave. While the central role played by black women in the development of this new feminism has gone virtually ignored in the mainstream media's representation of third-wave feminism, so has the fact that it was the Thomas hearings which provided the catalyst for the declaration of a third wave of feminism. In making this claim I do not mean to

163

suggest that the emergence of a third wave wasn't, in great part, a reaction against the "feminist backlash" years of the 1980s, to use Susan Faludi's term.[47] The calling for a new wave was undoubtedly a response to the previous decade of feminist inactivity and conservatism generally. Yet the fact that it was the Thomas hearings—where race, gender, class, and sexuality converged—which generated the third wave suggests that this new wave shares a common history with the two preceding waves of U.S. feminism. The first and second waves both emerged from and followed African-American, anti-racist social justice movements: the first wave from the abolitionist movement and the second from the civil rights movement. In examining the development of all three waves of women's activism, then, we see that race and gender are inextricably linked within U.S. feminism. The struggle for gender equality is not independent from the struggle for racial equality; race isn't merely some earlier, and thus disposable, concern which helps to launch feminism. Rather, race is intrinsic to feminism, always there when it begins, always essential to whatever shape feminism takes.

Although the Thomas hearings certainly didn't lead to a large-scale movement like abolitionism or civil rights, it lit the fuse for a national discussion on race and gender that would lead to Rebecca Walker's call for a third wave. To regard this latest wave of U.S. feminism as having its roots in an event so deeply about both race and gender is to suggest that the third wave, like the first and the second, owes its development not just to gender consciousness but to race consciousness as well. It is impossible to separate out questions of race from questions of gender in the development of feminism, nor should we forget that women of color have been actively involved in every wave of feminism.

Given this fact, it is vital that feminist scholars and activists challenge the notion, held by mainstream America and some feminists alike, that "the Feminism that gets to wear a capital 'F,'" to quote Gina Dent, is one produced and advocated by white women.[48] The influence that second-wave feminists of color have had on this new generation must be acknowledged alongside the recognition of the central role that young African-American, Asian, and Latina women play in this burgeoning third wave. Many of the writers included in third-wave anthologies, writers of all races, describe how their understanding of feminist theory and feminist practice was profoundly shaped by second-wave feminists of color. In their introduction to *Colonize This! Young Women of Color on Today's Feminism,* editors Daisy Hernández and Bushra Rehman describe having "grown up with a body of literature created by women of color in the last thirty years—Alice Walker's words about womanism, Gloria Anzaldúa's theories about living in the borderlands and Audre Lorde's writings about silences and survival."[49] Paula Kamen's landmark 1991 study of Generation X's attitudes about feminism also points to the important role of these feminist foremothers. Writing when the third wave was just in its infancy, Kamen notes, "The authors with the most undeniable influence on my generation . . . are women of color."[50]

This influence can be seen in many of the hallmarks of third-wave writing, most noticeably its celebration of contradictions. As Leslie Heywood and Jennifer Drake argue in their introduction to *Third Wave Agenda: Being Feminist, Doing Feminism,* what many describe as the "newness" of the third wave is not, in fact, a radical departure from previous feminisms but rather a by-product of nearly two decades worth of theorizing by black feminists and other feminists of color throughout the late 1970s and 1980s:

> [I]t was U.S. third world feminism that modeled a language and a politics of hybridity that can account for our lives at the century's turn. These are lives marked by the realities of multicultural exchange, fusion, and conflict, lives that combine blackness, whiteness, brownness, gayness, bisexuality, straightness.[51]

In works such as the Combahee River Collective's "A Black Feminist Statement" (1977); *This Bridge Called My Back: Writings by Radical Women of Color* (Moraga and Anzaldúa, 1983); *Home Girls: A Black Feminist Anthology* (Smith, 1983); bell hooks's *Feminist Theory from Margin to Center* (1984); Audre Lorde's *Sister Outsider* (1984); and *Making Face, Making Soul: Creative and Critical Perspectives by Feminists of Color* (Anzaldúa, 1990), along with many other examples, we see the very feminism that is now being celebrated as "third wave": one defined by contradiction, multiplicity, and coalition.[52] Some third-wave feminists, particularly feminists of color, have made this connection to the past explicit, such as when Hernández and Rehman describe *Colonize This!* as "a way to continue the conversations among young women of color found in earlier books like *This Bridge Called My Back* and *Making Face, Making Soul.*"[53] The fact that young writers have developed their feminism on the foundation created by these earlier texts points to the influential role that black feminists and other feminists of color have played in shaping the next generation of feminism.[54]

Yet the fact that this earlier work often goes uncredited in the celebration of the new feminism seems to point to a larger problem about the ways in which feminism is conceptualized. It may not seem all that remarkable that in its coverage of the third wave, the mainstream media would continue its long history of portraying feminism as a white women's movement.[55] What is surprising is how third-wave feminists *themselves* participate in this representation when they habitually portray second-wave feminism—the feminism from which they are trying to differentiate themselves—as being a white thing. In arguing for a new feminism of complexity and contradiction, third-wavers seem to need a "mother feminism" to rebel against. By describing second-wave feminism in terms associated with a controlling mother—regulating, puritanical, and moralistic—they create just such a maternal figure. It appears, however, that this "mother feminism" must also be white for this generational break to work. Although third-wavers routinely cite the influence of writers such as Gloria Anzaldúa, bell hooks, Audre Lorde, Cherríe Moraga, and Barbara Smith, these writers are not allowed to represent second-wave feminism in the capital F sense of the word. As Rebecca Hurdis asks in her essay "Heartbroken: Women of Color Feminism and the Third Wave": "Is it possible to construct a feminist genealogy that maintains inclusivity?"[56]

We are left with a paradox. Feminist theory produced by women of color is foundational to third-wave feminism, yet third-wavers cannot use the very feminists who created this theory to exemplify second-wave feminism lest they dilute the argument third-wavers make about the limits of the previous generation. In order to argue for a new, "real" feminism, young feminists need an old, out-of-touch feminism to whom they can shout "get real." As an example of how this works, consider bell hooks. Even though she is one of the most widely taught, published, and anthologized feminist theorists of the last 20-plus years, and even though many younger feminists of all races cite her as an extremely important influence on their own formulation of what feminism is and means to them, third-wave feminists cannot see her as representing second-wave feminism if their arguments against the previous wave are to hold up.

Although some young writers may neglect second-wave feminists of color because they simply don't recognize them as fellow feminists—Katie Roiphe's work comes to mind here—others appear to ignore many of these theorists because doing so facilitates a sharp critique of feminism's whiteness as well as its "rules." That is, by ignoring feminists of color, it is easy to argue that feminism is too white. If third-wave feminists were to reformulate their representation of second-wave feminism to include feminists of color—not to mention queer feminists, anti-censorship feminists, and many, many other types of second-wave feminists—they would not be able to create such an easy target for their criticism.[57]

The ways in which the mother-daughter relationship are mapped onto current feminist generational struggles must also be read in terms of race. I would argue that feminism's "whiteness" is *intrinsic* to its caricaturization as a puritanical mother. Third-wavers describe this maternal feminism as prudish, embittered, and moralistic in a way that is clearly indebted to stereotypes of a certain form of uptight, white femininity. (It is no coincidence that the person most often used to exemplify this feminism is Catherine MacKinnon.) Not only is the mother feminism put forward by the third wave ideologically at odds with black feminism, but the puritanical, stern mother used to depict this feminism is herself distinctly white, representing a particular version of white womanhood.

Given the third wave's obvious debts to black and other non-white feminisms, however, it does seem puzzling that the very feminism that gave birth to this wave is not described as its mother. It may be that second-wave feminism must be read as white in order for the various claims against it to be made, yet there seems to be more behind this conceptualization of feminism's history than just the creation of an easy target. If, in fact, hooks, Lorde, Moraga, and countless others have been so influential to third-wave writers, why do third-wavers not refer to them when they describe "mother feminism"?

In "The Occult of True Black Womanhood," Ann duCille critiques a particular mode by which white feminists describe their relationship to black feminists, one in which the former plays the role of "white child" to the latter's role of "mammy." In this metaphoric relationship, "it is black mammy," according to duCille,

> who takes the ignorant white infant into enlightenment. Often as the youthful, sometimes guilty witness to the silent martyrdom of the older other, the privileged white person inherits a wisdom, an agelessness, even a racelessness that entitles him or her to the raw materials of another's life and culture but, of course, not to the other's condition.[58]

DuCille uses the mammy metaphor to critique what she sees as white feminists' cooption and fetishization of their relationship to black feminists. She argues that white feminists are able to mine the raw materials of black women's lives, art, and theory for their own academic success without having either to engage with black women directly or to reciprocate the exchange.

Although DuCille uses this metaphoric relationship to criticize white feminists, I want to try to put her description of the black mammy in dialogue with what I have been describing as white mother feminism. The black mammy plays an important nurturing and pedagogical role in the life of "the ignorant white infant," but once her wisdom has been learned, the white child is free to break from her. While the black mammy is a mother figure, she is a surrogate; she may mother the children in her care, but mother with a capital M remains white. Within this new feminism, we can see a kind of triangular relationship between child (third-wave feminists), mother (white second-wave feminists), and surrogate mother or "mammy" (black second-wave feminists). Black feminism nurtures, inspires, and bequeaths wisdom to the third wave's infant feminism, yet black feminism cannot take white feminism's place as mother feminism—the Feminism that gets to wear a capital "F."

While this conceptualization of feminism makes possible a critique of its racism and its whiteness, it inevitably leaves black feminists and other feminists of color in what duCille describes as a mammylike role—allowed to nurture and educate this new generation of feminists without ever getting recognized for their labor.[59] The fact that feminists of color don't get the credit for second-wave feminism, however, also means that they rarely—if ever—get the accompanying blame that constitutes so much third-wave discourse. That is, it is only white mother feminism which gets recognized; similarly it is only white mother feminism which gets held responsible for all the perceived problems of contemporary feminism. Thus, while much current writing by young feminists is devoted to rebelling against the second wave, this rebellion cannot accurately be read as a revolt against feminists of color. The "mothers" under siege are white.

Second-wave feminists of color are thus left in a paradoxical position. Central to the development of feminist theory over the last thirty years, they are nevertheless unrecognized as such. Left out on the margins, they are not allowed to occupy feminism's center. Yet this relegation to the margins also means that they escape the arrow aimed at the perceived center of feminism: white, "anti-sex," "victim" feminism.

MOTHERS, DAUGHTERS, AND FEMINISM

Historically, white women have had difficulty in viewing black feminists as the foremothers to their own feminism. In turning to the first wave to create a history for themselves, many white second-wave feminists overlooked the black women involved in the suffrage movement. This neglect may have been the result of more than just ignorance. Within contemporary feminism, we see a repetition of this scenario in the way in which many third-wave feminists represent the second wave. Within the writing by young black feminists, however, the racing of second-wave feminism as white must also be understood in light of the fact that, as Tricia Rose notes, "for black women, feminism often reads white feminism and consequently represents a movement that has contributed to sustaining their oppression while claiming to speak on their behalf."[60]

Given the perception of feminism—and women's studies—as white and often racist, the active embracing of the term "feminist" by this new generation of black women writers can be seen as a challenge to feminism's whiteness. In their (re)claiming of the term, these young women recoup the black women who have participated in U.S. feminism throughout its long history but whose role within feminism has often been erased. They reveal as a lie the notion that feminism is the sole province of white women. As Tiya Miles, a writer included in the 1995 anthology *Listen Up*, notes:

> Many black women are unaware that we have deep roots in feminist consciousness and that our foremothers have always been involved in feminist

struggle. Our misinformation about feminist history—the false idea that feminist thought and activism in the United States have been exclusive to white women—led some of us in [Radcliffe's black student organization] to reject feminism immediately and refuse to work with white women who claimed the label.[61]

As Miles and others discuss, these "foremothers of feminist struggle" grant young black women a history—one which makes feminism their own and not just something they are borrowing from white women. Many young black feminists have described how they didn't discover these foremothers until college. In a revelatory description, Veronica Chambers writes of her introduction to black feminist thought in college: "When I bought Barbara Smith's *Home Girls: A Black Feminist Anthology*, I carried it like a prayer book."[62] Other writers, such as the editors of *Colonize This!* describe not discovering fellow feminists of color until after college:

> Like many other women of color, the two of us first learned the language of feminism in college through a white, middle-class perspective, one form of colonization. . . . It was only after college, through word of mouth from other women of color, that we learned about another kind of feminism. These groups practiced women of color feminism, sometimes naming it as such and sometimes not saying it at all.[63]

Rehman and Hernández describe the ways in which certain forms of feminism—namely white, middle-class forms—are institutionalized in higher learning through women's studies classes and feminist theory textbooks, while "another kind of feminism" goes unrecognized within the curriculum.

In her description of reading *Home Girls*, Chambers describes how studying black feminist thought empowered her while also educating her about the persistent presence of racism within feminism:

> As I continued my readings, I realized that in all incarnations of the women's movement, black women were there. . . . When white women talked about equality, we insisted that they mean black women too. But as it was, at any table of discussion our specific issues were—and still often are—low on the list of priorities. Even among feminists, we are "minorities." That simply isn't good enough. . . . White feminists of earlier generations have passed these values onto [sic] their daughters. The young women I went to school with, for all their notions of feminism, still basked in the glory and privilege of their whiteness.[64]

Chambers aligns herself with black feminists of the past by including herself in the "we" and "our" used to describe them; that is, she identifies herself as part of an ongoing feminist movement, as part of the second wave. She tentatively situates herself within a new generation—"the young women I went to school with"—while simultaneously criticizing the white "daughters" of the second wave for their racism. Chambers offers a different model of feminist identification than that seen in many of the third-wave texts described earlier, where generational bonds supercede feminist ideology. She identifies with Smith and other black second-wave feminists over her white feminist contemporaries, suggesting that race complicates the easy generational split between the second and third waves, particularly when there is nothing new about the racial politics practiced by the white "daughters" of the second wave.

In describing the white women she went to college with as the "daughters" of feminists, Chambers points out that they are second-generation feminists; their mothers' values are passed down to them. In describing her relationship with her own mother, however, she describes a different kind of inheritance.

> Like many young women of all colors and ethnic backgrounds, I had my first feminist awakening at college. . . . I come from a family of strong black women, but to my mother, feminism was a four-letter word. To the people in my neighborhood, feminists were man-haters. . . . To be strong, smart, independent and unashamed were necessary elements for survival in the Brooklyn of my youth. The black women I knew growing up embodied these qualities with the wiles and grace of Amazon warriors. They were, in other words, sisters who didn't take no shit. I knew strength, and I was taught from birth, "Don't allow no man to walk all over you."[65]

Here Chambers describes two different kinds of education in how to be a feminist: the one she received in college, officially called feminism, and the one she received growing up with women who considered feminism irrelevant. What she learned as a child—what was modeled to her—was strength, intelligence, and independence. This point is echoed by Joan Morgan in *When Chickenheads Come Home to Roost:*

> Feminism claimed me long before I claimed it. The foundation was laid by women who had little use for the word. . . . I did not know that feminism is what you called it when black warrior women moved mountains and walked on water. Growing up in their company, I considered these things ordinary. . . . The spirits of these women were nowhere to be found in the feminism I discovered in college.[66]

This theme has been further developed in more recent third-wave work by women of color, such as the 2002 anthology *Colonize This!* in which many of the contributors make similar claims regarding the differences between the feminism of home and the feminism of the academy: "The everyday feminism that I grew up with was missing from my classes; the women had the theory but not the practice."[67] And, "My mother taught me everything I know about 'feminism' even if she didn't think she was teaching me."[68] Like Chambers, these writers point to the tension between the term "feminism" and actually living feminism, whatever one calls it. They characterize the women of their childhoods as warriors, women who had little use for the word "feminism" but who nevertheless embodied many of the qualities they later came to associate with the term in college.

In their descriptions of the divergence between this "college feminism" and the feminism—though it was not called that—practiced at home, Morgan and Chambers seem to echo a point made by Katie Roiphe in *The Morning After*. In her 1993 text, Roiphe argues that the feminism she encountered in college bore no resemblance to the feminism she learned at home from her feminist mother. Although the feminism Roiphe describes is clearly quite different from that depicted by Morgan and Chambers, all three authors describe feeling surprised and let down by the feminism they discovered away from home. For Chambers and Morgan, however, the disconnect between the feminism of college and the feminism of home is even more glaring because only one is authorized to wear the title of feminism with a capital "F." In modeling both economic and emotional independence, the mothers described by black third-wave writers pass down to their daughters the very values that a generation of white feminists sought to achieve in the women's liberation movement.

In *Mama's Girl*, Chambers's moving memoir about her relationship with her often-distant and emotionally unavailable mother, she describes learning how to be strong and independent mainly through her mother's instruction on how to make it on her own without anyone's help, including her mother's. "There is a saying that black women mother their sons and raise their daughters," Chambers writes. "When it comes to my mother, the saying is too true. My mother raised me—there were a lot of hard times, times when we both were hurt and angry, nevertheless

I am the woman I am today because of her."[69] In *Mama's Girl*, the black daughter becomes a feminist even though "to [her] mother, feminism was a four-letter word."[70]

Black feminist theorists writing on the mother-daughter relationship, such as Gloria Joseph and Patricia Hill Collins, have argued that black mothers socialize their daughters to survive in a world that is both racist and sexist, a world in which it is essential that they learn to take care of themselves.[71] As Joseph says of her research into black mother-daughter relationships:

> The daughters showed tremendous respect, concern, and love for their mothers. The positive feelings that were expressed did not imply that all was sweet, kind, and loving between them. Rather, what was expressed was an undeniable respect and admiration for their mothers' accomplishments and struggles against overwhelming odds; their economic ability to make ends meet; their personal relationships with men; for having raised their families as a single parent or head of household and having encouraged them to be independent and get an education. The mothers were role models for their daughters.[72]

The experience of seeing their mothers as powerful and frequently feminist role models—even when the mothers themselves don't identify as feminists—provides an important contrast to the often-antagonistic mother-daughter relationship, whether literal or metaphoric, described in much white third-wave discourse.[73] As Madelyn Detloff points out, "Indeed, white women may have something to learn from women of color when it comes to fostering generational dynamics that facilitate individuation in a self-with-other manner, rather than a self-versus-other dialectic."[74] In the writing by third-wave feminists of color, we see a model of generational relationships that is less about cutting off ties in order to assert the originality of the young than it is about stressing the empowering effects of connections to others, whether biological or metaphorical foremothers. Paraphrasing *Manifesta*'s claim that for Generation X feminism is in the water, a contributor to *Colonize This!* writes, "If feminism is in the water I drink, my mom's herstory is the dry land that pushes me to swallow."[75]

In *To Be Real*, contributor Veronica Webb describes what she learned from her mother:

> My mother worked really really really really hard to make sure I was educated in a way that would teach me to think and which would allow me to compete on a lot of different levels and to have entrée into a lot of different places.

... [I]t wasn't until much later in life that intellectually it clicked, and it was because of *A Room of One's Own.* I realized that without any rhetoric or expectation of payback, my mother had basically set up a room of my own for me. Pushing me to find my own way was what my mother gave me.[76]

In her reference to Virginia Woolf's feminist classic, Webb connects the feminism learned at home with the feminism learned from books and in college: both encourage self-reliance and independence. Her mother gave her "the room of one's own" that Woolf argued was necessary for female autonomy and freedom. Webb describes finding feminism as an adult—in college, in books—and then reading back her childhood through this lens. Like other young feminists of color, she depicts a childhood in which she was raised to be strong and independent, but one which she only interpreted as feminist after it "intellectually clicked" much later. As Kristina Gray describes her childhood in *Colonize This!*

Growing up in a black household, I never heard the F-word used too much. Like my love of Mötley Crüe, most black women in my life saw feminism as a white thing. It wasn't meant for us and it didn't include us. But even though they couldn't quite quote Gloria Steinem, the women in my family led by example, showing me how to defiantly make my way in a world that told black women we didn't matter.[77]

In naming their mothers' lessons "feminist," these daughters challenge both their black mothers' rejection of feminism as white and white feminists' power to name what gets called feminism. By tracing their feminism back to their mothers, these African-American daughters also broaden our vision of feminist lineage. Feminism can be inherited from mothers who view feminism as "a four-letter word." Such mothers do not need to be rejected in order for daughters to move forward.

All this is not to suggest that every young black feminist sees her mother as a nascent feminist, however. The woman most associated with third-wave feminism, Rebecca Walker, has a feminist mother—and a second-wave icon at that. Like Katie Roiphe, Walker grew up with feminism; the practice and theory she learned at home was explicitly named as such. This experience has profoundly shaped the ways in which she argues for a new, third wave of feminism and provided her authority to proclaim "*I am* the Third Wave" in 1992.

In her introduction to *To Be Real,* Walker writes of the need for a new generation of feminists, one that is willing to challenge many of the old orthodoxies of the previous generation. Yet while simultaneously proclaiming the need for a new wave, she also expresses her fear that to challenge the second wave's definition of what she calls "good feminism" is to risk rejection:

> Linked with my desire to be a good feminist was, of course, not just a desire to change my behavior to change the world, but a deep desire to be accepted, claimed, and loved by a feminist community that included my mother, god-mother, aunts, and close friends. For all intents and purposes their beliefs were my own, and we mirrored each other in the most affirming of ways. As is common in familial relationships, I feared that our love was dependent upon that mirroring.[78]

Walker's representation of feminism in this passage suggests that feminism is itself part of her "familial relationships"; feminism is central to what she means by family. This is so not only because her mother and other relatives are feminists but also because her description of her deep desire to be accepted by her family is intertwined with her desire to be accepted as "a good feminist." In other words, her relationship to feminism is always bound up with her relationship to her mother.

"Because feminism has always been so close to home," Walker continues, "I worried that I might also be banished from there."[79] Walker describes a fear of being cast out on her own, yet the "there" that concludes the sentence, coming as it does after a description of feminism as "so close to home," suggests that her feared banishment would be both from feminism and from her family. She risks being kicked out of her home, both her literal familial home and the metaphoric home of feminism. In Walker's case, these two homes may be one and the same.

Published a few months prior to *To Be Real*, a 1995 article in *Essence* magazine entitled "The Two of Us" has Rebecca and Alice Walker writing about their relationship on the occasion of the daughter's twenty-fifth birthday. Rebecca writes of her lifelong "fear of her mother's abandonment," tracing this anxiety back to something that happened when she was eight years old.[80] She describes a childhood memory of lying in bed with her mother, notepad in hand, while Alice dictated the instructions for her own funeral: "[M]ake sure I am buried in a simple pine box. And play lots of Stevie Wonder." She goes on to write:

> I am not sure if the pine-box incident marked the beginning of my fear of my mother's abandonment of me, or if it was the first time that I silenced my own apprehensions in order to soothe hers. I do know that this memory captures how I have always felt, deep down, about my relationship with my

mother: If I don't do what she wants me to do, she will be gone, she will leave me. . . . The plan I devised in response was simple: I would be too perfect to leave. . . . I instinctively made myself into what I perceived to be "a good daughter," often silencing or ignoring my own needs.[81]

There are obvious parallels between Walker's relationship to her mother and her relationship to feminism. Both involve the fear of being abandoned. Both center on the idea that to be accepted, one must behave properly, whether as "good daughter" or "good feminist." In fact, the descriptions she gives of being a "good daughter" and a "good feminist" are remarkably similar: both require following mother's wishes.

In both *To Be Real* and the *Essence* article, the daughter's fear is of rejection, of being left out on her own. Yet, as Rebecca Walker goes on to say in the *Essence* article, the daughter must step out on her own if she is to become her own person and develop her own identity. "While I knew that I would have to stop always being the 'good daughter' in order to reach an adulthood I could be proud of, I fretted unconsciously for a few years, taking tentative steps out of my mother's orbit."[82] Here Walker suggests that she must give up the "good daughter" role in order to create her own sense of self; she describes the difficult yet ultimately necessary process of developing an identity separate from her mother's daughter.[83]

In her introduction to *To Be Real,* Walker describes an equally necessary break—in this case with feminism itself. Even as she worries that to make this break is to be what she calls "a bad feminist," she implores young feminists to abandon their role as dutiful daughters to the second wave.[84] In order to realize a new, "real" feminism, she argues that the third wave must face "the dreaded confrontation with some of the people who presently define and represent feminism."[85] In Walker's admittedly noteworthy case, her own mother is just such a person, someone who "presently defines and represents feminism" for millions of people.

Alice Walker's 1983 anthology *In Search of Our Mothers' Gardens* has been central to feminist scholarship on mother-daughter relationships. Dedicated to Rebecca, her only child, *In Search of Our Mothers' Gardens* addresses Walker's relationship to her own mother, a woman whom she describes as expressing her curtailed creativity in the one outlet granted her: her garden. In the title essay of this collection, Walker writes: "[N]o song or poem will bear my mother's name. Yet so many of the stories that I write, that we all write, are my mother's stories."[86] The black daughter who comes of age during the women's liberation and civil rights movements, Walker says, has opportunities never given to her mother. This daughter has an obligation to tell her mother's stories, which would otherwise disappear.

In another essay from this collection, entitled "One Child of One's Own," Walker turns her attention to her own experience of motherhood, writing now as a mother rather than as a daughter. She describes Rebecca as a child who "by the age of seven, at the latest, is one's friend and can be told of the fears one has, that she can, by listening to one . . . help allay." Walker describes a relationship with her daughter in which the young Rebecca is her friend, confidante, and political ally: "We are together, my child and I. Mother and child, yes, but sisters really, against whatever denies us all that we are."[87] By moving from "mother and child" to "sisters really," Walker aligns herself with Rebecca in a mutual fight for feminist and racial justice; they are sisters in the struggle. Yet this shift to "sisters really" seems to express an uneasiness on Walker's part in writing from the position of mother about her daughter. More than that, when read alongside the description of Rebecca as her mother's companion, this shift to "sisters really" seems to eclipse Rebecca as daughter, making her and Alice contemporaries, members of the same generation.[88] There is no mention of the Rebecca who "silenced [her] own apprehensions in order to soothe [Alice's]."

In the *Essence* article, Alice Walker concludes her piece with the following description of her relationship to her daughter:

> Rebecca has made me a mother. Because of her, I've reunited with banished bits of my own life. I know again the daughter and the mother I was, and feel pity and empathy for both. I appreciate the admirable daughter courage that, although self-denying and therefore painful, still springs from a valiant solidarity with the mother, who, in this world, always has too much to do and too few to help her. I've also discovered the world is full of mothers who've done their best and still hurt their daughters: that we have daughters everywhere.[89]

Although this passage begins with the statement "Rebecca has made me a mother," in its description of "reuniting with the daughter I was" and its "appreciation of admirable daughter courage," Walker again seems to shift to an identification with the daughter's position. Moreover, her conclusion—"we have daughters everywhere"—appears to universalize the experience of her particular "hurt daughter," suggesting that she is herself the daughter of a mother "who did her best."

In the divergence between Walker's writing as a daughter and her writing as a mother, something important is revealed about feminist subjectivity. As Marianne Hirsch has noted, feminism often reads like the daughter's story.[90] Second-wave daughters of pre-feminist mothers authorized themselves to tell their mothers' stories—whether to distance themselves from their mothers' lives, as in the case of many white feminists, or to celebrate their mothers as unsung heroines, as in the example of Walker and others. Because feminism had ensured the daughter's differentiation from her mother, the daughter who came of age during the second wave could unambiguously celebrate (or denigrate) her mother. She didn't take the risk of telling a life story that her mother would contest. Her mother would never be her rival.

In Alice Walker's case, for example, she could celebrate her mother's life without anxiety that her own life would be eclipsed in the process. "And so our mothers and grandmothers have, more often than not anonymously, handed on the creative spark, the seed of the flower that they themselves never hoped to see: or like a sealed letter they could not plainly read."[91] Walker would get to reap the benefits of the creative seed planted by her mother; she could found her feminism, and her career, on the basis of celebrating her mother. Being the good daughter could serve as her entry into feminism. Like some of the third-wave feminists discussed earlier—those *without* self-identified feminist mothers—Walker was able to affirm her mother while simultaneously moving beyond her. She had nothing to lose in telling her mother's story.

For her daughter Rebecca, however, defining feminism through a celebration of her mother will never entail the same rewards. Unlike Alice's invisible and unsung mother, Rebecca's mother is decidedly present, decidedly visible. Differentiation for Rebecca will necessarily require rejecting the "good daughter" role, since to play this role would mean merely accepting her mother's feminism and thus never moving beyond it.[92] More important, since her mother represents feminism in the capital F sense of the word, Rebecca's struggle for individuation will necessarily involve feminism as well. Whereas Alice could use feminism as a way to move beyond her own mother, the only way that Rebecca can remain a feminist and yet distinguish herself from her mother is to try to chart new territory *within* feminism: "*I* am the Third Wave." It is either that or rejecting feminism altogether, and, as she says in her introduction to *To Be Real,* "[n]either myself nor the young women and men in this book have bowed out" from a confrontation with feminism.[93]

Walker's description of trying to forge a new feminism for a new generation is not without risk and anxiety. She says that completing the anthology forced her "to confront that childlike and almost irrational fear of being different and therefore unacceptable."[94] Walker's writing provides a clarifying example of the problem of feminist generations since the second wave: the daughter who grows up taking feminism for granted sees it as her own to criticize and reshape, yet she is nevertheless always in her mother's shadow. She can never truly define feminism on her own—as her mother's generation appeared to do—because both second-wave feminism and her mother continue to be dominant shaping forces in her life. The question Walker's example raises is how one can be a second-generation feminist daughter without merely being a "good daughter." How can the daughters of the second wave continue their mothers' feminism without losing themselves in it?

In hindsight, it seems consistent that it would take the daughter of a well-known second-wave feminist to proclaim the emergence of a third wave. Although in many ways Katie Roiphe shares some of these daughterly features with Rebecca Walker—both have feminist writers for mothers, both describe feminism as "something assumed, something deep in [their] foundations"—the individualistic, almost self-obsessed, bent of Roiphe's feminism has never been about generating a new movement in the collective sense of the word.[95] In this she represents one dominant strain within much of this new feminist writing: individualism and a focus on self-definition. Walker, in contrast, seems emblematic of other key themes within the third wave: the struggle to maintain generational ties while simultaneously incorporating new identities and new complexities into feminism, the struggle to have a collective movement in the face of radical individuality. Biracial and bisexual, she literally embodies the very notion of identity as involving multiplicity that is being heralded in so much of this new work.[96] In both her work and her very presence she relocates black women from the margin to the center of feminism. While her mother was often relegated to the position of token black woman within white second-wave feminism, Rebecca defines the third wave as one of its most famous and visible spokespersons.

In the *Essence* piece, Rebecca Walker describes how she and her mother eventually overcame the obstacles between them, particularly her fear that if she wasn't "a good daughter" she risked abandonment.

> By articulating and talking about my childhood fears and feelings with my mother over the past few years, I have tested my childhood assumptions and found that . . . both my mother and my mother's love are here to stay. . . . I am no longer the powerless child at the mercy of my mother's moods. . . . These truths will neither kill nor divide us but will instead set us free. *Being honest, being real with each other* helps us to be true to ourselves and more accepting of what is real in all of our relationships.[97]

In her assessment that "being honest, being real with each other" is what helped to heal her sometimes painful relationship to her mother, Walker's resolution to her personal problem resonates with what she says is needed to take feminism in a new direction. In *To Be Real,* she argues that the next generation must do "the difficult work of being real . . . and telling the truth."[98] In both her relationship to her mother and her relationship to feminism, being real is offered as the solution. It is being real which might allow third-wave daughters to have a relationship to their mothers' feminism and to simultaneously reshape that feminism from within. Like its other meanings, this illustration of what it means to be real entails contradiction: love and fear, safety and risk, intimacy and distance, connection and separation. Rather than being pushed aside in favor of "good daughter" or "good feminist" obedience, these contradictions can be used to transform feminism.

In her writing and thinking through these contradictions—creating her own feminist identity while simultaneously maintaining a connection to second-wave feminism—Rebecca Walker provides a hopeful example for future generational dialogue. Too often, feminists writing about generational relationships within feminism have written merely as "mothers" or "daughters"—wise elders or insolent rebels. While Walker does not provide an escape from writing as a daughter within feminism's family, nor is she particularly interested in trying to do so, she suggests that there is insight to be gained in thinking through the second-generation feminist daughter's position. Unlike Phyllis Chesler's often-patronizing advice to younger feminists or Katie Roiphe's often-haughty disdain for feminists of all ages, what Walker adds to the discussion of contemporary feminism is the desire to both listen and be heard. As I talk to other feminists of all ages, I sense a similar longing. When all of our voices—and all of our various ways of being feminist—can be part of the dialogue, feminism will truly move forward.

Afterword

It's so easy for people to want to make it sexy and juicy by turning it into this kind of Greek tragedy of daughter against mother and matricide and all that. And that's not really what it is at all. It's about trying to strengthen the relationships between mothers and daughters by allowing the difference and respecting the difference and really working through that difference.[1]

—Rebecca Walker

One of the great ironies of writing about generations—particularly when the topic is so contemporary—is that one inevitably finds one's own generation being replaced. In the years it has taken me to finish this project, I have watched the "new" generation of which I am a part become eclipsed by something even more current: the next generation of American youth, variably called Generation Y or the Millennial Generation.[2] Within feminism, a similar replacement may soon be occurring. As one of my students recently reported back from the Feminist Majority's "Feminist Expo," there is now talk of a "fourth wave" of feminism among women in their late teens and early twenties. While admittedly isolated, pronouncements of a feminist "fourth wave" make me recall Rosi Braidotti's comment that "[i]t's strange how quickly one ages within feminism." As she continues, "[H]ere I am: barely 40, still sexually active but having to represent the 'older generation'—how did this happen?"[3]

The inevitability of such generational replacement should be a caution. The mother-daughter trope is an impoverished model of generational relations, one that allows for only two possible points of identification: mother or daughter. Within the familial structure used to describe feminist generations, it is inevitable, then, that those who are now feminism's daughters will, over time, become its mothers—and given the negative image associated with such mothers, who would want such a fate?

While feminism's familial language is, in fact, figurative, the metaphors we use to describe feminism have real effects in the world and in the ways that feminists develop intergenerational relationships and participate in intergenerational dialogue. What does it mean, for example, for "younger" feminists to view "older" feminists—whether they are their friends, lovers, teachers, colleagues, or adversaries—as mothers? When we remain stuck in feminism's imagined family, we lose sight of the myriad relations feminists have with one another as well as the possibility of cross-generational identification and similarities. As Susan Fraiman argues, there "is a difference less between seventies and nineties *feminists* than between seventies and nineties *feminisms*—a difference that finds mothers and daughters alike more apt in the nineties to boot up than sit in and that calls for ideological rather than oedipal diagnosis."[4] The focus on generational differences has also limited our ability to recognize the various ideological and political differences among and between feminists and feminisms, reducing such differences to the singular difference of age and generation. "Attributing our differences to generation rather than to politics," writes Lisa Marie Hogeland, "sets us firmly into psychologized thinking, and into versions of mother/daughter relations—somehow, we are never sisters who might have things to teach each other across our differences and despite our rivalries."[5]

In arguing against the dominant matrophor used to describe "the persistent nature of maternal metaphors in feminism," some feminists have maintained that we should return to the language of sisterhood as "an alternative to the divisive mother-daughter model."[6] While itself quite reductive, the sororal metaphor at least allows for a language of collectivity, something not seen in much of the "daughter" discourse examined here. Yet while I sympathize with the desire to break out of the mother-daughter dyad, I am not so optimistic that a return to sisterhood will solve the problem. This trope has its own troubled history, the least of which is its inability to recognize differences among women. While the mother-daughter dyad seems hopelessly fixated on the notion of difference—"I'm not like you"—the sisterhood trope seems to offer us the opposite problem—"We're the same."

As feminism has been made into a mother, the qualities that have been attributed to this maternal figure are disturbing, to say the least. While "younger" feminists may wish to depict feminists of the past as "dated and dowdy" in order to represent themselves as new and cutting-edge, such representations of "mother feminism" invariably conform to a conservative image of motherhood: one where mothers are moralistic, asexual prudes. For younger feminists who may not be mothers themselves, representing the maternal in these terms may seem an effective way to make feminism the repository of all that is to be rebelled against.[7] Ultimately, however, this representation only serves to maintain a conservative and ideologically suspect view of motherhood, one we should resist.

Finally, and potentially most troubling, the ubiquitous focus in recent feminist discourse on generational differences between women has ensured that much energy has gone into internal conflicts within feminism rather than external battles against sexism, racism, and homophobia, among other pressing concerns. As such, the focus on feminism's mother-daughter duo has meant that the father, as it were, has dropped out of the picture altogether.[8] As Judith Roof writes:

> Seeing relationships among feminists as generational means adopting the metaphor of the patriarchal family in the throes of its illusory battle against mortality. Our enticement by this model with its chimera of order and all-too-real Oedipal drama focuses blame, energies, and even the dilemma of women's relationships in the wrong place: among women themselves.[9]

Conflict within feminism, even when posited as generational, should not be avoided. Some of feminism's current struggles may very well be among women themselves and thus vitally necessary for feminists to examine in more detail. Unlike Roof, then, I do not think the solution to our current generational impasse is to sidestep the problem of generations in order to move on. Rather, we must continue to examine our generational differences and alliances in order to understand their psychological power for feminists.[10] Where I am in agreement with Roof, however, is that the attention on generational differences has dramatically shifted feminism's focus from external enemies to internal ones. If feminism is indeed like a family, it would be wise of us not to forget its absent father.

Notes

Introduction

1. B. Ruby Rich, "Feminism and Sexuality in the 1980s," *Feminist Studies* 12, no. 3 (Fall 1986): 529. Wisely anticipating what was to become a dominant trope within the next decade, Rich's essay predates the contemporary discussion of feminist "mothers" and "daughters" discussed here.

2. As Susan Fraiman has characterized this ubiquitous mother-daughter feud: "'Why are they attacking me? Where is their gratitude?' the mothers ask. 'Why won't they listen to us? Why can't they see our separateness?' the daughters cry." Fraiman, "Feminism Today: Mothers, Daughters, Emerging Sisters," *American Literary History* 11, no. 3 (Fall 1999): 527.

3. Rebecca Dakin Quinn, "An Open Letter to Institutional Mothers," in *Generations: Academic Feminists in Dialogue*, ed. Devoney Looser and Ann Kaplan (Minneapolis: University of Minnesota Press, 1997), 179.

4. Quinn, "An Open Letter to Institutional Mothers," 179.

5. Texts from the 1990s, in chronological order, that describe feminism in generational terms include (but are certainly not limited to) Barbara Christian, Ann duCille, Sharon Marcus, Elaine Marks, Nancy K. Miller, Sylvia Schafer, and Joan W. Scott, "Conference Call," *differences* 2, no. 3 (1990): 52–108; Jane Gallop, Marianne Hirsch, and Nancy K. Miller, "Criticizing Feminist Criticism," in *Conflicts in Feminism*, ed. Marianne Hirsch and Evelyn Fox Keller (New York: Routledge, 1990), 349–369; Renate D. Klein, "Passion and Politics in Women's Studies in the Nineties," *Women's Studies International Forum* 14, no. 3 (1991): 125–134; Nancy K. Miller, "Decades," *South Atlantic Quarterly* 91, no. 1 (Winter 1992): 65–86; Madelon Sprengnether, "Generational Differences: Reliving Mother-Daughter Conflicts," in *Changing Subjects: The Making of Feminist Literary Theory*, ed. Gayle Greene and Coppélia Kahn (New York: Routledge, 1993), 201–208; Rosi Braidotti, "Generations of Feminists, or, Is There Life after Post-Modernism?" *Found Object* 16 (1995): 55–62; Catharine R. Stimpson, "Women's Studies and Its Discontents," *Dissent* 42 (Winter 1996): 67–75; Devoney Looser and Ann Kaplan, eds., *Generations: Academic Feminists in Dialogue* (Minneapolis: University of Minnesota Press, 1997); Anna Bondoc and Meg Daly, eds., *Letters of Intent: Women Cross the Generations to Talk about Family, Work, Sex, Love and the Future of Feminism* (New York: Simon & Schuster, 1999); and Fraiman, "Feminism Today."

6. Conferences on third-wave feminism and/or generational relationships within feminism that I've attended over the last few years include Third Wave Feminism, University of Exeter, United Kingdom, July 2002; Third Wave Feminism, Purdue University, April 2002; Women @ 2K: Pasts, Presents, Futures, Tulane University, March 1999; Generations of Change, Valdosta State University, March 1999; and, what I believe was the first academic conference on the subject, Feminist Generations, Bowling Green State University, February 1996. There have also been numerous panels

and papers given on these subjects at National Women's Studies Association (NWSA) conferences over the last decade, as well as panels and papers at a wide range of discipline-specific conferences.

7. See Marilyn Jacoby Boxer, *When Women Ask the Questions: Creating Women's Studies in America* (Baltimore: Johns Hopkins University Press, 1998); Florence Howe, ed., *The Politics of Women's Studies: Testimony from 30 Founding Mothers* (New York: The Feminist Press, 2000); Ellen Messer-Davidow, *Disciplining Feminism: From Social Activism to Academic Discourse* (Durham, N.C.: Duke University Press, 2002); Joan Wallach Scott, ed., *differences: A Journal of Feminist Cultural Studies* 9, no. 3 (1997), special issue: *Women's Studies on the Edge;* The Social Justice Group at the Center for Advanced Feminist Studies, University of Minnesota, ed., *Is Academic Feminism Dead? Theory in Practice* (New York: New York University Press, 2000); and Robyn Wiegman, ed., *Women's Studies on Its Own: A Next Wave Reader in Institutional Change* (Durham, N.C.: Duke University Press, 2002). See also *Women's Studies Quarterly* 25, nos. 1 and 2 (Spring/Summer 1997), special issue: *Looking Back, Moving Forward: 25 Years of Women's Studies History.*

8. Recent second-wave memoirs include (but are by no means limited to): Susan Brownmiller, *In Our Time: Memoir of a Revolution* (New York: The Dial Press, 1999); Roxanne Dunbar-Ortiz, *Outlaw Woman: A Memoir of the War Years, 1960–1975* (San Francisco: City Lights, 2002); Rachel Blau DuPlessis and Ann Snitow, eds., *The Feminist Memoir Project: Voices from Women's Liberation* (New York: Three Rivers Press, 1998); Andrea Dworkin, *Heartbreak: The Political Memoir of a Feminist Militant* (New York: Basic Books, 2001); Jane Gallop, *Feminist Accused of Sexual Harassment* (Durham, N.C.: Duke University Press, 1997); bell hooks, *Wounds of Passion: A Writing Life* (New York: Henry Holt, 1997); Gerda Lerner, *Fireweed: A Political Autobiography* (Philadelphia: Temple University Press, 2002); and Robin Morgan, *Saturday's Child: A Memoir* (New York: W.W. Norton & Company, 2001).

9. Although not explicitly discussed here, the question of generations within academe—particularly the relationship between "junior" and "senior" feminist scholars—has also become an increasingly important one within feminism over the last decade. See Christian et al., "Conference Call"; Gallop, Hirsch, and Miller, "Criticizing Feminist Criticism"; Sprengnether, "Generational Differences"; Looser and Kaplan, eds., *Generations.*

10. For more on the dyadic nature of generations, see Kathleen Woodward, "Inventing Generational Models: Psychoanalysis, Feminism, Literature," in *Figuring Age: Women, Bodies, Generations,* ed. Kathleen Woodward (Bloomington: Indiana University Press, 1999), 149–168.

11. Mary Russo, "Aging and the Scandal of Anachronism," in Woodward, ed., *Figuring Age,* 24.

12. Karl Mannheim, "The Problem of Generations," in *Essays on the Sociology of Knowledge,* ed. Paul Kecskemeti (New York: Oxford University Press, 1952), 278, 290.

13. According to Judith Roof, this is precisely why we should avoid speaking of feminism in generational terms. See Roof, "Generational Difficulties; or, the Fear of a Barren History," in Looser and Kaplan, eds., *Generations,* 69–87. See also Lisa Marie Hogeland, "Against Generational Thinking, or, Some Things that 'Third Wave' Feminism Isn't," *Women's Studies in Communication* 24, no. 1 (Spring 2001): 107–121.

14. According to the *American Heritage Dictionary of the English Language* (3rd ed.), the cutoff birthdate for Generation X is 1972; however, most other sources place this date around 1981. See, for example, Neil Howe and William Strauss, "The New Generation Gap," *Atlantic Monthly*, December 1992, 67–89. The term "Generation X" is attributed to Douglas Coupland, who coined the term in his novel *Generation X: Tales for an Accelerated Culture* (New York: St. Martin's Press, 1992). For more on Generation X, see Eric Liu, ed., *Next: Young American Writers on the New Generation* (New York: W.W. Norton & Company, 1994).

15. Arlie Russell Hochschild, "Coming of Age, Seeking an Identity," *New York Times*, March 8, 2000, D1.

16. Mannheim, "The Problem of Generations," 281.

17. See Gallop et al., "Criticizing Feminist Criticism"; and Miller, "Decades."

18. For more on how generations function as markets within a capitalist economy, see Dana Heller, "The Anxiety of Affluence: Movements, Markets, and Lesbian Feminist Generation(s)," in Looser and Kaplan, eds., *Generations*, 309–326.

19. For more on aging and ageism within feminism, see Braidotti, "Generations of Feminists"; Baba Copper, *Over the Hill: Reflections on Ageism between Women* (Freedom, Calif.: Crossing Press, 1988); Mary Wilson Carpenter, "Female Grotesques in Academia: Ageism, Antifeminism, and Feminists on the Faculty," in *Antifeminism in the Academy*, ed. Vèvè Clark, Shirley Nelson Garner, Margaret Higonnet, and Ketu H. Katrak (New York: Routledge, 1996), 141–165; Devoney Looser, "Introduction 2: Gen X Feminists? Youthism, Careerism, and the Third Wave," in Looser and Kaplan, eds., *Generations*, 31–54; E. Ann Kaplan, "Introduction 2: Feminism, Aging, and Changing Paradigms," in Looser and Kaplan, eds., *Generations*, 13–29; E. Ann Kaplan and Devoney Looser, "Introduction 1: An Exchange," in Looser and Kaplan, eds., *Generations*, 1–12; Barbara Macdonald with Cynthia Rich, *Look Me in the Eye: Old Women, Aging, and Ageism* (San Francisco: Spinsters, Ink, 1983); Russo, "Aging and the Scandal of Anachronism"; and Woodward, "Inventing Generational Models."

20. Joan Scott et al., "Conference Call," 83. This point is echoed by Lisa Marie Hogeland when she writes, "The rhetoric of generational differences in feminism works to mask real political differences—fundamental differences in our visions of feminism's task and accomplishments." Hogeland, "Against Generational Thinking," 107.

21. Hogeland, "Against Generational Thinking," 110.

22. Mannheim, "The Problem of Generations," 292.

23. This also opens up the possibility that one can identify with a generation other than the one placed into by date of birth. This point has been addressed by both second- and third-wave writers. Rita Alfonso reminds us, "There are women of my age group who identify with the struggles of the second wave of feminists in a straightforward manner, and there are women of the baby boomer generation who are acutely aware of the experiences and issues informing a third wave of feminism." Rita Alfonso in Alfonso and Jo Trigilio, "Surfing the Third Wave: A Dialogue between Two Third Wave Feminists," *Hypatia: A Journal of Feminist Philosophy* 12, no. 3 (Summer 1997): 9.

24. A book that makes feminism a "mother" in just such a way is Rose L. Glickman, *Daughters of Feminists* (New York: St. Martin's Press, 1993). See also Christina Looper Baker and Christina Baker Kline, eds., *The Conversation Begins: Mothers and Daughters Talk about Living Feminism* (New York: Bantam Books, 1996); Louise D'Arcens, "Mothers, Daughters, Sisters," in *Talking Up: Young Women's Take on*

Feminism, ed. Rosamund Else-Mitchell and Naomi Flutter (North Melbourne, Australia: Spinifex Press, 1998), 103–116; Andrea O'Reilly and Sharon Abbey, eds., *Mothers and Daughters: Connection, Empowerment, and Transformation* (Boston: Rowman & Littlefield Publishers, 2000).

25. Diane Fuss, *Identification Papers* (New York: Routledge, 1995), 7. For more on the concept of disidentification, although from a boy's point of view, see Ralph R. Greenson, "Dis-Identifying from Mother: Its Special Importance for the Boy," *International Journal of Psychoanalysis* 49 (1968): 370–374.

26. Ann Snitow, "A Gender Diary," in Hirsch and Fox Keller, eds., *Conflicts in Feminism,* 32. The next line of this passage is "Black women whose ties to their mothers were more often a mutual struggle for survival rarely shared this particular emotion." For more on how feminism allowed second-wave feminists to escape their mothers' fate, see many of the essays in DuPlessis and Snitow, eds., *The Feminist Memoir Project.*

27. Marianne Hirsch, *The Mother/Daughter Plot: Narrative, Psychoanalysis, Feminism* (Bloomington: Indiana University Press, 1989), 11.

28. Phyllis Chesler, *Letters to a Young Feminist* (New York: Four Walls Eight Windows, 1997), 1.

29. Chesler's instruction might point toward what Diane Elam has called the "dutiful daughter complex" in which "[d]aughters are not allowed to invent new ways of thinking and doing feminism for themselves; feminist politics should take the same shape that it always has." Elam, "Sisters Are Doing It to Themselves," in Looser and Kaplan, eds., *Generations,* 62.

30. Looser, "Introduction 2," 34.

31. As Jennifer Baumgardner and Amy Richards emphatically declare to second-wave feminists, "'You're not our mothers.' We want to reprieve you from your mother guilt." Baumgardner and Richards, *Manifesta: Young Women, Feminism, and the Future* (New York: Farrar, Straus and Giroux, 2000), 233.

32. Chesler, *Letters to a Young Feminist,* 55. In a recently published letter to her former research assistant, Chesler writes, "You want nurturing from older feminists, most of whom have, at least psychologically, themselves committed matricide. Like the mythic Electra, who helped kill her mother Clytemnestra, they may be especially wary of daughters and daughter-figures as potentially matricidal." Chesler in Liza Featherstone and Phyllis Chesler, "Why Is There So Much Tension between Feminist Bosses and Their Female Assistants?" in Bondoc and Daly, eds., *Letters of Intent,* 119.

33. Naomi Wolf, *The Beauty Myth: How Images of Beauty Are Used against Women* (New York: William Morrow and Company, 1991), 281.

34. The phrase "next generation" has been used by many commentators to describe the generation of young women who were in their twenties and thirties in the 1990s. See, for example, Barbara Findlen, *Listen Up: Voices from the Next Feminist Generation* (Seattle: Seal Press, 1995).

35. Rene Denfeld, *The New Victorians: A Young Woman's Challenge to the Old Feminist Order* (New York: Warner Books, 1995), 263. As Sara Evans remarks, third-wavers "never experienced feminism as a sisterhood of sameness. Indeed they stumbled over saying 'we.'" Evans, *Tidal Wave: How Women Changed America at Century's End* (New York: The Free Press, 2003), 230.

36. As Katha Pollitt recently asked, "When did sisterhood become mother-daugh-

terhood?" Pollitt in Emily Gordon and Katha Pollitt, "Does Your Generation Resent Up-and-Coming Young Women?" in Bondoc and Daly, eds., *Letters of Intent*, 31.

37. Hirsch, *The Mother/Daughter Plot*, 136.

38. Adrienne Rich, *Of Woman Born: Motherhood as Experience and Institution* (New York: W.W. Norton & Company, 1976), 236, 235, emphasis in original. For more on the concept of matrophobia, see Hirsch, *The Mother/Daughter Plot*.

39. Fraiman, "Feminism Today," 527.

40. Braidotti, "Generations of Feminists," 56.

41. Writing in 1990, Joan W. Scott argues: "Why are we talking about generations at a time when other divisions among feminists seem (at least to me) so much more apparent, so much more troubling, and so much more interesting?" Scott et al., "Conference Call," 83. See also Hogeland, "Against Generational Thinking"; and Roof, "Generational Difficulties."

42. Elam, "Sisters Are Doing It to Themselves," 58.

43. Looser, "Introduction 2," 33, emphasis in original. Jacquelyn N. Zita reiterates the necessity of this discussion: "To me the most pressing task for the feminisms of our time, both inside and outside academe, is this cross-generational moment: a passage of legacy, wisdom, memory, and yet unanswered questions and unresolved conflicts belonging to political and intellectual struggles that are much larger than life and much too important to leave behind without dialogue across the generations." Zita, "Third Wave Feminisms: An Introduction," *Hypatia: A Journal of Feminist Philosophy* 12, no. 3 (Summer 1997): 1.

44. As DuPlessis and Snitow write in their introduction to *The Feminist Memoir Project:* "If we insist on a family metaphor for our politics, then feminism becomes a mother who did not give enough, and whose shortcomings and slowdowns we regard with contempt. But when we criticize the family metaphor and go beyond that familiar, familial rage, feminism's strengths and weaknesses become a collective and political responsibility" (20).

45. Katie King, "Lesbianism as Feminism's Magical Sign," in King, *Theory in Its Feminist Travels: Conversations in U.S. Women's Movements* (Bloomington: Indiana University Press, 1994), 124.

46. Elam, "Sisters Are Doing It to Themselves," 67.

1. Daughterhood Is Powerful

1. I am borrowing this phrase from Jane Gallop's *Around 1981*, in which she describes the importance of decades in defining feminist generational structures. Gallop, *Around 1981: Academic Feminist Literary Theory* (New York: Routledge, 1992).

2. I discuss the role of the Thomas hearings in more detail in chapter 5. For more on the effects of the Thomas confirmation hearings on the development of third-wave feminism, see Naomi Wolf, *Fire with Fire: The New Female Power and How It Will Change the 21st Century* (New York: Random House, 1993), 5–6; and Catherine M. Orr, "Charting the Current of the Third Wave," *Hypatia: A Journal of Feminist Philosophy* 12, no. 3 (Summer 1997): 30.

3. Of course, many feminist hopes about Bill Clinton were dashed by the sex scandals that seemed to dog him throughout his two terms in office. In particular, his relationship with former White House intern and employee Monica Lewinsky

generated a lot of debate among feminists. Katie Roiphe, one of the third-wave feminist writers discussed at length in this chapter, wrote a *New York Times* op-ed piece about Lewinsky in which she argues that it is a mistake to view the former White House intern as an innocent victim. See Roiphe, "Monica Lewinsky, Career Woman," *New York Times*, September 15, 1998, A27.

4. Susan Faludi, *Backlash: The Undeclared War against American Women* (New York: Crown Publishers, 1991); Naomi Wolf, *The Beauty Myth: How Images of Beauty Are Used against Women* (New York: William Morrow and Company, 1991). According to *Publisher's Weekly*, *Backlash* was a top bestseller during 1991–1992. Two other popular feminist books published in 1991 were Paula Kamen's study of young women's attitudes about feminism, *Feminist Fatale: Voices from the "Twentysomething" Generation Explore the Future of the "Women's Movement"* (New York: Donald I. Fine, 1991), and the anthology *Angry Women*, ed. Andrea Juno and V. Vale (San Francisco: Re/Search Publications, 1991).

5. Wolf, *Fire with Fire*, xxv.

6. *Ms.* went through a second revamping when it ceased publication for several months at the end of 1998. The magazine returned in May 1999 with a new publisher, an all-feminist consortium led by Gloria Steinem. It has since gone through another transition; at the end of 2001, the Feminist Majority Foundation assumed ownership of *Ms.* and moved its base of operation from New York to the Foundation's offices in Los Angeles and Arlington, Virginia.

7. Robin Morgan, "Ms. Lives!" *Ms.*, July/August 1990, 1. For more on the way in which advertisers influenced the depoliticization of *Ms.*'s feminist content, see Gloria Steinem, "Sex, Lies and Advertising," *Ms.*, July/August 1990, 18–28.

8. To give but one example of this tendency to proclaim feminism's death, Erica Jong has pointed out that *Time* has claimed the death of feminism at least 119 times since 1969. Quoted in Jennifer Baumgardner and Amy Richards, *Manifesta: Young Women, Feminism, and the Future* (New York: Farrar, Straus and Giroux, 2000), 93.

9. Susan Bolotin, "Views from the Postfeminist Generation," *New York Times Magazine*, October 17, 1982, 29+. In this piece one can see signs of a generational gap within feminism that seems to foreshadow later such gaps but one that has since become obliterated by the almost-exclusive focus on the second and third waves. The ubiquity of the term "post-feminism" in popular discourse about feminism during the 1980s is also discussed by Deborah Rosenfelt and Judith Stacey in "Second Thoughts on the Second Wave," *Feminist Studies* 13, no. 2 (Summer 1987): 341. See also Tania Modleski, *Feminism without Women: Culture and Criticism in a "Postfeminist" Age* (New York: Routledge, 1991).

10. For more on the ebbs and flows of feminism and the women's movement in the twentieth century, see Leila J. Rupp and Verta Taylor, *Survival in the Doldrums: The American Women's Rights Movement, 1945 to the 1960s* (Oxford: Oxford University Press, 1987); and Verta Taylor, "Social Movement Continuity: The Women's Movement in Abeyance," *American Sociological Review* 54 (October 1989): 761–775.

11. Cited in Nancy F. Cott, *The Grounding of Modern Feminism* (New Haven, Conn.: Yale University Press, 1987), 282.

12. Cott, *The Grounding of Modern Feminism*, 281. As witnessed in countless national opinion polls, Cott's description of female individualism and its limits can

easily be applied to the attitudes of many young women—feminist and non-feminist alike—who came of age in the 1980s and 1990s.

13. As Nancy Whittier writes, the generation after the second wave "came of age in an era that was simultaneously more hostile to feminism and less restrictive of women." Whittier, *Feminist Generations: The Persistence of the Radical Women's Movement* (Philadelphia: Temple University Press, 1995), 3.

14. Rosenfelt and Stacey, "Second Thoughts on the Second Wave," 349.

15. Bolotin, "Views from the Postfeminist Generation," 115, emphasis added.

16. For more on the conservative politics of young women during the Reagan-Bush years, see Kamen, *Feminist Fatale*, 117–118.

17. A number of articles during the early 1990s attempted to characterize this "new generation" of young women and their relationship to feminism. See Karen Avenoso, "Feminism's Newest Foot Soldiers," *Elle*, March 1993, 114–118; Phoebe Hoban, "Big WAC Attack," *New York*, August 3, 1992, 30–35; bell hooks, Gloria Steinem, Urvashi Vaid, and Naomi Wolf, "Let's Get Real about Feminism: The Backlash, the Myths, the Movement," *Ms.*, September/October 1993, 34–43; Anna Seaton Huntington, "These Women Do Not Fear the Twenty-First Century," *Harper's Bazaar*, September 1995, 384–389; Wendy Kaminer, "Feminism's Third Wave: What Do Young Women Want?" *New York Times Book Review*, June 4, 1995, 3+; Katherine Pushkar, "Pro Feminism," *Village Voice*, October 4, 1994, 14; Joannie M. Schrof, "Feminism's Daughters," *U.S. News and World Report*, September 27, 1993, 6+; and "Young Feminists Speak for Themselves," *Ms.*, March/April 1991, 28–34. For an article from the end of the 1990s on the same subject, see Naomi Wolf, "The Future Is Ours to Lose," *New York Times Magazine*, May 16, 1999, 134+. For more on young women and feminism, see Jean O'Barr and Mary Wyer, eds., *Engaging Feminism: Students Speak Up and Speak Out* (Charlottesville: University Press of Virginia, 1992).

18. An article which highlights self-defined young feminist women and men in the early 1980s, including a young Naomi Wolf, is Diane Salvatore et al., "Young Feminists Speak for Themselves," *Ms.*, April 1983, 43+.

19. A 1998 *Time* poll found that from 1989 to 1998, the number of women calling themselves feminists dropped from approximately 33 percent to 26 percent. See Ginia Bellafante, "Feminism: It's All about Me!" *Time*, June 29, 1998, 58. Similarly, a CNN poll found that the percentage of self-identified feminists dropped from 31 percent of women in 1992 to only 20 percent of women in 1999. See Kathleen Koch, "Feminists Meet to Discuss Future of the Movement," April 2, 2000, available online at http://www.cnn.com/2000/US/04/01/feminist.majority.

20. Faludi, *Backlash*, x–xi. The argument that feminism failed women—and that various branches of feminism led to the downfall of a "true" women's movement focused on women's equality—is also the position put forward by two writers who gained notoriety in the 1990s: Camille Paglia and Christina Hoff Sommers. In terms of their generational location, these writers are not part of the group of feminists I examine here; however, the feminism advocated by them, as well as the alliances they have made with third-wavers such as Katie Roiphe, make them important figures in the debates within feminism during this period. See Camille Paglia, *Vamps and Tramps: New Essays* (New York: Vintage Books, 1994); and Christina Hoff Sommers, *Who Stole Feminism? How Women Have Betrayed Women* (New York: Touchstone Books, 1994).

For a critique of Paglia and her "anti-feminist feminism," see Ruby B. Rich, "Top Girl," *Village Voice*, October 8, 1991, 29–33. For critiques of Sommers, see Nina Auerbach, "Sisterhood Is Fractious," *New York Times Book Review*, June 12, 1994, 13; and *Democratic Culture* 3, no. 4 (Fall 1994), special issue: *Symposium on* Who Stole Feminism? How Women Have Betrayed Women *by Christina Hoff Sommers*. Two books written by academic feminists also made similar arguments about the state of contemporary feminism and the rise of "victimism": see Elizabeth Fox-Genovese, *"Feminism Is Not the Story of My Life": How Today's Feminist Elite Has Lost Touch with the Real Concerns of Women* (New York: Anchor Books, 1996); and Daphne Patai and Noretta Koertge, *Professing Feminism: Cautionary Tales from the Strange World of Women's Studies* (New York: Basic Books, 1994). Three late-1990s books by women the same age as the third-wavers discussed in this chapter also argue that feminism has failed women: Danielle Crittenden, *What Our Mothers Didn't Tell Us: Why Happiness Eludes the Modern Woman* (New York: Simon & Schuster, 1999); Karen Lehrman, *The Lipstick Proviso: Women, Sex and Power in the Real World* (New York: Anchor Books, 1997); and Wendy Shalit, *A Return to Modesty: Discovering the Lost Virtue* (New York: Simon & Schuster, 1999).

21. See for example, Nina J. Easton, "'I'm not a feminist, but . . .': Can the Women's Movement March into the Mainstream?" *Los Angeles Times Magazine*, February 2, 1992, 12–16; Nancy Gibbs, "The War against Feminism," *Time*, March 9, 1992, 50–56; Vivian Gornick, "Who Says We Haven't Made a Revolution? A Feminist Takes Stock," *New York Times Magazine*, April 15, 1990, 24+; Germaine Greer, "The Backlash Myth," *New Republic*, October 5, 1992, 20–22; Jane Gross, "Does She Speak for Today's Women?" *New York Times Magazine*, March 1, 1992, 17+; Wendy Kaminer, "Feminism's Identity Crisis," *The Atlantic*, October 1993, 51–68; Karen Lehrman, "Off Course," *Mother Jones*, September/October 1993, 45+; John Leo, "The Trouble with Feminism," *U.S. News and World Report*, February 10, 1992, 19; Daphne Patai, "The Struggle for Feminist Purity Threatens the Goals of Feminism," *Chronicle of Higher Education*, February 5, 1992, B1+; and Laura Shapiro, "Sisterhood Was Powerful," *Newsweek*, June 20, 1994, 68+. In more-academic journals, this terrain was covered by articles such as Johanna Brenner, "The Best of Times, The Worst of Times: U.S. Feminism Today," *New Left Review* 200 (July/August 1993): 101–159; Elizabeth Fox-Genovese and Nancy Hewitt, "Rethinking Feminism," *Tikkun*, June 1992, 29+; and Renate D. Klein, "Passion and Politics in Women's Studies in the Nineties," *Women's Studies International Forum* 14, no. 3 (1991): 125–134. See previous note 17 for articles that specifically address young women's relationships to feminism during the early to mid-1990s.

22. See for example, Sarah Crichton, "Sexual Correctness: Has It Gone Too Far?" *Newsweek*, October 25, 1993, 52–56. See also Adele M. Stan's edited collection, which contains many of the key essays surrounding this debate: *Debating Sexual Correctness: Pornography, Sexual Harassment, Date Rape, and the Politics of Sexual Equality* (New York: Delta Books, 1995).

23. For more on this history, see Lisa Duggan and Nan D. Hunter, *Sex Wars: Sexual Dissent and Political Culture* (New York: Routledge, 1995); B. Ruby Rich, "Feminism and Sexuality in the 1980s," *Feminist Studies* 12, no. 3 (Fall 1986): 525–561; Lynne Segal, *Straight Sex: Rethinking the Politics of Pleasure* (Berkeley: University of California Press, 1994); Carole S. Vance, "Pleasure and Danger: Toward a Politics of Sexuality," in *Pleasure and Danger: Exploring Female Sexuality*, ed. Carole S. Vance

(Boston: Routledge and Kegan Paul, 1985), 1–27; and Ellen Willis, "Toward a Feminist Sexual Revolution," *Social Text* 2, no. 3 (Fall 1982): 3–21.

24. This is a major claim in Susan Faludi's "I'm Not a Feminist but I Play One on TV," *Ms.*, March/April 1995, 30–49. For two examples from the popular press which prove Faludi's point regarding the often-dismissive representation of conflicts between feminists, see Barbara Brotman, "Sibling Rivalry," *Chicago Tribune*, July 17, 1994, sec. 6, 1+; and Anthony Flint, "New Breed of Feminist Challenges Old Guard," *Boston Globe*, May 29, 1994, 1+.

25. Rebecca Walker, "Becoming the Third Wave," *Ms.*, January/February 1992, 39–41; "Doing the Third Wave," *Ms.* (September/October 1992), 87. According to information found on the Third Wave Foundation's website, it is "the only organization created by and for young women" (http://www.thirdwavefoundation.org). The Third Wave Foundation's first major event was to register voters in poor communities of color before the 1992 elections; the group named this event "Freedom Ride 1992," a name which pays homage to the 1960s civil rights movement. See also Meri Nana-Ama Danquah, "Keeping the Third Wave Afloat," *Los Angeles Times*, December 6, 1995, E1.

26. Rosenfelt and Stacey, "Second Thoughts on the Second Wave," 359. This 1987 article is the first use of the term "third wave" I have come across in my research.

27. Wolf, *The Beauty Myth*, 276. Around the same time as Wolf and Walker, Laurie Ouellette also uses the term in her "Building the Third Wave: Reflections of a Young Feminist," *On the Issues* 14 (Fall 1992): 9+.

28. Leslie Heywood and Jennifer Drake, "Introduction," in *Third Wave Agenda: Being Feminist, Doing Feminism*, ed. Leslie Heywood and Jennifer Drake (Minneapolis: University of Minnesota Press, 1997), 1.

29. Lisa Albrecht, e-mail to the author, January 10, 2000.

30. For texts that refer to *The Third Wave: Feminist Perspectives on Racism* in this manner, see Rory Dicker and Alison Piepmeier, "Introduction," in *Catching a Wave: Reclaiming Feminism for the 21st Century*, ed. Rory Dicker and Alison Piepmeier (Boston: Northeastern University Press, 2003), 7–8; Heywood and Drake, "Introduction," 1; Orr, "Charting the Current of the Third Wave," 30; Kayann Short, "Coming to the Table: The Differential Politics of *This Bridge Called My Back*," *Genders* 20 (1994): 14–16; and Kimberly Springer, "Third Wave Black Feminism?" *Signs: Journal of Women in Culture and Society* 27, no. 4 (Summer 2002): 1063.

31. While *The Third Wave: Feminist Perspectives on Racism* never went into print, the editors of this collection ultimately did publish a text remarkably similar to the one they had envisioned: *Sing, Whisper, Shout, Pray! Feminist Visions for a Just World*, ed. Jacqui M. Alexander, Lisa Albrecht, Sharon Day, and Mab Segrest (Fort Bragg, Calif.: EdgeWork Books, 2003). By this text's publication date in 2003, the term "third wave" had apparently become completely identified with a generational division within feminism, and the new collection has lost its editors' earlier formulation of this term.

32. The term "second wave" was first coined by Marsha Weinman Lear in "The Second Feminist Wave," *New York Times Magazine*, March 10, 1968, 24+.

33. For more on the metaphor of the wave as it has been used within feminist discourse, see Cathryn Bailey, "Making Waves and Drawing Lines: The Politics of Defining the Vicissitudes of Feminism," *Hypatia: A Journal of Feminist Philosophy* 12, no. 3 (Summer 1997): 17–28; Anita Harris, "Not Waving or Drowning: Young Women, Feminism, and the Limits of the Next Wave Debate," *Outskirts: Feminisms along the*

Edge 8 (May 2001), available online at http://www.chloe.uwa.edu.au/outskirts/archive/VOL8/article4.html (accessed June 3, 2003); and Elizabeth Sarah, "Towards a Reassessment of Feminist History," *Women's Studies International Forum* 6 (1982): 519–523.

34. Walker, "Becoming the Third Wave," 41.

35. Rebecca Walker, "Being Real: An Introduction," in *To Be Real: Telling the Truth and Changing the Face of Feminism,* ed. Rebecca Walker (New York: Anchor Books, 1995), xxxiii.

36. Walker's authority in proclaiming a new feminism may be attributed to the fact that she is the daughter of a celebrated second-wave feminist, something I discuss in more detail in chapter 5.

37. Wolf, *The Beauty Myth,* 281.

38. In fact, I would argue that while *The Beauty Myth* is a key text in the resurgence of popular feminism that I am discussing here, this text is far more aligned with second-wave feminism than third, both in the feminism it advocates and in its relationship to second-wave feminism and feminists. Wolf would dramatically shift gears with *Fire with Fire.*

39. I discuss Walker's relationship to her mother, Alice, in more detail in chapter 5. For more on the relationship between Wolf and her mother, see Deborah Wolf, "A Mother's Story" and Naomi Wolf, "A Daughter's Story," in *The Conversation Begins: Mothers and Daughters Talk about Living Feminism,* ed. Christina Looper Baker and Christina Baker Kline (New York: Bantam Books, 1996), 142–147 and 148–155.

40. Wolf says of the 1980s: "I grew up in the heart of the second wave, when exciting things were happening, but as a young woman in the 1980s I saw that feminism for my generation was dead." Wolf, "A Daughter's Story," 152.

41. For the 1994 paperback edition, Wolf's subtitle was slightly altered to *The New Female Power and How to Use It*—a change that, in my opinion, is fitting, given the self-help nature of the book. Subsequent references are to the paperback edition.

42. "Power" and "victim" feminism are terms which are used almost exclusively by those advocating "power feminism" in order to criticize so-called victim feminism.

43. See Martha Duffy, "Tremors of Genderquake," *Time,* December 27, 1993, 76–78; Maggie Gallagher, "Party Girl," *National Review,* November 29, 1993, 66–67; Lesley Hazleton, "Power Politics," *Women's Review of Books,* February 1994, 1–4; bell hooks, "Dissident Heat: Fire with Fire," in hooks, *Outlaw Culture: Resisting Representations* (New York: Routledge, 1994), 91–100; "Who's Afraid of Naomi Wolf?" *The Economist,* January 22, 1994, 95–96. For an article on Wolf and her bipartisan training center for future women leaders, see Jennifer Senior, "Decrying Wolf," *Mirabella,* February 2000, 84+.

44. Gallagher, "Party Girl," 66. Wolf's attempt to open the doors to feminism so that everyone may walk through them is, on its face, admirable. Rather than open the doors, however, she knocks them down. She argues for a feminism so devoid of politics that anyone—no matter how anti-gay, anti-choice, or racist—can claim it for herself, as long as she's for "power feminism." In *Catching a Wave,* Dicker and Piepmeier argue against the third-wave tendency to water down feminism in order to make it palpable: "We think that the third wave impulse to challenge certain perceptions of what feminism is or how it should be performed is valid, as is the impulse to make feminism as inviting as possible to a broad range of people. However, we contend that this invitation to feminism must be politically rigorous; rather than emptying feminism of its political

content, we must embrace feminism's potential to transform our lives and our world." Dicker and Piepmeier, "Introduction," 18.

45. Katie Roiphe, *The Morning After: Sex, Fear, and Feminism on Campus* (Boston: Little, Brown and Company, 1993). The title lost the words "on campus" for the 1994 paperback edition. Subsequent references are to the paperback edition.

46. Katie Roiphe, "Date Rape Hysteria," *New York Times*, November 20, 1991, A29; Katie Roiphe, "Date Rape's Other Victim," *New York Times Magazine*, June 13, 1993, 26+. For articles by Katie Roiphe after *The Morning After*, see "Making the Incest Scene," *Harper's*, November 1995, 68–71; "The Independent Woman (and Other Lies)," *Esquire*, February 1997, 84–87; "The End of Innocence," *Vogue*, January 1998, 38+; "A Grandmother's Biological Clock," *New York Times Magazine*, February 2, 1998, 80.

47. See Deborah A. Cohen, "An Intellectual Home," *Women's Review of Books*, February 1994, 16–17; Margaret Emery, "Feminism Under Fire," *Time*, September 20, 1993, 82–84; Stephanie Gutmann, "Unhand Us, Miss MacKinnon!" *National Review*, October 18, 1993, 66–68; bell hooks, "Katie Roiphe: A Little Feminist Excess Goes a Long Way," in hooks, *Outlaw Culture*, 101–108; Carol Iannone, "Sex and the Feminists," *Commentary* 96, no. 3 (September 1993): 51–54; Paula Kamen, "Acquaintance Rape: Revolution and Reaction," in *"Bad Girls"/"Good Girls": Women, Sex, and Power in the Nineties*, ed. Nan Bauer Maglin and Donna Perry (New Brunswick, N.J.: Rutgers University Press, 1996), 137–149; Paula Kamen, "Erasing Rape: Media Hype an Attack on Sexual-Assault Research," *Extra!* November/December 1993, 10–11; Wendy Kaminer, "What Is This Thing Called Rape?" *New York Times Book Review*, September 19, 1993, 1+; Felicia Kornbluh, "After *The Morning After*," *Women's Review of Books*, February 1994, 14–15; Devoney Looser, "This Feminism Which Is Not One," *The Minnesota Review* 11, no. 5 (Fall 1993/Spring 1994): 108–117; Laura Wright, "Anti-Feminism Generation X-Style," *The Minnesota Review* 11, no. 5 (Fall 1993/Spring 1994): 129–132; Elizabeth Kamarch Minnich, "Feminist Attacks on Feminisms: Patriarchy's Prodigal Daughters," *Feminist Studies* 24, no. 1 (Spring 1998): 159–175.

48. Kaminer, "What Is This Thing Called Rape?" Roiphe's mother, Anne Roiphe, is herself a well-known writer, and it has been suggested that much of the attention given to Roiphe was due to her mother's connections as much as to her book's controversial (and conservative support–winning) content. See Karen Angel, "A Bounty of Fruit Falls from the Literary Tree: Young Authors Profit from Their Last Names," *New York Times*, April 25, 2000, B1+. For more on Roiphe's publication history, see Baumgardner and Richards, *Manifesta*, 236–240.

49. Kaminer, "What Is This Thing Called Rape?" 1.

50. Iannone, "Sex and the Feminists," 51.

51. Carolyn Sorisio argues, "By refusing to name the feminist theorists she implicates or to analyze their ideas seriously, Roiphe creates an inaccurately monolithic portrayal of what is a very complex, dynamic, and contentious field." Sorisio, "A Tale of Two Feminisms: Power and Victimization in Contemporary Feminist Debate," in Heywood and Drake, eds., *Third Wave Agenda*, 140.

52. Roiphe, *The Morning After*, xxii.

53. Kaminer, "Feminism's Third Wave," 22.

54. For more on the anti–"victim feminism" of Wolf, Roiphe, and Denfeld, see Alyson M. Cole, "'There Are No Victims in This Class': On Female Suffering and Anti-'Victim Feminism,'" *NWSA Journal* 11, no. 1 (Spring 1999): 72–96; and Joan D. Mandle, "Sisterly Critics," *NWSA Journal* 11, no. 1 (Spring 1999): 97–109.

55. Heywood and Drake, "Introduction," 1. Joan Mandle furthers this point: "To label these critics as part of a backlash . . . is simply to dismiss them and refuse to engage in a critical examination of their views of feminism. This troubles me, particularly because some of their arguments, I believe, are sufficiently strong to warrant serious consideration. Furthermore, feminism would benefit from a public dialogue that includes debate and argumentation with all those who address feminist issues, regardless of their definition of or position on feminism." Mandle, "Sisterly Critics," 97–98.

56. Baumgardner and Richards, *Manifesta*, 240.

57. In her discussion of this trio, Elizabeth Minnich writes that "they are working hard to discredit the feminisms that make them uncomfortable, rather than arguing with them in a scholarly and sisterly fashion." Minnich, "Feminist Attacks on Feminisms," 160. Rather than merely discredit Roiphe, Wolf, and Denfeld's construction of feminism, I hope to analyze it in precisely such a "scholarly and sisterly fashion."

58. *Third Wave Agenda* and *Catching a Wave* were published by academic presses, whereas the majority of self-described "third wave" texts have been published by smaller commercial publishing houses and marketed to both academics and nonacademics alike.

59. Barbara Findlen, "Introduction," in *Listen Up: Voices from the Next Feminist Generation*, ed. Barbara Findlen (Seattle: Seal Press, 1995), xv.

60. For another third-wave "anthology" from this period, although in journal form, see *Hypatia: A Journal of Feminist Philosophy* 12, no. 3 (Summer 1997). This is a special issue entitled *Third Wave Feminisms*, edited by Jacquelyn N. Zita.

61. For example, *Letters of Intent* is "a book of letters between twenty- and thirtysomething women and their 'foremothers.'" Unfortunately, as the editors also acknowledge, the book is structured so that these "foremothers" get the last word in every essay. Anna Bondoc in Anna Bondoc and Meg Daly, "Introduction," in *Letters of Intent: Women Cross the Generations to Talk about Family, Work, Sex, Love and the Future of Feminism*, ed. Anna Bondoc and Meg Daly (New York: Simon & Schuster, 1999), 6. A similar last word is made by Angela Davis in *To Be Real* (where Gloria Steinem has the first word). Angela Y. Davis, "Afterword," in Walker, ed., *To Be Real*, 279–284; Gloria Steinem, "Foreword," in Walker, ed., *To Be Real*, xiii–xxviii. See also Katha Pollitt and Jennifer Baumgardner, "Afterword: A Correspondence between Katha Pollitt and Jennifer Baumgardner," in Dicker and Piepmeier, eds., *Catching a Wave*, 309–319; and Cherríe Moraga, "Foreword: 'The War Path of Greater Empowerment,'" in *Colonize This! Young Women of Color on Today's Feminism*, ed. Daisy Hernández and Bushra Rehman (New York: Seal Press, 2002), xi–xv.

62. *Bust* began in 1992, *Bitch: Feminist Response to Popular Culture* in 1996. Marcelle Karp and Debbie Stoller, the founders of *Bust*, describe why they started their magazine: "Except for an outspoken group of younger women who were calling themselves 'Riot Grrls,' it looked like our generation of feminists was getting swept under the rug. Out of sight, out of mind. . . . Not only did we want to let the younger girls know that we older girls had never given up on feminism, but we also wanted to create a place where girls of all ages could let their voices be heard, in all their fierce, funny, feminist glory. Thus, the idea for *BUST* was born. . . . A magazine for broads who weren't afraid of any f-words—from feminism to fucking to fashion." Karp and Stoller, eds., *The Bust Guide to the New Girl Order* (New York: Penguin Books, 1999), xii–xiii.

63. For more on third-wave cultural productions, see Ednie Kaeh Garrison, "U.S. Feminism-Grrrl Style! Young (Sub)Cultures and the Technologies of the Third Wave," *Feminist Studies* 26, no. 1 (Spring 2000): 141–170; Melissa Klein, "Duality and Redefinition: Young Feminism and the Alternative Music Community," in Heywood and Drake, eds., *Third Wave Agenda,* 207–225; and Jen Smith, "Doin' It for the Ladies—Youth Feminism: Cultural Productions/Cultural Activism," in Heywood and Drake, eds., *Third Wave Agenda,* 226–238. On the Riot Grrrl movement, see Hillary Carlip, *Girl Power: Young Women Speak Out!* (New York: Warner Books, 1995), 31–63; Nina Malkin, "It's a Grrrl Thing," *Seventeen,* May 1991, 80–82; Jessica Rosenberg and Gitana Garofalo, "Riot Grrrl: Revolutions from Within," *Signs: A Journal of Women in Culture and Society* 23, no. 3 (Spring 1998): 809–841; and Gayle Wald, "Just a Girl? Rock Music, Feminism, and the Cultural Construction of Female Youth," *Signs: A Journal of Women in Culture and Society* 23, no. 3 (Spring 1998): 585–610. For more on the importance of music to this new feminism, see *The Righteous Babes,* dir. Pratibha Parmar, Women Make Movies, New York, 1997.

64. For Australian feminism, see Kathy Bail, ed., *DIY Feminism* (Sydney, Australia: Allen and Unwin, 1996); Rosamund Else-Mitchell and Naomi Flutter, eds., *Talking Up: Young Women's Take on Feminism* (North Melbourne, Australia: Spinifex Press); and Virginia Trioli, *Generation f: Sex, Power, and the Young Feminist* (Melbourne, Australia: Minerva, 1996). For an example of Canadian third-wave feminism, see Allyson Mitchell, Lisa Bryn Rundle, and Lara Karaian, eds., *Turbo Chicks: Talking Young Feminisms* (Toronto: Sumach Press, 2001). For more on young women's feminism in the United Kingdom during the 1990s, see Natasha Walter, *The New Feminism* (London: Little, Brown and Company, 1998); and Natasha Walter, ed., *On the Move: Feminism for a New Generation* (London: Virago Press, 1999).

65. Dicker and Piepmeier, "Introduction," 5.

66. For a critique of *Manifesta*'s politics, see Michelle Jensen, "Riding the Third Wave," *The Nation,* December 11, 2000, 24–30.

67. See bell hooks's critique of Roiphe, where she writes that the coalitional politics of the late 1970s and 1980s "risks being undone and undermined by some of the current feminist writing by young white privileged women who strive to create a narrative of feminism (not feminist movement) that denies race or class differences." hooks, "Feminist Opportunism or Commitment to Struggle?" *Z*, January 1994, 1.

68. Orr, "Charting the Current of the Third Wave," 37. See also the section entitled "From the Third World to the Third Wave: Our Debts" in Heywood and Drake, "Introduction," in *Third Wave Agenda,* 8–13.

69. Chela Sandoval, "U.S. Third World Feminism: The Theory and Method of Oppositional Consciousness in the Postmodern World," *Genders* 10 (Spring 1991): 4.

70. As Cherríe Moraga describes the writers in *Colonize This!*: "They are young sisters (our daughters) who . . . have read and been schooled by the feminist writings and works of the women of color who preceded them, and as such are free to ask questions of feminism more deeply than we could have imagined twenty years ago." Moraga, "Foreword: 'The War Path of Greater Empowerment,'" xi.

71. Garrison, "U.S. Feminism-Grrrl Style!" 145. For more on the history of the third wave, see Baumgardner and Richards, *Manifesta,* 77–80; and Dicker and Piepmeier, "Introduction."

72. I discuss this point in more detail in chapter 5.

73. Patricia Justine Tumang, *"Nasaan ka anak ko?* A Queer Filipina-American Feminist's Tale of Abortion and Self-Recovery," in Hernández and Rehman, eds., *Colonize This!*, 379.

74. Lisa Marie Hogeland, "Against Generational Thinking, or, Some Things that 'Third Wave' Feminism Isn't," *Women's Studies in Communication* 24, no. 1 (Spring 2001), 118.

75. This point is eloquently made by JeeYeun Lee in *Listen Up*, where she writes: "I want to emphasize that the feminism that I and other young women come to today is one that is at least sensitive to issues of exclusion. If perhaps twenty years ago charges of racism, classism, and homophobia were not taken seriously, today they are the cause of extreme anguish and soul-searching. I am profoundly grateful to older feminists of color and their white allies who struggled to bring U.S. feminist movements to this point." Lee, "Beyond Bean Counting," in Findlen, ed., *Listen Up*, 208.

76. Claims about the third wave's anti-racism and diversity have been made at all of the conferences on third-wave feminism I've attended.

77. It is interesting that *To Be Real* includes an essay by bell hooks who, by virtue of her birth year of 1952, is not "third wave" in the generational sense of the term. hooks, "Beauty Laid Bare: Aesthetics in the Ordinary," in Walker, ed., *To Be Real*, 157–166.

78. Helene Shugart goes even farther in arguing that "third-wave feminism is more appropriately understood as a *subculture of* the larger rhetorical phenomenon of Generation X rather than a phase or contemporary incarnation of feminism." I disagree with Shugart on this point: one, because I think there is more diversity within third-wave feminism than discussed in her article, and two, because in focusing only on third-wavers whose rhetoric exhibits Generation X–type qualities, such as irony, she ignores other forms of third-wave feminism, particularly by third-wave feminists of color. For more on the whiteness of Generation X as a generational term, see chapter 5. Helene A. Shugart, "Isn't It Ironic? The Intersection of Third-Wave Feminism and Generation X," *Women's Studies in Communication* 24, no. 2 (Fall 2001): 134, emphasis added. For more on the relationship between Generation X and third-wave feminism, see Findlen, "Introduction"; and Leslie Heywood and Jennifer Drake, "We Learn America Like a Script: Activism in the Third Wave; or, Enough Phantoms of Nothing," in Heywood and Drake, eds., *Third Wave Agenda*, 40–54.

79. Baumgardner and Richards, eds., *Manifesta*, 234. Third Wave Foundation, http://www.thirdwavefoundation.org/programs/default.htm.

80. For more on how second- and third-wave debates are structured around age, see "What Younger Women Think about Older Women," *The Oprah Winfrey Show*, Harpo Productions, Chicago, aired January 16, 2002. This episode features Jennifer Baumgardner, Amy Richards, Rebecca Walker, and Naomi Wolf.

81. Heywood and Drake, "Introduction," 3. For more on the relationship between third-wave feminism and beauty culture, see Amy Richards, "Body Image: Third Wave Feminism's Issue?" in *Adiós Barbie: Young Women Write about Body Image and Identity*, ed. Ophira Edut (Seattle: Seal Press, 1998), 196–200.

82. Dicker and Piepmeier, "Introduction," 10.

83. For more on how the term "third wave" functions as an ideological, versus generational, concept, see Hogeland, "Against Generational Thinking."

84. Carol Siegel, *New Millennial Sexstyles* (Bloomington: Indiana University Press, 2000), 3. For more on cross-generational identification, see Eileen Myles, "My Intergeneration," *Village Voice*, June 27, 2000, 68.

85. E. Ann Kaplan, keynote address at Third Wave Feminism, a conference held at the University of Exeter, United Kingdom, July 2002.

86. Garrison, "U.S. Feminism-Grrrl Style!" 164.

87. Rene Denfeld, *The New Victorians: A Young Woman's Challenge to the Old Feminist Order* (New York: Warner Books, 1995), 21.

88. Adds Barbara Findlen, this is "the kind of experience *only* a woman of this generation could have had. We are the first generation for whom feminism has been entwined in the fabric of our lives; it is natural that many of us are feminists." Findlen, "Introduction," xii.

89. Denfeld, *The New Victorians*, 252.

90. Gornick, "Who Says We Haven't Made a Revolution?" 27. For another perspective on this nostalgia about making a difference, see Nancy K. Miller's "Decades," in which she writes, "I will admit to a certain homesickness for the gestures of those years in feminism that now have come to seem transparent, like being called Ms. I sometimes long for the conviction we had then that changing the language counted for something." Miller, "Decades," *South Atlantic Quarterly* 91, no. 1 (Winter 1992): 75.

91. Shani Jamila, "Can I Get a Witness? Testimony from a Hip Hop Feminist," in Hernández and Rehman, eds., *Colonize This!* 393.

92. Melissa Silverstein, "WAC-ing Operation Rescue," in Findlen, ed., *Listen Up*, 241.

93. As Deborah L. Siegel points out, many third-wave narratives "are compelled by nostalgia for an ideal of collectivity, the dream of a common language, which was foundational to certain strains of second wave feminism." Siegel, "The Legacy of the Personal: Generating Theory in Feminism's Third Wave," *Hypatia: A Journal of Feminist Philosophy* 12, no. 3 (Summer 1997): 58–59.

94. Meg Daly in Bondoc and Daly, "Introduction," 3. See also Tayari Jones's letter in *Letters of Intent;* comparing herself to her parents' involvement in the civil rights movement, she writes, "I, on the other hand, have risked nothing. I feel as though I am assigned as the keeper of a flame that I have not fanned." Tayari Jones and Pearl Cleage, "Which Come First, Our Paychecks or Our Principles?" in Bondoc and Daly, eds., *Letters of Intent*, 37.

95. Laurie Ouellette argues that second-wave texts such as *The Feminine Mystique, Sisterhood Is Powerful,* and *Sexual Politics* "simultaneously captivat[ed] and exclud[ed] me." Ouellette, "Building the Third Wave," 10. For more on younger feminists' sense of being adrift and without a movement of their own, see AnnJanette Rosga and Meg Satterthwaite, "Notes from the Aftermath," in *The Feminist Memoir Project: Voices from Women's Liberation,* ed. Rachel Blau DuPlessis and Ann Snitow (New York: Three Rivers Press, 1998), 469–476.

96. Ellen Neuborne, "Imagine My Surprise," in Findlen, ed., *Listen Up*, 35.

97. As Nancy K. Miller remarks, "Our generation had no women ahead of us: We were rebelling against father figures, and that was simpler in some ways. Now I'm the same age of some of my students' mothers, and I stir some of those feelings of identification and repudiation you might expect." Nancy K. Miller quoted in Margaret Talbot, "A Most Dangerous Method," *Lingua Franca* 4, no. 2 (January/February 1994): 30.

98. Roiphe, *The Morning After*, 171.

99. As Jennifer Baumgardner recently joked, "the second wave was the patriarchy to me." Personal conversation with the author, June 2003.

100. Baumgardner and Richards, *Manifesta*, 17.

101. Denfeld, *The New Victorians*, 2.

102. Roiphe, *The Morning After*, 4.

103. Walker, "Being Real," xxx–xxxi.

104. Iannone, "Sex and the Feminists," 51.

105. As Rose Glickman has noted, "To be a feminist is one among many options for [women in their twenties and early thirties], because they do not recognize it as a process, as a perspective that informs other choices. They interpret the word as an end in itself." Glickman, *Daughters of Feminists* (New York: St. Martin's Press, 1993), 5.

106. On the generational difference regarding consciousness-raising, Denfeld writes: "While CR might have been helpful for women raised in eras where women didn't talk about their experiences with sexism—let alone talk about sex—my generation often finds it redundant. Unlike our mothers, we grew up in a world where issues such as sex discrimination, sexual harassment, abortion, birth control, homosexuality, and relationships are openly discussed. My friends and I have the kind of explicit talk about our sex lives and personal experiences that would give Jerry Falwell a heart attack. . . . Yet my mother tells me such a thing would have been unthinkable in her day." Denfeld, *The New Victorians*, 204–205.

107. Findlen, "Introduction," xii. See also Laurie Ouellette, who writes, "I am a member of the first generation of women to benefit from the gains of the 1970s' women's movement without having participated in its struggles." Ouellette, "Building the Third Wave," 10.

108. Steinem, "Foreword," xxvi.

109. For more on this process of reinvention, see Orr, "Charting the Current of the Third Wave," 32–33.

110. Adrienne Rich, *Of Woman Born: Motherhood as Experience and Institution* (New York: W.W. Norton & Company, 1976), 236. For more on the concept of matrophobia, see the introduction to this volume.

111. Rene Denfeld, "Feminism 2000: What Does It Really Mean (to You)?" *Sassy* 9 (May 1996): 60.

112. Wolf, *Fire with Fire*, 137.

113. Nancy Chodorow, a feminist psychoanalyst and sociologist, is the main proponent of this theory, known as object-relations theory. See, for example, *The Reproduction of Mothering: Psychoanalysis and the Sociology of Gender* (Berkeley: University of California Press, 1978).

114. In comparison to the large body of feminist work which stresses the positive aspects of female gender individuation, there has been relatively little work which focuses on the more negative aspects of this individuation and the mother-daughter relationship generally. One important exception is Luce Irigaray's "And the One Doesn't Stir without the Other," *Signs* 7, no. 1 (1981): 60–67. For another example of someone trying to write the mother-daughter relationship in such a way that it includes both similarity and difference, see Joan Nestle, "My Mother Liked to Fuck," in *Powers of Desire: The Politics of Sexuality*, ed. Ann Snitow, Christine Stansell, and Sharon Thompson (New York: Monthly Review Press, 1983), 468–470; and Nestle's essays on her mother in *A Restricted Country* (Ithaca, N.Y.: Firebrand Books, 1987).

115. Madelyn Detloff, "Mean Spirits: The Politics of Contempt between Feminist Generations," *Hypatia: A Journal of Feminist Philosophy* 12, no. 3 (Summer 1997): 92.

116. While the writers who are my focus here clearly see feminism as limiting their individuality—feminism as Big Sister or, more accurately, Big Mother—other third-wave writers offer a different understanding of what feminism has meant to them. For these writers, such as several featured in *Listen Up* and *To Be Real,* feminism is described as something which enables them to *acquire* individuality. In other words, feminism is depicted as an empowering force in their lives, allowing them to question society's rules about how they should be in the world. I would argue that this identification with feminism is much more like the descriptions offered by early second-wave writers who describe the process of becoming feminists in positive terms, emphasizing, in Steinem's words, "the joyful freedom" found in coming into feminism. It is interesting, however, that even this more positive third-wave understanding of what feminism has to offer seems inextricably linked to the mother-daughter relationship. See, for example, Sharon Lennon's essay in *Listen Up:* "My mother, who had allowed and encouraged me to be who I was through most of my youth, viewed [my interest in feminism] as a major point of contention between us. . . . In my quest for individuality through feminism, there were a lot of screaming matches between my mother and me." Lennon, "What Is Mine," in Findlen, ed., *Listen Up,* 127.

117. Walker, "To Be Real," xxxiii.

118. Adds Paula Kamen, "The vast majority of people of my generation have little patience for anything that seems too ideological, dogmatic, or revolutionary. It smacks of extremist, shortsighted rhetoric from the late sixties. We mistrust such either-or, black-or-white thinking that renders us inflexible to changing conditions." Kamen, "My 'Bourgeois' Brand of Feminism," in *Next: Young American Writers on the New Generation,* ed. Eric Liu (New York: W.W. Norton & Company, 1994), 87.

119. Heywood and Drake, "Introduction," 11.

120. Denfeld, *The New Victorians,* 263. Karen Lehrman adds, "the idea of a rigid political sisterhood—of a 'women's movement' with a distinct ideological agenda—has become not only anachronistic but counterproductive." Lehrman, *The Lipstick Proviso: Women, Sex and Power in the Real World* (New York: Anchor Books, 1997), 179.

121. Representing third-wave feminism as something individual feminists can define individually for themselves is also a key theme in and guiding structure of the documentary *Gloria Steinem, the Spice Girls, and Me: Defining the Third Wave of Feminism,* dir. Krista Longtin, 2002.

122. Walker, "Becoming the Third Wave," 39–41.

123. An exception can be found in *Catching a Wave,* where editors Dicker and Piepmeier explicitly describe their anthology's format as following the second-wave principle of consciousness-raising in order to move the reader from personal experience to theory and action. See Dicker and Piepmeier, "Introduction."

124. Findlen, "Introduction," xiv.

125. Elspeth Probyn, "New Traditionalism and Post-Feminism: TV Does the Home," *Screen* 31 (Summer 1990): 156.

126. In this regard, I find it interesting that the next books published by Denfeld, Roiphe, and Wolf moved away from policy or academic issues to more personal topics. Denfeld's *Kill the Body, the Head Will Fall: A Closer Look at Women and Aggression* (New York: Warner Books, 1997) addresses her experience training as a boxer; Roiphe's *Last Night in Paradise: Sex and Morals at the Century's End* (Boston: Little, Brown and Company, 1997) addresses HIV, AIDS, and sexual morality from a personal rather

than policy perspective; and Wolf's *Promiscuities: The Secret Struggle for Womanhood* (New York: Random House, 1997) addresses the sexual-coming-of-age stories of Wolf and friends. For reviews of these books, see Michiko Kakutani, "Feminism Lite: She Is Woman, Hear Her Mate," *New York Times*, June 10, 1997, B6 (review of *Promiscuities*); and Courtney Weaver, "Growing Up Sexual," *New York Times Book Review*, June 8, 1997, 12 (review of *Promiscuities* and *Last Night in Paradise*). See also Naomi Wolf, *Misconceptions: Truth, Lies, and the Unexpected Journey to Motherhood* (New York: Doubleday, 2001).

127. Lehrman, *The Lipstick Proviso*, 14, 5.

128. Lehrman, *The Lipstick Proviso*, 156, 154.

129. Naomi Wolf, for example, argues for a pro-capitalist form of feminism, encouraging us to make feminism "fun" and "lucrative." Wolf, *Fire with Fire*, 300.

130. Jennifer Harris, "Betty Friedan's Granddaughters: *Cosmo*, Ginger Spice & the Inheritance of Whiteness," in Mitchell, Rundle, and Karaian, eds., *Turbo Chicks*, 203.

131. Glickman, *Daughters of Feminists*, xiii, emphasis added.

132. Kaminer, "Feminism's Third Wave," 22.

133. Carroll Smith-Rosenberg, *Disorderly Conduct: Visions of Gender in Victorian America* (New York: Alfred A. Knopf, 1985), 248.

134. Bolotin, "Views from the Postfeminist Generation," 31.

135. For more on feminist mothers, see Marilyn Webb, "Our Daughters, Ourselves: How Feminists Can Raise Feminists," *Ms.*, November/December 1992, 30–35.

136. Glickman writes, "The daughters speak with one voice about how their parents instilled and nurtured their self-esteem, reminded them of their worth as women, affirmed their equality with men in ability, strength, and rights (at least in principle), and encouraged them to become self-sufficient. This is the strongest common denominator in the daughters' formative years." Glickman, *Daughters of Feminists*, 30.

137. Denfeld, for example, thanks her mother "for teaching me what feminism means." Denfeld, *The New Victorians*, acknowledgments.

138. Anne Roiphe writes of her daughter's feminism in *The Morning After:* "One of my daughters publishes a book. I hold it in my hand. I turn it over. There on the back is a picture of her. Her hair curls, disobedient thick locks, her eyes glare back at the photographer. What do I see? I see sass, energy, womanliness, but not the kind I was taught. I don't see helplessness, pretense, fear. I see clarity, brightness, and sexuality, her own, bold and strong, right there on the cover of her book. I turn pink, so pleased am I. I think my daughter's point of view is bold, humane, and right. My daughter is a critic of the revolution in which I was a foot soldier and she was a beneficiary. I agree with her criticism." Roiphe, *Fruitful: A Real Mother in the Modern World* (Boston: Houghton Mifflin Company, 1996), 231–232.

139. Roiphe, *The Morning After*, 140. For another use of the "aunt" trope to describe feminism, see Merri Lisa Johnson, who writes: "Growing up with feminism like an eccentric aunt always reminding us how smart we are, how we can do anything, be anyone, the women of my generation hesitate to own up to the romantic binds we find ourselves in. . . . For if feminism is right, and we *can* do anything, be anyone, it follows logically that the obstacles we face must reflect personal failures, individual shortcomings in the face of unlimited feminist possibility." Merri Lisa Johnson, "Fuck You and Your Untouchable Face: Third Wave Feminism and the Problem of Romance," in *Jane*

Sexes It Up: True Confessions of Feminist Desire, ed. Merri Lisa Johnson (New York: Four Walls Eight Windows, 2002), 14–15, emphasis in original.

140. In response to the idea that *The Morning After* is just a rebellion against her mother, Roiphe has said, "I had plenty of rebellions against my mother, but this isn't one." Quoted in Barbara Presley Noble, "One Daughter's Rebellion or Her Mother's Imprint?" *New York Times*, November 10, 1993, C1.

141. See Nancy Chodorow, *Feminism and Psychoanalytic Theory* (New Haven, Conn.: Yale University Press, 1989); Nancy Chodorow, *The Reproduction of Mothering;* Jessica Benjamin, *The Bonds of Love: Psychoanalysis, Feminism, and the Problem of Domination* (New York: Pantheon Books, 1988).

142. Susan Faludi quoted in Avenoso, "Feminism's Newest Foot Soldiers," *Elle*, March 1993, 114.

143. Gloria Steinem, "Why Young Women Are More Conservative," in Steinem, *Outrageous Acts and Everyday Rebellions* (New York: Holt, Rinehart and Winston, 1983), 216–217. See also L. A. Winokur's "Interview with Gloria Steinem," in which Steinem criticizes the conservative bent of third-wave writers such as Roiphe. *Progressive*, June 1995, 34–37.

144. Erica Duncan, "Mothers and Daughters," in *Competition: A Feminist Taboo?* ed. Valerie Miner and Helen E. Longino (New York: The Feminist Press, 1987), 133.

145. Duncan, "Mothers and Daughters," 131, 132.

146. Beth E. Schneider, "Political Generations and the Contemporary Women's Movement," *Sociological Inquiry* 58 (Winter 1988): 10.

147. Rebecca Walker quoted in Retha Powers, "Don't Ask Alice: Rebecca Walker Steps Out," *Girlfriends*, May/June 1996, 21.

148. Walker, "Being Real," xxx–xxxi.

149. Steinem, "Foreword," xviii.

150. Roiphe, *The Morning After*, 102–103.

151. Roiphe, *The Morning After*, 71–72.

152. Roiphe, *The Morning After*, xix.

153. Wolf, *Fire with Fire*, 207.

154. Roiphe, *The Morning After*, 63.

155. Roiphe, *The Morning After*, 83.

156. The grandmother trope is also used by Susie Bright to critique victim feminism: "I feel really let down by people voicing puritan attitudes I could have gotten from my Baptist grandmother, if I'd had one," Bright says. "What happened to the joyful '70s exploration of *Our Bodies, Ourselves?* When did that take-off-your-top-and-smash-the-state feeling die?" Quoted in Tad Friend, "Yes," *Esquire*, February 1994, 52.

157. As Roiphe writes, "This image of a delicate woman bears a striking resemblance to that fifties ideal my mother and the other women of her generation fought so hard to get away from." Roiphe, *The Morning After*, 6. And Denfeld argues, "Today's feminists have instituted a new set of confining rules for women, many of which smell suspiciously like the same repressive sexual mores that our mothers fought to escape." Denfeld, *The New Victorians*, 57.

158. Catherine MacKinnon is the main figure under attack in *The Morning After*, and she plays an important role in Roiphe's critique of feminism as both too childish and too old. MacKinnon represents the grandmother who patronizes women by treating them as children. Roiphe writes: "MacKinnon's is the sophisticated political version of the

classic grandparent's whine: you don't know what's good for you. . . . The infantilized position is one she reserves for other women." Roiphe, *The Morning After*, 148.

2. Finding Ourselves in the Past

1. It is beyond the scope of this project to investigate the effects of this formulation of the second wave's origins on the women's movement's relationship to other leftist movements during this period. Juliet Mitchell and Ann Oakley have argued that the desire to locate feminism's origins in the past had the effect of distancing the women's movement of the 1960s and 1970s from other liberation movements of that period, such as the black nationalist movement and the gay liberation movement. See Juliet Mitchell and Ann Oakley, "Introduction," in *What Is Feminism?* ed. Juliet Mitchell and Ann Oakley (Oxford: Basil Blackwell, 1986), 12.

2. Alice Echols, *Daring to Be Bad: Radical Feminism in America, 1967–1975* (Minneapolis: University of Minnesota Press, 1989), 113.

3. Echols, *Daring to Be Bad*, 107–108. For descriptions of the anti-inaugural protest written during the period in which it occurred, see Judith Hole and Ellen Levine, *Rebirth of Feminism* (New York: Quadrangle Books, 1971), 133; and Cellestine Ware, *Woman Power: The Movement for Women's Liberation* (New York: Tower Publications, 1970), 35. As with the other documents from this period which describe the protest, Hole and Levine and Ware are not critical of the motivations behind this action or the relationship between themselves and the suffragettes constructed by it.

4. Ellen Willis, "Women and the Left," in *Notes from the Second Year: Women's Liberation: Major Writings of the Radical Feminists* (New York, 1970), 55. Cellestine Ware says of this protest, "The theme of the women's liberation action was the failure of the vote to effect changes in the quality of life of American women. The century of struggle that ended in the vote had not brought forth the deterioration of the inequities that burden women in every area, in every class, and in every aspect of their identities." Ware, *Woman Power*, 35.

5. In her description of the anti-inaugural, Echols tells the following story about the feminist activists' relationship to the suffragettes: "In a display of remarkable chutzpah, they decided to contact the famous suffragist and founder of the National Women's Party, Alice Paul, to see if she would join them in 'giving back the vote.' As one might expect of someone who had endured jail for the suffrage cause, Paul was not interested in repudiating suffrage as 'a sop for women.' Indeed, when Shulamith Firestone asked her to join them on stage in burning their voter registration cards, Paul reportedly 'hit the ceiling.' To Paul, woman's suffrage constituted a significant breakthrough in women's struggle for equality. But to women's liberationists who had acquired their political education in the civil rights movement and the New Left, voting was a 'mockery of democracy,' and equality in a fundamentally unequal society an obscenity. Liberation, not equality, was their goal." Echols, *Daring to Be Bad*, 12.

6. From a photo of the protest (originally from Redstockings Women's Liberation Archives), reprinted in Echols, *Daring to Be Bad*.

7. Other founding members of New York Radical Feminists included Cellestine Ware and Ann Snitow.

8. New York Radical Feminists, "Organizing Principles of the New York Radical Feminists," in *Notes from the Second Year*, 119–122; and New York Radical Feminists,

"Politics of the Ego: A Manifesto for N.Y. Radical Feminists," in *Notes from the Second Year*, 124–126.

9. NYRF, "Organizing Principles," 119. Note that NYRF includes Simone de Beauvoir as a "feminist independent" in their list of who and what constitutes "the militant tradition of the old radical feminist movement," even though she is from a substantially different era than the other women listed and in fact was still very much alive and writing when NYRF wrote their statement. I discuss U.S. radical feminists' relationship to Beauvoir in more detail later in this chapter.

10. Hole and Levine, *Rebirth of Feminism*, 117. Five thousand women participated in this demonstration. For more on this protest, see Susan Brownmiller, *In Our Time: Memoir of a Revolution* (New York: The Dial Press, 1999), 22.

11. NYRF, "Organizing Principles," 120, emphasis in original.

12. What happened to New York Radical Feminists, particularly the Stanton-Anthony Brigade, is revealing. Approximately six months after the group's founding, the entire brigade system was dismantled because women who were not members of the founding brigade accused the women who had founded it (including Shulamith Firestone, Anne Koedt, and Cellestine Ware) of being elitist and of seeing themselves as the true leaders of the entire group. Susan Brownmiller, not a member of the founding brigade, recounts that the women in the Stanton-Anthony Brigade "believe[d] that they were the leaders and that I and the rest of us were the followers"; a "vanguard brigade was unnecessary, extraordinarily presumptuous, and silly and demeaning to the rest of us." Brownmiller quoted in Echols, *Daring to Be Bad*, 192. For more on the Stanton-Anthony Brigade, see Brownmiller, *In Our Time*, 78; and Ware, *Woman Power*, 56–57.

13. Marsha Weinman Lear, "The Second Feminist Wave," *New York Times Magazine*, March 10, 1968, 24.

14. Shulamith Firestone, *The Dialectic of Sex: The Case for Feminist Revolution* (New York: Bantam Books, 1970), 15.

15. Germaine Greer, *The Female Eunuch* (London: Granada Publishing Limited, 1971), 11.

16. Karl Mannheim, "The Problem of Generations," in *Essays on the Sociology of Knowledge*, ed. Paul Kecskemeti (New York: Oxford University Press, 1952), 281.

17. Leslie B. Tanner, "Preface," in *Voices from Women's Liberation*, ed. Leslie B. Tanner (New York: New American Library, 1970), 13.

18. Jennifer Baumgardner and Amy Richards, *Manifesta: Young Women, Feminism, and the Future* (New York: Farrar, Straus and Giroux, 2000), 17.

19. Marilyn Salzman Webb, "Women: We Have a Common Enemy," *New Left Notes*, June 10, 1968, 15.

20. Echols, *Daring to Be Bad*, 54.

21. It is curious that Firestone has been widely credited with this shift in perception of the first wave, yet her role in the development of a new relationship to women's history has gone relatively unaddressed by academic women's historians who have followed her.

22. Shulamith Firestone, "The Woman's Rights Movement in the U.S.: A New View," in Tanner, ed., *Voices from Women's Liberation*, 435. This essay was later expanded into the second chapter of Firestone's *The Dialectic of Sex*.

23. Firestone, *The Dialectic of Sex*, 30.

24. Firestone, "The Woman's Rights Movement in the U.S.," 434.

25. Firestone, *The Dialectic of Sex,* 37, emphasis added.

26. Echols, *Daring to Be Bad,* 54.

27. Firestone, *The Dialectic of Sex,* 16, 18.

28. Firestone, *The Dialectic of Sex,* 24.

29. Betty Friedan, *The Feminine Mystique* (1963; reprint, New York: Laurel Books, 1973), 95.

30. In its focus on appearance and heterosexual romance, I would also argue that this representation of "the feminist" is clearly linked to a homophobic anxiety about lesbianism.

31. Judith Hole and Ellen Levine, "The First Feminists," in *Radical Feminism,* ed. Anne Koedt, Ellen Levine, and Anita Rapone (New York: Quadrangle, 1973), 3–16. Originally published in *Notes from the Third Year* (New York, 1971), 5–10.

32. Similarly, Cellestine Ware notes the continuity between the two movements in a chapter she entitles "Nineteenth-Century Feminism and WLM [Women's Liberation Movement] as Different Phases in the Same Movement"; Ware, *Woman Power.* For more on the comparison between the two movements, see also Gerda Lerner, "The Feminists: A Second Look" (1970), in Lerner, *The Majority Finds Its Past: Placing Women in History* (New York: Oxford University Press, 1979), 31–47.

33. Tanner, ed., *Voices from Women's Liberation,* back cover.

34. NYRF, "Organizing Principles," 120, emphasis added.

35. Kathie Sarachild, "The Power of History," in Redstockings, *Feminist Revolution,* ed. Kathie Sarachild (1975; reprint, New York: Random House, 1978), 27.

36. Kate Millett, *Sexual Politics* (New York: Equinox Book, 1969), 84.

37. Friedan, *The Feminine Mystique,* 101.

38. Millett, *Sexual Politics,* 64.

39. Ware, *Woman Power,* 17.

40. For more on the way feminism has constructed its history, see Rosalind Delmar, "What Is Feminism?" in *What Is Feminism?* ed. Juliet Mitchell and Ann Oakley (Oxford: Basil Blackwell, 1986), 8–33; and Sara Evans, *Tidal Wave: How Women Changed America at Century's End* (New York: The Free Press, 2003).

41. Nancy F. Cott, *The Grounding of Modern Feminism* (New Haven, Conn.: Yale University Press, 1987); Ellen Carol DuBois, *Feminism and Suffrage: The Emergence of an Independent Women's Movement in America, 1848–1868* (Ithaca, N.Y.: Cornell University Press, 1978); DuBois, "The Radicalism of the Woman Suffrage Movement: Notes Toward the Reconstruction of Nineteenth-Century Feminism," *Feminist Studies* 3, nos. 1 and 2 (Fall 1975): 63–71; Carroll Smith-Rosenberg, *Disorderly Conduct: Visions of Gender in Victorian America* (New York: Alfred A. Knopf, 1985); Carroll Smith-Rosenberg, "The New Woman and the New History," *Feminist Studies* 3, nos. 1 and 2 (Fall 1975): 185–198.

42. Robin Morgan, "Women Disrupt the Miss America Pageant," in Morgan, *Going Too Far: The Personal Chronicle of a Feminist* (New York: Random House, 1977), 62. It was at this protest that women threw their bras and other "instruments of torture"—such as girdles, curlers, high-heeled shoes, false eyelashes, cosmetics, wigs, and magazines such as *Cosmopolitan* and *Playboy*—into a "Freedom Trash Can." The original plan was to light a fire in the can, but the protesters complied with the police's request not to endanger the wooden boardwalk. Although no bras were in fact burned

at this event, it is from the Miss America Protest that we get the pejorative term "bra burners" to describe feminists.

43. *Notes from the First Year* was edited by Shulamith Firestone and Anne Koedt.

44. For more on the importance of the year 1968, see Dana Densmore, "A Year of Living Dangerously: 1968," in *The Feminist Memoir Project: Voices from Women's Liberation*, ed. Rachel Blau DuPlessis and Ann Snitow (New York: Three Rivers Press, 1998), 71–89.

45. NOW's membership quadrupled in its first year, growing from 300 members in 1966 to 1,200 by the time of its first national convention in 1967. Miriam Schneir, ed., *Feminism in Our Time: The Essential Writings, World War II to the Present* (New York: Vintage, 1994), 96.

46. Ware, *Woman Power*, 21, emphasis added.

47. Firestone, *The Dialectic of Sex*, 33.

48. Greer, *The Female Eunuch*, 295. Radical feminists' aversion to liberalism also manifested itself in a disdain for groups such as NOW, magazines such as *Ms.*, and feminist leaders such as Friedan and Gloria Steinem. While liberal feminists sought to include women in the mainstream of U.S. politics, radical feminists who sought to change mainstream political structures rejected working within those structures.

49. Firestone, *The Dialectic of Sex*. For other tributes to Beauvoir, see Bonnie Kreps, "Radical Feminism 1," in Koedt, Levine, and Rapone, *Radical Feminism*, 234–239 (reprinted from *Notes from the Second Year*), where she uses Beauvoir as the basis for her analysis; see also *No More Fun and Games: A Journal of Female Liberation* 3 (November 1969), which has over twenty long passages from *The Second Sex* interspersed throughout the journal.

50. Redstockings, *Feminist Revolution*. For more on the relationship between second-wave U.S. feminists and Simone de Beauvoir, see *Daughters of de Beauvoir*, prod. Penny Foster, Women Make Movies, New York, 1989.

51. Kathie Sarachild, "The Power of History," in *Feminist Revolution: An Abridged Edition with Additional Writings*, ed. Kathie Sarachild (New York: Random House, 1978), 27.

52. Kreps, "Radical Feminism 1," 239.

53. Sarachild, "The Power of History," 28.

54. Paula Giddings, *When and Where I Enter: The Impact of Black Women on Race and Sex in America* (New York: Bantam Books, 1984), 305.

55. Ann Snitow, "A Gender Diary," in *Conflicts in Feminism*, ed. Marianne Hirsch and Evelyn Fox Keller (New York: Routledge, 1990), 32.

56. As two recent biographies of Friedan discuss in detail, her enduring association with the domestic sphere of home and family—Friedan as über-housewife, as it were—is more a product of her famous book's subject matter than her actual life experience. See Judith Hennessee, *Betty Friedan: Her Life* (New York: Random House, 1999); and Daniel Horowitz, *Betty Friedan and the Making of* The Feminine Mystique: *The American Left, the Cold War, and Modern Feminism* (Amherst: University of Massachusetts Press, 1999).

57. Sarachild, "The Power of History," 27, emphasis added.

58. Simone de Beauvoir was born in 1908, Betty Friedan in 1921.

59. That early second-wave feminists didn't recognize the ways in which feminism continued after 1920—albeit not in mass movement form—isn't surprising given the

paucity of women's history scholarship available to them in the late 1960s and early 1970s, when the academic field of U.S. women's history was in its infancy.

60. For an excellent examination of the changes within the women's movement and feminism after the Nineteenth Amendment was passed, see Cott, *Grounding of Modern Feminism*.

61. Firestone, *The Dialectic of Sex*, 30; Jo Freeman, "The New Feminists," *The Nation*, February 24, 1969, 241.

62. Barbara Epstein, "Ambivalence about Feminism," in *The Feminist Memoir Project*, ed. DuPlessis and Snitow, 128.

63. Beth E. Schneider, "Political Generations and the Contemporary Women's Movement," *Sociological Inquiry* 58 (Winter 1988): 7.

64. Sarachild, "The Power of History," 41.

65. As I argue in chapter 1, young women's declaration of themselves as feminism's third wave represents, in great part, a desire for a movement and political purpose of their own.

66. "The Trial of Susan B. Anthony" (1873), in *Notes from the Third Year*, 11–12; this account of Anthony's trial was later reprinted in Koedt, Levine, and Rapone, eds., *Radical Feminism*, 17–19.

67. The first-wave feminists in Tanner's volume include Elizabeth Blackwell, Sarah Moore Grimké, Lucretia Mott, Lucy Stone, and Sojourner Truth as well as Anthony and Stanton. See Tanner, ed., *Voices from Women's Liberation*.

68. "Declaration of Sentiments and Resolutions" (1848), in Tanner, ed., *Voices from Women's Liberation*, 43–47.

69. Hole and Levine's *The Rebirth of Feminism* also contains an analysis of the historical background of the second wave, with a particular focus on the radical/conservative divide in first-wave feminism that dominated much radical feminist discourse during the late 1960s, early 1970s period.

70. Shulamith Firestone and Anne Koedt, "Editorial," in *Notes from the Second Year*, 2.

71. Sarachild, "The Power of History," 26.

72. Firestone, *The Dialectic of Sex*, 29. This way of identifying movements for racial equality as the foundation for movements for gender equality can be seen in a number of essays and books from this period; for example, see Jo Freeman, "The Building of the Gilded Cage," in *Notes from the Third Year*, 44–55 (later reprinted in Koedt, Levine, and Rapone, eds., *Radical Feminism*, 127–150). This point is also made by Sara Evans in *Personal Politics: The Roots of Women's Liberation in the Civil Rights Movement and the New Left* (New York: Vintage Books, 1980).

73. Jo Freeman, *The Politics of Women's Liberation: A Case Study of an Emerging Social Movement and Its Relation to the Policy Process* (New York: Longman, 1975), 14.

74. From Gloria T. Hull, Patricia Bell-Scott, and Barbara Smith, eds., *All the Women Are White, All the Blacks Are Men, but Some of Us Are Brave: Black Women's Studies* (New York: The Feminist Press, 1982). See also bell hooks, *Ain't I a Woman: Black Women and Feminism* (Boston: South End Press, 1981), 7–8.

75. Frances Beale, "Double Jeopardy: To Be Black and Female," in *The Black Woman: An Anthology*, ed. Toni Cade (New York: Signet Books, 1970), 90–100; "Double Jeopardy" was also published in *Sisterhood Is Powerful: An Anthology of Writings from the Women's Liberation Movement*, ed. Robin Morgan (New York: Vintage Books, 1970), 340–353.

76. DuBois, *Feminism and Suffrage*.

77. Elizabeth Cady Stanton cited in Deborah K. King, "Multiple Jeopardy, Multiple Consciousness: The Context of a Black Feminist Ideology" (1988), in *Words of Fire: An Anthology of African American Feminist Thought*, ed. Beverly Guy-Sheftall (New York: The New Press, 1995), 295.

78. Beverly Jones and Judith Brown, "Toward a Female Liberation Movement," in Tanner, ed., *Voices from Women's Liberation*, 367.

79. Deborah King, "Multiple Jeopardy, Multiple Consciousness," 295–296.

80. Sojourner Truth, "The Women Want Their Rights" (1853), in Tanner, ed., *Voices from Women's Liberation*, 73–74.

81. Beale, "Double Jeopardy: To Be Black and Female"; Linda La Rue, "The Black Movement and Women's Liberation" (1970), in Guy-Sheftall, ed., *Words of Fire*, 164–173; Pauli Murray, "The Liberation of Black Women," in *Voices of the New Feminism*, ed. Mary Lou Thompson (Boston: Beacon Press, 1970), 87–102.

82. Cellestine Ware, one of the founding members of New York Radical Feminists, was one of the few black women involved in the radical women's liberation movement discussed in this chapter. As Ware herself notes, "The Women's Liberation Movement is a multitude of white women with an only occasional black sister to lend color to the meetings." Ware, *Woman Power*, 75.

83. I address this point in more detail in chapter 5 in my discussion of the third wave's racial politics.

84. See Firestone, *The Dialectic of Sex;* and Hole and Levine, *The Rebirth of Feminism*. One essay from the period that does attempt to address the racist turn in feminist politics of the nineteenth century, albeit in a limited way, is Connie Brown and Jane Seitz, "'You've Come a Long Way, Baby': Historical Perspectives," in Morgan, ed., *Sisterhood Is Powerful*, 3–28. Cellestine Ware also offers a limited critique of "the compromises that suffragists made to win backing for the vote." Ware, *Woman Power*, 158.

85. Willis, "Women and the Left," 56, emphasis added.

86. Firestone, *The Dialectic of Sex*, 108; Jones and Brown, "Toward a Female Liberation Movement," 388.

87. "Redstockings Manifesto," in Morgan, ed., *Sisterhood Is Powerful*, 535.

88. Toni Morrison, "What the Black Woman Thinks about Woman's Lib," *New York Times Magazine*, August 22, 1971, 64. See also Ware's chapter "The Relationship of Black Women to the Women's Liberation Movement," in *Woman Power*, 75–99.

89. La Rue, "The Black Movement and Women's Liberation," 164, emphasis in original.

90. It is interesting that many third-wave writers make the same sort of claim, describing second-wave feminism as overwhelmingly white in order to argue for the racial diversity of their own wave. I discuss this claim in more detail in chapters 1 and 5.

91. "Redstockings Manifesto," 535.

92. On sexuality generally, see Boston Women's Health Book Collective, *Our Bodies, Ourselves: A Book by and for Women* (New York: Simon & Schuster, 1971); and Greer, *The Female Eunuch*. On clitoral orgasms, see Anne Koedt, "The Myth of the Vaginal Orgasm," in Koedt, Levine, and Rapone, eds., *Radical Feminism*, 198–207 (originally published in *Notes from the First Year*); and Susan Lydon, "The Politics of Orgasm," in Morgan, ed., *Sisterhood Is Powerful*, 197–205. On lesbianism and bisexual-

ity, see Gene Damon, "The Least of These: The Minority Whose Screams Haven't Yet Been Heard," in Morgan, ed., *Sisterhood Is Powerful*, 297–306; Anne Koedt, "Lesbianism and Feminism," in *Notes from the Third Year*, 84–89; "Loving Another Woman," interview conducted by Anne Koedt, in *Notes from the Third Year*, 25–29; Radicalesbians, "The Woman Identified Woman," in *Notes from the Third Year*, 81–84; and Martha Shelly, "Notes of a Radical Lesbian," in Morgan, ed., *Sisterhood Is Powerful*, 306–311. On marriage and housework, see Sheila Cronan, "Marriage," in *Notes from the Third Year*, 62–65; Jones and Brown, "Toward a Female Liberation Movement"; Judy Syfers, "Why I Want a Wife," in *Notes from the Third Year*, 13–15; and Betsy Warrior, "Slavery or Labor of Love," in *Notes from the Third Year*, 68–71. On women's "nature," see Joreen, "The Bitch Manifesto," in *Notes from the Second Year*, 5–9; and Valerie Solanas, *SCUM Manifesto* (1968; reprint, London: The Matriarchy Study Group, 1983).

93. Friedan, *The Feminine Mystique*, 385.

94. Kate Millett, "Sexual Politics: A Manifesto for a Revolution," in Koedt, Levine, and Rapone, eds., *Radical Feminism*, 366. (Originally published in *Notes from the Second Year*.)

95. Greer, *The Female Eunuch*, 318 and 42, emphasis in original.

96. Echols, *Daring to Be Bad*, 12.

97. Koedt, "The Myth of the Vaginal Orgasm," 206.

98. Greer, *The Female Eunuch*, 306; Friedan, *The Feminine Mystique*, 389.

99. Koedt, "The Myth of the Vaginal Orgasm," 199.

100. For more on the effects of Koedt's essay on feminist thought and an important discussion of feminism's theories of sexuality generally, see Jane Gerhard, *Desiring Revolution: Second-Wave Feminism and the Rewriting of American Sexual Thought, 1920 to 1982* (New York: Columbia University Press, 2001).

101. Koedt, "The Myth of the Vaginal Orgasm," 203.

102. Information regarding the clitoris's role in female orgasm has certainly become much more accessible in the last thirty years; from *Our Bodies, Ourselves* to *Cosmopolitan* magazine to HBO's *Sex and the City*, discussions of the clitoris are ubiquitous these days. Yet every semester, I still encounter a number of undergraduate students who, upon reading Koedt's text for the first time, are just as thrilled and shocked by this information as I imagine the original readers of the essay were.

103. Baumgardner and Richards, *Manifesta*, 17.

104. Radicalesbians, "The Woman Identified Woman," 245.

105. Attributed to Ti-Grace Atkinson. See Koedt, "Lesbianism and Feminism," 246.

106. Ginny Berson, "The Furies" (1972), in *For Lesbians Only: A Separatist Anthology*, ed. Sarah Lucia Hoagland and Julia Penelope (London: Onlywomen Press, 1988), 26.

107. See Ellen Carol DuBois and Linda Gordon, "Seeking Ecstasy on the Battlefield: Danger and Pleasure in Nineteenth-Century Feminist Sexual Thought," in *Pleasure and Danger: Exploring Female Sexuality*, ed. Carole S. Vance (Boston: Routledge and Kegan Paul, 1985), 31–49.

108. Robin Morgan, "Lesbianism and Feminism: Synonyms or Contradictions?" in Morgan, *Going Too Far: The Personal Chronicle of a Feminist* (New York: Random House, 1977), 181, emphasis in original.

109. Abby Rockefeller, "Sex: The Basis of Sexism," *No More Fun and Games: A Journal of Female Liberation*, May 1973, 25, emphasis in original.

3. Taking Feminism to Bed

The subtitle of this chapter was adapted from Merri Lisa Johnson's phrase "Generation X does the Sex Wars," which she uses in "Jane Hocus, Jane Focus," in *Jane Sexes It Up: True Confessions of Feminist Desire,* ed. Merri Lisa Johnson (New York: Four Walls Eight Windows, 2002), 1.

1. Nan Bauer Maglin and Donna Perry, "Introduction," in *"Bad Girls"/"Good Girls": Women, Sex, and Power in the Nineties,* ed. Nan Bauer Maglin and Donna Perry (New Brunswick, N.J.: Rutgers University Press, 1996), xvi.

2. Other third-wave collections published by Seal Press over the last decade include, in chronological order, *Listen Up,* ed. Barbara Findlen (1995); *Adiós Barbie,* ed. Ophira Edut (1998); *Breeder: Real-Life Stories from the New Generation of Mothers,* ed. Ariel Gore and Bee Lavender (2001); *Young Wives' Tales: New Adventures in Love and Partnership,* ed. Jill Corral and Lisa Miya-Jervis (2001); and *Colonize This!* ed. Daisy Hernández and Bushra Rehman (2002). Seal Press also published Inga Muscio's *Cunt: A Declaration of Independence* (1998).

3. Lee Damsky, "Introduction," in *Sex and Single Girls: Straight and Queer Women on Sexuality,* ed. Lee Damsky (Seattle: Seal Press, 2000), xii–xiii.

4. Ann Snitow, Christine Stansell, and Sharon Thompson, eds., *Powers of Desire: The Politics of Sexuality* (New York: Monthly Review Press, 1983); and Carole S. Vance, ed., *Pleasure and Danger: Exploring Female Sexuality* (Boston: Routledge and Kegan Paul, 1985).

5. Damsky, "Introduction," xvi.

6. Lisa Duggan, "Introduction," in *Sex Wars: Sexual Dissent and Political Culture,* Lisa Duggan and Nan D. Hunter (New York: Routledge, 1995), 5. For more on feminism's sex wars, see Hannah Alderfer, Beth Jaker, and Marybeth Nelson, eds., *Diary of a Conference on Sexuality* (New York: Faculty Press, 1982); Caught Looking Inc., *Caught Looking: Feminism, Pornography and Censorship,* 2nd ed. (East Haven, Conn.: LongRiver Books, 1992); Carla Freccero, "Notes of a Post–Sex Wars Theorizer," in *Conflicts in Feminism,* ed. Marianne Hirsch and Evelyn Fox Keller (New York: Routledge, 1990), 305–325; B. Ruby Rich, "Feminism and Sexuality in the 1980s," *Feminist Studies* 12, no. 3 (Fall 1986): 525–561; Lynne Segal, *Straight Sex: Rethinking the Politics of Pleasure* (Berkeley: University of California Press, 1994); Vance, "Pleasure and Danger," in Vance, ed., *Pleasure and Danger,* 1–27; and Willis, "Toward a Feminist Sexual Revolution," *Social Text* 2, no. 3 (Fall 1982): 3–21.

7. Duggan, "Introduction," 6.

8. Damsky, "Introduction," xiii.

9. Paula Kamen, *Her Way: Young Women Remake the Sexual Revolution* (New York: Broadway Books, 2002), 3.

10. Rebecca Walker, "Lusting for Freedom," in *Listen Up: Voices from the Next Feminist Generation,* ed. Barbara Findlen (Seattle: Seal Press, 1995), 100.

11. Rene Denfeld, *The New Victorians: A Young Woman's Challenge to the Old Feminist Order* (New York: Warner Books, 1995), 2.

12. They continue: "We wrestle with marriage's sordid social and economic history. . . . We no longer see singlehood as some limbo to be rushed through headlong on the search for a mate. We no longer see those mates as necessarily male. We seek out romantic commitments for the personal and emotional satisfaction they can bring—not to avoid 'spinsterhood.'" Jill Corral and Lisa Miya-Jervis, "Introduction," in Corral and

Miya-Jervis, eds., *Young Wives' Tales*, xviii. For other third-wave takes on marriage, see Jennifer Allyn and David Allyn, "Identity Politics," in *To Be Real: Telling the Truth and Changing the Face of Feminism*, ed. Rebecca Walker (New York: Anchor Books, 1995), 143–156; and Naomi Wolf, "Brideland," in Walker, ed., *To Be Real*, 35–40.

13. Meg Daly, "The Allure of the One-Night Stand," in Damsky, ed., *Sex and Single Girls*, 196.

14. Katie Roiphe, *The Morning After: Sex, Fear, and Feminism on Campus* (Boston: Little, Brown and Company, 1993), 171.

15. See Roiphe, "Date Rape Hysteria," *New York Times*, November 20, 1991, A29; and "Date Rape's Other Victim," *New York Times Magazine*, June 13, 1993, 26+.

16. Baumgardner and Richards, *Manifesta*, 250, emphasis in original. For other third-wave critiques of Roiphe's arguments regarding date rape, see Katie J. Hogan, "'Victim Feminism' and the Complexities of AIDS," in Maglin and Perry, eds., *"Bad Girls"/"Good Girls,"* 68–89; Paula Kamen, "Acquaintance Rape: Revolution and Reaction," in Maglin and Perry, eds., *"Bad Girls"/"Good Girls";* and Kamen, "Erasing Rape: Media Hype an Attack on Sexual-Assault Research," *Extra!* November/December 1993.

17. Linda Garber, *Identity Poetics: Race, Class, and the Lesbian-Feminist Roots of Queer Theory* (New York: Columbia University Press, 2001), 210.

18. Abby Levine, "Better Living through Porn," in Damsky, ed., *Sex and Single Girls*, 326.

19. As Andrea Dworkin notes, "'Sex-negative' is the current secular *reductio ad absurdum* used to dismiss or discredit ideas, particularly political critiques, that might lead to detumescence." Dworkin, *Intercourse* (New York: The Free Press, 1987), 48.

20. Johnson, "Jane Hocus, Jane Focus," 1.

21. As Lisa Marie Hogeland reminds us, "the rhetoric of generational differences in feminism works to mask real political differences—fundamental differences in our visions of feminism's task and accomplishments." Lisa Marie Hogeland, "Against Generational Thinking, or, Some Things that 'Third Wave' Feminism Isn't," *Women's Studies in Communication* 24, no. 1 (Spring 2001): 107.

22. Merri Lisa Johnson, "Blow Job Queen," in Damsky, ed., *Sex and Single Girls*, 84.

23. Johnson, "Blow Job Queen," 84.

24. Johnson, "Blow Job Queen," 77.

25. Johnson, "Blow Job Queen," 83–84.

26. Johnson, "Blow Job Queen," 78–79.

27. Johnson, "Blow Job Queen," 77, 85.

28. Johnson, ed., *Jane Sexes It Up*, back cover. Citing Elizabeth Minnich's critique of the ways in which some young feminists posit themselves as on the cutting edge, Johnson writes, "The truth is, it has been hard to resist the urge to announce that the girls of *Jane* are 'today's truest and bravest feminists.'" Johnson, "Jane Hocus, Jane Focus," 360, note 3. See Elizabeth Kamarch Minnich, "Feminist Attacks on Feminisms: Patriarchy's Prodigal Daughters," *Feminist Studies* 24, no. 1 (Spring 1998): 159–175.

29. Johnson, "Jane Hocus, Jane Focus," 4. Johnson seems to mean the generation whose values are reflected in *Jane Sexes It Up* when she writes the term *"Jane* generation"—thus the italics for "Jane."

30. Denfeld, *The New Victorians*, 21.

31. Merri Lisa Johnson, "Pearl Necklace: The Politics of Masturbation Fantasies," in Johnson, ed., *Jane Sexes It Up*, 313.

32. Johnson, "Pearl Necklace," 316–317.

33. Gayle Rubin, "Thinking Sex: Notes for a Radical Theory of the Politics of Sexuality," in Vance, ed., *Pleasure and Danger*, 282.

34. Rubin, "Thinking Sex," 282.

35. Robin Morgan, "Lesbianism and Feminism: Synonyms or Contradictions?" (1973) in Morgan, *Going Too Far: The Personal Chronicle of a Feminist* (New York: Random House, 1977), 181.

36. Johnson, "Blow Job Queen," 84.

37. Johnson, "Pearl Necklace," 313. The relationship between feminist theory and sexual transgression is explored in more detail in chapter 4.

38. Johnson, "Jane Hocus, Jane Focus," 2, emphasis in original.

39. Johnson, "Pearl Necklace," 321, 322.

40. Johnson, "Pearl Necklace," 312.

41. Johnson, "Blow Job Queen," 78–79; Johnson, "Pearl Necklace," 312, 326. At other moments, Johnson replaces bravado with a different rhetorical style, revealing, "I would have done anything in exchange for traditional couplehood. This was, maybe still is, the weak spot in my practice of feminism." Johnson, "Fuck You and Your Untouchable Face: Third Wave Feminism and the Problem of Romance," in Johnson, ed., *Jane Sexes It Up*, 21.

42. This bad-girl-for-effect quality can also be seen in Johnson's author blurb for *Jane Sexes It Up*, where she describes herself as someone who has "earned her Ph.D. in English and has worked as a stripper." Indeed, stripping in particular and sex work generally have been major themes in third-wave discourse and cultural production, with the stripper/porn star becoming a sort of third-wave icon. For third-wave perspectives on sex work, see Kari Kesler, "The Plain-Clothes Whore," in Johnson, ed., *Jane Sexes It Up*, 231–240; Kirsten Pullen, "Co-Ed Call Girls," in Johnson, ed., *Jane Sexes It Up*, 207–230; Jocelyn Taylor, "Testimony of a Naked Woman," in Walker, ed., *To Be Real*, 219–237. See also the documentary *Live Nude Girls Unite*, dir. Julia Query and Vicky Funari, First Run Features, New York, 2000.

43. Catherine Millet, *The Sexual Life of Catherine M.*, trans. Adriana Hunter (New York: Grove Press, 2003), 163.

44. Stevi Jackson and Sue Scott, "Sexual Skirmishes and Feminist Factions," in *Feminism and Sexuality: A Reader*, ed. Stevi Jackson and Sue Scott (New York: Columbia University Press, 1996), 5. See also Ellen Willis, who argues that women must "destroy the association between sex and badness." Willis, "Toward a Feminist Sexual Revolution," 20.

45. As Lisa Miya-Jervis, the editor of *Bitch* magazine, notes, "The true promise of sex-positive feminism is not to make way for the triumph of the überbabe—that would just create new and different hoops for women to jump through. . . . No, the goal of sex-positive feminism is to enable all of us to express our sexuality to its fullest, live our sex lives as we want to, without guilt or stigma or external imperatives." Miya-Jervis, "A Celibate Sexpot Ties the Knot," in Damsky, ed., *Sex and Single Girls*, 287.

46. African-American women's absence from this feminist debate may have some-

thing to do with the ways in which black women's sexuality has been incorporated into feminism. As Hortense Spillers pointed out in the mid-1980s, "Black American women in the public/critical discourse of feminist thought have no acknowledged sexuality because they enter the historical stage from quite another angle of entrance from that of Anglo-American women." Spillers, "Interstices: A Small Drama of Words," in Vance, ed., *Pleasure and Danger*, 79.

47. Barbara McCaskill and Layli Phillips, "We Are All 'Good Woman!': A Womanist Critique of the Current Feminist Conflict," in Maglin and Perry, eds., *"Bad Girls"/"Good Girls,"* 116.

48. Jane Gerhard, *Desiring Revolution: Second-Wave Feminism and the Rewriting of American Sexual Thought, 1920 to 1982* (New York: Columbia University Press, 2001), 115.

49. Johnson, "Jane Hocus, Jane Focus," 4, emphasis in original.

50. Bailey, "Unpacking the Mother/Daughter Baggage: Reassessing Second- and Third-Wave Tensions," *Women's Studies Quarterly* 30, nos. 3 and 4 (2002): 140. For more on how feminism functions as an authority figure, see Rosi Braidotti, "Generations of Feminists, or, Is There Life after Post-Modernism?" *Found Object* 16 (1995): 55–62. For a discussion of senior academic feminists' power and authority, particularly in relation to junior faculty and graduate students, see Jane Gallop and Elizabeth Francis, "Talking Across," in *Generations: Academic Feminists in Dialogue*, ed. Devoney Looser and Ann Kaplan (Minneapolis: University of Minnesota Press, 1997), 103–131; and Jane Gallop, *Feminist Accused of Sexual Harassment* (Durham, N.C.: Duke University Press, 1997).

51. Bailey, "Unpacking the Mother/Daughter Baggage," 150.

52. As I will discuss in more detail in chapter 5, the phrase "the Feminism that gets to wear a capital 'F'" comes from Gina Dent's "Missionary Position," in Walker, ed., *To Be Real*, 62.

53. Bailey, "Unpacking the Mother/Daughter Baggage," 141.

54. Pat Califia, "Feminism and Sadomasochism," *Heresies 12* (1981): 32; special issue: *Sex Issue*.

55. Roiphe, *The Morning After*, 84.

56. Denfeld, *The New Victorians*, 91.

57. Denfeld, *The New Victorians*, 112, 122.

58. Roiphe, *The Morning After*, 84.

59. Denfeld, *The New Victorians*, 54.

60. Roiphe, *The Morning After*, 81; Denfeld, *The New Victorians*, 115, 35.

61. Denfeld, *The New Victorians*, 55.

62. Denfeld, *The New Victorians*, 11–12. Describing the notion that women *must be* lesbians to be feminists, Denfeld writes, "A radical concept in the mid-seventies, this theory gained mainstream popularity in the eighties through women's studies, feminist literature, and conferences on sexual violence. Today it is entrenched as a major feminist tenet in the places young women encounter the movement—especially in women's studies classes." *The New Victorians*, 31.

63. For an analysis of the ways in which lesbian-baiting is used to keep women from identifying as feminists, see Lisa Marie Hogeland, "Fear of Feminism: Why Young Women Get the Willies," *Ms.*, November/December 1994, 18–21; and Donna

Minkowitz, "The Newsroom Becomes a Battleground: Is the Media's Siege on Lesbians in the Women's Movement a Desperate Attempt to Undermine Feminism?" *The Advocate*, May 19, 1992, 30–37. For more discussion on how feminism connotes lesbianism for many young women, see also Naomi Wolf, *Fire with Fire: The New Female Power and How It Will Change the 21st Century* (New York: Random House, 1993), 62; and Rose L. Glickman, *Daughters of Feminists* (New York: St. Martin's Press, 1993), 6–17.

64. Nancy F. Cott, *The Grounding of Modern Feminism* (New Haven, Conn.: Yale University Press, 1987), 279.

65. Susan Bolotin, "Views from the Postfeminist Generation," *New York Times Magazine*, October 17, 1982, 30.

66. Denfeld, *The New Victorians*, 35.

67. Denfeld, *The New Victorians*, 57.

68. Roiphe, "Men: What's to Be Afraid of?" *Chatelaine*, July 1994, 56–57.

69. Dworkin, for example, routinely refers to her life partner, writer John Stoltenberg, in both interviews and essays. See Norah Vincent, "Sex, Love & Politics," interview with Andrea Dworkin, *New York Press*, February 4, 1998, 40–42. For an interesting article on Catherine MacKinnon's heterosexuality, see Dinitia Smith, "Love Is Strange: The Crusading Feminist and the Repentant Womanizer," *New York*, March 22, 1993, 36–43.

70. Willis, "Toward a Feminist Sexual Revolution," 8.

71. For Denfeld's discussion of Nestle, see *The New Victorians*, 113–114.

72. Denfeld, *The New Victorians*, 215–216; Gayle Rubin, "The Leather Menace: Comments on Politics and S/M," in *Coming to Power: Writings and Graphics on Lesbian S/M*, ed. Samois (Berkeley: Samois, 1981), 192–225. See also Pat Califia's discussion, one that predates Denfeld's, of the ways in which feminism is Victorian and old-fashioned; Califia, *Public Sex: The Culture of Radical Sex* (Pittsburgh: Cleis Press, 1994), 110–111.

73. Quoted in Johnson, "Pearl Necklace," 311.

74. Califia, "Feminism and Sadomasochism," 30.

75. Califia, "Feminism and Sadomasochism," 30.

76. Pat Califia is now Patrick Califia, so these feminine pronouns no longer describe his current gender status. However, since I am writing about Califia's earlier work before his gender transition, I refer to Califia using feminine pronouns.

77. Bailey, "Unpacking the Mother/Daughter Baggage," 150.

78. Ellen Willis, "Villains and Victims: 'Sexual Correctness' and the Repression of Feminism," in Maglin and Perry, eds., *"Bad Girls"/"Good Girls,"* 52–53.

79. Johnson, "Jane Hocus, Jane Focus," 3, emphasis in original.

80. Alyssa Harad, "Reviving Lolita; or, Because Junior High Is Still Hell," in *Catching a Wave: Reclaiming Feminism for the 21st Century*, ed. Rory Dicker and Alison Piepmeier (Boston: Northeastern University Press, 2003), 84.

81. Johnson, "Pearl Necklace," 313.

82. Carol Siegel, *New Millennial Sexstyles* (Bloomington: Indiana University Press, 2000), 134–135, emphasis added.

83. Patricia Payette, "The Feminist Wife? Notes from a Political 'Engagement,'" in Johnson, ed., *Jane Sexes It Up*, 141.

84. Damsky, "Introduction," xiii.

85. For more on the relationship between HBO's *Sex and the City* and third-wave feminism, see my essay "Orgasms and Empowerment: *Sex and the City* and Third Wave Feminism," in *Reading Sex and the City*, ed. Kim Akass and Janet McCabe (London: I. B. Tauris, 2003), 65–82.

86. Debbie Stoller, "Sex and the Thinking Girl," in *The Bust Guide to the New Girl Order*, ed. Marcelle Karp and Debbie Stoller (New York: Penguin Books, 1999), 79.

87. Rachel Lehmann-Haupt, "How to Talk Dirty and Influence People: The Selling of the Female Orgasm," *Paper*, February 2000, 64.

88. Stoller, "Sex and the Thinking Girl," 84.

89. Alex Kuczynski, "The New Feminist Mystique," *New York Times*, September 10, 2001, C1.

90. Glossing this stereotype, Paula Kamen, in her 1991 *Feminist Fatale*, found that when she asked 103 "nonactivists" "What do you associate with the word 'feminist'?" the responses she got went like this: "I imagine: bra-burning, hairy-legged, amazon, castrating, militant-almost-antifeminine, communist, Marxist, separatist, female skinheads, female supremacists, he-woman types, bunch-a-lesbians, you-know-dykes, man-haters, man-bashers, wanting-men's-jobs, wanting-to-dominate men, want-to-be-men, wear-short-hair-to-look-unattractive, bizarre-chicks-running-around-doing-kooky-thing, i-am-woman-hear-me-roar, uptight, angry, white-middle-class radicals." Kamen, *Feminist Fatale: Voices from the "Twentysomething" Generation Explore the Future of the "Women's Movement"* (New York: Donald I. Fine, 1991), 23.

91. Kathy Bail, ed., *DIY Feminism* (Sydney, Australia: Allen and Unwin, 1996), 5.

92. Tad Friend, "Yes," *Esquire*, February 1994, 50.

93. Friend, "Yes," 48.

94. Patricia Ireland quoted in Friend, "Yes," 50.

95. As Anna Quindlen describes "babe feminism": "we're young, we're fun, we do what we want in bed." "It has a shorter shelf life than the feminism of sisterhood. I've been a babe, and I've been a sister. Sister lasts longer." Quindlen, "And Now, Babe Feminism" (1994), in Maglin and Perry, eds., *"Bad Girls"/"Good Girls,"* 4.

96. Wendy Kaminer coins the term "bimbo feminism" in her "Bimbo Feminism," in Kaminer, *True Love Waits: Essays and Criticism* (Reading, Mass.: Addison-Wesley, 1996), 22–28.

97. Leah Rumack, "Lipstick," in *Turbo Chicks: Talking Young Feminisms*, ed. Allyson Mitchell, Lisa Bryn Rundle, and Lara Karaian (Toronto: Sumach Press, 2001), 99.

98. Wolf, *Fire with Fire*, 184.

99. Johnson, "Jane Hocus, Jane Focus," 7, emphasis in original.

100. As Jo Triglio writes, "Second wave feminism has not been successful at producing new, interesting forms of sexuality." She continues, "This leaves young feminists either alienated, confused, or in the sex shop, spending lots of money on overpriced sex toys." Jo Trigilio in Rita Alfonso and Jo Trigilio, "Surfing the Third Wave: A Dialogue between Two Third Wave Feminists," *Hypatia: A Journal of Feminist Philosophy* 12, no. 3 (Summer 1997): 12.

101. Naomi Wolf, "Radical Heterosexuality . . . or How to Love a Man and Save Your Soul," *Ms.*, July/August 1992, 29–31. See also Wolf, "Brideland."

102. Willis, "Toward a Feminist Sexual Revolution," 9.

103. Natasha Walter, *The New Feminism* (London: Little, Brown and Company, 1998), 113. This point is echoed by Carol Siegel, writing as a "heterosexual feminist critic," who notes: "Current feminist narratives of heterosexuality almost never allow that sex can be an area of women's lives in which we experiment fairly freely with various roles, including exercising direct power over males. We need to recognize that some of us not only can but often do use sex in ways traditionally associated with masculine freedom: that is, to feel powerful in relation to another person and as a form of physical recreation through which we experience our bodies and other peoples' as sources of our own pleasure." Siegel, *New Millennial Sexstyles*, 4.

104. Sarah Smith, "A Cock of One's Own: Getting a Firm Grip on Feminist Sexual Power," in Johnson, ed., *Jane Sexes It Up*, 303.

105. Feminists for Fornication, "Mission Statement," Milwaukee, July 1996.

106. I discuss this point in more detail in chapter 4.

107. Paula Kamen rightly cautions us against viewing women's sexual "progress" in solely positive terms: "Instead of living up to the standards set by men, a woman with real sexual power lives up to those standards derived from within herself. She has the confidence and self-esteem to take precautions against unwanted pregnancy, steer sex toward her own satisfaction, and stand up for her rights in a relationship. . . . [This] is reinforced by outside forces, including support from men and a community of women, who provide validation, political consciousness, and greater knowledge of sexual choices. Furthermore, sexual power requires economic power, to make choices out of desire and not of desperation. When more women recognize these types of sexual power, they will experience a real sexual revolution." Kamen, *Her Way*, 248.

108. Pandora L. Leong, "Living Outside the Box," in Hernández and Rehman, eds., *Colonize This!* 353.

109. Joan Nestle quoted in *Hand on the Pulse*, dir. Joyce Warshow, Frameline Distribution, San Francisco, 2002.

4. Neither My Mother nor My Lover

1. Naomi Wolf, *Fire with Fire: The New Female Power and How It Will Change the 21st Century* (New York: Random House, 1993), 184.

2. Sharon Marcus rightly critiques this supposition when she asks, "Can an erotic model be an alternative to a familial one, when we can seldom peel erotic and familial structures apart from one another?" Marcus in Barbara Christian et al., "Conference Call," *differences: A Journal of Feminist Cultural Studies* 2, no. 3 (1990): 99.

3. Rebecca Dakin Quinn, "An Open Letter to Institutional Mothers," in *Generations: Academic Feminists in Dialogue*, ed. Devoney Looser and Ann Kaplan (Minneapolis: University of Minnesota Press), 179.

4. Lillian Faderman, "Afterword," in *Cross Purposes: Lesbians, Feminists, and the Limits of Alliance*, ed. Dana Heller (Bloomington: Indiana University Press, 1997), 221.

5. See, for example, Nancy Chodorow, *The Reproduction of Mothering: Psycho-analysis and the Sociology of Gender* (Berkeley: University of California Press, 1978).

6. For example, Chodorow argues that lesbian relationships "tend to recreate mother-daughter emotions and connections." Chodorow, *The Reproduction of Mothering*, 200.

7. Adrienne Rich, "Compulsory Heterosexuality and Lesbian Existence," in Rich, *Blood, Bread, and Poetry: Selected Prose 1979–1985* (New York: W.W. Norton & Company, 1985), 54.

8. Quoted in Adrienne Rich, *Of Woman Born: Motherhood as Experience and Institution* (New York: W.W. Norton & Company, 1976), 232. This point is also echoed in a recent anthology by second-wave lesbians writing about their mothers, in which the editor writes, "I have wanted to find my mother in every woman I've ever loved. I have ached to find traces of her smell, her touch, the way she would cradle the back of my head, her songs." Catherine Reid, "Introduction," in *Every Woman I've Ever Loved: Lesbian Writers on Their Mothers*, ed. Catherine Reid and Holly Iglesias (San Francisco: Cleis Press, 1997), ix. The relationship between lesbianism and mother-love is also sarcastically pointed out by Camille Paglia who writes, "[l]esbianism, seeking a lost state of blissful union with the mother, is cozy, regressive, and, I'm sorry to say, too often intellectually enervating, tending toward the inert." Paglia, "Homosexuality at the Fin de Siècle," in Paglia, *Sex, Art, and American Culture* (New York: Vintage Books, 1992), 24.

9. As Lynne Segal writes about the queer turn in lesbian life, "Gay girls were being urged to keep up with the boys." Segal, *Straight Sex: Rethinking the Politics of Pleasure* (Berkeley: University of California Press, 1994), 206.

10. For example, many lesbians were involved in the direct action group ACT UP, which eventually spawned both Queer Nation and the Lesbian Avengers. The latter group began organizing in the summer of 1992 and had its first action that fall. For more on the Lesbian Avengers, see Sarah Schulman, *My American Life: Lesbian and Gay Life during the Reagan/Bush Years* (New York: Routledge, 1994), 277–319. For more on women and ACT UP, see ACT UP/NY Women and AIDS Book Group, *Women, AIDS, and Activism*, ed. Cynthia Chris and Monica Pearl (Boston: South End Press, 1990).

11. For more on the sex segregation of the homophile movement, see John D'Emilio, "Dual Identity and Lesbian Autonomy: The Beginning of Separate Organizing among Women," in John D'Emilio, *Sexual Politics, Sexual Communities: The Making of a Homosexual Minority in the United States, 1940–1970*, 2nd ed. (Chicago: University of Chicago Press, 1998). For more on this early period of gay and lesbian history and the gay and lesbian civil rights movement generally, see D'Emilio, *Sexual Politics, Sexual Communities;* Martin Duberman, Martha Vicinus, and George Chauncey, Jr., eds., *Hidden from History: Reclaiming the Gay and Lesbian Past* (New York: Penguin Books, 1989); Martin Duberman, *Stonewall* (New York: Plume, 1994); Lillian Faderman, *Odd Girls and Twilight Lovers: A History of Lesbian Life in Twentieth-Century America* (New York: Penguin Books, 1991); Lillian Faderman, *Surpassing the Love of Men: Romantic Friendship and Love between Women from the Renaissance to the Present* (New York: William Morrow and Company, 1981); and Neil Miller, *Out of the Past: Gay and Lesbian History from 1869 to the Present* (New York: Vintage Books, 1995).

12. Ruth L. Schwartz, "New Alliances, Strange Bedfellows: Lesbians, Gay Men,

and AIDS," in *Sisters, Sexperts, Queers: Beyond the Lesbian Nation,* ed. Arlene Stein (New York: Plume, 1993), 235.

13. Schwartz, "New Alliances, Strange Bedfellows," 235, emphasis in original.

14. For one example of lesbians describing their sexuality as being shaped by gay male sexual practices and gay male porn, see Kris Franklin and Sarah E. Chinn, "Ms. Strangelove, or, How I Stopped Worrying and Learned to Love Gay Male Porn," in *Generation Q: Gays, Lesbians, and Bisexuals Born around 1969's Stonewall Riots Tell Their Stories of Growing Up in the Age of Information,* ed. Robin Bernstein and Seth Clark Silberman (Los Angeles: Alyson Publications, 1996), 168–173. See also Julia Creet, "Lesbian Sex/Gay Sex: What's the Difference?" *Outlook* 11 (Winter 1991): 28–34. See also Abby Levine's "Better Living through Porn" in which she argues that "gay male porn charges my sexual energy." In *Sex and Single Girls: Straight and Queer Women on Sexuality,* ed. Lee Damsky (Seattle: Seal Press, 2000), 329.

15. Although it is beyond the scope of this project to analyze the point, the apparent rise in the number of female-to-male gender transitions over the last decade, particularly among former self-identified lesbians, is also part of this new attitude toward men.

16. One critical commentator asks of 1990s lesbians: "Is it really good enough to base your whole sexuality on what you do in bed?" Cited in Emma Healey, *Lesbian Sex Wars* (London: Virago Press, 1996), 33.

17. Radicalesbians, "The Woman Identified Woman," in *Notes from the Third Year: Women's Liberation* (New York, 1971), 81–84; Adrienne Rich, "Compulsory Heterosexuality and Lesbian Existence." For more on Rich's essay and a debate about the lesbian continuum, see Ann Ferguson, "Patriarchy, Sexual Identity, and the Sexual Revolution," *Signs: A Journal of Women in Culture and Society* 7, no. 1 (Autumn 1981): 158–172; Jacquelyn N. Zita, "Historical Amnesia and the Lesbian Continuum," *Signs* 7, no. 1 (Autumn 1981): 172–187; and Kathryn Pyne Addelson, "Words and Lives," *Signs* 7, no. 1 (Autumn 1981): 187–199.

18. Arlene Stein, "All Dressed Up, but No Place to Go? Style Wars and the New Lesbianism," *Outlook* 4 (Winter 1989): 39.

19. Arlene Stein, "Introduction," in Stein, ed., *Sisters, Sexperts, Queers,* 5.

20. Elizabeth Wilson, "Is Transgression Transgressive?" in *Activating Theory: Lesbian, Gay, Bisexual Politics,* ed. Joseph Bristow and Angelia R. Wilson (London: Lawrence & Wisehart, 1993), 11.

21. Beth Elliott, "Bisexuality: The Best Thing that Ever Happened to Lesbian-Feminism?" in *Bi Any Other Name: Bisexual People Speak Out,* ed. Lorraine Hutchins and Lani Kaahumanu (Boston: Alyson Publications, 1991), 325.

22. Elliott, "Bisexuality," 326.

23. Riki Anne Wilchins, "The Menace Statement to Janice Raymond," in Wilchins, *Read My Lips: Sexual Subversion and the End of Gender* (Ithaca, N.Y.: Firebrand Books, 1997), 61.

24. Linda Semple quoted in Cherry Smyth, *Lesbians Talk Queer Notions* (London: Scarlet Press, 1992), 26. For an important discussion of the ways in which feminism can be used to hurt other feminists, see Dorothy Allison, *Skin: Talking about Sex, Class & Literature* (Ithaca, N.Y.: Firebrand Books, 1994).

25. Natasha Gray, "Bored with the Boys: Cracks in the Queer Coalition," *NYQ,* April 26, 1992, 27.

26. Debi Sundahl, "Battle Scars," *On Our Backs,* September/October 1994, 32.

27. Arlene Stein, "All Dressed Up, but No Place to Go?" 34–43. For more on the important role that fashion has played in defining various generations and "types" of lesbians, see the documentary *Framing Lesbian Fashion,* dir. Karen Everett, Frameline, San Francisco, 1992. For more on "lesbian chic" in the 1990s, and a prime example of the popular media's fascination with it, see Jeanie Russell Kasindorf, "Lesbian Chic: The Bold, Brave New World of Gay Women," *New York,* May 10, 1993, 30–37.

28. Peggy Sue quoted in *Outlook* 11 (Winter 1991): 18.

29. Letter by Yvonne Zylan, *Outlook* 8 (Spring 1990): 4.

30. In describing current generational conflict among lesbians, Alisa Solomon writes: "We dykes are rebels. . . . [W]hy, then, should we tie each other down with a new set of rules drawn up by our sisters? This is a question many young dykes are asking, with no small measure of venom. The result has been a new split in the lesbian community—between women whose analysis of sexuality was based on a model of oppression and victimization, and women whose model is Madonna—an emblem of autonomy and sexual taboo. My generation rebelled against patriarchy; the 'new' lesbians are rebelling against *us.*" Alisa Solomon, "Dykotomies: Scents and Sensibility," in Stein, ed., *Sisters, Sexperts, Queers,* 213, emphasis in original.

31. For more on feminism as an anti-sex "symbolic mother," see Julia Creet, "Daughter of the Movement: The Psychodynamics of Lesbian S/M Fantasy," *differences: A Journal of Feminist Cultural Studies* 3, no. 2 (Summer 1991): 143.

32. Tracy Morgan, "Butch-Femme and the Politics of Identity," in Stein, ed., *Sisters, Sexperts, Queers,* 39. See also Jeannine Delombard, "Femmenism," in *To Be Real: Telling the Truth and Changing the Face of Feminism,* ed. Rebecca Walker (New York: Anchor Books, 1995), 21–33. Delombard argues that her femme identity is a rebellious reaction to both her mother's feminism and the lesbian-feminist lesbian identities available to her.

33. Susie Bright, *Sexual State of the Union* (New York: Simon & Schuster, 1997), 131.

34. Pat Califia, *Macho Sluts* (Boston: Alyson Publications, 1988), 13.

35. B. Ruby Rich, "Feminism and Sexuality in the 1980s," *Feminist Studies* 12, no. 3 (Fall 1986): 532.

36. For more on this protest, in which a group of lesbians interrupted the Second Congress to Unite Women, see Alice Echols, *Daring to Be Bad: Radical Feminism in America, 1967–1975* (Minneapolis: University of Minnesota, 1989), 214–216.

37. See Katie King, "Lesbianism as Feminism's Magical Sign," in King, *Theory in Its Feminist Travels: Conversations in U.S. Women's Movements* (Bloomington: Indiana University Press, 1994), 124–137; and King, "Producing Sex, Theory, and Culture: Gay/Straight Remappings in Contemporary Feminism," in *Conflicts in Feminism,* ed. Marianne Hirsch and Evelyn Fox Keller (New York: Routledge, 1990), 82–101.

38. Joan Nestle, *A Restricted Country* (Ithaca, N.Y.: Firebrand Books, 1987), 124.

39. Nestle, *A Restricted Country,* 106–107.

40. Jan Clausen, "My Interesting Condition," *Outlook* 7 (Winter 1990): 15.

41. Charlotte Ashton, "Getting Hold of the Phallus: 'Post-Lesbian' Power Negotiations," in *Assaults on Convention: Essays on Lesbian Transgressors,* ed. Nicola Godwin, Belinda Hollows, and Sheridan Nye (London: Cassell, 1996), 159.

42. Healey, *Lesbian Sex Wars*, 35.

43. Eve Sedgwick quoted in "Identity Crisis: Queer Politics in the Age of Possibilities," *Village Voice*, June 30, 1992, 28.

44. Warner, "Introduction," in *Fear of a Queer Planet: Queer Politics and Social Theory*, ed. Michael Warner (Minneapolis: University of Minnesota Press, 1993), xxvii, emphasis in original.

45. This point is also noted by Judith Butler, who writes, "If the 'sex' which feminism is said to study constitutes one dimension of the multidimensional 'sex' that lesbian and gay research is said to study, then the implicit argument is that lesbian and gay studies does precisely what feminism is said to do but does it in a more *expansive and complex* way." "Against Proper Objects," in *Feminism Meets Queer Theory*, ed. Elizabeth Weed and Naomi Schor (Bloomington: Indiana University Press, 1997), 7, emphasis added.

46. Lucia Hicks quoted in Arlene Stein, *Sex and Sensibility: Stories of a Lesbian Generation* (Berkeley: University of California Press, 1997), 186.

47. Maria Maggenti, "Wandering through Herland," in Stein, ed., *Sisters, Sexperts, Queers*, 246. See also Mocha Jean Herrup, "Virtual Identity," in Walker, ed., *To Be Real*, 239–251; and Arlene Stein, "Sisters and Queers: The Decentering of Lesbian Feminism," *Socialist Review* 22, no. 1 (1992): 52.

48. Although the term "queer" has been around for many years as a derogatory term for "homosexual," in its recent reappropriated positive use, "queer" became popularized in the late 1980s and early 1990s. See Annamarie Jagose, *Queer Theory: An Introduction* (New York: New York University Press, 1996), 76. The term "queer theory" is attributed to Teresa de Lauretis and her essay "Queer Theory: Lesbian and Gay Sexualities," *differences: A Journal of Feminist Cultural Studies. Queer Theory: Lesbian and Gay Sexualities* 3, no. 2 (Summer 1991): iii–xviii.

49. Jagose, *Queer Theory*, 112.

50. Maggenti, "Wandering through Herland," 245–253. Also, Maggenti, "Women as Queer Nationals," *Outlook* 11 (Winter 1991): 20–23. For more on the ways in which the term "queer" ends up repeating the same mistakes and divisions around gender that plagued the gay liberation movement, see Mary McIntosh, "Queer Theory and the War of the Sexes," in Bristow and Wilson, eds., *Activating Theory*, 30–52.

51. Smyth, *Lesbians Talk Queer Notions*, 41–42; Stein, "Introduction," in Stein, ed., *Sisters, Sexperts, Queers*, xv.

52. Smyth, *Lesbians Talk Queer Notions*, 38; Stein, "Introduction," xv.

53. For more on queerness and bisexuality, see Elizabeth Däumer, "Queer Ethics, or the Challenge of Bisexuality to Lesbian Ethics," *Hypatia: A Journal of Feminist Philosophy* 7, no. 4 (Fall 1992): 91–105; Hutchins and Kaahumanu, eds., *Bi Any Other Name*; Carol Queen, "Strangers at Home: Bisexuals in the Queer Movement," *Outlook* 16 (Spring 1992): 23–33; Gabriel Rotello, "Bi Any Means Necessary," *Village Voice*, June 30, 1992, 37–38; and Elizabeth Reba Weise, ed., *Closer to Home: Bisexuality and Feminism* (Seattle: Seal Press, 1992). For more on queer and transgender identities, see Kate Bornstein, *Gender Outlaw: On Men, Women, and the Rest of Us* (New York: Vintage Books, 1994); and Wilchins, *Read My Lips*. For more on the heterosexual queer, see Calvin Thomas, "Straight with a Twist: Queer Theory and the Subject of Heterosexuality," *The Gay '90s: Disciplinary and Interdisciplinary Formations in Queer Studies*, ed. Thomas Foster, Carol Siegel, and Ellen E. Berry (New York: New York

University Press, 1997), 83–115; and Thomas, ed., *Straight with a Twist: Queer Theory and the Subject of Heterosexuality* (Urbana: University of Illinois Press, 2000).

54. Lisa Power, "Forbidden Fruit," in *Anti-Gay*, ed. Mark Simpson (London: Freedom Editions, 1996), 55–65.

55. Christy Calame and Robbie Scott Phillips, "Fuck Your Healthy Gay Lifestyle (The FRINGE Manifesto—Freaks, Radicals, and Inverts Nail Gay Elite)," in Bernstein and Silberman, eds., *Generation Q*, 235, emphasis in original.

56. Linda Semple quoted in Smyth, *Lesbians Talk Queer Notions*, 20–21.

57. Warner, "Introduction," x.

58. The national gay press "have been either oblivious or hostile to queer theory." Lauren Berlant and Michael Warner, "What Does Queer Theory Teach Us about X?" *PMLA* 110, no. 3 (May 1995): 347.

59. Sarah E. Chinn and Kris Franklin, "The (Queer) Revolution Will Not Be Liberalized," *Minnesota Review* 40 (Spring/Summer 1993): 141.

60. Sue-Ellen Case, "Toward a Butch-Feminist Retro-Future," in Heller, ed., *Cross Purposes*, 213.

61. Anonymous Queers, "Queers Read This" (1990), in *We Are Everywhere: A Historical Sourcebook of Gay and Lesbian Politics*, ed. Mark Blasius and Shane Phelan (New York: Routledge, 1997), 774.

62. King, "Lesbianism as Feminism's Magical Sign," 124. See also Scott Bravmann, *Queer Fictions of the Past: History, Culture, and Difference* (New York: Cambridge University Press, 1997).

63. For more on the relationship between queer and lesbian feminism—and the denial thereof—see Linda Garber, *Identity Poetics: Race, Class, and the Lesbian-Feminist Roots of Queer Theory* (New York: Columbia University Press, 2001). The analogy between queer and gay liberation is frequently made by arguing that both were a reaction to the more reformist politics of their day. For example, Cherry Smyth argues: "Just as queer politics perceives itself in opposition to the more assimilationist approaches of elements of lesbian and gay politics such as the Stonewall Group, GLF [Gay Liberation Front] too saw itself as revolutionary compared to the homophile campaigns for civil rights of the 50s and 60s." Smyth, *Lesbians Talk Queer Notions*, 14.

64. This relationship to the past has a lot in common with the early second wave's relationship to the first wave discussed in chapter 2.

65. One exception to this rule is Jagose's *Queer Theory*. While clearly advocating a queer position, Jagose nevertheless manages to write an account of queer theory's history and lineage that does not reject all that is past in favor of "the new"; rather, Jagose attempts to trace all of the previous movements and schools of thought that led to queer theory.

66. Healey, *Lesbian Sex Wars*, 2. For more on the construction of both lesbian identities and lesbian communities since the late 1960s, see Kristin G. Esterberg, *Lesbian and Bisexual Identities: Constructing Communities, Constructing Selves* (Philadelphia: Temple University Press, 1997); Vera Whisman, *Queer by Choice: Lesbians, Gay Men, and the Politics of Identity* (New York: Routledge, 1996); and Stein, ed., *Sisters, Sexperts, Queers*.

67. For more on a group of young British lesbian separatists in the 1990s, see Gerry Doyle, "No Man's Land: Lesbian Separatism Revisited," in *Assaults on Convention: Essays on Lesbian Transgressors*, ed. Nicola Godwin, Belinda Hollows, and Sheridan Nye (London: Cassell, 1996), 178–197.

68. This point is stressed by Bonnie Zimmerman who, in a critique of *Sisters, Sexperts, Queers*, argues: "Much of what I hear and read these days about lesbian feminism is written by women who criticize it without apparently having had much firsthand experience of the movement and era they condemn. So, increasingly, young women learn about lesbian feminism through parodic representations of it." Zimmerman, "'Confessions' of a Lesbian Feminist," in Heller, ed., *Cross Purposes*, 163.

69. Morgan, "Lesbianism and Feminism: Synonyms or Contradictions?" in Morgan, *Going Too Far: The Personal Chronicle of a Feminist* (New York: Random House, 1977), 181, emphasis in original.

70. Sue Katz cited in Echols, *Daring to Be Bad*, 217–218.

71. During this period, for example, sadomasochism was intensely debated within feminist and lesbian-feminist writing, culminating in a proliferation of texts for and against S/M. For example, see the two defining anthologies on this debate: Samois, ed., *Coming to Power: Writings and Graphics on Lesbian S/M* (Berkeley: Samois, 1981); and Robin Ruth Linden, Darlene R. Pagano, Diana E. H. Russell, and Susan Leigh Star, eds., *Against Sadomasochism: A Radical Feminist Analysis* (San Francisco: Frog in the Well, 1982). The latter book was published in response to the former; thus they serve as a perfect example of both this dialogue/debate within feminism and the way in which this debate tends to get played out in very polarized ways; you're either for or against S/M. See also Laura Lederer, ed., *Take Back the Night: Women on Pornography* (New York: William Morrow and Company, 1980). For more on the central role of S/M within the debate around lesbian sexual politics, see also Healey, *Lesbian Sex Wars*, 89–112. I agree with B. Ruby Rich, who notes that within feminist discourse on sexuality "it is indeed peculiar that the debate on sadomasochism should have arisen as a lesbian issue when the practice is so widespread among heterosexuals." Rich, "Feminism and Sexuality in the 1980s," 535.

72. For more on this argument, see Andrea Dworkin, *Intercourse* (New York: The Free Press, 1987).

73. Esther Newton and Shirley Walton, "The Misunderstanding: Toward a More Precise Sexual Vocabulary," in *Pleasure and Danger: Exploring Female Sexuality*, ed. Carole S. Vance (Boston: Routledge and Kegan Paul, 1985), 250.

74. Sarah Smith, "A Cock of One's Own: Getting a Firm Grip on Feminist Sexual Power," in *Jane Sexes It Up: True Confessions of Feminist Desire*, ed. Merri Lisa Johnson (New York: Four Walls Eight Windows, 2002), 295.

75. As Vera Whisman notes, claims made about sexuality and sexual practice often rely on not recognizing that sexual diversity always exists within generations: "Lesbian feminists were rigid and dead wrong in claiming that lesbians wanted only a diffuse, process-oriented sexuality. But when lesbian queers try to liberate sexuality without recognizing that some women do want that sort of sexuality, they just erect a new barrier, and a new category of the false: false lesbian sex. (You may think that what you're doing is having sex, but it's too tame to be the real thing.)" Vera Whisman, "Identity Crises: Who Is a Lesbian, Anyway?" in Stein, ed., *Sisters, Sexperts, Queers*, 58.

76. Healey, *Lesbian Sex Wars*, 195.

77. Healey, *Lesbian Sex Wars*, 181.

78. An interesting site of generational antagonism: in the British sex-toy catalog *Thrilling Bits*, a dildo is named after the notoriously anti-porn, anti-queer lesbian feminist Sheila Jeffreys. It is called "The Sheila—the Spinster's best friend," named after her book *The Spinster and Her Enemies*. Healey, *Lesbian Sex Wars*, 135.

79. Fanny Fatale, "This Is What Fanny's G-Spot Looks Like!" *On Our Backs,* September/October 1992, 8+. Also see *How to Female Ejaculate,* dir. Fanny Fatale, Fatale Productions, Fatale Media Inc., San Rafael, Calif., 1992.

80. Koedt, "The Myth of the Vaginal Orgasm," in *Radical Feminism,* ed. Anne Koedt, Ellen Levine, and Anita Rapone (New York: Quadrangle, 1973).

81. For more on the G-spot and generational shifts with sexual practice, see Shannon Bell, "Liquid Fire: Female Ejaculation and Fast Feminism," in Johnson, ed., *Jane Sexes It Up,* 327–345.

82. To consider the change in attitude toward the G-spot that took place during this period, one need only compare 1990s lesbian writing with the discussion of the G-spot in Pat Califia's 1980 *Sapphistry,* a book that is, on the whole, uniquely non-judgmental and open to all forms of sexual practice, particularly considering its publication date at the beginning of the sex wars. Califia questions the existence of the G-spot and is skeptical about the "Freudian" investment in proving that vaginal orgasms exist. Califia, *Sapphistry: The Book of Lesbian Sexuality* (Tallahassee, Fla.: Naiad Press, 1980), 78.

83. Alison quoted in Ashton, "Getting Hold of the Phallus," 161–162, emphasis added.

84. The author of the essay, Charlotte Ashton, uses the term to mean "a new broader definition of lesbianism," suggesting that the "post" in the term indicates expansiveness, as with the term "post-feminism" perhaps? Ashton, "Getting Hold of the Phallus," 158.

85. Judith Butler, "The Lesbian Phallus and the Morphological Imaginary," in Butler, *Bodies that Matter: On the Discursive Limits of "Sex"* (New York: Routledge, 1993), 85.

86. Pat Califia, *Public Sex: The Culture of Radical Sex* (Pittsburgh: Cleis Press, 1994), 188.

87. This point is also made by Tamsin Wilton and Carol Queen, who note that because penises "come attached to male people and demonstrate a troublesome tendency to resist both the burden of phallic power (they may become soft and flaccid at the most inconvenient moments) and the imposition of disciplinary power (they are not easily controlled or directed by their 'owner'), it is not hard to see that dildos may be perceived as superior." Cited in Smith, "A Cock of One's Own," 298.

88. For more on the distinction between the phallus and the penis, particularly as it relates to female sexuality, see Jane Gallop, "Beyond the Phallus," in Gallop, *Thinking through the Body* (New York: Columbia University Press, 1988), 119–133; and Butler, "The Lesbian Phallus and the Morphological Imaginary," 57–91.

89. Laura quoted in Stein, ed., *Sex and Sensibility,* 168.

90. For more on this phenomenon within lesbian culture, see chapter 6 of Arlene Stein's *Sex and Sensibility,* entitled "Sleeping with the Enemy?"

91. It should be noted, of course, that the title *On Our Backs* is a response to the title of the feminist magazine *off our backs* and thus is itself a "traitorous" action in response to a certain kind of feminism.

92. Sundahl writes, "Penetration was traitorous to the lesbian nation." Debi Sundahl, "Battle Scars," *On Our Backs,* September/October 1994, 34, 32.

93. Sundahl, "Battle Scars," 34.

94. Clausen, "My Interesting Condition," 15. For more on Jan Clausen's story, see her memoir *Apples and Oranges: My Journey through Sexual Identity* (Boston: Houghton Mifflin, 1999).

95. In describing the experience of one of the lesbians interviewed for her study, Arlene Stein notes: "The fact that heterosexual love was so forbidden in her friendship circle made it even more powerful." *Sex and Sensibility*, 168.

96. Karen Bullock-Jordan, "Eternal Novice," in Damsky, ed., *Sex and Single Girls*, 239.

97. For a different variation of the intersection between queerness and hetero-sexuality—or the queering of heterosexuality—see Eve Kosofsky Sedgwick, "Queer and Now," in Sedgwick, *Tendencies* (Durham, N.C.: Duke University Press, 1993), 9–10; and Thomas, "Straight with a Twist." See also Pat Califia's comment that gay sex occurs whenever two gay people (regardless of their individual genders) have sex. Califia, *Public Sex*, 185–186.

98. Califia, *Public Sex*, 181.

99. Califia, *Public Sex*, 177.

100. Califia, *Public Sex*, 177.

101. Laura Doan, ed., *The Lesbian Postmodern* (New York: Columbia University Press, 1994).

102. Kathleen Martindale, *Un/Popular Culture: Lesbian Writing after the Sex Wars* (Albany: State University of New York Press, 1997), 25. For more on the relation-ship between postmodernism, gay identity, and queer identity, see Steven Seidman, "Identity and Politics in a 'Postmodern' Gay Culture: Some Historical and Conceptual Notes," in Warner, ed., *Fear of a Queer Planet*, 105–142.

103. Carol Queen and Lawrence Schimel, *PoMoSexuals: Challenging Assumptions about Gender and Sexuality* (San Francisco: Cleis Press, 1997), 112.

104. Robyn Wiegman, "Introduction: Mapping the Lesbian Postmodern," in Doan, ed., *The Lesbian Postmodern*, 2.

105. On the prevalence of this metaphor, see Jane Gallop, "The Attraction of Mat-rimonial Metaphor," in Gallop, *Around 1981: Academic Feminist Literary Theory* (New York: Routledge, 1992), 177–205. For another example of how this metaphor is used to describe the relationship between lesbians and gay men, see Jacquelyn N. Zita, "Gay and Lesbian Studies: Yet Another Unhappy Marriage?" in *Tilting the Tower: Lesbians Teaching Queer Subjects*, ed. Linda Garber (New York: Routledge, 1994), 258–276.

106. Gayle Rubin, "Thinking Sex: Notes for a Radical Theory of the Politics of Sexuality," in Vance, ed., *Pleasure and Danger*, 300. See also Amber Hollibaugh and Cherríe Moraga, who describe the inability of feminism to theorize sexuality as "the failure of feminism." Hollibaugh and Moraga, "What We're Rolling around in Bed With: Sexual Silences in Feminism," in *Powers of Desire: The Politics of Sexuality*, ed. Ann Snitow, Christine Stansell, and Sharon Thompson (New York: Monthly Review Press, 1983), 395.

107. Warner, "Introduction," viii. For more on the development of queer theory, see Michael Warner, "From Queer to Eternity: An Army of Theorists Cannot Fail," *Village Voice Literary Supplement*, June 1992, 18–19.

108. Garber, *Identity Poetics*, 176.

109. On the back cover of *Coming Out of Feminism*, a book explicitly concerned

with the relationship between queer theory and feminism, the following description is offered: "the 70s women's movement acting as mother or midwife to the 90s generation of queers." Mandy Merck, Naomi Segal, and Elizabeth Wright, eds., *Coming Out of Feminism* (Oxford: Blackwell Publishers, 1998).

110. Elizabeth Weed, "Introduction," in Weed and Schor, eds., *Feminism Meets Queer Theory*, vii. The material in this book was originally published as a special issue of *differences* (6, nos. 2 and 3 [Summer–Fall 1994]) entitled *More Gender Trouble: Feminism Meets Queer Theory*.

111. Dana Heller, "Purposes: An Introduction," in Heller, ed., *Cross Purposes*, 11.

112. Biddy Martin, "Extraordinary Homosexuals and the Fear of Being Ordinary," in Martin, *Femininity Played Straight: The Significance of Being Lesbian* (New York: Routledge, 1996), 45–46.

113. Martin, "Extraordinary Homosexuals," 70.

114. Lillian Faderman, "Afterword," 225.

115. Sherri Paris, rev. of *A Lure of Knowledge: Lesbian Sexuality and Theory*, by Judith Roof, and *Inside/Out: Lesbian Theories, Gay Theories*, ed. Diana Fuss, *Signs: A Journal of Women in Culture and Society* 18, no. 4 (Summer 1993): 988.

116. For more on the ways in which charges of elitism and utopianism are used by those both for and against queer, see Jagose, *Queer Theory*, 106.

117. For example, see Janice G. Raymond, "Putting the Politics Back into Lesbianism," *Women's Studies International Forum* 12, no. 2 (1989): 149–156; Susan J. Wolfe and Julia Penelope, "Sexual Identity/Textual Politics: Lesbian (De/Com)positions," in *Sexual Practice, Textual Theory: Lesbian Cultural Criticism*, ed. Susan J. Wolfe and Julia Penelope (Cambridge, Mass.: Blackwell Publishers, 1993), 5; Julia Penelope, *Call Me Lesbian: Lesbian Lives, Lesbian Theory* (Freedom, Calif.: The Crossing Press, 1992).

118. Sheila Jeffreys, "The Queer Disappearance of Lesbians: Sexuality in the Academy," *Women's Studies International Forum* 17, no. 5 (1994): 459. See also Sheila Jeffreys, "How Orgasm Politics Has Hijacked the Women's Movement," *On the Issues* (Spring 1996): 18+.

119. Perhaps Jeffreys's fear stems from such comments as "the postmodern lesbian is not another lesbian but the *end of lesbianism as we know it*—as a distinct, minority sexual orientation." And "[t]he demise of lesbian feminism may be seen as the end—the climax and collapse—of modern lesbianism, ushering in the new day of the postmodern lesbian." Colleen Lamos, "The Postmodern Lesbian Position: *On Our Backs*," in Doan, ed., *The Lesbian Postmodern*, 94, emphasis added.

120. Jeffreys, "The Queer Disappearance of Lesbians," 471.

5. To Be, or Not to Be, Real

1. Rebecca Walker, "Being Real: An Introduction," in *To Be Real: Telling the Truth and Changing the Face of Feminism*, ed. Rebecca Walker (New York: Anchor Books, 1995), xl.

2. Walker, "Being Real," xxix.

3. In fact, racial diversity has become a hallmark of the third-wave anthology genre.

4. It is interesting that all the writers discussed in this chapter use the word "feminist," as opposed to "womanist" or some other term. They echo the sentiment expressed

by Beverly Guy-Sheftall in *Words of Fire,* where she argues: "I use the term 'feminist' to capture the emancipatory vision and acts of resistance among a diverse group of African American women who attempt in their writings to articulate their understanding of the complex nature of black womanhood, the interlocking nature of the oppressions black women suffer, and the necessity of sustained struggle in their quest for self-definition, the liberation of black people, and gender equality." Guy-Sheftall, "Preface," in *Words of Fire: An Anthology of African-American Feminist Thought,* ed. Beverly Guy-Sheftall (New York: The New Press, 1995), xiv.

5. Walker, "Being Real," xxx–xxxi.

6. Walker, "Being Real," xxxvi–xxxvii.

7. Walker, "Being Real," xxxiv, emphasis added.

8. Danzy Senna, "To Be Real," in Walker, ed., *To Be Real,* 5–6. See also Danzy Senna, "The Color of Love," *O: The Oprah Magazine,* May/June 2000, 117+. Senna's novel *Caucasia* (New York: Riverhead Books, 1997) incorporates many autobiographical elements in its discussion of growing up as the biracial black daughter of a white mother and a black father.

9. Senna, "To Be Real," 13.

10. This point is echoed by many other third-wave writers. Veronica Chambers writes in her 1996 memoir: "Reading about black history, watching documentaries on T.V., it seemed that all the big black battles were over by the time I was born. My parents would talk about black people having to sit on [*sic*] the back of the bus and drink out of separate fountains, but that was so long ago. . . . As bad as those times were, I wished sometimes that there was some sort of protest or something important I could get involved with." Chambers, *Mama's Girl* (New York: Riverhead Books), 52. In describing going to see the twentieth anniversary of Ntozake Shange's *for colored girls who have considered suicide/when the rainbow is enuf,* Joan Morgan writes: "I'd come into the theater hoping to finally feel what my mother must have over two decades ago. I wanted Shange's language to arm me with the awesome power of self-definition. I left realizing this was impossible. As much as I appreciated the artistic, cultural, and historical significance of this moment it wasn't mine to claim. As a child of the post-Civil Rights, post-feminist, post-soul hip-hop generation, my struggle songs consisted of the same notes but they were infused with distinctly different rhythms. What I wanted was a *for colored girls . . .* of my own. The problem was that I was waiting around for someone else to write it." Joan Morgan, *When Chickenheads Come Home to Roost: My Life as a Hip-Hop Feminist* (New York: Simon & Schuster, 1999), 21–22.

11. Senna, "To Be Real," 18.

12. Senna, "To Be Real," 13–14.

13. Senna, "To Be Real," 20.

14. Kristal Brent Zook, "A Manifesto of Sorts for a Black Feminist Movement," *New York Times Magazine,* November 12, 1995, 88.

15. Morgan, *When Chickenheads,* 62. In its 2000 paperback edition, the subtitle of Morgan's book is changed from "My Life as a Hip-Hop Feminist" to "A Hip-Hop Feminist Breaks It Down."

16. Morgan, *When Chickenheads,* 76.

17. Morgan, *When Chickenheads,* 37.

18. Morgan, *When Chickenheads,* 59. A different take on their generation is offered by Daisy Hernández and Bushra Rehman in their introduction to *Colonize This!*: "As

young women of color, we have both a different and similar relationship to feminism as the women in our mothers' generation. We've grown up with legalized abortion, the legacy of the Civil Rights movement and gay liberation, but we still deal with sexual harassment, racist remarks from feminists and the homophobia within our communities. The difference is that now we talk about these issues in women's studies classes, in classrooms that are both multicultural but xenophobic, and in a society that pretends to be racially integrated but remains racially profiled." Rehman and Hernández, "Introduction," in *Colonize This! Young Women of Color on Today's Feminism*, ed. Daisy Hernández and Bushra Rehman (New York: Seal Press, 2002), xxiv.

19. Second-wave feminists Johnnetta Betsch Cole and Beverly Guy-Sheftall make the following comment on Morgan's text: "What is clear to us is that hip-hop generationers have a different conception of feminism than we do, or are perhaps more suspicious of its values, especially with respect to what women might have to surrender in these gender wars." Cole and Guy-Sheftall, *Gender Talk: The Struggle for Women's Equality in African American Communities* (New York: Ballantine Books, 2003), 212.

20. This is worth noting for several reasons. First, Morgan's broad vision of who has contributed to second-wave feminism is refreshing given the almost exclusive focus on white, second-wave feminists within most third-wave critiques. Second, although she does not directly say as much, one can read Naomi Wolf's discussion of "victim feminism" in *Fire with Fire* as describing a particularly white version of feminism—and femininity. With the exception of Audre Lorde, Wolf exclusively singles out white women for their promotion of this breed of feminist thought; additionally, she argues that the image of womanhood advanced in victim feminism is one which has its roots in Victorian notions of white womanhood.

21. I disagree with Kimberly Springer when she argues that other than Michele Wallace's work, "few sources speak of conflicts or distinctions between Black feminists of different generations." Kimberly Springer, "Third Wave Black Feminism?" *Signs: Journal of Women in Culture and Society* 27, no. 4 (Summer 2002): 1064.

22. Morgan, *When Chickenheads*, 26.

23. Morgan, *When Chickenheads*, 56–57.

24. In his *The Hip Hop Generation: Young Blacks and the Crisis in African-American Culture*, Bakari Kitwana describes these generational differences as follows: "For our parents' generation, the political ideas of civil rights and Black power are central to their worldview. Our parents' generation placed family, spirituality, social responsibility, and Black pride at the center of their identity as Black Americans. They, like their parents before them, looked to their elders for values and identity. The core set of values shared by a large segment of the hip-hop generation . . . stands in contrast to our parents' worldview. For the most part, we have turned to ourselves, our peers, global images and products, and the new realities we face for guidance." (New York: Basic Civitas Books, 2002), 6–7. For more on hip-hop as a generational phenomenon, see Mark Anthony Neal, *Soul Babies: Black Popular Culture and Post-Soul Aesthetic* (New York: Routledge, 2002).

25. Shani Jamila, "Can I Get a Witness? Testimony from a Hip Hop Feminist," in Hernández and Rehman, eds., *Colonize This!* 391.

26. For more on the ways in which Generation X functions as an ideological rather

than a demographic term, see Helene A. Shugart, "Isn't It Ironic? The Intersection of Third-Wave Feminism and Generation X," *Women's Studies in Communication* 24, no. 2 (Fall 2001): 162.

27. Of course, hip-hop is widely embraced by people of all races and ethnicities, so I do not mean to imply that it is only used as a generational term by African Americans. However, within the work discussed here, it is primarily African-American feminists who use the term.

28. Springer, "Third Wave Black Feminism?" 1060, emphasis in original. Springer's article doesn't address the key role that Rebecca Walker has played in bringing the term "third wave"—and the subsequent third-wave movement—to life; in fact she does not refer to the 1992 *Ms.* article in which Walker proclaims "I am the Third Wave," nor does she discuss the role of the Thomas hearings in spurring Walker to make this claim. Springer's thesis is that the term third wave "excludes feminists of color." While I too am wary of the ways in which the wave structure has obscured the participation of women of color within feminist movements, I disagree with Springer on this point. Springer, "Third Wave Black Feminism?" 1059.

29. For more on the relationship between third-wave feminism and hip-hop, see Eisa Davis, "Sexism and the Art of Feminist Hip-Hop Maintenance," in Walker, ed., *To Be Real*, 127–142; Gwendolyn D. Pough, "Do the Ladies Run This . . . ? Some Thoughts on Hip-Hop Feminism," in *Catching a Wave: Reclaiming Feminism for the 21st Century*, ed. Rory Dicker and Alison Piepmeier (Boston: Northeastern University Press, 2003), 232–243; Gwendolyn D. Pough, "Love Feminism but Where's My Hip Hop?" in Hernández and Rehman, eds., *Colonize This!* 85–95; Tara Roberts and Eisa Nefertari Ulen, "Sisters Spin Talk on Hip-Hop: Can the Music Be Saved?" *Ms.*, February/March 2000, 69–74; and Eisa Nefertari Ulen and Angela Y. Davis, "What Happened to Your Generation's Promise of 'Love and Revolution'?" in *Letters of Intent: Women Cross the Generations to Talk about Family, Work, Sex, Love and the Future of Feminism*, ed. Anna Bondoc and Meg Daly (New York: Simon & Schuster, 1999), 99–108. On gender relations and black feminism in hip-hop, see also Cole and Guy-Sheftall, "No Respect: Gender Politics and Hip-Hop," in Cole and Guy-Sheftall, *Gender Talk*, 182–215.

30. Morgan, *When Chickenheads*, 56, 59.

31. Morgan, *When Chickenheads*, 62. It should also be noted that an attention to "gray areas" is also a central theme within Katie Roiphe's argument against what she calls the "rape crisis movement" in *The Morning After*.

32. It is interesting that although Rene Denfeld, the author of *The New Victorians*, is also biracial, she mentions this point only in passing and deliberately seems to choose not to identify herself with other biracial black feminists. For more on this next generation's biraciality, see Kristal Brent Zook, "Light Skinned-ded Naps," in *Making Face, Making Soul: Creative and Critical Perspectives by Women of Color*, ed. Gloria Anzaldúa (San Francisco: Aunt Lute Foundation Books, 1990), 85–96.

33. Rebecca Hurdis, "Heartbroken: Women of Color Feminism and the Third Wave," in Hernández and Rehman, eds., *Colonize This!* 292.

34. Walker, "Being Real," xxxiii. See also Zook's essay, where she writes: "Growing up after civil rights, women's lib and the sexual revolution, my generation of black

women is not necessarily obsessed with the Man in the same ways that the old guard was. Some of us live among, and even love, white people. Some of us are biracial. And some are bisexual." Zook, "A Manifesto of Sorts," 88.

35. For more on this generation's relationship to race relations, see Farai Chideya, *The Color of Our Future* (New York: William Morrow and Company, 1999).

36. Marilyn Milloy also criticizes feminist writing for being unnecessarily academic in "The New Feminism," *Essence*, September 1997, 117+.

37. For more on the effects of the Thomas confirmation hearings on the development of third-wave feminism, see Naomi Wolf, *Fire with Fire: The New Female Power and How It Will Change the 21st Century* (New York: Random House, 1993), 5–6; and Catherine M. Orr, "Charting the Current of the Third Wave," *Hypatia: A Journal of Feminist Philosophy* 12, no. 3 (Summer 1997): 30.

38. Rebecca Walker, "Becoming the Third Wave," *Ms.*, January/February 1992, 41. Walker's piece was one of several essays featured in a special section of the magazine devoted to feminist reactions to the Thomas-Hill hearings. According to Jennifer Baumgardner and Amy Richards, "In April 1992, Hunter College in New York City was the site of a conference entitled 'I Believe Anita Hill,' which featured a panel on Third Wave Feminism." Baumgardner and Richards, *Manifesta*, 78. See also Meri Nana-Ama Danquah, "Keeping the Third Wave Afloat," *Los Angeles Times*, December 6, 1995, E1.

39. Beverly Guy-Sheftall, "Introduction: The Evolution of Feminist Consciousness among African American Women," in Guy-Sheftall, ed., *Words of Fire*, 19. For more on the Thomas hearings, see "Clarence Thomas and Anita Hill: Public Hearing, Private Pain," prod. Ofra Bizel, *Frontline*, PBS, aired October 13, 1992; Toni Morrison, ed., *Race-ing Justice, En-gendering Power: Essays on Anita Hill, Clarence Thomas, and the Construction of Social Reality* (New York: Pantheon Books, 1992); Robert Chrisman and Robert L. Allen, eds., *Court of Appeal: The Black Community Speaks Out on the Racial and Sexual Politics of Clarence Thomas vs. Anita Hill* (New York: Ballantine Books, 1992); Geneva Smitherman, ed., *African American Women Speak Out on Anita Hill-Clarence Thomas* (Detroit: Wayne State University Press, 1995); and Anita Hill, *Speaking Truth to Power* (New York: Doubleday, 1997).

40. "African American Women in Defense of Ourselves," *New York Times*, November 17, 1991, A53. All subsequent references to this text are from this page.

41. Guy-Sheftall, "Introduction," 20.

42. The Combahee River Collective, "A Black Feminist Statement" (1977) in *All the Women Are White, All the Blacks Are Men, but Some of Us Are Brave*, ed. Gloria T. Hull, Patricia Bell Scott, and Barbara Smith (New York: The Feminist Press, 1982), 16.

43. Lisa Jones, "The Invisible Ones" (1991), in Jones, *Bulletproof Diva: Tales of Race, Sex, and Hair* (New York: Anchor Books, 1994), 121, 123.

44. See Zook, "A Manifesto of Sorts"; Rebecca Walker, "Changing the Face of Feminism," *Essence*, January 1996, 123; and "The Complexities of Black Feminism: Ain't I a Womanist?" *Village Voice*, February 13, 1996, 26–40, which includes Joan Morgan's essay, "Fly Girls, Bitches, and Hos: Notes of a Hip-Hop Feminist," 32–33. See also Marilyn Milloy, "The New Feminism," *Essence*, September 1997: 117+; and Joan Morgan, "White Noise," *Ms.*, August/September, 1999, 96.

45. Although she doesn't identify herself as a feminist per se, rap star Sister Souljah's *No Disrespect* (New York: Time Books, 1994) can be seen as part of the publishing boom I am describing here.

46. Here I am picking up on the title of bell hooks's *Feminist Theory from Margin to Center* (Boston: South End Press, 1984). For other multiracial third-wave anthologies, see Bondoc and Daly, eds., *Letters of Intent;* Ophira Edut, ed., *Adiós Barbie: Young Women Write about Body Image and Identity* (Seattle: Seal Press, 1998); and Hernández and Rehman, eds., *Colonize This!*

47. For more on the term "backlash" and this pre-third-wave period, see chapter 1.

48. Gina Dent, "Missionary Position," in Walker, ed., *To Be Real,* 62.

49. Rehman and Hernández, "Introduction," xxiiv.

50. Paula Kamen, *Feminist Fatale: Voices from the "Twentysomething" Generation Explore the Future of the "Women's Movement"* (New York: Donald I. Fine, 1991), 17. Merri Lisa Johnson says of hooks and her frequent citation by third-wavers that she's "like the big sister who understands the world better than we do." Johnson, "Pearl Necklace: The Politics of Masturbation Fantasies," in *Jane Sexes It Up: True Confessions of Feminist Desire,* ed. Merri Lisa Johnson (New York: Four Walls Eight Windows, 2002), 319.

51. Leslie Heywood and Jennifer Drake, "Introduction," *Third Wave Agenda: Being Feminist, Doing Feminism,* ed. Leslie Heywood and Jennifer Drake (Minneapolis: University of Minnesota Press, 1997), 13.

52. In particular, Audre Lorde's work seems to have had a profound effect on much third-wave theorizing, specifically her writing on the complexity of identity. Compare, for example, what Danzy Senna writes about how she "can no longer allow these parts of myself to be compartmentalized" to Lorde in "Age, Race, Class, and Sex: Women Redefining Difference," where she writes: "I find I am constantly being encouraged to pluck out some one aspect of myself and present this as the meaningful whole, eclipsing or denying the other parts of self. But this is a destructive and fragmenting way to live. My fullest concentration of energy is available to me only when I integrate all the parts of who I am, openly, allowing power from particular sources of my living to flow back and forth freely through all my different selves, without the restrictions of externally imposed definition." Senna, "To Be Real," 18; Lorde, *Sister Outsider: Essays and Speeches* (Trumansburg, N.Y.: Crossing Press, 1984), 120–121.

53. Rehman and Hernández, "Introduction," xxi.

54. Linda Garber makes a similar point when she writes: "I am of a generation of lesbian scholars whose 'higher education,' both inside and outside the academy, include Lorde, Anzaldúa, *This Bridge Called My Back, Home Girls,* and a variety of other works by women of color in the 1980s. It was not something added on later. . . . [These writers] were the leading voices of feminist and lesbian theory. From our privileged positions in a mostly white academy and a white-dominated movement, my peers and I could choose to ignore them, but many of us didn't. Their critiques of racism within feminism were widely accepted as true by the time I heard about them. . . . What remained for my generation, then, was a choice of what to do with this work." Garber, *Identity Poetics: Race, Class, and the Lesbian-Feminist Roots of Queer Theory* (New York: Columbia University Press, 2001), 4. See also Beverly Guy-Sheftall, "Other Mothers of Women's Studies," in *The Politics of Women's Studies: Testimony from 30 Founding Mothers,* ed. Florence Howe (New York: The Feminist Press, 2000), 216–226.

55. For example, see the 1998 *Time* cover story on feminism in the late 1990s (June 29, 1998). On the cover are the photographs of four white women's heads: Susan B. Anthony, Betty Friedan, Gloria Steinem, and the fictional television character Ally

McBeal, played by actress Calista Flockhart. Underneath the photos is the caption: "Is Feminism Dead?" In both this cover and the articles that accompany it, *Time* represents contemporary feminism as the province of white women. See Ginia Bellafante, "Feminism: It's All About Me!" *Time*, June 29, 1998, 54–62.

56. Hurdis continues: "Does feminism still exist for women of color or is it just a 'white thing'? Are generation X women of color participating in feminisms?" Hurdis, "Heartbroken," 287. She poses these questions while critiquing what she sees as the white bias of Baumgardner and Richards's *Manifesta*.

57. For more on the representation of feminism's sexuality, see chapters 3 and 4.

58. Ann duCille, "The Occult of True Black Womanhood," in duCille, *Skin Trade* (Cambridge, Mass.: Harvard University Press, 1996), 108. For more on the ways in which black feminists and black feminism are taken up by white feminists, see Patricia Hill Collins, "What's in a Name? Womanism, Black Feminism, and Beyond," *Black Scholar* 26, no. 1–2 (Winter/Spring 1996): 9–18; and Hazel Carby, "The Multicultural Wars," in *Black Popular Culture*, ed. Gina Dent (Seattle: Bay Press, 1992), 187–199.

59. It may be useful to apply this mammy metaphor to thinking about what counts as feminist theory generally. As Deborah McDowell and Michele Wallace, among others, have pointed out, black feminism is rarely viewed as contributing to the high world of theory but rather "gets constructed as 'practice' or 'politics,' the negative obverse of 'theory.'" In this division, what black feminists write is relegated to the nitty-gritty, everyday world of practice, while what white feminists write is treated as theory. This theory/practice split seems to share some features with the mother/mammy split. Deborah E. McDowell, "Transferences: Black Feminist Thinking: The 'Practice' of Theory," in McDowell, *"The Changing Same": Black Women's Literature, Criticism, and Theory* (Bloomington: Indiana University Press, 1995), 158. See also Michele Wallace, "Introduction: Negative/Positive Images" and "Twenty Years Later," in Wallace, *Invisibility Blues: From Pop to Theory* (New York: Verso Press, 1990), 1–10 and 159–171. For more on what counts as theory with feminism, see also bell hooks, "Theory as Liberatory Practice," in hooks, *Teaching to Transgress: Education as the Practice of Freedom* (New York: Routledge, 1994), 59–75; and Valerie Smith, *Not Just Race, Not Just Gender: Black Feminist Readings* (New York: Routledge, 1998).

60. Tricia Rose, *Black Noise: Rap Music and Black Culture in Contemporary America* (Hanover, N.H.: Wesleyan University Press, 1994), 181.

61. Tiya Miles, "Lessons from a Young Feminist Collective," in *Listen Up: Voices from the Next Feminist Generation*, ed. Barbara Findlen (Seattle: Seal Press, 1995), 173.

62. Veronica Chambers, "Betrayal Feminism," in Findlen, ed., *Listen Up*, 24.

63. Rehman and Hernández, "Introduction," xxii–xxiii.

64. Chambers, "Betrayal Feminism," 24.

65. Chambers, "Betrayal Feminism," 23. For more on Chambers's relationship with her mother, see her memoir, *Mama's Girl*.

66. Morgan, *When Chickenheads*, 33–35.

67. Siobhan Brooks, "Black Feminism in Everyday Life: Race, Mental Illness, Poverty and Motherhood," in Hernández and Rehman, eds., *Colonize This!* 115.

68. Paula Austin, "Femme-Inism: Lessons of My Mother," in Hernández and Rehman, eds., *Colonize This!* 157.

69. Chambers, *Mama's Girl*, 181.

70. The mothers' rejection of the term feminism raises a host of issues I do not

address here. As many black feminists have noted, the myth that African-American women don't need feminism because, unlike white women, they are already "liberated" has been used to keep black women from organizing around their needs and from building coalitions with feminist women of other races. What Michele Wallace called "the myth of the superwoman" is central to the idea of black matriarchy that has been forwarded by both the black nationalist left and the conservative white right wing. See Paula Terrelonge, "Feminist Consciousness and Black Women" (1984), in Guy-Sheftall, ed., *Words of Fire*, 490–501; E. Frances White, "Africa on My Mind: Gender, Counterdiscourse, and African American Nationalism," in Guy-Sheftall, ed., *Words of Fire*, 504–524; and Michele Wallace, *Black Macho and the Myth of the Superwoman* (1979; reprint, New York: Verso Press, 1990).

71. Patricia Hill Collins, *Black Feminist Thought: Knowledge, Consciousness, and the Politics of Empowerment* (New York: Routledge, 1990); Patricia Hill Collins, "The Meaning of Motherhood in Black Culture and Black Mother-Daughter Relationships," in *Double Stitch: Black Women Write about Mothers & Daughters*, ed. Patricia Bell-Scott, Beverly Guy-Sheftall, Jacqueline Jones Royster, Janet Sims-Wood, Miriam DeCosta-Willis, and Lucille P. Fultz (New York: HarperPerennial, 1991), 42–60; Stanlie M. James, "Mothering: A Possible Black Feminist Link to Social Transformation?" in *Theorizing Black Feminisms: The Visionary Pragmatism of Black Women*, ed. Stanlie M. James and Abena P. A. Busia (New York: Routledge, 1993), 44–54; Gloria I. Joseph, "Black Mothers and Daughters: Traditional and New Perspectives," in Bell-Scott et al., eds., *Double Stitch*, 94–106; Fabian Clements Worsham, "The Poetics of Matrilineage: Mothers and Daughters in the Poetry of African American Women, 1965–1985," in *Women of Color: Mother-Daughter Relationships in 20th-Century Literature*, ed. Elizabeth Brown-Guillory (Austin: University of Texas Press, 1996), 117–131.

72. Joseph, "Black Mothers and Daughters," 95–96.

73. See, for example, the essays in the second section of *Colonize This!* entitled "Our Mothers, Refugees from a World on Fire."

74. Madelyn Detloff, "Mean Spirits: The Politics of Contempt between Feminist Generations," *Hypatia: A Journal of Feminist Philosophy* 12, no. 3 (Summer 1997): 79. For more on the positive relationships between young black women and their political and biological foremothers, see Springer, "Third Wave Black Feminism?"

75. Baumgardner and Richards, *Manifesta*, 17. Lourdes-marie Prophete, "Feminist Musings on the No. 3 Train," in Hernández and Rehman, eds., *Colonize This!* 170.

76. Veronica Webb in Rebecca Walker, "How Does a Supermodel Do Feminism? An Interview with Veronica Webb," in Walker, ed., *To Be Real*, 213.

77. Kristina Gray, "I Sold My Soul to Rock and Roll," in Hernández and Rehman, eds., *Colonize This!* 261.

78. Walker, "Being Real," xxxi.

79. Walker, "Being Real," xxxi.

80. Walker also explores this theme in her essay in *Listen Up*, where she describes being left alone much of the time while she was growing up—"[b]ecause my mother was often away, leaving me with a safe and private space to bring my boyfriends"—and so had the freedom to explore her sexuality. Rebecca Walker, "Lusting for Freedom," in Findlen, ed., *Listen Up*, 98. For more on her sense of abandonment as a child, see also Walker's memoir *Black, White, and Jewish: Autobiography of a Shifting Self* (New York: Riverhead Books, 2001).

81. Rebecca Walker in Alice Walker and Rebecca Walker, "The Two of Us," *Essence*, May 1995, 173, 254.

82. Rebecca Walker in Walker and Walker, "The Two of Us," 254.

83. As an aside, it is worth noting that Rebecca made a matrilineal claim at the age of seventeen when she changed her surname from Levanthal, her father's last name, to Walker. Danquah, "Keeping the Third Wave Afloat," E1.

84. Walker, "Being Real," xxxix.

85. Walker, "Being Real," xxxiv.

86. Alice Walker, "In Search of Our Mothers' Gardens," in Walker, *In Search of Our Mothers' Gardens: Womanist Prose* (New York: Harcourt Brace Jovanovich, 1983), 240.

87. Alice Walker, "One Child of One's Own: A Meaningful Digression within the Work(s)," in Walker, *In Search of Our Mothers' Gardens*, 382.

88. For more on Rebecca's erasure in this essay devoted to Walker's mothering of her, see Marianne Hirsch, *The Mother/Daughter Plot: Narrative, Psychoanalysis, Feminism* (Bloomington: Indiana University Press, 1989), 191–196.

89. Alice Walker in Walker and Walker, "The Two of Us," 254.

90. See Hirsch, *The Mother/Daughter Plot*.

91. Walker, "In Search of Our Mothers' Gardens," 240.

92. Although generationally not representative of a second-wave–third-wave relationship, the mother-daughter pair of Faith Ringgold and Michele Wallace also provides an interesting example of feminist familial and generational conflict. Like Alice and Rebecca Walker, both Ringgold and Wallace are self-identified feminists and writer-artists, and both often write about their relationship as it intersects with feminism. For example, in her 1995 memoir, Ringgold describes Wallace's *Black Macho and the Myth of the Superwoman* as a "book that would deny my presence as a feminist role model in her life." She argues that Wallace "made me look like a controlling stereotypical black matriarch whose daughter became a feminist in spite of her. She gave me no credit as a role model for learning how to be both a woman and a political activist. There is no greater defeat to a woman who is a mother than to have her value as a mother denied. I had produced two very talented children, why not give me credit?" Faith Ringgold, *We Flew Over the Bridge: The Memoirs of Faith Ringgold* (Boston: Bulfinch Press, 1995), 94. For more on their relationship from Wallace's point of view, see her introduction to the reissue of *Black Macho*.

93. Walker, "Being Real," xxxiv.

94. Walker, "Being Real," xxxviii.

95. Roiphe, *The Morning After*, 4.

96. On Walker's bisexuality, see Rebecca Walker, "Serial Lover," in *Here Lies My Heart: Essays on Why We Marry, Why We Don't, and What We Find There*, ed. Deborah Chasman and Catherine Jhee (Boston: Beacon Press, 1999), 46–49. See also Retha Powers, "Don't Ask Alice: Rebecca Walker Steps Out," *Girlfriends*, May/June 1996, 20–21.

97. Rebecca Walker in Walker and Walker, "The Two of Us," 256, emphasis added.

98. Walker, "Being Real," xxxiv.

Afterword

1. Rebecca Walker quoted in Meri Nana-Ama Danquah, "Keeping the Third Wave Afloat," *Los Angeles Times,* December 6, 1995, E1.

2. It's worth noting that the Millennial Generation, or Generation Y, is a substantially bigger demographic group than Generation X and is thus more like the Baby Boom generation in its population size.

3. Rosi Braidotti, "Generations of Feminists, or, Is There Life after Post-Modernism?" *Found Object* 16 (1995): 55. This point is echoed by Jacquelyn Zita in her introduction to the *Hypatia* special issue on third-wave feminisms, where she writes, "Strangely, I have become an 'old timer' as I look back now on more than a quarter century of feminist theory and politics." Zita, "Third Wave Feminisms: An Introduction," *Hypatia: A Journal of Feminist Philosophy* 12, no. 3 (Summer 1997): 1.

4. Susan Fraiman, "Feminism Today: Mothers, Daughters, Emerging Sisters," *American Literary History* 11, no. 3 (Fall 1999): 532, emphasis in original.

5. Lisa Marie Hogeland, "Against Generational Thinking, or, Some Things that 'Third Wave' Feminism Isn't," *Women's Studies in Communication* 24, no. 1 (Spring 2001): 118.

6. Rebecca Dakin Quinn, "An Open Letter to Institutional Mothers," in *Generations: Academic Feminists in Dialogue,* ed. Devoney Looser and Ann Kaplan (Minneapolis: University of Minnesota Press, 1997), 179; Louise D'Arcens, "Mothers, Daughters, Sisters," in *Talking Up: Young Women's Take on Feminism,* ed. Rosamund Else-Mitchell and Naomi Flutter (North Melbourne, Australia: Spinifex Press, 1998), 114. Susan Fraiman makes a similar call to return to sisterhood in her praise of *Third Wave Agenda* for "usefully direct[ing] our attention away from mother-daughter tensions and back to sisterly ties." Fraiman, "Feminism Today," 543.

7. For more positive images of motherhood, see recent texts by third-wave mothers, such as Spike Gillespie's "Sex and the Single Mom," in *Sex and Single Girls: Straight and Queer Women on Sexuality,* ed. Lee Damsky (Seattle: Seal Press, 2000), 357–367. See also editors Ariel Gore and Bee Lavender's anthology, *Breeder: Real-Life Stories from the New Generation of Mothers* (Seattle: Seal Press, 2001).

8. For more on the "father" within feminist familial discourse, see Helena Michie, "Not One of the Family: The Repression of the Other Woman in Feminist Theory," in *Discontented Discourses: Feminism, Textual Intervention, Psychoanalysis,* ed. Marleen S. Barr and Richard Feldstein (Urbana: University of Illinois Press, 1989), 15–28.

9. Judith Roof, "Generational Difficulties; or, the Fear of a Barren History," in Looser and Kaplan, eds., *Generations,* 85.

10. Here I am echoing Devoney Looser's point in *Generations: Academic Feminists in Dialogue,* where she writes, "we should continue to examine what are already quite entrenched and *perceived* feminist generational differences and alliances. These deserve to be further theorized now, even if they are ultimately cast out of our critical vocabulary." Looser, "Introduction 2," in Looser and Kaplan, eds., *Generations,* 33, emphasis in original.

Bibliography

ACT UP/NY Women and AIDS Book Group and Marion Banzhof et al. *Women, AIDS, and Activism*. Boston: South End Press, 1990.

Addelson, Kathryn Pyne. "Words and Lives." *Signs: A Journal of Women in Culture and Society* 7, no. 1 (Autumn 1981): 187–199.

"African American Women in Defense of Ourselves." *New York Times*, November 17, 1991, A53.

Alderfer, Hannah, Beth Jaker, and Marybeth Nelson, eds. *Diary of a Conference on Sexuality*. New York: Faculty Press, 1982.

Alexander, M. Jacqui, Lisa Albrecht, Sharon Day, and Mab Segrest, eds. *Sing, Whisper, Shout, Pray! Feminist Visions for a Just World*. Fort Bragg, Calif.: EdgeWork Books, 2003.

Alfonso, Rita, and Jo Trigilio. "Surfing the Third Wave: A Dialogue between Two Third Wave Feminists." *Hypatia: A Journal of Feminist Philosophy* 12, no. 3 (Summer 1997): 7–16.

Allison, Dorothy. *Skin: Talking about Sex, Class & Literature*. Ithaca, N.Y.: Firebrand Books, 1994.

Allyn, David. *Make Love, Not War: The Sexual Revolution, An Unfettered History*. Boston: Little, Brown and Company, 2000.

———, and Jennifer Allyn. "Identity Politics." In *To Be Real: Telling the Truth and Changing the Face of Feminism*, ed. Rebecca Walker, 143–156. New York: Anchor Books, 1995.

Angel, Karen. "A Bounty of Fruit Falls from the Literary Tree: Young Authors Profit from Their Last Names." *New York Times*, April 25, 2000, B1+.

Anonymous Queers. "I Hate Straights" (1990). In *We Are Everywhere: A Historical Sourcebook of Gay and Lesbian Politics*, ed. Mark Blasius and Shane Phelan, 779–780. New York: Routledge, 1997.

———. "Queers Read This" (1990). In *We Are Everywhere: A Historical Sourcebook of Gay and Lesbian Politic*, ed. Mark Blasius and Shane Phelan, 773–779. New York: Routledge, 1997.

Ashton, Charlotte. "Getting Hold of the Phallus: 'Post-Lesbian' Power Negotiations." In *Assaults on Convention: Essays on Lesbian Transgressors*, ed. Nicola Godwin, Belinda Hollows, and Sheridan Nye, 158–174. London: Cassell, 1996.

Auerbach, Nina. "Sisterhood Is Fractious." *New York Times Book Review*, June 12, 1994, 13. Review of Christina Hoff Sommers, *Who Stole Feminism?*

Austin, Paula. "Femme-Inism: Lessons of My Mother." In *Colonize This! Young Women of Color on Today's Feminism*, ed. Daisy Hernández and Bushra Rehman, 157–169. New York: Seal Press, 2002.

Avenoso, Karen. "Feminism's Newest Foot Soldiers." *Elle*, March 1993, 114–118.

Bail, Kathy, ed. *DIY Feminism*. Sydney, Australia: Allen and Unwin, 1996.

Bailey, Cathryn. "Making Waves and Drawing Lines: The Politics of Defining the Vicissitudes of Feminism." *Hypatia: A Journal of Feminist Philosophy* 12, no. 3 (Summer 1997): 17–28.

———. "Unpacking the Mother/Daughter Baggage: Reassessing Second- and Third-Wave Tensions." *Women's Studies Quarterly* 30, nos. 3 and 4 (2002): 138–154.

Baker, Christina Looper, and Christina Baker Kline, eds. *The Conversation Begins: Mothers and Daughters Talk about Living Feminism.* New York: Bantam Books, 1996.

Banks, Olive. *Becoming a Feminist: The Social Origins of "First Wave" Feminism.* London: Wheatsheaf Books, 1986.

Baumgardner, Jennifer, and Amy Richards. *Manifesta: Young Women, Feminism, and the Future.* New York: Farrar, Straus and Giroux, 2000.

Beale, Frances. "Double Jeopardy: To Be Black and Female." In *The Black Woman: An Anthology,* ed. Toni Cade, 90–100. New York: Signet Books, 1970.

Beauvoir, Simone de. *The Second Sex.* 1952. Reprint, New York: Random House, 1974.

Bell, Laurie, ed. *Good Girls/Bad Girls: Feminists and Sex Trade Workers Face to Face.* Seattle: Seal Press, 1987.

Bell, Shannon. "Liquid Fire: Female Ejaculation and Fast Feminism." In *Jane Sexes It Up: True Confessions of Feminist Desire,* ed. Merri Lisa Johnson, 327–345. New York: Four Walls Eight Windows, 2002.

Bellafante, Ginia. "Feminism: It's All about Me!" *Time,* June 29, 1998, 54–62.

Bell-Scott, Patricia, Beverly Guy-Sheftall, Jacqueline Jones Royster, Janet Sims-Wood, Miriam DeCosta-Willis, and Lucille P. Fultz, eds. *Double Stitch: Black Women Write about Mothers & Daughters.* New York: HarperPerennial, 1991.

Benjamin, Jessica. *The Bonds of Love: Psychoanalysis, Feminism, and the Problem of Domination.* New York: Pantheon Books, 1988.

Berlant, Lauren, and Michael Warner. "What Does Queer Theory Teach Us about X?" *PMLA* 110, no. 3 (May 1995): 343–349.

Bernstein, Robin, and Seth Clark Silberman, eds. *Generation Q: Gays, Lesbians, and Bisexuals Born around 1969's Stonewall Riots Tell Their Stories of Growing Up in the Age of Information.* Los Angeles: Alyson Publications, 1996.

Berson, Ginny. "The Furies" (1972). In *For Lesbians Only: A Separatist Anthology,* ed. Sarah Lucia Hoagland and Julia Penelope, 24–27. London: Onlywomen Press, 1988.

Bolotin, Susan. "Views from the Postfeminist Generation." *New York Times Magazine,* October 17, 1982, 29+.

Bondoc, Anna, and Meg Daly. "Introduction." In *Letters of Intent: Women Cross the Generations to Talk about Family, Work, Sex, Love and the Future of Feminism,* ed. Anna Bondoc and Meg Daly, 1–8. New York: Simon & Schuster, 1999.

———, eds. *Letters of Intent: Women Cross the Generations to Talk about Family, Work, Sex, Love and the Future of Feminism.* New York: Simon & Schuster, 1999.

Bornstein, Kate. *Gender Outlaw: On Men, Women, and the Rest of Us.* New York: Vintage Books, 1994.

Boston Women's Health Book Collective. *Our Bodies, Ourselves: A Book by and for Women.* New York: Simon & Schuster, 1971.

Boxer, Marilyn Jacoby. *When Women Ask the Questions: Creating Women's Studies in America.* Baltimore: Johns Hopkins University Press, 1998.

Braidotti, Rosi. "Generations of Feminists, or, Is There Life After Post-modernism?" *Found Object* 16 (1995): 55–62.

Bravmann, Scott. *Queer Fictions of the Past: History, Culture, and Difference.* New York: Cambridge University Press, 1997.

Brenner, Johanna. "The Best of Times, the Worst of Times: U.S. Feminism Today." *New Left Review* 200 (July/August 1993): 101–159.

Bright, Susie. *Sexual State of the Union.* New York: Simon & Schuster, 1997.

Brooks, Siobhan. "Black Feminism in Everyday Life: Race, Mental Illness, Poverty and Motherhood." In *Colonize This! Young Women of Color on Today's Feminism,* ed. Daisy Hernández and Bushra Rehman, 99–118. New York: Seal Press, 2002.

Brotman, Barbara. "Sibling Rivalry." *Chicago Tribune,* July 17, 1994, 6:1+.

Brown, Connie, and Jane Seitz. "'You've Come a Long Way, Baby': Historical Perspectives." In *Sisterhood Is Powerful: An Anthology of Writings from the Women's Liberation Movement,* ed. Robin Morgan, 3–28. New York: Vintage Books, 1970.

Brownmiller, Susan. *In Our Time: Memoir of a Revolution.* New York: The Dial Press, 1999.

Bullock-Jordan, Karen. "Eternal Novice." In *Sex and Single Girls: Straight and Queer Women on Sexuality,* ed. Lee Damsky, 232–240. Seattle: Seal Press, 2000.

Butler, Judith. "Against Proper Objects." In *Feminism Meets Queer Theory,* ed. Elizabeth Weed and Naomi Schor, 1–30. Bloomington: Indiana University Press, 1997.

———. *Gender Trouble: Feminism and the Subversion of Identity.* New York: Routledge, 1990.

———. "The Lesbian Phallus and the Morphological Imaginary." In Judith Butler, *Bodies that Matter: On the Discursive Limits of "Sex,"* 57–91. New York: Routledge, 1993.

Cade, Toni, ed. *The Black Woman: An Anthology.* New York: Signet Books, 1970.

Calame, Christy, and Robbie Scott Phillips. "Fuck Your Healthy Gay Lifestyle (The FRINGE Manifesto—Freaks, Radicals, and Inverts Nail Gay Elite)." In *Generation Q: Gays, Lesbians, and Bisexuals Born around 1969's Stonewall Riots Tell Their Stories of Growing Up in the Age of Information,* ed. Robin Bernstein and Seth Clark Silberman, 233–236. Los Angeles: Alyson Publications, 1996.

Califia, Pat. "Feminism and Sadomasochism." *Heresies* 12 (1981): 30–34. Special Issue: *The Sex Issue.*

———. *Macho Sluts.* Boston: Alyson Publications, 1988.

———. *Public Sex: The Culture of Radical Sex.* Pittsburgh: Cleis Press, 1994.

———. *Sapphistry: The Book of Lesbian Sexuality.* Tallahassee, Fla.: Naiad Press, 1980.

Caraway, Nancie. *Segregated Sisterhood: Racism and the Politics of American Feminism.* Knoxville: University of Tennessee Press, 1991.

Carby, Hazel. "The Multicultural Wars." In *Black Popular Culture,* ed. Gina Dent, 187–199. Seattle: Bay Press, 1992.

Carlip, Hillary. *Girl Power: Young Women Speak Out!* New York: Warner Books, 1995.

Carpenter, Mary Wilson. "Female Grotesques in Academia: Ageism, Antifeminism, and Feminists on the Faculty." In *Antifeminism in the Academy,* ed. Vèvè Clark, Shirley Nelson Garner, Margaret Higonnet, and Ketu H. Katrak, 141–165. New York: Routledge, 1996.

Case, Sue-Ellen. "Toward a Butch-Feminist Retro-Future." In *Cross Purposes: Lesbians, Feminists, and the Limits of Alliance,* ed. Dana Heller, 205–220. Bloomington: Indiana University Press, 1997.

Caught Looking Inc. *Caught Looking: Feminism, Pornography and Censorship.* 3rd ed. East Haven, Conn.: LongRiver Books, 1992.

Chambers, Veronica. "Betrayal Feminism." In *Listen Up: Voices from the Next Feminist Generation,* ed. Barbara Findlen, 21–28. Seattle: Seal Press, 1995.

———. *Mama's Girl.* New York: Riverhead Books, 1996.

Chesler, Phyllis. *Letters to a Young Feminist.* New York: Four Walls Eight Windows, 1997.

Chideya, Farai. *The Color of Our Future.* New York: William Morrow and Company, 1999.

Chinn, Sarah E., and Kris Franklin. "The (Queer) Revolution Will Not Be Liberalized." *Minnesota Review* 40 (Spring/Summer 1993): 138–150.

Chodorow, Nancy. *Feminism and Psychoanalytic Theory.* New Haven, Conn.: Yale University Press, 1989.

———. *The Reproduction of Mothering: Psychoanalysis and the Sociology of Gender.* Berkeley: University of California Press, 1978.

Chrisman, Robert, and Robert L. Allen, eds. *Court of Appeal: The Black Community Speaks Out on the Racial and Sexual Politics of Clarence Thomas vs. Anita Hill.* New York: Ballantine Books, 1992.

Christian, Barbara, Ann DuCille, Sharon Marcus, Elaine Marks, Nancy K. Miller, Sylvia Schafer, and Joan W. Scott. "Conference Call." *differences: A Journal of Feminist Cultural Studies* 2, no. 3 (1990): 52–108.

"Clarence Thomas and Anita Hill: Public Hearing, Private Pain." Prod. Ofra Bizel. *Frontline,* PBS, October 13, 1992.

Clausen, Jan. *Apples and Oranges: My Journey through Sexual Identity.* Boston: Houghton Mifflin Company, 1999.

———. "My Interesting Condition." *Outlook* 7 (Winter 1990): 11–21.

Cohen, Deborah A. "An Intellectual Home." *Women's Review of Books* 6, no. 5 (February 1994): 16–17.

Cole, Alyson M. "'There Are No Victims in This Class': On Female Suffering and Anti-'Victim' Feminism." *NWSA Journal* 11, no. 1 (Spring 1999): 72–96.

Cole, Johnnetta Betsch, and Beverly Guy-Sheftall. *Gender Talk: The Struggle for Women's Equality in African American Communities.* New York: Ballantine Books, 2003.

Collins, Patricia Hill. *Black Feminist Thought: Knowledge, Consciousness, and the Politics of Empowerment.* New York: Routledge, 1990.

———. "The Meaning of Motherhood in Black Culture and Black Mother-Daughter Relationships." In *Double Stitch: Black Women Write about Mothers & Daughters,* ed. Patricia Bell-Scott, Beverly Guy-Sheftall, Jacqueline Jones Royster, Janet Sims-Wood, Miriam DeCosta-Willis, and Lucille P. Fultz, 42–60. New York: HarperPerennial, 1991.

———. "What's in a Name? Womanism, Black Feminism, and Beyond." *Black Scholar* 26, nos. 1 and 2 (Winter/Spring 1996): 9–18.

The Combahee River Collective. "A Black Feminist Statement" (1977). In *All the Women Are White, All the Blacks Are Men, but Some of Us Are Brave: Black Women's Studies,* ed. Gloria T. Hull, Patricia Bell Scott, and Barbara Smith, 13–22. Old Westbury, N.Y.: The Feminist Press, 1982.

"The Complexities of Black Feminism: Ain't I a Womanist?" *Village Voice,* February 13, 1996, 26–40.

Copper, Baba. *Over the Hill: Reflections on Ageism between Women.* Freedom, Calif.: Crossing Press, 1988.

Corral, Jill, and Lisa Miya-Jervis, eds. "Introduction." In *Young Wives' Tales: New Adventures in Love and Partnership,* ed. Jill Corral and Lisa Miya-Jervis, xvii–xxii. Seattle: Seal Press, 2001.

———, eds. *Young Wives' Tales: New Adventures in Love and Partnership.* Seattle: Seal Press, 2001.

Cott, Nancy F. "Feminist Theory and Feminist Movements: The Past before Us." In *What Is Feminism?* ed. Juliet Mitchell and Ann Oakley, 49–62. Oxford: Basil Blackwell, 1986.

———. *The Grounding of Modern Feminism.* New Haven, Conn.: Yale University Press, 1987.

Coupland, Douglas. *Generation X: Tales for an Accelerated Culture.* New York: St. Martin's Press, 1992.

Creet, Julia. "Daughter of the Movement: The Psychodynamics of Lesbian S/M Fantasy." *differences: A Journal of Feminist Cultural Studies* 3, no. 2 (Summer 1991): 135–159.

———. "Lesbian Sex/Gay Sex: What's the Difference?" *Outlook* 11 (Winter 1991): 28–34.

Crichton, Sarah. "Sexual Correctness: Has It Gone Too Far?" *Newsweek,* October 25, 1993, 52–56.

Crittenden, Danielle. *What Our Mothers Didn't Tell Us: Why Happiness Eludes the Modern Woman.* New York: Simon & Schuster, 1999.

Cronan, Sheila. "Marriage." In *Notes from the Third Year: Women's Liberation,* 62–65. New York, 1971.

Daly, Meg. "The Allure of the One-Night Stand." In *Sex and Single Girls: Straight and Queer Women on Sexuality,* ed. Lee Damsky, 194–204. Seattle: Seal Press, 2000.

Damon, Gene. "The Least of These: The Minority Whose Screams Haven't Yet Been Heard." In *Sisterhood Is Powerful: An Anthology of Writings from the Women's Liberation Movement,* ed. Robin Morgan, 297–306. New York: Vintage Books, 1970.

Damsky, Lee, ed. "Introduction." In *Sex and Single Girls: Straight and Queer Women on Sexuality,* ed. Lee Damsky, xi–xx. Seattle: Seal Press, 2000.

———, ed. *Sex and Single Girls: Straight and Queer Women on Sexuality.* Seattle: Seal Press, 2000.

Danquah, Meri Nana-Ama. "Keeping the Third Wave Afloat." *Los Angeles Times,* December 6, 1995, E1.

D'Arcens, Louise. "Mothers, Daughters, Sisters." In *Talking Up: Young Women's Take on Feminism,* ed. Rosamund Else-Mitchell and Naomi Flutter, 103–116. North Melbourne, Australia: Spinifex Press, 1998.

Daughters of de Beauvoir. Prod. Penny Foster. Women Make Movies, New York, 1989.

Däumer, Elizabeth. "Queer Ethics, or the Challenge of Bisexuality to Lesbian Ethics." *Hypatia: A Journal of Feminist Philosophy* 7, no. 4 (Fall 1992): 91–105.

Davis, Angela Y. "Afterword." In *To Be Real: Telling the Truth and Changing the Face of Feminism,* ed. Rebecca Walker, 279–284. New York: Anchor Books, 1995.

Davis, Eisa. "Sexism and the Art of Feminist Hip-Hop Maintenance." In *To Be Real: Telling the Truth and Changing the Face of Feminism,* ed. Rebecca Walker, 127–142. New York: Anchor Books, 1995.

De Lauretis, Teresa. "Queer Theory: Lesbian and Gay Sexualities." *differences: A Journal of Feminist Cultural Studies. Queer Theory: Lesbian and Gay Sexualities* 3, no. 2 (Summer 1991): iii–xviii.

"Declaration of Sentiments and Resolutions" (1848). In *Voices from Women's Liberation,* ed. Leslie B. Tanner, 43–47. New York: New American Library, 1970.

Delmar, Rosalind. "What Is Feminism?" In *What Is Feminism?* ed. Juliet Mitchell and Ann Oakley, 8–33. Oxford: Basil Blackwell, 1986.

Delombard, Jeannine. "Femmenism." In *To Be Real: Telling the Truth and Changing the Face of Feminism,* ed. Rebecca Walker, 21–33. New York: Anchor Books, 1995.

D'Emilio, John. *Sexual Politics, Sexual Communities: The Making of a Homosexual Minority in the United States, 1940–1970.* 2nd ed. Chicago: University of Chicago Press, 1998.

Denfeld, Rene. "Feminism 2000: What Does It Really Mean (to You)?" *Sassy* 9 (May 1996): 60.

———. *Kill the Body, the Head Will Fall: A Closer Look at Women and Aggression.* New York: Warner Books, 1997.

———. *The New Victorians: A Young Woman's Challenge to the Old Feminist Order.* New York: Warner Books, 1995.

Densmore, Dana. "A Year of Living Dangerously: 1968." In *The Feminist Memoir Project: Voices from Women's Liberation,* ed. Rachel Blau DuPlessis and Ann Snitow, 71–89. New York: Three Rivers Press, 1998.

Dent, Gina. "Missionary Position." In *To Be Real: Telling the Truth and Changing the Face of Feminism,* ed. Rebecca Walker, 61–75. New York: Anchor Books, 1995.

Detloff, Madelyn. "Mean Spirits: The Politics of Contempt between Feminist Generations." *Hypatia: A Journal of Feminist Philosophy* 12, no. 3 (Summer 1997): 76–99.

Dicker, Rory, and Alison Piepmeier. "Introduction." In *Catching a Wave: Reclaiming Feminism for the 21st Century,* ed. Rory Dicker and Alison Piepmeier, 3–28. Boston: Northeastern University Press, 2003.

———, eds. *Catching a Wave: Reclaiming Feminism for the 21st Century.* Boston: Northeastern University Press, 2003.

Doan, Laura. *The Lesbian Postmodern.* New York: Columbia University Press, 1994.

"Doing the Third Wave." *Ms.,* September/October 1992, 87.

Doyle, Gerry. "No Man's Land: Lesbian Separatism Revisited." In *Assaults on Convention: Essays on Lesbian Transgressors,* ed. Nicola Godwin, Belinda Hollows, and Sheridan Nye, 178–197. London: Cassell, 1996.

Duberman, Martin. *Stonewall.* New York: Plume, 1994.

———, Martha Vicinus, and George Chauncey, Jr., eds. *Hidden from History: Reclaiming the Gay and Lesbian Past.* New York: Penguin Books, 1989.

DuBois, Ellen Carol. *Feminism and Suffrage: The Emergence of an Independent Women's Movement in America, 1848–1868.* Ithaca, N.Y.: Cornell University Press, 1978.

———. "The Radicalism of the Woman Suffrage Movement: Notes toward the Reconstruction of Nineteenth-Century Feminism." *Feminist Studies* 3, nos. 1 and 2 (Fall 1975): 63–71.

———, and Linda Gordon. "Seeking Ecstasy on the Battlefield: Danger and Pleasure in Nineteenth-Century Feminist Sexual Thought." In *Pleasure and Danger: Exploring Female Sexuality,* ed. Carole S. Vance, 31–49. Boston: Routledge and Kegan Paul, 1985.

DuCille, Ann. *Skin Trade.* Cambridge, Mass.: Harvard University Press, 1996.

Due, Linnea. *Joining the Tribe: Growing Up Gay and Lesbian in the '90s.* New York: Anchor Books, 1995.

Duffy, Martha. "Tremors of Genderquake." *Time,* December 27, 1993, 76–78. Review of Naomi Wolf, *Fire with Fire.*

Duggan, Lisa. "Introduction." In Lisa Duggan and Nan D. Hunter, *Sex Wars: Sexual Dissent and Political Culture,* 1–14. New York: Routledge, 1995.

———. "Making It Perfectly Queer." *Socialist Review* 22, no. 1 (1992): 9–31.

———, and Nan D. Hunter. *Sex Wars: Sexual Dissent and Political Culture.* New York: Routledge, 1995.

Dunbar-Ortiz, Roxanne. *Outlaw Woman: A Memoir of the War Years, 1960–1975.* San Francisco: City Lights, 2002.

Duncan, Erica. "Mothers and Daughters." In *Competition: A Feminist Taboo?* ed. Valerie Miner and Helen E. Longino, 131–140. New York: The Feminist Press, 1987.

DuPlessis, Rachel Blau, and Ann Snitow. "A Feminist Memoir Project." In *The Feminist Memoir Project: Voices from Women's Liberation,* ed. Rachel Blau DuPlessis and Ann Snitow, 3–24. New York: Three Rivers Press, 1998.

——, eds. *The Feminist Memoir Project: Voices from Women's Liberation.* New York: Three Rivers Press, 1998.

Dworkin, Andrea. *Heartbreak: The Political Memoir of a Feminist Militant.* New York: Basic Books, 2001.

——. *Intercourse.* New York: The Free Press, 1987.

Easton, Nina J. "'I'm not a Feminist, but . . .': Can the Women's Movement March into the Mainstream?" *Los Angeles Times Magazine,* February 2, 1992, 12–16.

Echols, Alice. *Daring to Be Bad: Radical Feminism in America, 1967–1975.* Minneapolis: University of Minnesota, 1989.

——. "The New Feminism of Yin and Yang." In *Powers of Desire: The Politics of Sexuality,* ed. Ann Snitow, Christine Stansell, and Sharon Thompson, 439–459. New York: Monthly Review Press, 1983.

——. "The Taming of the Id: Feminist Sexual Politics, 1968–83." In *Pleasure and Danger: Exploring Female Sexuality,* ed. Carole S. Vance, 50–72. Boston: Routledge and Kegan Paul, 1985.

Edut, Ophira, ed. *Adiós Barbie: Young Women Write about Body Image and Identity.* Seattle: Seal Press, 1998.

Elam, Diane. "Sisters Are Doing It to Themselves." In *Generations: Academic Feminists in Dialogue,* ed. Devoney Looser and Ann Kaplan, 55–68. Minneapolis: University of Minnesota Press, 1997.

——, and Robyn Wiegman, eds. *Feminism Beside Itself.* New York: Routledge, 1995.

Elliott, Beth. "Bisexuality: The Best Thing that Ever Happened to Lesbian-Feminism?" In *Bi Any Other Name: Bisexual People Speak Out,* ed. Lorraine Hutchins and Lani Kaahumanu, 324–328. Boston: Alyson Publications, 1991.

Else-Mitchell, Rosamund, and Naomi Flutter, eds. *Talking Up: Young Women's Take on Feminism.* North Melbourne, Australia: Spinifex Press, 1998.

Emery, Margaret. "Feminism under Fire." *Time,* September 20, 1993, 82–84. Review of Katie Roiphe, *The Morning After.*

English, Deirdre, Amber Hollibaugh, and Gayle Rubin. "Talking Sex: A Conversation on Sexuality and Feminism." In *Sexuality: A Reader,* ed. Feminist Review, 63–81. London: Virago Press Limited, 1987.

Epstein, Barbara. "Ambivalence about Feminism." In *The Feminist Memoir Project: Voices from Women's Liberation,* ed. Rachel Blau DuPlessis and Ann Snitow, 124–148. New York: Three Rivers Press, 1998.

Esterberg, Kristin G. *Lesbian and Bisexual Identities: Constructing Communities, Constructing Selves.* Philadelphia: Temple University Press, 1997.

Evans, Sara. *Personal Politics: The Roots of Women's Liberation in the Civil Rights Movement and the New Left.* New York: Vintage Books, 1980.

——. *Tidal Wave: How Women Changed America at Century's End.* New York: The Free Press, 2003.

Faderman, Lillian. "Afterword." In *Cross Purposes: Lesbians, Feminists, and the Limits of Alliance,* ed. Dana Heller, 221–229. Bloomington: Indiana University Press, 1997.

——. *Odd Girls and Twilight Lovers: A History of Lesbian Life in Twentieth-Century America.* New York: Penguin Books, 1991.

——. *Surpassing the Love of Men: Romantic Friendship and Love between Women from the Renaissance to the Present.* New York: William Morrow and Company, 1981.

Faludi, Susan. *Backlash: The Undeclared War against American Women.* New York: Crown Publishers, 1991.

———. "I'm Not a Feminist but I Play One on TV." *Ms.,* March/April 1995, 30–49.

Fatale, Fanny. "This Is What Fanny's G-Spot Looks Like!" *On Our Backs,* September/October 1992, 8+.

Featherstone, Liza, and Phyllis Chesler. "Why Is There So Much Tension between Feminist Bosses and Their Female Assistants?" In *Letters of Intent: Women Cross the Generations to Talk about Family, Work, Sex, Love and the Future of Feminism,* ed. Anna Bondoc and Meg Daly, 109–120. New York: Simon & Schuster, 1999.

Feminists for Fornication. "Mission Statement." Milwaukee, July 1996.

Ferguson, Ann. "Patriarchy, Sexual Identity, and the Sexual Revolution." *Signs: A Journal of Women in Culture and Society* 7, no. 1 (Autumn 1981): 158–172.

Findlen, Barbara. "Introduction." In *Listen Up: Voices from the Next Feminist Generation,* ed. Barbara Findlen, xi–xvi. Seattle: Seal Press, 1995.

———, ed. *Listen Up: Voices from the Next Feminist Generation.* Seattle: Seal Press, 1995.

Firestone, Shulamith. *The Dialectic of Sex: The Case for Feminist Revolution.* New York: Bantam Books, 1970.

———. "The Woman's Rights Movement in the U.S.: A New View." In *Voices from Women's Liberation,* ed. Leslie B. Tanner, 433–443. New York: New American Library, 1970.

———, and Anne Koedt. "Editorial." In *Notes from the Second Year: Women's Liberation. Major Writings of the Radical Feminists,* 2. New York, 1970.

Flint, Anthony. "New Breed of Feminist Challenges Old Guard." *Boston Globe,* May 29, 1994, 1+.

Fox-Genovese, Elizabeth. *"Feminism Is Not the Story of My Life": How Today's Feminist Elite Has Lost Touch with the Real Concerns of Women.* New York: Anchor Books, 1996.

———, and Nancy Hewitt. "Rethinking Feminism." *Tikkun,* June 1992, 29+.

Fraiman, Susan. "Feminism Today: Mothers, Daughters, Emerging Sisters." *American Literary History* 11, no. 3 (Fall 1999): 525–544.

Framing Lesbian Fashion. Dir. Karen Everett. Frameline, San Francisco, 1992.

Franklin, Kris, and Sarah E. Chinn. "Ms. Strangelove, or, How I Stopped Worrying and Learned to Love Gay Male Porn." In *Generation Q: Gays, Lesbians, and Bisexuals Born around 1969's Stonewall Riots Tell Their Stories of Growing Up in the Age of Information,* ed. Robin Bernstein and Seth Clark Silberman, 168–173. Los Angeles: Alyson Publications, 1996.

Freccero, Carla. "Notes of a Post–Sex Wars Theorizer." In *Conflicts in Feminism,* ed. Marianne Hirsch and Evelyn Fox Keller, 305–325. New York: Routledge, 1990.

Freeman, Jo. "The Building of the Gilded Cage." In *Notes from the Third Year: Women's Liberation,* 44–55. New York, 1971.

———. "Generation Gap in the Feminist Movement." *Sojourner,* November 1979, 7+.

———. "The New Feminists." *The Nation,* February 24, 1969, 241–244.

———. *The Politics of Women's Liberation: A Case Study of an Emerging Social Movement and Its Relation to the Policy Process.* New York: McKay Views, 1975.

Friedan, Betty. *The Feminine Mystique.* 1963. Reprint, New York: Laurel Books, 1983.

Friend, Tad. "Yes." *Esquire,* February 1994, 48–56.

Fuss, Diane. *Identification Papers.* New York: Routledge, 1995.

———, ed. *Inside/Out: Lesbian Theories, Gay Theories.* New York: Routledge, 1991.

Gallagher, Maggie. "Party Girl." *National Review*, November 29, 1993, 66–67. Review of Naomi Wolf, *Fire with Fire*.

Gallop, Jane. *Around 1981: Academic Feminist Literary Theory*. New York: Routledge, 1992.

———. *Feminist Accused of Sexual Harassment*. Durham, N.C.: Duke University Press, 1997.

———. *Thinking through the Body*. New York: Columbia University Press, 1988.

———, and Elizabeth Francis. "Talking Across." In *Generations: Academic Feminists in Dialogue*, ed. Devoney Looser and Ann Kaplan, 103–131. Minneapolis: University of Minnesota Press, 1997.

———, Marianne Hirsch, and Nancy K. Miller. "Criticizing Feminist Criticism." In *Conflicts in Feminism*, ed. Marianne Hirsch and Evelyn Fox Keller, 349–369. New York: Routledge, 1990.

Garber, Linda. *Identity Poetics: Race, Class, and the Lesbian-Feminist Roots of Queer Theory*. New York: Columbia University Press, 2001.

Garrison, Ednie Kaeh. "U.S. Feminism-Grrrl Style! Young (Sub)Cultures and the Technologies of the Third Wave." *Feminist Studies* 26, no. 1 (Spring 2000): 141–170.

Gerhard, Jane. *Desiring Revolution: Second-Wave Feminism and the Rewriting of American Sexual Thought, 1920 to 1982*. New York: Columbia University Press, 2001.

Gibbs, Nancy. "The War against Feminism." *Time*, March 9, 1992, 50–56.

Giddings, Paula. *When and Where I Enter: The Impact of Black Women on Race and Sex in America*. New York: Bantam Books, 1984.

Glickman, Rose L. *Daughters of Feminists*. New York: St. Martin's Press, 1993.

Gloria Steinem, the Spice Girls, and Me: Defining the Third Wave of Feminism. Dir. Krista Longtin. 2002.

Gordon, Emily, and Katha Pollitt. "Does Your Generation Resent Up-and-Coming Young Women?" In *Letters of Intent: Women Cross the Generations to Talk about Family, Work, Sex, Love and the Future of Feminism*, ed. Anna Bondoc and Meg Daly, 21–32. New York: Simon & Schuster, 1999.

Gore, Ariel, and Bee Lavender, eds. *Breeder: Real-Life Stories from the New Generation of Mothers*. Seattle: Seal Press, 2001.

Gornick, Vivian. *Essays in Feminism*. New York: Harper & Row, 1978.

———. "Who Says We Haven't Made a Revolution? A Feminist Takes Stock." *New York Time Magazine*, April 15, 1990, 24+.

Gray, Kristina. "I Sold My Soul to Rock and Roll." In *Colonize This! Young Women of Color on Today's Feminism*, ed. Daisy Hernández and Bushra Rehman, 257–267. New York: Seal Press, 2002.

Gray, Natasha. "Bored with the Boys: Cracks in the Queer Coalition." *NYQ*, April 26, 1992, 26–30.

Greenson, Ralph R. "Dis-Identifying from Mother: Its Special Importance for the Boy." *International Journal of Psychoanalysis* 49 (1968): 370–374.

Greer, Germaine. "The Backlash Myth." *New Republic*, October 5, 1992, 20–22.

———. *The Female Eunuch*. London: Granada Publishing, 1971.

Gross, Jane. "Does She Speak for Today's Women?" *New York Times Magazine*, March 1, 1992, 17+.

Gutmann, Stephanie. "Unhand Us, Miss MacKinnon!" *National Review*, October 18, 1993, 66–68. Review of Katie Roiphe, *The Morning After*.

Guy-Sheftall, Beverly. "Introduction: The Evolution of Feminist Consciousness among African American Women." In *Words of Fire: An Anthology of African-American Feminist Thought*, ed. Beverly Guy-Sheftall, 1–22. New York: The New Press, 1995.

————. "Other Mothers of Women's Studies." In *The Politics of Women's Studies: Testimony from 30 Founding Mothers*, ed. Florence Howe, 216–226. New York: The Feminist Press, 2000.

————. "Preface." In *Words of Fire: An Anthology of African-American Feminist Thought*, ed. Beverly Guy-Sheftall, xiii–xx. New York: The New Press, 1995.

————, ed. *Words of Fire: An Anthology of African-American Feminist Thought*. New York: The New Press, 1995.

Hand on the Pulse. Dir. Joyce Warshow. Frameline Distribution, San Francisco, 2002.

Harad, Alyssa. "Reviving Lolita; or, Because Junior High Is Still Hell." In *Catching a Wave: Reclaiming Feminism for the 21st Century*, ed. Rory Dicker and Alison Piepmeier, 81–98. Boston: Northeastern University Press, 2003.

Harris, Anita. "Not Waving or Drowning: Young Women, Feminism, and the Limits of the Next Wave Debate." *Outskirts: Feminisms along the Edge* 8 (May 2001). Available online at http://www.chloe.uwa.edu.au/outskirts/archive/VOL8/article4.html. Accessed December 4, 2003.

Harris, Jennifer. "Betty Friedan's Granddaughters: *Cosmo*, Ginger Spice & the Inheritance of Whiteness." In *Turbo Chicks: Talking Young Feminisms*, ed. Allyson Mitchell, Lisa Bryn Rundle, and Lara Karaian, 195–206. Toronto: Sumach Press, 2001.

Harris, Laura, and Elizabeth Crocker, eds. *Fem(me): Feminists, Lesbians, and Bad Girls*. New York: Routledge, 1997.

Hazleton, Lesley. "Power Politics." *Women's Review of Books* 6, no. 5 (February 1994): 1–4. Review of Naomi Wolf, *Fire with Fire*.

Healey, Emma. *Lesbian Sex Wars*. London: Virago Press, 1996.

Heller, Dana. "The Anxiety of Affluence: Movements, Markets, and Lesbian Feminist Generation(s)." In *Generations: Academic Feminists in Dialogue*, ed. Devoney Looser and Ann Kaplan, 309–326. Minneapolis: University of Minnesota Press, 1997.

————. "Purposes: An Introduction." In *Cross Purposes: Lesbians, Feminists, and the Limits of Alliance*, ed. Dana Heller, 1–18. Bloomington: Indiana University Press, 1997.

————, ed. *Cross Purposes: Lesbians, Feminists, and the Limits of Alliance*. Bloomington: Indiana University Press, 1997.

Hennessee, Judith. *Betty Friedan: Her Life*. New York: Random House, 1999.

Hennessy, Rosemary. "Queer Theory: A Review of the *differences* Special Issue and Wittig's *The Straight Mind*." *Signs: A Journal of Women in Culture and Society* 18, no. 4 (Summer 1993): 964–973.

Henry, Astrid. "Orgasms and Empowerment: *Sex and the City* and Third Wave Feminism." In *Reading Sex and the City*, ed. Kim Akass and Janet McCabe, 65–82. London: I. B. Tauris, 2004.

Hernández, Daisy, and Bushra Rehman, eds. *Colonize This! Young Women of Color on Today's Feminism*. New York: Seal Press, 2002.

Herrup, Mocha Jean. "Virtual Identity." In *To Be Real: Telling the Truth and Changing the Face of Feminism*, ed. Rebecca Walker, 239–251. New York: Anchor Books, 1995.

Heywood, Leslie, and Jennifer Drake. "Introduction." In *Third Wave Agenda: Being Feminist, Doing Feminism*, ed. Leslie Heywood and Jennifer Drake, 1–20. Minneapolis: University of Minnesota Press, 1997.

————. "We Learn America Like a Script: Activism in the Third Wave; or, Enough Phantoms of Nothing." In *Third Wave Agenda: Being Feminist, Doing Feminism*, ed. Leslie Heywood and Jennifer Drake, 40–54. Minneapolis: University of Minnesota Press, 1997.

———, eds. *Third Wave Agenda: Being Feminist, Doing Feminism*. Minneapolis: University of Minnesota Press, 1997.

Hill, Anita. *Speaking Truth to Power*. New York: Doubleday, 1997.

Hirsch, Marianne. *The Mother/Daughter Plot: Narrative, Psychoanalysis, Feminism*. Bloomington: Indiana University Press, 1989.

Hirsch, Marianne, and Evelyn Fox Keller, eds. *Conflicts in Feminism*. New York: Routledge, 1990.

Hoagland, Sarah Lucia, and Julia Penelope, eds. *For Lesbians Only: A Separatist Anthology*. London: Onlywomen Press, 1988.

Hoban, Phoebe. "Big WAC Attack." *New York*, August 3, 1992, 30–35.

Hochschild, Arlie Russell. "Coming of Age, Seeking an Identity." *New York Times*, March 8, 2000, D1+.

Hogan, Katie J. "'Victim Feminism' and the Complexities of AIDS." In *"Bad Girls"/"Good Girls": Women, Sex, and Power in the Nineties*, ed. Nan Bauer Maglin and Donna Perry, 68–89. New Brunswick, N.J.: Rutgers University Press, 1996.

Hogeland, Lisa Marie. "Against Generational Thinking, or, Some Things that 'Third Wave' Feminism Isn't." *Women's Studies in Communication* 24, no. 1 (Spring 2001): 107–121.

———. "Fear of Feminism: Why Young Women Get the Willies." *Ms.*, November/December 1994, 18–21.

———. *Feminism and Its Fictions: The Consciousness-Raising Novel and the Women's Liberation Movement*. Philadelphia: University of Pennsylvania Press, 1998.

Hole, Judith, and Ellen Levine. "The First Feminists." In *Radical Feminism*, ed. Anne Koedt, Ellen Levine, and Anita Rapone, 3–16. New York: Quadrangle, 1973.

———. *Rebirth of Feminism*. New York: Quadrangle Books, 1971.

Hollibaugh, Amber, and Cherríe Moraga. "What We're Rolling around in Bed With: Sexual Silences in Feminism." In *Powers of Desire: The Politics of Sexuality*, ed. Ann Snitow, Christine Stansell, and Sharon Thompson, 394–405. New York: Monthly Review Press, 1983.

hooks, bell. *Ain't I a Woman: Black Women and Feminism*. Boston: South End Press, 1981.

———. "Beauty Laid Bare: Aesthetics in the Ordinary." In *To Be Real: Telling the Truth and Changing the Face of Feminism*, ed. Rebecca Walker, 157–166. New York: Anchor Books, 1995.

———. "Dissident Heat: Fire with Fire." In bell hooks, *Outlaw Culture: Resisting Representations*, 91–100. New York: Routledge, 1994.

———. "Feminist Opportunism or Commitment to Struggle?" *Z*, January 1994, 1.

———. *Feminist Theory from Margin to Center*. Boston: South End Press, 1984.

———. "Katie Roiphe: A Little Feminist Excess Goes a Long Way." In bell hooks, *Outlaw Culture: Resisting Representations*, 101–108. New York: Routledge, 1994.

———. "Theory as Liberatory Practice." In bell hooks, *Teaching to Transgress: Education as the Practice of Freedom*, 59–75. New York: Routledge, 1994.

———. *Wounds of Passion: A Writing Life*. New York: Henry Holt, 1997.

———, Gloria Steinem, Urvashi Vaid, and Naomi Wolf. "Let's Get Real about Feminism: The Backlash, the Myths, the Movement." *Ms.*, September/October 1993, 34–43.

Horowitz, Daniel. *Betty Friedan and the Making of* The Feminine Mystique: *The American Left, the Cold War, and Modern Feminism*. Amherst: University of Massachusetts Press, 1999.

How to Female Ejaculate. Dir. Fanny Fatale. Fatale Media Inc., San Rafael, Calif., 1992.

Howe, Florence, ed. *The Politics of Women's Studies: Testimony from 30 Founding Mothers.* New York: The Feminist Press, 2000.

Howe, Neil, and William Strauss. "The New Generation Gap." *Atlantic Monthly,* December 1992, 67–89.

Hull, Gloria 'T., Patricia Bell Scott, and Barbara Smith, eds. *All the Women Are White, All the Blacks Are Men, but Some of Us Are Brave: Black Women's Studies.* New York: The Feminist Press, 1982.

Huntington, Anna Seaton. "These Women Do Not Fear the Twenty-First Century." *Harper's Bazaar,* September 1995, 384–389.

Hurdis, Rebecca. "Heartbroken: Women of Color Feminism and the Third Wave." In *Colonize This! Young Women of Color on Today's Feminism,* ed. Daisy Hernández and Bushra Rehman, 279–292. New York: Seal Press, 2002.

Hutchins, Lorraine, and Lani Kaahumanu, eds. *Bi Any Other Name: Bisexual People Speak Out.* Boston: Alyson Publications, 1991.

Iannone, Carol. "Sex and the Feminists." *Commentary* 96, no. 3 (September 1993): 51–54. Review of Katie Roiphe, *The Morning After.*

"Identity Crisis: Queer Politics in the Age of Possibilities." *Village Voice,* June 30, 1992, 27+.

Irigaray, Luce. "And the One Doesn't Stir without the Other." *Signs: A Journal of Women in Culture and Society* 7, no. 1 (1981): 60–67.

Jackson, Stevi, and Sue Scott. "Sexual Skirmishes and Feminist Factions." In *Feminism and Sexuality: A Reader,* ed. Stevi Jackson and Sue Scott, 1–31. New York: Columbia University Press, 1996.

Jagose, Annamarie. *Queer Theory: An Introduction.* New York: New York University Press, 1996.

James, Stanlie M. "Mothering: A Possible Black Feminist Link to Social Transformation?" In *Theorizing Black Feminisms: The Visionary Pragmatism of Black Women,* ed. Stanlie M. James and Abena P. A. Busia, 44–54. New York: Routledge, 1993.

Jamila, Shani. "Can I Get a Witness? Testimony from a Hip Hop Feminist." In *Colonize This! Young Women of Color on Today's Feminism,* ed. Daisy Hernández and Bushra Rehman, 382–394. New York: Seal Press, 2002.

Jeffreys, Sheila. *Anticlimax: A Feminist Perspective on the Sexual Revolution.* New York: New York University Press, 1990.

———. "How Orgasm Politics Has Hijacked the Women's Movement." *On the Issues,* Spring 1996, 18+.

———. "The Queer Disappearance of Lesbians: Sexuality in the Academy." *Women's Studies International Forum* 17, no. 5 (1994): 459–472.

Jensen, Michelle. "Riding the Third Wave." *The Nation,* December 11, 2000, 24–30. Review of Jennifer Baumgardner and Amy Richards, *Manifesta: Young Women Feminism and the Future.*

Johnson, Merri Lisa. "Blow Job Queen." In *Sex and Single Girls: Straight and Queer Women on Sexuality,* ed. Lee Damsky, 76–86. Seattle: Seal Press, 2000.

———. "Fuck You and Your Untouchable Face: Third Wave Feminism and the Problem of Romance." In *Jane Sexes It Up: True Confessions of Feminist Desire,* ed. Merri Lisa Johnson, 13–50. New York: Four Walls Eight Windows, 2002.

———. "Jane Hocus, Jane Focus." In *Jane Sexes It Up: True Confessions of Feminist Desire,* ed. Merri Lisa Johnson, 1–11. New York: Four Walls Eight Windows, 2002.

———. "Pearl Necklace: The Politics of Masturbation Fantasies." In *Jane Sexes It Up: True Confessions of Feminist Desire*, ed. Merri Lisa Johnson, 311–326. New York: Four Walls Eight Windows, 2002.

———, ed. *Jane Sexes It Up: True Confessions of Feminist Desire*. New York: Four Walls Eight Windows, 2002.

Jones, Beverly, and Judith Brown. "Toward a Female Liberation Movement." In *Voices from Women's Liberation*, ed. Leslie B. Tanner, 362–415. New York: New American Library, 1970.

Jones, Lisa. *Bulletproof Diva: Tales of Race, Sex, and Hair*. New York: Anchor Books, 1994.

Jones, Tayari, and Pearl Cleage. "Which Come First, Our Paychecks or Our Principles?" In *Letters of Intent: Women Cross the Generations to Talk about Family, Work, Sex, Love and the Future of Feminism*, ed. Anna Bondoc and Meg Daly, 33–41. New York: Simon & Schuster, 1999.

Joreen. "The Bitch Manifesto." In *Notes from the Second Year: Women's Liberation. Major Writings of the Radical Feminists*, 5–9. New York, 1970.

———. "The Tyranny of Structurelessness" (1972). In *Radical Feminism*, ed. Anne Koedt, Ellen Levine, and Anita Rapone, 285–299. New York: Quadrangle, 1973.

Joseph, Gloria I. "Black Mothers and Daughters: Traditional and New Perspectives." In *Double Stitch: Black Women Write about Mothers & Daughters*, ed. Patricia Bell-Scott, Beverly Guy-Sheftall, Jacqueline Jones Royster, Janet Sims-Wood, Miriam DeCosta-Willis, and Lucille P. Fultz, 94–106. New York: HarperPerennial, 1991.

Juno, Andrea, and V. Vale, eds. *Angry Women*. San Francisco: Re/Search Publications, 1991.

Kakutani, Michiko. "Feminism Lite: She Is Woman, Hear Her Mate." *New York Times*, June 10, 1997, B6. Review of Naomi Wolf, *Promiscuities: The Secret Struggle for Womanhood*.

Kamen, Paula. "Acquaintance Rape: Revolution and Reaction." In *"Bad Girls"/"Good Girls": Women, Sex, and Power in the Nineties*, ed. Nan Bauer Maglin and Donna Perry, 137–149. New Brunswick, N.J.: Rutgers University Press, 1996.

———. "Erasing Rape: Media Hype an Attack on Sexual-Assault Research." *Extra!* November/December 1993, 10–11.

———. *Feminist Fatale: Voices from the "Twentysomething" Generation Explore the Future of the "Women's Movement."* New York: Donald I. Fine, 1991.

———. *Her Way: Young Women Remake the Sexual Revolution*. New York: Broadway Books, 2002.

———. "My 'Bourgeois' Brand of Feminism." In *Next: Young American Writers on the New Generation*, ed. Eric Liu, 81–94. New York: W.W. Norton & Company, 1994.

Kaminer, Wendy. "Bimbo Feminism." In Wendy Kaminer, *True Love Waits: Essays and Criticism*, 22–28. Reading, Mass.: Addison-Wesley, 1996.

———. "Feminism's Identity Crisis." *Atlantic*, October 1993, 51–68.

———. "Feminism's Third Wave: What Do Young Women Want?" *New York Times Book Review*, June 4, 1995, 3+.

———. "What Is This Thing Called Rape?" *New York Times Book Review*, September 19, 1993, 1+. Review of Katie Roiphe, *The Morning After*.

Kaplan, E. Ann. "Introduction 2: Feminism, Aging, and Changing Paradigms." In *Generations: Academic Feminists in Dialogue*, ed. Devoney Looser and Ann Kaplan, 13–29. Minneapolis: University of Minnesota Press, 1997.

————, and Devoney Looser. "Introduction 1: An Exchange." In *Generations: Academic Feminists in Dialogue*, ed. Devoney Looser and Ann Kaplan, 1–12. Minneapolis: University of Minnesota Press, 1997.

Karp, Marcelle, and Debbie Stoller, eds. *The Bust Guide to the New Girl Order*. New York: Penguin Books, 1999.

Kasindorf, Jeanie Russell. "Lesbian Chic: The Bold, Brave New World of Gay Women." *New York*, May 10, 1993, 30–37.

Katz, Jonathan Ned. *The Invention of Heterosexuality*. New York: Plume, 1996.

Kesler, Kari. "The Plain-Clothes Whore." In *Jane Sexes It Up: True Confessions of Feminist Desire*, ed. Merri Lisa Johnson, 231–240. New York: Four Walls Eight Windows, 2002.

King, Deborah K. "Multiple Jeopardy, Multiple Consciousness: The Context of a Black Feminist Ideology." In *Words of Fire: An Anthology of African-American Feminist Thought*, ed. Beverly Guy-Sheftall, 294–317. New York: The New Press, 1995. Originally published in *Signs: A Journal of Women in Culture and Society* 14 (Autumn 1988): 47–72.

King, Katie. "Producing Sex, Theory, and Culture: Gay/Straight Remappings in Contemporary Feminism." In *Conflicts in Feminism*, ed. Marianne Hirsch and Evelyn Fox Keller, 82–101. New York: Routledge, 1990.

————. *Theory in Its Feminist Travels: Conversations in U.S. Women's Movements*. Bloomington: Indiana University Press, 1994.

Kiss & Tell. *Drawing the Line: Lesbian Sexual Politics on the Wall*. Vancouver, B.C.: Press Gang Publishers, 1991.

Kitwana, Bakari. *The Hip Hop Generation: Young Blacks and the Crisis in African-American Culture*. New York: Basic Civitas Books, 2002.

Klein, Melissa. "Duality and Redefinition: Young Feminism and the Alternative Music Community." In *Third Wave Agenda: Being Feminist, Doing Feminism*, ed. Leslie Heywood and Jennifer Drake, 207–225. Minneapolis: University of Minnesota Press, 1997.

Klein, Renate D. "Passion and Politics in Women's Studies in the Nineties." *Women's Studies International Forum* 14, no. 3 (1991): 125–134.

Koch, Kathleen. "Feminists Meet to Discuss Future of the Movement." April 2, 2000. Available online at http://www.cnn.com/2000/US/04/01/feminist.majority/. Accessed December 4, 2003.

Koedt, Anne. "Lesbianism and Feminism." In *Notes from the Third Year: Women's Liberation*, 84–89. New York, 1971.

————. "Loving Another Woman." In *Notes from the Third Year: Women's Liberation*, 25–29. New York, 1971.

————. "The Myth of the Vaginal Orgasm." In *Radical Feminism*, ed. Anne Koedt, Ellen Levine, and Anita Rapone, 198–207. New York: Quadrangle, 1973. Originally published in *Notes from the First Year*. New York, 1968.

————, Ellen Levine, and Anita Rapone, eds. *Radical Feminism*. New York: Quadrangle, 1973.

Kornbluh, Felicia. "After *The Morning After*." *Women's Review of Books* 6, no. 5 (February 1994): 14–15. Review of Katie Roiphe, *The Morning After*.

Kreps, Bonnie. "Radical Feminism 1." In *Radical Feminism*, ed. Anne Koedt, Ellen Levine, and Anita Rapone, 234–239. New York: Quadrangle, 1973.

Kuczynski, Alex. "The New Feminist Mystique." *New York Times*, September 10, 2001, C1+.

La Rue, Linda. "The Black Movement and Women's Liberation." In *Words of Fire: An Anthology of African-American Feminist Thought*, ed. Beverly Guy-Sheftall, 164–173. New York: The New Press, 1995. Originally published in *Black Scholar* (May 1970): 36–42.

Lamos, Colleen. "The Postmodern Lesbian Position: *On Our Backs.*" In *The Lesbian Postmodern,* ed. Laura Doan, 85–103. New York: Columbia University Press, 1994.

Lear, Marsha Weinman. "The Second Feminist Wave." *New York Times Magazine,* March 10, 1968, 24+.

Lederer, Laura, ed. *Take Back the Night: Women on Pornography.* New York: William Morrow and Company, 1980.

Lee, JeeYeun. "Beyond Bean Counting." In *Listen Up: Voices from the Next Feminist Generation,* ed. Barbara Findlen, 205–211. Seattle: Seal Press, 1995.

Lehmann-Haupt, Rachel. "How to Talk Dirty and Influence People: The Selling of the Female Orgasm." *Paper,* February 2000, 61+.

Lehrman, Karen. *The Lipstick Proviso: Women, Sex and Power in the Real World.* New York: Anchor Books, 1997.

———. "Off Course." *Mother Jones,* September/October 1993, 45+.

Lennon, Sharon. "What Is Mine." In *Listen Up: Voices from the Next Feminist Generation,* ed. Barbara Findlen, 120–131. Seattle: Seal Press, 1995.

Leo, John. "The Trouble with Feminism." *U.S. News and World Report,* February 10, 1992, 19.

Leong, Pandora L. "Living Outside the Box." In *Colonize This! Young Women of Color on Today's Feminism,* ed. Daisy Hernández and Bushra Rehman, 343–356. New York: Seal Press, 2002.

Lerner, Gerda. *Fireweed: A Political Autobiography.* Philadelphia: Temple University Press, 2002.

———. *The Majority Finds Its Past: Placing Women in History.* New York: Oxford University Press, 1979.

Levine, Abby. "Better Living through Porn." In *Sex and Single Girls: Straight and Queer Women on Sexuality,* ed. Lee Damsky, 321–330. Seattle: Seal Press, 2000.

Levine, Suzanne, and Harriet Lyons. *The Decade of Women: A Ms. History of the Seventies in Words and Pictures.* New York: Putnam, 1980.

Linden, Robin Ruth, Darlene R. Pagano, Diana E. H. Russell, and Susan Leigh Star, eds. *Against Sadomasochism: A Radical Feminist Analysis.* San Francisco: Frog in the Well, 1982.

Liu, Eric, ed. *Next: Young American Writers on the New Generation.* New York: W.W. Norton & Company, 1994.

Live Nude Girls Unite. Dir. Julia Query and Vicky Funari. First Run Features, New York, 2000.

Looking Back, Moving Forward: 25 Years of Women's Studies History. Special issue of *Women's Studies Quarterly* 25, nos. 1 and 2 (Spring/Summer 1997).

Looser, Devoney. "Introduction 2: Gen X Feminists? Youthism, Careerism, and the Third Wave." In *Generations: Academic Feminists in Dialogue,* ed. Devoney Looser and Ann Kaplan, 31–54. Minneapolis: University of Minnesota Press, 1997.

———. "This Feminism Which Is Not One." *Minnesota Review* 11, no. 5 (Fall 1993/Spring 1994): 108–117.

———, and Ann Kaplan, eds. *Generations: Academic Feminists in Dialogue.* Minneapolis: University of Minnesota Press, 1997.

Lorde, Audre. *Sister Outsider: Essays and Speeches.* Trumansburg, N.Y.: Crossing Press, 1984.

———. *Zami: A New Spelling of My Name.* Trumansburg, N.Y.: The Crossing Press, 1982.

Lydon, Susan. "The Politics of Orgasm." In *Sisterhood Is Powerful: An Anthology of Writings from the Women's Liberation Movement,* ed. Robin Morgan, 197–205. New York: Vintage Books, 1970.

Macdonald, Barbara, with Cynthia Rich. *Look Me in the Eye: Old Women, Aging, and Ageism.* San Francisco: Spinsters, Ink, 1983.

Maggenti, Maria. "Wandering through Herland." In *Sisters, Sexperts, Queers: Beyond the Lesbian Nation,* ed. Arlene Stein, 245–255. New York: Plume, 1993.

———. "Women as Queer Nationals." *Outlook* 11 (Winter 1991): 20–23.

Maglin, Nan Bauer, and Donna Perry. "Introduction." In *"Bad Girls"/"Good Girls": Women, Sex, and Power in the Nineties,* ed. Nan Bauer Maglin and Donna Perry, xiii–xxvi. New Brunswick, N.J.: Rutgers University Press, 1996.

———, eds. *"Bad Girls"/"Good Girls": Women, Sex, and Power in the Nineties.* New Brunswick, N.J.: Rutgers University Press, 1996.

Malkin, Nina. "It's a Grrrl Thing." *Seventeen,* May 1991, 80–82.

Mandle, Joan D. "Sisterly Critics." *NWSA Journal* 11, no. 1 (Spring 1999): 97–109.

Mannheim, Karl. "The Problem of Generations." In *Essays on the Sociology of Knowledge,* ed. Paul Kecskemeti, 276–320. New York: Oxford University Press, 1952.

Martin, Biddy. *Femininity Played Straight: The Significance of Being Lesbian.* New York: Routledge, 1996.

Martindale, Kathleen. *Un/Popular Culture: Lesbian Writing after the Sex Wars.* Albany, N.Y.: State University of New York Press, 1997.

McCaskill, Barbara, and Layli Phillips. "We Are All 'Good Woman'!: A Womanist Critique of the Current Feminist Conflict." In *"Bad Girls"/"Good Girls": Women, Sex, and Power in the Nineties,* ed. Nan Bauer Maglin and Donna Perry, 106–122. New Brunswick, N.J.: Rutgers University Press, 1996.

McDowell, Deborah E. *"The Changing Same": Black Women's Literature, Criticism, and Theory.* Bloomington: Indiana University Press, 1995.

McIntosh, Mary. "Queer Theory and the War of the Sexes." In *Activating Theory: Lesbian, Gay, Bisexual Politics,* ed. Joseph Bristow and Angelia R. Wilson, 30–52. London: Lawrence & Wisehart, 1993.

Merck, Mandy, Naomi Segal, and Elizabeth Wright, eds. *Coming Out of Feminism.* Oxford: Blackwell Publishers, 1998.

Messer-Davidow, Ellen. *Disciplining Feminism: From Social Activism to Academic Discourse.* Durham, N.C.: Duke University Press, 2002.

Michie, Helena. "Not One of the Family: The Repression of the Other Woman in Feminist Theory." In *Discontented Discourses: Feminism, Textual Intervention, Psychoanalysis,* ed. Marleen S. Barr and Richard Feldstein, 15–28. Urbana: University of Illinois Press, 1989.

Miles, Tiya. "Lessons from a Young Feminist Collective." In *Listen Up: Voices from the Next Feminist Generation,* ed. Barbara Findlen, 167–176. Seattle: Seal Press, 1995.

Miller, Nancy K. "Decades." *South Atlantic Quarterly* 91, no. 1 (Winter 1992): 65–86.

Miller, Neil. *Out of the Past: Gay and Lesbian History from 1869 to the Present.* New York: Vintage Books, 1995.

Millet, Catherine. *The Sexual Life of Catherine M.* Trans. Adriana Hunter. New York: Grove Press, 2003.

Millett, Kate. *Sexual Politics.* New York: Equinox Books, 1969.

———. "Sexual Politics: A Manifesto for a Revolution." In *Radical Feminism,* ed. Anne Koedt, Ellen Levine, and Anita Rapone, 356–367. New York: Quadrangle, 1973.

Milloy, Marilyn. "The New Feminism." *Essence,* September 1997, 117+.

Miner, Valerie, and Helen E. Longino, eds. *Competition: A Feminist Taboo?* New York: The Feminist Press, 1987.

Minkowitz, Donna. "The Newsroom Becomes a Battleground: Is the Media's Siege on Lesbians in the Women's Movement a Desperate Attempt to Undermine Feminism?" *Advocate,* May 19, 1992, 30–37.

Minnich, Elizabeth Kamarch. "Feminist Attacks on Feminisms: Patriarchy's Prodigal Daughters." *Feminist Studies* 24, no. 1 (Spring 1998): 159–175.

Mitchell, Allyson, Lisa Bryn Rundle, and Lara Karaian, eds. *Turbo Chicks: Talking Young Feminisms.* Toronto: Sumach Press, 2001.

Mitchell, Juliet, and Ann Oakley. "Introduction." In *What Is Feminism?* ed. Juliet Mitchell and Ann Oakley, 1–7. Oxford: Basil Blackwell, 1986.

————, eds. *What Is Feminism?* Oxford: Basil Blackwell, 1986.

Miya-Jervis, Lisa. "A Celibate Sexpot Ties the Knot." In *Sex and Single Girls: Straight and Queer Women on Sexuality,* ed. Lee Damsky, 280–287. Seattle: Seal Press, 2000.

Modleski, Tania. *Feminism without Women: Culture and Criticism in a "Postfeminist" Age.* New York: Routledge, 1991.

Moraga, Cherríe. "Foreword: 'The War Path of Greater Empowerment.'" In *Colonize This! Young Women of Color on Today's Feminism,* ed. Daisy Hernández and Bushra Rehman, xi–xv. New York: Seal Press, 2002.

Morgan, Joan. "Fly Girls, Bitches, and Hos: Notes of a Hip-Hop Feminist." *Village Voice,* February 13, 1996, 32–33.

————. *When Chickenheads Come Home to Roost: My Life as a Hip-Hop Feminist.* New York: Simon & Schuster, 1999.

————. "White Noise." *Ms.,* August/September 1999, 96.

Morgan, Robin. *Going Too Far: The Personal Chronicle of a Feminist.* New York: Random House, 1977.

————. "Lesbianism and Feminism: Synonyms or Contradictions?" (1973). In Robin Morgan, *Going Too Far: The Personal Chronicle of a Feminist,* 170–188. New York: Random House, 1977.

————. "Ms. Lives!" *Ms.,* July/August 1990, 1–2.

————. *Saturday's Child: A Memoir.* New York: W.W. Norton & Company, 2001.

————. "Women Disrupt the Miss America Pageant." (1968). In *Going Too Far: The Personal Chronicle of a Feminist,* 62–67. New York: Random House, 1977.

————, ed. *Sisterhood Is Powerful: An Anthology of Writings from the Women's Liberation Movement.* New York: Vintage Books, 1970.

Morgan, Tracy. "Butch-Femme and the Politics of Identity." In *Sisters, Sexperts, Queers: Beyond the Lesbian Nation,* ed. Arlene Stein, 35–46. New York: Plume, 1993.

Morrison, Toni, ed. *Race-ing Justice, En-gendering Power: Essays on Anita Hill, Clarence Thomas, and the Construction of Social Reality.* New York: Pantheon Books, 1992.

————. "What the Black Woman Thinks about Woman's Lib." *New York Times Magazine,* August 22, 1971, 14+.

Murray, Pauli. "The Liberation of Black Women." In *Voices of the New Feminism,* ed. Mary Lou Thompson, 87–102. Boston: Beacon Press, 1970.

Muscio, Inga. *Cunt: A Declaration of Independence.* Seattle: Seal Press, 1998.

Myles, Eileen. "My Intergeneration." *Village Voice,* June 27, 2000, 68.

Neal, Mark Anthony. *Soul Babies: Black Popular Culture and Post-Soul Aesthetic.* New York: Routledge, 2002.

Nestle, Joan. "My Mother Liked to Fuck." In *Powers of Desire: The Politics of Sexuality,* ed. Ann Snitow, Christine Stansell, and Sharon Thompson, 468–470. New York: Monthly Review Press, 1983.

————. *A Restricted Country.* Ithaca, N.Y.: Firebrand Books, 1987.

————, ed. *The Persistent Desire: A Femme-Butch Reader.* Boston: Alyson Publications, 1992.

New York Radical Feminists. *Notes from the Second Year: Women's Liberation. Major Writings of the Radical Feminists.* New York, 1970.

————. *Notes from the Third Year: Women's Liberation.* New York, 1971.

Newton, Esther, and Shirley Walton. "The Misunderstanding: Toward a More Precise Sexual Vocabulary." In *Pleasure and Danger: Exploring Female Sexuality*, ed. Carole S. Vance, 242–250. Boston: Routledge and Kegan Paul, 1985.

Noble, Barbara Presley. "One Daughter's Rebellion or Her Mother's Imprint?" *New York Times*, November 10, 1993, C1+.

O'Barr, Jean, and Mary Wyer, eds. *Engaging Feminism: Students Speak Up and Speak Out*. Charlottesville: University Press of Virginia, 1992.

O'Reilly, Andrea, and Sharon Abbey, eds. *Mothers and Daughters: Connection, Empowerment, and Transformation*. Boston: Rowman & Littlefield, 2000.

Orr, Catherine M. "Charting the Current of the Third Wave." *Hypatia: A Journal of Feminist Philosophy* 12, no. 3 (Summer 1997): 29–45.

Ouellette, Laurie. "Building the Third Wave: Reflections of a Young Feminist." *On the Issues* 14 (Fall 1992): 9+.

Paglia, Camille. *Sex, Art, and American Culture*. New York: Vintage Books, 1992.

———. *Vamps and Tramps: New Essays*. New York: Vintage Books, 1994.

Paris, Sherri. Review of *A Lure of Knowledge: Lesbian Sexuality and Theory*, by Judith Roof, and *Inside/Out: Lesbian Theories, Gay Theories*, ed. Diana Fuss. *Signs: A Journal of Women in Culture and Society* 18, no. 4 (Summer 1993): 984–988.

Patai, Daphne. "The Struggle for Feminist Purity Threatens the Goals of Feminism." *Chronicle of Higher Education* (February 5, 1992): B1+.

Patai, Daphen, and Noretta Koertge. *Professing Feminism: Cautionary Tales from the Strange World of Women's Studies*. New York: Basic Books, 1994.

Payette, Patricia. "The Feminist Wife? Notes from a Political 'Engagement.'" In *Jane Sexes It Up: True Confessions of Feminist Desire*, ed. Merri Lisa Johnson, 139–167. New York: Four Walls Eight Windows, 2002.

Penelope, Julia. *Call Me Lesbian: Lesbian Lives, Lesbian Theory*. Freedom, Calif.: The Crossing Press, 1992.

Phelan, Shane. *Getting Specific: Postmodern Lesbian Politics*. Minneapolis: University of Minnesota Press, 1994.

———. *Identity Politics: Lesbian Feminism and the Limits of Community*. Philadelphia: Temple University Press, 1989.

———, ed. *Playing with Fire: Queer Politics, Queer Theories*. New York: Routledge, 1997.

Pollitt, Katha, and Jennifer Baumgardner. "Afterword: A Correspondence between Katha Pollitt and Jennifer Baumgardner." In *Catching a Wave: Reclaiming Feminism for the 21st Century*, ed. Rory Dicker and Alison Piepmeier, 309–319. Boston: Northeastern University Press, 2003.

Pough, Gwendolyn D. "Do the Ladies Run This . . . ? Some Thoughts on Hip-Hop Feminism." In *Catching a Wave: Reclaiming Feminism for the 21st Century*, ed. Rory Dicker and Alison Piepmeier, 232–243. Boston: Northeastern University Press, 2003.

———. "Love Feminism but Where's My Hip Hop?" In *Colonize This! Young Women of Color on Today's Feminism*, ed. Daisy Hernández and Bushra Rehman, 85–95. New York: Seal Press, 2002.

Power, Lisa. "Forbidden Fruit." In *Anti-Gay*, ed. Mark Simpson, 55–65. London: Freedom Editions, 1996.

Powers, Retha. "Don't Ask Alice: Rebecca Walker Steps Out." *Girlfriends*, May/June 1996, 20–21.

Probyn, Elspeth. "New Traditionalism and Post-Feminism: TV Does the Home." *Screen* 31 (Summer 1990): 147–159.

Prophete, Lourdes-marie. "Feminist Musings on the No. 3 Train." In *Colonize This!*

Young Women of Color on Today's Feminism, ed. Daisy Hernández and Bushra Rehman, 170–181. New York: Seal Press, 2002.

Pullen, Kirsten. "Co-Ed Call Girls." In *Jane Sexes It Up: True Confessions of Feminist Desire,* ed. Merri Lisa Johnson, 207–230. New York: Four Walls Eight Windows, 2002.

Pushkar, Katherine. "Pro Feminism." *Village Voice,* October 4, 1994, 14.

Queen, Carol. *Real Live Nude Girl: Chronicles of a Sex-Positive Culture.* San Francisco: Cleis Press, 1997.

———. "Strangers at Home: Bisexuals in the Queer Movement." *Outlook* 16 (Spring 1992): 23–33.

———, and Lawrence Schimel, eds. *PoMoSexuals: Challenging Assumptions about Gender and Sexuality.* San Francisco: Cleis Press, 1997.

Quindlen, Anna. "And Now, Babe Feminism." In *"Bad Girls"/"Good Girls": Women, Sex, and Power in the Nineties,* ed. Nan Bauer Maglin and Donna Perry, 3–5. New Brunswick, N.J.: Rutgers University Press, 1996. Originally published in the *New York Times,* January 19, 1994, A21.

Quinn, Rebecca Dakin. "An Open Letter to Institutional Mothers." In *Generations: Academic Feminists in Dialogue,* ed. Devoney Looser and Ann Kaplan, 174–182. Minneapolis: University of Minnesota Press, 1997.

Radicalesbians. "The Woman Identified Woman." In *Notes from the Third Year: Women's Liberation,* 81–84. New York, 1971.

Rapp, Rayna, and Ellen Ross. "The Twenties Backlash: Compulsory Heterosexuality, the Consumer Family, and the Waning of Feminism." In *Class, Race, and Sex: The Dynamics of Control,* ed. Amy Swerdlow and Hanna Lessinger, 93–107. Boston: G. K. Hall, 1983.

Raymond, Janice G. "Putting the Politics Back into Lesbianism." *Women's Studies International Forum* 12, no. 2 (1989): 149–156.

Reagon, Bernice Johnson. "Coalition Politics: Turning the Century." In *Home Girls: A Black Feminist Anthology,* ed. Barbara Smith, 356–368. New York: Kitchen Table, A Woman of Color Press, 1983.

Redstockings. *Feminist Revolution: An Abridged Edition with Additional Writings,* ed. Kathie Sarachild. 1975. Reprint, New York: Random House, 1978.

———. "Redstockings Manifesto." In *Sisterhood Is Powerful: An Anthology of Writings from the Women's Liberation Movement,* ed. Robin Morgan, 533–536. New York: Vintage Books, 1970.

Rehman, Bushra, and Daisy Hernández. "Introduction." In *Colonize This! Young Women of Color on Today's Feminism,* ed. Daisy Hernández and Bushra Rehman, xvii–xxviii. New York: Seal Press, 2002.

Reid, Catherine. "Introduction." In *Every Woman I've Ever Loved: Lesbian Writers on Their Mothers,* ed. Catherine Reid and Holly Iglesias, ix–xviii. San Francisco: Cleis Press, 1997.

Rich, Adrienne. "Compulsory Heterosexuality and Lesbian Existence." In *Blood, Bread, and Poetry: Selected Prose 1979–1985.* New York: W.W. Norton & Company, 1985. 23–68. Originally published in *Signs: A Journal of Women in Culture and Society* 5, no. 4 (Summer 1980): 631–660.

———. *Of Woman Born: Motherhood as Experience and Institution.* New York: W.W. Norton & Company, 1976.

Rich, B. Ruby. "Feminism and Sexuality in the 1980s." *Feminist Studies* 12, no. 3 (Fall 1986): 525–561.

———. "Top Girl." *Village Voice,* October 8, 1991, 29–33.

Richards, Amy. "Body Image: Third Wave Feminism's Issue?" In *Adiós Barbie: Young*

Women Write about Body Image and Identity, ed. Ophira Edut, 196–200. Seattle: Seal Press, 1998.

The Righteous Babes. Dir. Pratibha Parmar. Women Make Movies, New York, 1997.

Ringgold, Faith. *We Flew over the Bridge: The Memoirs of Faith Ringgold.* Boston: Bulfinch Press, 1995.

Roberts, Tara, and Eisa Nefertari Ulen. "Sisters Spin Talk on Hip-Hop: Can the Music Be Saved?" *Ms.,* February/March 2000, 69–74.

Rockefeller, Abby. "Sex: The Basis of Sexism." *No More Fun and Games: A Journal of Female Liberation,* May 1973.

Roiphe, Anne. *Fruitful: A Real Mother in the Modern World.* Boston: Houghton Mifflin Company, 1996.

Roiphe, Katie. "Date Rape Hysteria." *New York Times,* November 20, 1991, A29.

———. "Date Rape's Other Victim." *New York Times Magazine,* June 13, 1993, 26+.

———. "The End of Innocence." *Vogue,* January 1998, 38+.

———. "A Grandmother's Biological Clock." *New York Times Magazine,* February 2, 1998, 80.

———. "The Independent Woman (and Other Lies)." *Esquire,* February 1997, 84–87.

———. *Last Night in Paradise: Sex and Morals at the Century's End.* Boston: Little, Brown and Company, 1997.

———. "Making the Incest Scene." *Harper's,* November 1995, 68–71.

———. "Men: What's to Be Afraid of?" *Chatelaine,* July 1994, 56–57.

———. "Monica Lewinsky, Career Woman." *New York Times,* September 15, 1998, A27.

———. *The Morning After: Sex, Fear, and Feminism on Campus.* Boston: Little, Brown and Company, 1993.

Roof, Judith. "Generational Difficulties; or, the Fear of a Barren History." In *Generations: Academic Feminists in Dialogue,* ed. Devoney Looser and Ann Kaplan, 69–87. Minneapolis: University of Minnesota Press, 1997.

Rose, Tricia. *Black Noise: Rap Music and Black Culture in Contemporary America.* Hanover, N.H.: Wesleyan University Press, 1994.

Rosenberg, Jessica, and Gitana Garofalo. "Riot Grrrl: Revolutions from Within." *Signs: A Journal of Women in Culture and Society* 23, no. 3 (Spring 1998): 809–841.

Rosenfelt, Deborah, and Judith Stacey. "Second Thoughts on the Second Wave." *Feminist Studies* 13, no. 2 (Summer 1987): 341–361.

Rosga, AnnJanette, and Meg Satterthwaite. "Notes from the Aftermath." In *The Feminist Memoir Project: Voices from Women's Liberation,* ed. Rachel Blau DuPlessis and Ann Snitow, 469–476. New York: Three Rivers Press, 1998.

Rotello, Gabriel. "Bi Any Means Necessary." *Village Voice,* June 30, 1992, 37–38.

Rubin, Gayle. "The Leather Menace: Comments on Politics and S/M." In *Coming to Power: Writings and Graphics on Lesbian S/M,* ed. Samois, 192–225. Berkeley: Samois, 1981.

———. "Thinking Sex: Notes for a Radical Theory of the Politics of Sexuality." In *Pleasure and Danger: Exploring Female Sexuality,* ed. Carole S. Vance, 267–319. Boston: Routledge and Kegan Paul, 1985.

Rumack, Leah. "Lipstick." In *Turbo Chicks: Talking Young Feminisms,* ed. Allyson Mitchell, Lisa Bryn Rundle, and Lara Karaian, 93–100. Toronto: Sumach Press, 2001.

Rupp, Leila J., and Verta Taylor. *Survival in the Doldrums: The American Women's Rights Movement, 1945 to the 1960s.* Oxford: Oxford University Press, 1987.

Russo, Mary. "Aging and the Scandal of Anachronism." In *Figuring Age: Women, Bodies, Generations,* ed. Kathleen Woodward, 20–33. Bloomington: Indiana University Press, 1999.

Salvatore, Diane, et al. "Young Feminists Speak for Themselves." *Ms.*, April 1983, 43+.

Samois, ed. *Coming to Power: Writings and Graphics on Lesbian S/M.* Berkeley: Samois, 1981.

Sandoval, Chela. "U.S. Third World Feminism: The Theory and Method of Oppositional Consciousness in the Postmodern World." *Genders* 10 (Spring 1991): 1–24.

Sarachild, Kathie. "The Power of History." In Redstockings, *Feminist Revolution: An Abridged Edition with Additional Writings*, ed. Kathie Sarachild, 12–43. New York: Random House, 1978.

Sarah, Elizabeth. "Towards a Reassessment of Feminist History." *Women's Studies International Forum* 6 (1982): 519–523.

Schneider, Beth E. "Political Generations and the Contemporary Women's Movement." *Sociological Inquiry* 58 (Winter 1988): 4–21.

Schneir, Miriam, ed. *Feminism in Our Time: The Essential Writings, World War II to the Present.* New York: Vintage, 1994.

Schrof, Joannie M. "Feminism's Daughters." *U.S. News and World Report*, September 27, 1993, 6+.

Schulman, Sarah. *My American Life: Lesbian and Gay Life during the Reagan/Bush Years.* New York: Routledge, 1994.

Schwartz, Ruth L. "New Alliances, Strange Bedfellows: Lesbians, Gay Men, and AIDS." In *Sisters, Sexperts, Queers: Beyond the Lesbian Nation*, ed. Arlene Stein, 230–244. New York: Plume, 1993.

Scott, Joan Wallach, ed. *differences: A Journal of Feminist Cultural Studies* 9, no. 3 (1997). Special issue: *Women's Studies on the Edge.*

Sedgwick, Eve Kosofsky. *Epistemology of the Closet.* Berkeley: University of California Press, 1990.

———. *Tendencies.* Durham, N.C.: Duke University Press, 1993.

Segal, Lynne. *Straight Sex: Rethinking the Politics of Pleasure.* Berkeley: University of California Press, 1994.

Seidman, Steven. "Identity and Politics in a 'Postmodern' Gay Culture: Some Historical and Conceptual Notes." In *Fear of a Queer Planet: Queer Politics and Social Theory*, ed. Michael Warner, 105–142. Minneapolis: University of Minnesota Press, 1993.

Senior, Jennifer. "Decrying Wolf." *Mirabella*, February 2000, 84+.

Senna, Danzy. *Caucasia.* New York: Riverhead Books, 1997.

———. "The Color of Love." *O: The Oprah Magazine*, May/June 2000, 117+.

———. "To Be Real." In *To Be Real: Telling the Truth and Changing the Face of Feminism*, ed. Rebecca Walker, 5–20. New York: Anchor Books, 1995.

Shalit, Wendy. *A Return to Modesty: Discovering the Lost Virtue.* New York: Simon & Schuster, 1999.

Shapiro, Laura. "Sisterhood Was Powerful." *Newsweek*, June 20, 1994, 68+.

Shelly, Martha. "Notes of a Radical Lesbian." In *Sisterhood Is Powerful: An Anthology of Writings from the Women's Liberation Movement*, ed. Robin Morgan, 306–311. New York: Vintage Books, 1970.

———. "Subversion in the Women's Movement: What Is to Be Done." *On Our Backs* 1, no. 13 (1970): 5–7.

Short, Kayann. "Coming to the Table: *The Differential Politics of This Bridge Called My Back.*" *Genders* 20 (1994): 3–44.

Shugart, Helene A. "Isn't It Ironic? The Intersection of Third-Wave Feminism and Generation X." *Women's Studies in Communication* 24, no. 2 (Fall 2001): 131–168.

Siegel, Carol. *New Millennial Sexstyles*. Bloomington: Indiana University Press, 2000.

Siegel, Deborah L. "The Legacy of the Personal: Generating Theory in Feminism's Third Wave." *Hypatia: A Journal of Feminist Philosophy* 12, no. 3 (Summer 1997): 46–75.

———. "Reading between the Waves: Feminist Historiography in a 'Postfeminist Moment.'" In *Third Wave Agenda: Being Feminist, Doing Feminism*, ed. Leslie Heywood and Jennifer Drake, 55–82. Minneapolis: University of Minnesota Press, 1997.

Silverstein, Melissa. "WAC-ing Operation Rescue." In *Listen Up: Voices from the Next Feminist Generation*, ed. Barbara Findlen, 239–248. Seattle: Seal Press, 1995.

Smith, Barbara, ed. *Home Girls: A Black Feminist Anthology*. New York: Kitchen Table, A Woman of Color Press, 1983.

Smith, Dinitia. "Love Is Strange: The Crusading Feminist and the Repentant Womanizer." *New York*, March 22, 1993, 36–43.

Smith, Jen. "Doin' It for the Ladies—Youth Feminism: Cultural Productions/Cultural Activism." In *Third Wave Agenda: Being Feminist, Doing Feminism*, ed. Leslie Heywood and Jennifer Drake, 226–238. Minneapolis: University of Minnesota Press, 1997.

Smith, Sarah. "A Cock of One's Own: Getting a Firm Grip on Feminist Sexual Power." In *Jane Sexes It Up: True Confessions of Feminist Desire*, ed. Merri Lisa Johnson, 293–309. New York: Four Walls Eight Windows, 2002.

Smith, Valerie. *Not Just Race, Not Just Gender: Black Feminist Readings*. New York: Routledge, 1998.

Smitherman, Geneva, ed. *African American Women Speak Out on Anita Hill-Clarence Thomas*. Detroit: Wayne State University Press, 1995.

Smith-Rosenberg, Carroll. *Disorderly Conduct: Visions of Gender in Victorian America*. New York: Alfred A. Knopf, 1985.

———. "The New Woman and the New History." *Feminist Studies* 3, nos. 1 and 2 (Fall 1975): 185–198.

Smyth, Cherry. *Lesbians Talk Queer Notions*. London: Scarlet Press, 1992.

Snitow, Ann. "A Gender Diary." In *Conflicts in Feminism*, ed. Marianne Hirsch and Evelyn Fox Keller, 9–43. New York: Routledge, 1990.

———, Christine Stansell, and Sharon Thompson, eds. *Powers of Desire: The Politics of Sexuality*. New York: Monthly Review Press, 1983.

The Social Justice Group at the Center for Advanced Feminist Studies, University of Minnesota, ed. *Is Academic Feminism Dead? Theory in Practice*. New York: New York University Press, 2000.

Solanas, Valerie. *SCUM Manifesto*. 1968. Reprint, London: The Matriarchy Study Group, 1983.

Solomon, Alisa. "Dykotomies: Scents and Sensibility." In *Sisters, Sexperts, Queers: Beyond the Lesbian Nation*, ed. Arlene Stein, 210–217. New York: Plume, 1993.

Sommers, Christina Hoff. *Who Stole Feminism? How Women Have Betrayed Women*. New York: Touchstone Books, 1994.

Sorisio, Carolyn. "A Tale of Two Feminisms: Power and Victimization in Contemporary Feminist Debate." In *Third Wave Agenda: Being Feminist, Doing Feminism*, ed. Leslie Heywood and Jennifer Drake, 134–149. Minneapolis: University of Minnesota Press, 1997.

Souljah, Sister. *No Disrespect*. New York: Time Books, 1994.

Spillers, Hortense. "Interstices: A Small Drama of Words." In *Pleasure and Danger: Exploring Female Sexuality*, ed. Carole S. Vance, 73–100. Boston: Routledge and Kegan Paul, 1985.

Sprengnether, Madelon. "Generational Differences: Reliving Mother-Daughter Conflicts." In *Changing Subjects: The Making of Feminist Literary Theory,* ed. Gayle Greene and Coppélia Kahn, 201–208. New York: Routledge, 1993.

Springer, Kimberly. "Third Wave Black Feminism?" *Signs: Journal of Women in Culture and Society* 27, no. 4 (Summer 2002): 1059–1082.

Stan, Adele M., ed. *Debating Sexual Correctness: Pornography, Sexual Harassment, Date Rape, and the Politics of Sexual Equality.* New York: Delta Books, 1995.

Stein, Arlene. "All Dressed Up, but No Place to Go? Style Wars and the New Lesbianism." *Outlook* 4 (Winter 1989): 34–43.

———. "Introduction." In *Sisters, Sexperts, Queers: Beyond the Lesbian Nation,* ed. Arlene Stein, xi–xvii. New York: Plume, 1993.

———. *Sex and Sensibility: Stories of a Lesbian Generation.* Berkeley: University of California Press, 1997.

———. "Sisters and Queers: The Decentering of Lesbian Feminism." *Socialist Review* 22, no. 1 (1992): 33–55.

———, ed. *Sisters, Sexperts, Queers: Beyond the Lesbian Nation.* New York: Plume, 1993.

Steinem, Gloria. "Foreword." In *To Be Real: Telling the Truth and Changing the Face of Feminism,* ed. Rebecca Walker, xiii–xxviii. New York: Anchor Books, 1995.

———. "Sex, Lies and Advertising." *Ms.,* July/August 1990, 18–28.

———. "Why Young Women Are More Conservative." In Gloria Steinem, *Outrageous Acts and Everyday Rebellions,* 211–218. New York: Holt, Rinehart and Winston, 1983.

Stimpson, Catharine R. "Women's Studies and Its Discontents." *Dissent* 42 (Winter 1996): 67–75.

Stoller, Debbie. "Sex and the Thinking Girl." In *The Bust Guide to the New Girl Order,* ed. Marcelle Karp and Debbie Stoller, 74–84. New York: Penguin Books, 1999.

Sundahl, Debi. "Battle Scars." *On Our Backs* (September/October 1994): 32–36.

Syfers, Judy. "Why I Want a Wife." In *Notes from the Third Year: Women's Liberation,* 13–15. New York, 1971.

A Symposium on Who Stole Feminism? How Women Have Betrayed Women *by Christina Hoff Sommers.* Special issue of *Democratic Culture* 3, no. 4 (Fall 1994).

Talbot, Margaret. "A Most Dangerous Method." *Lingua Franca* 4, no. 2 (January/February 1994): 1, 24–40.

Tanner, Leslie B. "Foreword." In *Voices from Women's Liberation,* ed. Leslie B. Tanner, 25–30. New York: New American Library, 1970.

———. "Preface." In *Voices from Women's Liberation,* ed. Leslie B. Tanner, 13–16. New York: New American Library, 1970.

———, ed. *Voices from Women's Liberation.* New York: New American Library, 1970.

Taylor, Jocelyn. "Testimony of a Naked Woman." In *To Be Real: Telling the Truth and Changing the Face of Feminism,* ed. Rebecca Walker, 219–237. New York: Anchor Books, 1995.

Taylor, Verta. "Social Movement Continuity: The Women's Movement in Abeyance." *American Sociological Review* 54 (October 1989): 761–775.

Terrelonge, Paula. "Feminist Consciousness and Black Women." (1984). In *Words of Fire: An Anthology of African-American Feminist Thought,* ed. Beverly Guy-Sheftall, 490–501. New York: The New Press, 1995.

Thomas, Calvin. "Straight with a Twist: Queer Theory and the Subject of Heterosexuality." In *The Gay '90s: Disciplinary and Interdisciplinary Formations in Queer Studies,* ed. Thomas Foster, Carol Siegel, and Ellen E. Berry, 83–115. New York: New York University Press, 1997.

————, ed. *Straight with a Twist: Queer Theory and the Subject of Heterosexuality*. Urbana: University of Illinois Press, 2000.

"The Trial of Susan B. Anthony." (1873). In *Notes from the Third Year: Women's Liberation*, 11–12. New York, 1971.

Trioli, Virginia. *Generation f: Sex, Power, and the Young Feminist*. Melbourne, Australia: Minerva, 1996.

Truth, Sojourner. "The Women Want Their Rights." (1853). In *Voices from Women's Liberation*, ed. Leslie B. Tanner, 73–74. New York: New American Library, 1970.

Tumang, Patricia Justine. "*Nasaan ka anak ko?* A Queer Filipina-American Feminist's Tale of Abortion and Self-Recovery." In *Colonize This! Young Women of Color on Today's Feminism*, ed. Daisy Hernández and Bushra Rehman, 370–381. New York: Seal Press, 2002.

Ulen, Eisa Nefertari, and Angela Y. Davis. "What Happened to Your Generation's Promise of 'Love and Revolution'?" In *Letters of Intent: Women Cross the Generations to Talk about Family, Work, Sex, Love and the Future of Feminism*, ed. Anna Bondoc and Meg Daly, 99–108. New York: Simon & Schuster, 1999.

Vance, Carole S. "Pleasure and Danger: Toward a Politics of Sexuality." In *Pleasure and Danger: Exploring Female Sexuality*, ed. Carole S. Vance, 1–27. Boston: Routledge and Kegan Paul, 1985.

————, ed. *Pleasure and Danger: Exploring Female Sexuality*. Boston: Routledge and Kegan Paul, 1985.

Vincent, Norah. "Sex, Love & Politics." *New York Press*, February 4, 1998, 40–42. Interview with Andrea Dworkin.

Wald, Gayle. "Just a Girl? Rock Music, Feminism, and the Cultural Construction of Female Youth." *Signs: A Journal of Women in Culture and Society* 23, no. 3 (Spring 1998): 585–610.

Walker, Alice. "In Search of Our Mothers' Gardens." In Alice Walker, *In Search of Our Mothers' Gardens: Womanist Prose*, 231–243. New York: Harcourt Brace Jovanovich, 1983.

————. "One Child of One's Own: A Meaningful Digression within the Work(s)." In Alice Walker, *In Search of Our Mothers' Gardens: Womanist Prose*, 361–383. New York: Harcourt Brace Jovanovich, 1983.

————, and Rebecca Walker. "The Two of Us." *Essence*, May 1995, 172+.

Walker, Lisa M. "How to Recognize a Lesbian: The Cultural Politics of Looking Like What You Are." *Signs: A Journal of Women in Culture and Society* 18, no. 4 (Summer 1993): 866–890.

Walker, Rebecca. "Becoming the Third Wave." *Ms.*, January/February 1992, 39–41.

————. "Being Real: An Introduction." In *To Be Real: Telling the Truth and Changing the Face of Feminism*, ed. Rebecca Walker, xxix–xl. New York: Anchor Books, 1995.

————. *Black, White, and Jewish: Autobiography of a Shifting Self*. New York: Riverhead Books, 2001.

————. "Changing the Face of Feminism." *Essence*, January 1996, 123.

————. "How Does a Supermodel Do Feminism? An Interview with Veronica Webb." In *To Be Real: Telling the Truth and Changing the Face of Feminism*, ed. Rebecca Walker, 209–218. New York: Anchor Books, 1995.

————. "Lusting for Freedom." In *Listen Up: Voices from the Next Feminist Generation*, ed. Barbara Findlen, 95–101. Seattle: Seal Press, 1995.

————. "Serial Lover." In *Here Lies My Heart: Essays on Why We Marry, Why We Don't, and What We Find There*, ed. Deborah Chasman and Catherine Jhee, 46–49. Boston: Beacon Press, 1999.

———, ed. *To Be Real: Telling the Truth and Changing the Face of Feminism.* New York: Anchor Books, 1995.

Wall, Cheryl, ed. *Changing Our Own Words: Essays on Criticism, Theory, and Writing by Black Women.* New Brunswick, N.J.: Rutgers University Press, 1989.

Wallace, Michele. *Black Macho and the Myth of the Superwoman.* 1979. Reprint, New York: Verso Press, 1990.

———. *Invisibility Blues: From Pop to Theory.* New York: Verso Press, 1990.

———. "Memoirs of a Premature Bomb-Thrower." *Village Voice,* February 13, 1996, 35–36.

Walter, Natasha. *The New Feminism.* London: Little, Brown and Company, 1998.

———, ed. *On the Move: Feminism for a New Generation.* London: Virago Press, 1999.

Ware, Cellestine. *Woman Power: The Movement for Women's Liberation.* New York: Tower Publications, 1970.

Warner, Michael, ed. *Fear of a Queer Planet: Queer Politics and Social Theory.* Minneapolis: University of Minnesota Press, 1993.

———. "From Queer to Eternity: An Army of Theorists Cannot Fail." *Village Voice Literary Supplement,* June 1992, 18–19.

———. "Introduction." In *Fear of a Queer Planet: Queer Politics and Social Theory,* ed. Michael Warner, vii–xxxi. Minneapolis: University of Minnesota Press, 1993.

———. *The Trouble with Normal: Sex, Politics, and the Ethics of Queer Life.* New York: The Free Press, 1999.

Warrior, Betsy. "Slavery or Labor of Love." In *Notes from the Third Year: Women's Liberation,* 68–71. New York, 1971.

Weaver, Courtney. "Growing Up Sexual." *New York Times Book Review,* June 8, 1997, 12. Review of Naomi Wolf, *Promiscuities: The Secret Struggle for Womanhood* and Katie Roiphe, *Last Night in Paradise: Sex and Morals at the Century's End.*

Webb, Marilyn. "Our Daughters, Ourselves: How Feminists Can Raise Feminists." *Ms.,* November/December 1992, 30–35.

Webb, Marilyn Salzman. "Women: We Have a Common Enemy." *New Left Notes,* June 10, 1968, 15.

Weed, Elizabeth. "Introduction." In *Feminism Meets Queer Theory,* ed. Elizabeth Weed and Naomi Schor, vii–xiii. Bloomington: Indiana University Press, 1997.

———, and Naomi Schor, eds. *Feminism Meets Queer Theory.* Bloomington: Indiana University Press, 1997.

Weise, Elizabeth Reba, ed. *Closer to Home: Bisexuality and Feminism.* Seattle: Seal Press, 1992.

"What Younger Women Think about Older Women." *The Oprah Winfrey Show.* Harpo Productions, Chicago, January 16, 2002.

"What's Feminism? A Cross-Generational Dialogue." *Sojourner* 21, no. 4 (December 1995): 7–11.

Whisman, Vera. "Identity Crises: Who Is a Lesbian, Anyway?" In *Sisters, Sexperts, Queers: Beyond the Lesbian Nation,* ed. Arlene Stein, 47–60. New York: Plume, 1993.

———. *Queer by Choice: Lesbians, Gay Men, and the Politics of Identity.* New York: Routledge, 1996.

White, E. Frances. "Africa on My Mind: Gender, Counterdiscourse, and African American Nationalism." In *Words of Fire: An Anthology of African-American Feminist Thought,* ed. Beverly Guy-Sheftall, 504–524. New York: The New Press, 1995.

Whittier, Nancy. *Feminist Generations: The Persistence of the Radical Women's Movement.* Philadelphia: Temple University Press, 1995.

"Who's Afraid of Naomi Wolf?" *Economist,* January 22, 1994, 95–96. Review of Katie Roiphe, *The Morning After* and Naomi Wolf, *Fire with Fire.*

Wiegman, Robyn. "Introduction: Mapping the Lesbian Postmodern." In *The Lesbian Postmodern,* ed. Laura Doan, 1–20. New York: Columbia University Press, 1994.

———, ed. *Women's Studies on Its Own: A Next Wave Reader in Institutional Change.* Durham, N.C.: Duke University Press, 2002.

Wilchins, Riki Anne. *Read My Lips: Sexual Subversion and the End of Gender.* Ithaca, N.Y.: Firebrand Books, 1997.

Willis, Ellen. "Toward a Feminist Sexual Revolution." *Social Text* 2, no. 3 (Fall 1982): 3–21.

———. "Villains and Victims: 'Sexual Correctness' and the Repression of Feminism." In *"Bad Girls"/"Good Girls": Women, Sex, and Power in the Nineties,* ed. Nan Bauer Maglin and Donna Perry, 44–53. New Brunswick, N.J.: Rutgers University Press, 1996.

———. "Women and the Left." In *Notes from the Second Year: Women's Liberation. Major Writings of the Radical Feminists,* 55–56. New York, 1970.

Wilson, Elizabeth. "Is Transgression Transgressive?" In *Activating Theory: Lesbian, Gay, Bisexual Politics,* ed. Joseph Bristow and Angelia R. Wilson, 107–117. London: Lawrence & Wisehart, 1993.

Winokur, L. A. "Interview with Gloria Steinem." *Progressive,* June 1995, 34–37.

Wolf, Deborah. "A Mother's Story." In *The Conversation Begins: Mothers and Daughters Talk about Living Feminism,* ed. Christina Looper Baker and Christina Baker Kline, 142–147. New York: Bantam Books, 1996.

Wolf, Naomi. *The Beauty Myth: How Images of Beauty Are Used against Women.* New York: William Morrow and Company, 1991.

———. "Brideland." In *To Be Real: Telling the Truth and Changing the Face of Feminism,* ed. Rebecca Walker, 35–40. New York: Anchor Books, 1995.

———. "A Daughter's Story." In *The Conversation Begins: Mothers and Daughters Talk about Living Feminism,* ed. Christina Looper Baker and Christina Baker Kline, 148–155. New York: Bantam Books, 1996.

———. *Fire with Fire: The New Female Power and How It Will Change the 21st Century.* New York: Random House, 1993.

———. "The Future Is Ours to Lose." *New York Times Magazine,* May 16, 1999, 134+.

———. *Misconceptions: Truth, Lies, and the Unexpected Journey to Motherhood.* New York: Doubleday, 2001.

———. *Promiscuities: The Secret Struggle for Womanhood.* New York: Random House, 1997.

———. "Radical Heterosexuality . . . or How to Love a Man and Save Your Soul." *Ms.,* July/August 1992, 29–31.

Wolfe, Susan J., and Julia Penelope. "Sexual Identity/Textual Politics: Lesbian (De/Com)positions." In *Sexual Practice, Textual Theory: Lesbian Cultural Criticism,* ed. Susan J. Wolfe and Julia Penelope, 1–24. Cambridge, Mass.: Blackwell Publishers, 1993.

Women's Action Coalition. *WAC Stats: The Facts about Women.* New York: The New Press, 1993.

Woodward, Kathleen. "Inventing Generational Models: Psychoanalysis, Feminism, Literature." In *Figuring Age: Women, Bodies, Generations,* ed. Kathleen Woodward, 149–168. Bloomington: Indiana University Press, 1999.

———, ed. *Figuring Age: Women, Bodies, Generations.* Bloomington: Indiana University Press, 1999.

Worsham, Fabian Clements. "The Poetics of Matrilineage: Mothers and Daughters in the Poetry of African American Women, 1965–1985." In *Women of Color: Mother-Daughter Relationships in 20th-Century Literature,* ed. Elizabeth Brown-Guillory, 117–131. Austin: University of Texas Press, 1996.

Wright, Laura. "Anti-Feminism Generation X-Style." *Minnesota Review* 11, no. 5 (Fall 1993/Spring 1994): 129–132. Review of Katie Roiphe, *The Morning After.*

Wurtzel, Elizabeth. *Bitch: In Praise of Difficult Women.* New York: Doubleday, 1996.

"Young Feminists Speak for Themselves." *Ms.,* March/April 1991, 28–34.

Zimmerman, Bonnie. "'Confessions' of a Lesbian Feminist." In *Cross Purposes: Lesbians, Feminists, and the Limits of Alliance,* ed. Dana Heller, 157–168. Bloomington: Indiana University Press, 1997.

Zita, Jacquelyn N. "Gay and Lesbian Studies: Yet Another Unhappy Marriage?" In *Tilting the Tower: Lesbians Teaching Queer Subjects,* ed. Linda Garber, 258–276. New York: Routledge, 1994.

———. "Historical Amnesia and the Lesbian Continuum." *Signs: A Journal of Women in Culture and Society* 7, no. 1 (Autumn 1981): 172–187.

———. "The Male Lesbian and the Postmodernist Body." *Hypatia: A Journal of Feminist Philosophy* 7, no. 4 (Fall 1992): 106–127.

———. "Third Wave Feminisms: An Introduction." *Hypatia: A Journal of Feminist Philosophy* 12, no. 3 (Summer 1997): 1–6.

———, ed. *Hypatia: A Journal of Feminist Philosophy* 12, no. 3 (Summer 1997). Special Issue: *Third Wave Feminisms.*

Zook, Kristal Brent. "Light Skinned-ded Naps." In *Making Face, Making Soul: Creative and Critical Perspectives by Women of Color,* ed. Gloria Anzaldúa, 85–96. San Francisco: Aunt Lute Foundation Books, 1990.

———. "A Manifesto of Sorts for a Black Feminist Movement." *New York Times Magazine,* November 12, 1995, 86–89.

Index

Astrid Henry is Assistant Professor of
Women's Studies and English at Saint Mary's College in Indiana,
where she also serves as the coordinator of the Program in Women's
Studies. Her essays on third-wave feminism and feminist generations
have appeared in *Reading Sex and the City* (2004); *Catching a Wave:
Reclaiming Feminism for the 21st Century* (2003); and *Mothers and
Daughters: Connection, Empowerment, and Transformation* (2000).